D1336944

MICROPROCESSORS/MICROCOMPUTERS
An Introduction

McGraw-Hill Series in Electrical Engineering

Consulting Editor
Stephen W. Director, Carnegie-Mellon University

Networks and Systems
Communications and Information Theory
Control Theory
Electronics and Electronic Circuits
Power and Energy
Electromagnetics
Computer Engineering and Switching Theory
Introductory and Survey
Radio, Television, Radar, and Antennas

Previous Consulting Editors

Ronald M. Bracewell, Colin Cherry, James F. Gibbons, Willis W. Harman, Hubert Heffner, Edward W. Herold, John G. Linvill, Simon Ramo, Ronald A. Rohrer, Anthony E. Siegman, Charles Susskind, Frederick E. Terman, John G. Truxal, Ernst Weber, and John R. Whinnery.

Computer Engineering and Switching Theory

Bartee: *Digital Computer Fundamentals*
Bell and Newell: *Computer Structures Readings and Examples*
Clare: *Designing Logic Systems Using State Machines*
Garland: *Introduction to Microprocessor System Design*
Givone: *Introduction to Switching Circuit Theory*
Givone and Roesser: *Microprocessors/Microcomputers: An Introduction*
Hamacher, Vranesic, and Zaky: *Computer Organization*
Hayes: *Computer Organization and Architecture*
Kohavi: *Switching and Finite Automata Theory*
McCluskey: *Introduction to the Theory of Switching Circuits*
Peatman: *Design of Digital Systems*
Peatman: *Microcomputer Based Design*
Sandige: *Digital Concepts Using Standard Integrated Circuits*
Scott: *Electronic Computer Technology*
Woollons: *Introduction to Digital Computer Design*

MICROPROCESSORS/ MICROCOMPUTERS

An Introduction

Donald D. Givone

Associate Professor of Electrical Engineering
State University of New York at Buffalo

Robert P. Roesser

Associate Professor of Electrical Engineering
University of Detroit

McGraw-Hill Book Company

New York   St. Louis   San Francisco   Auckland   Bogotá   Düsseldorf
Johannesburg   London   Madrid   Mexico   Montreal   New Delhi
Panama   Paris   São Paulo   Singapore   Sydney   Tokyo   Toronto

This book was set in Times Roman.
The editors were Charles E. Stewart and Stephen Wagley;
the cover was designed by Antonia Goldmark;
the production supervisor was John Mancia.
The drawings were done by Santype International Limited.
Fairfield Graphics was printer and binder.

MICROPROCESSORS/MICROCOMPUTERS: AN INTRODUCTION

1234567890FGFG7832109

Library of Congress Cataloging in Publication Data

Givone, Donald D
    Microprocessors/microcomputers: an introduction.

    (McGraw-Hill series in electrical engineering)
    Bibliography: p.
    Includes index.
    1. Microprocessors. 2. Microcomputers.
I. Roesser, Robert P., joint author. II. Title.
QA76.5.G516 001.6'4'04   79-13543
ISBN 0-07-023326-8

To our wives
Louise and Patricia

CONTENTS

PREFACE

Since the development of the integrated circuit in 1959, there has been continuous interest in the fabrication of new electronic devices capable of performing complex functions. One of the most dramatic consequences of integrated circuit technology was the microprocessor in 1971. Although originally developed as calculator chips, microprocessors soon were recognized as having great potential as the heart of dedicated digital processors because of their low cost and programmable capability. In essence, the central processing unit of the digital computer was encompassed in the form of an integrated circuit.

It is the intent of this book to provide the reader with a foundation on digital computer principles with emphasis on the behavior, operation, and applications of microprocessors and microcomputers. This book develops in detail the basic concepts that are important in the design of most microcomputer-based systems. These concepts include microcomputer architecture, memory structure, input/output facility, interfacing, and programming. No background computer knowledge is assumed. Material on number systems, Boolean algebra, and electronic circuits is included in order to make the text self-contained. However, some knowledge in electrical circuits is assumed.

Perhaps the most difficult decision we had to make in the writing of this book concerned the selection of a microprocessor for illustrative purposes. Since our objective is to provide fundamental concepts in microcomputer design, we feel that a noncommercial microprocessor best serves our purposes. In this way, we hope that the microprocessor itself will not mask the concepts being developed. Although a chapter expounding upon the commercially available microprocessors could have been included, we feel this information is best obtained from the various manufacturers.

The material in this book is suitable for a one-semester or two-quarter course on the junior or senior level in electrical or computer engineering. Since it is self-contained, the book is also well-suited for self study. It is realized that some of the material in Chaps. 2, 3, and 4 will most probably have been included in previous courses. However, to maintain completeness and to allow for different backgrounds, these chapters provide detailed development of their material. It should therefore not be necessary to cover certain portions of these chapters.

We would like to express our thanks to the many people who have helped and encouraged us during the writing of this book. A special acknowledgment is given to our children who did not always understand why we could not spend more time with them while engaged in this project. We hope they will be rewarded with a better tomorrow built out of the new advances of today. Finally, we would like to express our appreciation to Mrs. Marilyn Hutchings for her patient typing of the final manuscript.

Donald D. Givone
Robert P. Roesser

MICROPROCESSORS AND MICROCOMPUTERS: AN OVERVIEW

Microprocessors are new and fascinating logic devices that are having pronounced effects upon our lives. Microprocessors can be found in pocket calculators, checkout terminals in stores, home appliances, office equipment, scientific instruments, medical equipment, and video games, to name just a few occurrences. Furthermore, every day new applications are being found and new microprocessor-based products are being developed. Their potential effects upon our lives are almost beyond imagination. This book will introduce the reader to the internal workings of microprocessors and larger systems that contain microprocessors. This introduction requires some exposure to logic design principles, electronics, and programming. These concepts are applied where they are necessary for the effective utilization of these new logic devices.

This chapter will provide an overview of the behavior and structure of microprocessors and microcomputers. A great deal of terminology will be introduced during this discussion. The intent, at this time, is to establish in the reader a general feeling for the numerous concepts involved in microprocessor systems and the interrelationships of these concepts. In the ensuing chapters, the details will be developed and exemplified. However, if during the course of study the broad picture established in this chapter is kept in mind, the reader will be able to appreciate more fully the operation and design of a microprocessor system.

1.1 A NEW ERA OF COMPUTATION

Digital computers have had a great deal of influence upon our society and manner of living since 1951, when the first commercial digital computer (Univac I) became available. A new technology had emerged. Such terms as "digital computation," "logic design," and "programming" became concepts integral to science and engineering. However, the diversity of these concepts frequently caused a split in interest. For example, there were those whose interest was in using or programming computers (software), while there were others whose interest was in designing computers (hardware). Although this dichotomy in interest may have real foundations in the case of large-scale computers, the problems facing application programmers and computer designers became more interrelated with the introduction of minicomputers in 1965. These computers were no longer intended solely for data processing and problem solving, but were to become a part of systems requiring immediate computer decisions, called *real-time systems.*

The introduction of the microprocessor in 1971 closed this interest gap even further. An era of software logic design, or programmed logic, has resulted. In this era, programming concepts and logic design principles have merged to the point that their interactions require scientists and engineers to have complete familiarity with both the software and hardware principles of computers to utilize fully the potential of the microprocessor. It is toward an understanding of these principles and their interrelation that this book is directed, with the hope that the full beneficial potential of microprocessors can be realized.

1.2 MICROPROCESSORS AND MICROCOMPUTERS

Since this book is about microprocessors and microcomputers, let us begin by defining these two words. Precise and detailed definitions are really impossible since microprocessors and microcomputers deal with a dynamic technology, and as this technology changes, so must their definitions be modified.

One of the results of the advancement in solid-state technology is the capability of fabricating very large numbers of transistors (say, 1000 and over) within a single silicon chip. This is known as *large-scale integration.* A direct consequence of large-scale integration is the microprocessor. In general, a *microprocessor* is a programmable logic device fabricated according to the concept of large-scale integration. As will be seen, a microprocessor has a large degree of flexibility built into it. By itself it cannot perform a given task, but must be programmed and connected to a set of additional system devices. These additional system devices usually include memory elements and input/output devices. In general, a set of system devices, including the microprocessor, memory, and input/output elements, interconnected for the purpose of performing some well-defined function, is known as a *microcomputer* or *microprocessor system.*

Although microcomputers have the general characteristics of digital computers, a notable property of microcomputers is their relatively low cost and small size. This has greatly contributed to their popularity and success. While large mainframe computers and minicomputers have more computational power than microcomputers, this power is not always needed in every application. Further, the cost of large computers and minicomputers has often precluded their adoption into certain electronic systems which would have otherwise benefited from their inclusion. The microprocessor has now made it possible to use a programmable device in a logic system where cost constraints, rather than speed and computational power, are important.

Microprocessors are finding new applications every day. Currently, they are used for instrumentation, point-of-sale terminals, intelligent terminals, and calculators. They are also vital elements in the control of machines, chemical processes, computer peripherals, traffic systems, major appliances, and automobiles. Finally, in the recreational area, these devices are responsible for a new group of hobbyists who are building their own computers.

1.3 A BASIC MICROCOMPUTER ORGANIZATION

A basic computer system consists of five functional units: the *input unit*, the *memory unit*, the *arithmetic unit*, the *control unit*, and the *output unit*. One such basic system is illustrated in Fig. 1.1.

The physical components and circuits that comprise a computer system are known as its *hardware*. These circuits are capable of performing only a small number of different operations. Any additional operational capabilities of the computer must be accomplished by *programming*. A *program* is an organized collection of elementary computer operations, called *instructions*, that manipulate

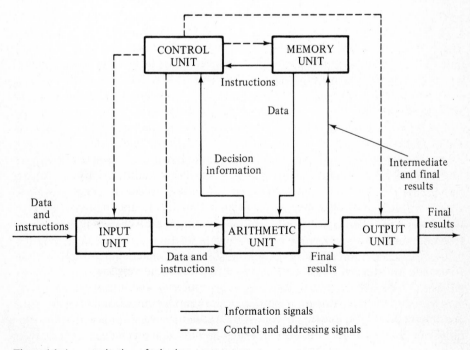

Figure 1.1 An organization of a basic computer system.

information, called *data*. The programs that are written for a computer are called its *software*.

The program and data are first stored in the memory unit via the input unit. The individual instructions of the program are then automatically entered, one at a time, into the control unit, where they are interpreted and executed. The execution usually requires data to be entered into the arithmetic unit, where the circuitry necessary for manipulating the data is contained. During the course of computation or at its completion, the derived results are sent to the output unit. The arithmetic unit and control unit together are normally called the *central processing unit* (CPU). The central processing unit of a microcomputer system is the microprocessor.

In addition to the memory unit, the other computer units are also capable of storing information. Information is stored as groups of binary digits (called *bits*) in storage devices called *registers*. Essentially the operation of a computer can be regarded as a series of information transfers from register to register with possible information modification (e.g., addition) being performed between transfers. The group of binary digits handled all at the same time by the computer is known as a *word*, and the number of binary digits that make up the word is the *word length*. A word is the basic logical unit of information in a computer. An instruction or data consist of one or more words. Microprocessors are typically available with 4, 8, 12, and 16 binary-digit word lengths. Since an 8 binary-digit word length is so common, it is given the special name *byte*.

The Memory Unit

The bulk of the information storage is in the memory unit. This unit is divided into substorage units, also called *registers*, each capable of holding one computer word. The place in the memory where each substorage unit appears is known as a *location*. Each of these locations is identified by an *address*. The address is simply an integral number that uniquely designates a substorage unit. Since only one computer word is stored at each location, this word is referred to as the *content* of the location.

An important characteristic of digital computers is that both the data and program are stored in its memory. This has led to two basic design philosophies. In one case, the computer has two separate and distinct memories. The program is always within one of these memories, and the data are always in the other. Computers designed according to this two-memory philosophy are called *Harvard-type* computers. In the second philosophy, the distinction between a program memory and a data memory is not made; these machines are called *Von Neumann-* or *Princeton-type* computers. In this case, the program can appear anywhere within the memory, and it becomes the responsibility of the programmer to maintain the distinction between the two types of information, i.e., data and instructions. The advantage gained by this design philosophy is that instructions can be treated as data, so that the computer is allowed to modify its own instructions. Microcomputers have been designed according to both philosophies. This book will always assume Von Neumann-type computers.

Because of their low cost, microprocessors are playing a significant role in dedicated applications. Large general-purpose digital computers are continually reprogrammed so that they can be used for solving a large variety of problems. Microcomputers in a dedicated application do not need this flexibility. Once the program is written and tested, it usually is not subject to further change. Thus, microcomputers frequently have two different forms of memory within the memory unit. There is the *read-only memory* (ROM) and the *read/write memory* (RWM).† Once information is placed into a read-only memory it cannot be modified easily, if at all. The read-only memory, with its lower cost, is used to hold the program and any constant data, while the read/write memory is used for holding information that is subject to change.‡

The Arithmetic Unit

The arithmetic unit is where most of the data manipulations occur. These manipulations involve both arithmetic and logic computations. As will be seen in Chap. 7, where a typical microprocessor is described, the allowable computations are very elementary. The more complex mathematical operations have to be performed by means of a program which utilizes the allowable operations.

Typically, the most important register in the arithmetic unit is the *accumulator*. This register normally contains one of the operands prior to a computation and the result after the computation.§ In addition, several auxiliary registers, called *scratchpad registers*, frequently appear in the arithmetic unit to facilitate the writing of programs.

Also included in the arithmetic unit are *flag bits*. These bits provide status-type information that can be important for determining the course of computation. For example, a flag indicating that the result of a computation is 0 might be provided. The programmer can then use the detection of this condition for decision making. Typically, if a particular computation produces a result of 0, one set of future computations is performed; if the result is not 0, an alternate set of future computations is performed. The set of flag bits indicating the results of computa-

---

† It has become conventional to refer to read/write memory as *random-access memory* (RAM), even though both read-only and read/write memories generally have the property of random access. Random access refers to the fact that all locations within the memory are accessible in the same amount of time.

‡ The reader should be careful to note that the existence of a read-only memory does not imply a Harvard-type computer. In a Von Neumann-type computer the ROM locations may appear anywhere within the memory unit. The key point is that the microprocessor does not know whether it is getting its information from ROM or RWM.

§ In some microprocessor designs, there are several accumulators, called *general-purpose registers*, that are used for the computational processes.

tions and tests is often kept (along with other machine status information) in a special register called the *program status word* (PSW).

The Control Unit

The function of the control unit is to oversee the operation of the computer. It automatically receives the instructions, one at a time, from the memory unit. Then it decodes each instruction and generates the necessary signals to provide for its execution. For the control unit to obtain an instruction, it must first know the instruction's location in the memory. Normally the instructions are in sequential order, and their location is indicated by a *program counter* within the control unit. Furthermore, to decode and provide for instruction execution, the control unit must hold the current instruction. It is the *instruction register* that stores the instruction within the control unit for these purposes.

In order for the control unit to interpret an instruction correctly, the instruction must have a definite organization, called the *instruction format*. The exact instruction format is dependent on the particular microprocessor. However, certain information must be included within an instruction. Most significant are the *operation code* and, in some instructions, an *address*. The operation code is a set of binary digits that uniquely define what operation is to be performed during the execution of the instruction. The address portion of an instruction, if it exists, indicates the location (e.g., in memory) that must be accessed to execute the instruction. For example, if an addition operation is to be performed, the address portion of the instruction may indicate the location of the addend.

It is important that the reader fully understand the use of the word "address" and the difference between the address of a location and the content of the location. There is an address portion in the format of some instructions. This is the numerical designator of a location associated with an operand. However, prior to the execution of an instruction, the instruction itself is stored in the memory. Thus, the instruction itself has an address associated with it. In general, this address is not the same as the address portion in the instruction format.

Maintaining synchronization between the various computer units is another function of the control unit. This is achieved by means of a *clock*. Several clock periods are needed to handle an instruction. In general, an instruction must be fetched from memory, decoded, and then executed. The fetching, decoding, and executing of an instruction is broken down into several time intervals. Each of these intervals, involving one or more clock periods, is called a *machine cycle*. The entire period of time associated with the fetching, decoding, and executing of an instruction is called an *instruction cycle*.

The Input/Output Units

The final two units of a computer are the input and output units. These units are the contact between the computer and the outside world. They act as buffers, translating information between the different speeds and languages with which computers and humans, or other systems, operate. The input unit receives data and instructions from the outside world, which eventually are entered into the memory unit. The output unit receives the computed results and communicates them to the operator or to another system. The input and output devices are known as *peripherals*. Examples are paper-tape readers/punches and typewriters. The places of contact between the input/output devices and the microprocessor are called the *input/output ports*. The input and output ports are also addressable so that several input and output devices can be connected to the microprocessor.

It is characteristic of *digital* computer operation that all information is handled in discrete form, i.e., with finite numbers. Frequently a digital computer must communicate with another system not capable of handling discrete information. Nondiscrete information is termed *analog* or *continuous*. In such a case there must be a transformation between continuous and discrete information. The input and output devices capable of performing this type of transformation are called *analog-to-digital converters* and *digital-to-analog converters*.

Figure 1.1 indicates that the input and output units directly communicate with the arithmetic unit. This is not the only possible organization. To achieve greater overall speed in a computer, it is frequently desirable to allow the input and output units to access memory directly rather than via the arithmetic unit. This is known as *direct memory access* (DMA). The direct memory access concept will be developed in Chap. 9.

Buses

In a microcomputer the various units are connected by *buses*. A bus is a set of lines over which information is transferred from any of several sources to any of several destinations. One common bus structure of a microcomputer is shown in Fig. 1.2.

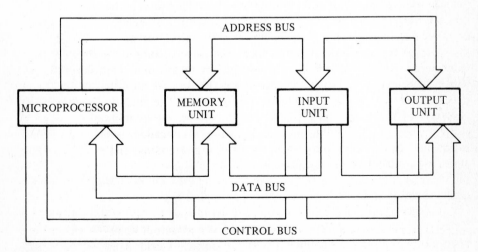

Figure 1.2 The bus structure of a typical microcomputer.

This structure consists of three buses. The *address bus* is unidirectional; i.e., information flows in only one direction. This bus is used to transmit an address from the microprocessor to the memory, input, or output unit. The *data bus* is bidirectional; i.e., information can flow in either direction on these lines, and is the path for data flow. Finally, the *control bus* is the set of lines over which signals travel to maintain timing and status information. Some of these lines are bidirectional, while others are unidirectional. For this reason, no direction for this bus has been indicated in the figure.

1.4 MICROCOMPUTER OPERATION

In the previous section, the functions of the various computer units were explained. In this section, let us consider the way in which the units interact and the dynamics of information flow.

The control unit progresses through three phases of operation: fetch, decode, and execute. After the program and data have been entered into the memory, the address of the first instruction to be executed is placed into the program counter, and the control unit is set to its fetch phase. At this time, the content of the program counter is placed onto the address bus so that the corresponding instruction can be retrieved from memory. The instruction stored at the location specified by the address in the program counter is sent to the instruction register in the control unit via the data bus. Since the instructions are stored in sequential order, the program counter is then incremented by 1 so that it will contain the address of the next word in the program. The control unit now decodes the operation code in the instruction word just received. If it is determined that the instruction consists of more than one word, the fetch phase is repeated a sufficient number of times to retrieve the entire instruction. Each time the fetch phase is performed, the program counter is incremented. After the entire instruction has been fetched and decoded, the control unit enters its execute phase. At this time it proceeds to generate signals to activate the circuits that will perform the specified operation. If an address for an operand is given in the instruction, the control unit then proceeds to arrange for the transfer of the addressed information between the location specified by the instruction and the appropriate computer unit (e.g., the arithmetic unit or the output unit). This transfer is achieved by placing the address portion of the instruction onto the address bus and having the addressed information then appear on the data bus. Finally, the control unit supervises the actual performance of the operation. Upon completion of the operation, the control unit returns to its fetch phase and gets the next instruction from the memory, the address of which is in the program counter. The process is then repeated until the computer is instructed to halt.

In general, as indicated above, the instructions are executed in the sequential order in which they appear in the memory. However, there are occasions when it is desirable to ignore this sequential order, e.g., as the consequence of a decision based on a flag bit. In such a case the location of the next instruction may be other than the location immediately following that of the instruction currently being executed. Instructions that permit this deviation are called *jump* or *branch instructions*. In the case of a jump instruction, the address portion of the instruction contains the location of the next instruction to be fetched by the control unit if the change in sequential order is to be carried out. Thus, upon decoding a jump instruction and establishing that a deviation in the instruction sequence is to occur, the control unit places that part of the current instruction having the address of the next instruction into the program counter. In this way, when the control unit enters the fetch phase, the appropriate next instruction is obtained.

1.5 TWO ADDITIONAL COMPUTER CONCEPTS

Before we conclude this overview of microcomputers, two additional concepts that increase the computer's versatility should be introduced. These are the *stack* and *program interrupts*.

The Stack

It has already been mentioned that jump instructions are used to break away from the sequential ordering of instructions currently being executed. A type of jump instruction, which differs from those previously discussed, allows the repeated use of a specific subset of instructions, called a *subroutine.*

During the course of a (main program) computation, a subcomputation, written as a subroutine, may need to be performed. The computer must jump from the main program to the subroutine, perform the necessary subcomputation, and then return to the point of exit in the main program. A record must be kept of the program counter prior to the jump to ensure the correct return of the computer. This is precisely what is done by a *jump to subroutine* instruction. In particular, the content of the program counter is stored, and then the jump is executed. A special *return from subroutine* instruction is used to retrieve the stored program counter so that reentry into the main program can be made. The place of storage for the program counter is typically in a *stack*.

In general, a stack is a set of registers that accept and return information on a *last-in first-out* (LIFO) basis. This means that only the top of the stack (last-in) is immediately accessible. Depending upon the design of the computer, the stack may appear in the control unit or as part of the memory unit.

By allowing the stack to hold several addresses, the nesting of subroutines becomes possible. That is, a jump from a subroutine to another subroutine can be performed, and even a jump from a subroutine to itself (called *recursion*). Clearly, the degree of nesting is dependent upon the storage capacity of the stack.

Program Interrupts

In many microprocessor applications, it is desirable to interrupt the computing process to service an external device. An interrupt can be performed by having the external device requesting attention transmit a signal to the microprocessor. The microprocessor, in response, can then suspend the operation of its current program, maintain a record of its internal state (i.e., the content of the various registers, including the program counter), and then honor the request of the external device. Upon completion of the interrupt request, the microprocessor then returns to its normal computation by first retrieving the internal-state information previously recorded.

In cases where there are several external devices, a generalization of the interrupt concept is possible. In this case any of the devices may request attention. The actual processing of the requests may be on a first-come first-served basis, or a priority scheme may be established so that the execution of requests is in accordance with the degree of priority.

In any event, the capability of handling interrupts can be a very powerful tool in microprocessor applications. Since the information as to the current state of the microprocessor must be retained when servicing interrupts, the stack concept may again be applied. That is, the internal state of the microprocessor at the time of request, which includes the program counter, is placed into a stack. If a large enough stack is provided, a nesting of interrupts can be handled. In a sense, the interrupt concept is a jump to subroutine that is initiated by an external signal as opposed to an instruction in a program.

1.6 A PREVIEW

The basic structure and operation of a microprocessor and a microcomputer were overviewed in the previous sections. The remaining chapters of this book will elaborate upon the details of the structure and operation just described, as well as many of its variations.

To begin our study, Chap. 2 considers various computer number systems and the methods of performing arithmetic in these number systems. Since a digital computer is a number manipulator, this chapter is fundamental to much of the material that follows it.

Chapter 3 is concerned with an algebra that can serve as a mathematical model for logic networks. The application of this algebra is frequently useful in logic network design. In addition, it provides a convenient way to describe logic network behavior.

Basic digital electronic circuits are the main concern of Chap. 4. These circuits are the realizations of the various algebraic operations introduced in Chap. 3. Furthermore, since the operations have more than one realization, corresponding to different *logic families*, Chap. 4 compares the advantages and disadvantages offered by the various logic families. A knowledge of the logic families is important for the understanding of the electrical characteristics of microprocessors and some of the problems encountered when interconnecting the various units of a microcomputer.

The present chapter has stated that a microcomputer consists of several basic logic networks. For example, registers appear in every functional unit of a microcomputer. Furthermore, computer operation involves register-to-register transfers. In order to achieve these transfers it is necessary to make reference to the individual registers involved. This register selection is achieved by means of a basic logic network called a *decoder*. Decoders are also used to interpret an instruction prior to its execution. This chapter has also shown that an arithmetic capability is part of a microprocessor system. This arithmetic capability is typically achieved through the use of adders and subtractors. The logic details of registers, decoders, adders, and subtractors are studied in Chap. 5.

During the discussion of the memory unit of a computer, it was stated that, in general, two types of memories are used, i.e., read/write memory and read-only memory. In Chap. 6 these two memory types are studied from the point of view of both their electronic structure and their terminal behavior. Furthermore, not all read/write memory has the random-access property previously mentioned. In Chap. 6 the sequential-access memory is also considered.

Chapters 7 and 8 introduce a typical (but hypothetical) microprocessor. This microprocessor is used to illustrate the nature of the instructions that a microprocessor is capable of executing. In addition, the basic principles of microprocessor programming are explained. The microprocessor developed in these two chapters is later used in Chaps. 9 and 10, where microprocessor system design is considered.

Chapter 9 concerns the interconnection of a microprocessor with various system elements. When such elements are interconnected, it is necessary to provide for their compatibility, in regard to timing, data format, and signal type. In general, this compatibility is achieved by designing supplementary circuits known as an *interface*. Several interfacing concepts are studied in Chap. 9.

The final chapter of this book considers the design of three microprocessor systems. The intent is to illustrate microprocessor applications as well as to show how the material developed in the previous chapters is utilized.

TWO

COMPUTER NUMBER SYSTEMS AND ARITHMETIC

Fundamentally, a computer is a device that processes and manipulates information. This information can be either numeric or nonnumeric. In both cases, however, the representation within the computer is a string of 0s and 1s. The net effect is that all information appears as numbers, whether or not it is interpreted numerically.

This chapter covers the binary number system and other number systems closely related to it. Methods of performing arithmetic will be considered. Finally, it will be shown how nonnumeric information can also be represented by strings of 0 and 1 symbols.

2.1 POSITIONAL NUMBER SYSTEMS

Although we are all familiar with the decimal number system, it is not the only number system that can be defined. Actually, the conventional decimal number system is just one in a class of number systems known as *radix-weighted positional number systems*. These number systems utilize a finite number of distinct symbols. Each symbol, called a *digit*, denotes a quantity. The number of these distinct symbols is known as the *base* or *radix* of the number system. In order to denote quantities larger than those associated with the individual symbols, the digits are juxtaposed to form a *number*. The relative position of a digit within the number is then associated with a weighting factor.

Consider the familiar decimal number system. There are only 10 distinct digit symbols that are used in writing a number, i.e., 0, 1, ..., 9. Thus, the number 536.4 is really a shorthand notation for the polynomial

$$5 \times 10^2 + 3 \times 10^1 + 6 \times 10^0 + 4 \times 10^{-1}$$

Table 2.1 Number systems

Base	Number system	Digit symbols
2	Binary	0, 1
3	Ternary	0, 1, 2
4	Quaternary	0, 1, 2, 3
5	Quinary	0, 1, 2, 3, 4
8	Octal	0, 1, 2, 3, 4, 5, 6, 7
10	Decimal	0, 1, 2, 3, 4, 5, 6, 7, 8, 9
12	Duodecimal	0, 1, 2, 3, 4, 5, 6, 7, 8, 9, A, B
16	Hexadecimal	0, 1, 2, 3, 4, 5, 6, 7, 8, 9, A, B, C, D, E, F

Here, the digit symbol 5 is weighted by one hundred, the digit symbol 3 by ten, the digit symbol 6 by one, and the digit symbol 4 by one-tenth.

As an expansion of this idea, a number in a radix-weighted positional number system

$$N = d_{n-1} d_{n-2} \cdots d_1 d_0 . d_{-1} d_{-2} \cdots d_{-m}$$

can be represented by the polynomial

$$N = d_{n-1} b^{n-1} + d_{n-2} b^{n-2} + \cdots + d_{-m} b^{-m}$$

In this general form, the d_i's denote the digit symbols restricted to the range $0 \le d_i < b$, n is the number of digit symbols to the left of the *radix point*, m is the number of digit symbols to the right of the radix point, and b is the base of the number system.

Table 2.1 lists some of the more common number systems. By convention, the digit symbols in number systems whose base is less than 10 are the corresponding first digits of the decimal number system; while those number systems whose base is greater than 10 use the symbols of the decimal number system plus the first letters of the alphabet. It is understood that the relative ordering of the digit symbols in any of these systems is as indicated in the table.

Three radix-weighted positional number systems are of particular interest in the study of computers: the *binary*, *octal*, and *hexadecimal number systems*. Thus, using the digit symbols from Table 2.1, some numbers in these systems are

$$1011.101_2$$

$$372.46_8$$

$$C65F.B3_{16}$$

A decimal subscript following each number is used by convention to indicate the base of that number. The subscript is omitted when the base is understood from the context.

As in the decimal number system, numbers appear as the juxtaposition of the digit symbols associated with the system. The fractional and integral portions

Table 2.2 The first 32 numbers in the binary, octal, and hexadecimal number systems, and their decimal equivalents

Decimal	Binary	Octal	Hexadecimal
0	0	0	0
1	1	1	1
2	10	2	2
3	11	3	3
4	100	4	4
5	101	5	5
6	110	6	6
7	111	7	7
8	1000	10	8
9	1001	11	9
10	1010	12	A
11	1011	13	B
12	1100	14	C
13	1101	15	D
14	1110	16	E
15	1111	17	F
16	10000	20	10
17	10001	21	11
18	10010	22	12
19	10011	23	13
20	10100	24	14
21	10101	25	15
22	10110	26	16
23	10111	27	17
24	11000	30	18
25	11001	31	19
26	11010	32	1A
27	11011	33	1B
28	11100	34	1C
29	11101	35	1D
30	11110	36	1E
31	11111	37	1F

correspond to those parts to the right and left, respectively, of the radix point. In the case of the binary system, the symbols 0 and 1 are called *bits* as an abbreviation for *bi*nary digi*ts*.

Table 2.2 lists the first 32 integers in the binary, octal, and hexadecimal number systems, along with their decimal equivalents.

2.2 NUMBER CONVERSIONS

One interpretation of numbers is that of denoting quantities. Thus, it is interesting to determine the configuration of symbols in one number system that denotes the same quantity as the configuration of symbols in another number system. These two numbers can then be regarded as equivalent representations of the same quantity in different systems.

Number Conversion into Decimal

Let us first consider the conversion of any nondecimal number (in a radix-weighted positional number system) into its equivalent decimal form. This conversion can be achieved easily by evaluating the polynomial representation of the number. In particular, the conversion process is performed as follows:

1. Express the number in the polynomial form

$$d_{n-1}d_{n-2} \cdots d_0 . d_{-1} \cdots d_{-m} = d_{n-1}b^{n-1} + d_{n-2}b^{n-2} + \cdots$$
$$+ d_0 b^0 + d_{-1}b^{-1} + \cdots + d_{-m}b^{-m}$$

where b is the base of the number system expressed as a positive decimal integer, i.e., 2, 3, ... For those number systems having alphabetic digit symbols, the decimal equivalent of the alphabetic symbol is used in the polynomial, e.g., $A = 10$, $B = 11$, $C = 12$, ...
2. Evaluate the polynomial using decimal arithmetic.

To illustrate the binary-to-decimal conversion, consider the binary number 1110.1_2. Writing this number as a polynomial in powers of 2, i.e., in powers of the base of the number system, we get

$$1110.1_2 = 1 \times 2^3 + 1 \times 2^2 + 1 \times 2^1 + 0 \times 2^0 + 1 \times 2^{-1}$$
$$= 1 \times 8 + 1 \times 4 + 1 \times 2 + 0 \times 1 + 1 \times 0.5$$
$$= 8 + 4 + 2 + 0 + 0.5$$
$$= 14.5_{10}$$

Thus, 14.5 is the decimal equivalent of the binary number 1110.1.

As a second example, the hexadecimal number $D3F.4_{16}$ can be converted into a decimal number as follows:

$$D3F.4_{16} = D \times 16^2 + 3 \times 16^1 + F \times 16^0 + 4 \times 16^{-1}$$
$$= 13 \times 16^2 + 3 \times 16^1 + 15 \times 16^0 + 4 \times 16^{-1}$$
$$= 13 \times 256 + 3 \times 16 + 15 \times 1 + 4 \times 0.0625$$
$$= 3328 + 48 + 15 + 0.25$$
$$= 3391.25_{10}$$

Number Conversion from Decimal

The conversion of a decimal number into its equivalent form in some other number system, on the other hand, is slightly more difficult. This conversion requires treating the integral portion of the decimal number separately from the fractional portion.

Consider first the conversion of a decimal integer N_I into its equivalent base-b number (where b is a positive integer). Since the base-b number can be expressed as a polynomial in powers of b and the base-b digit symbols, we can write

$$N_I = d_{n-1}b^{n-1} + \cdots + d_1 b^1 + d_0 b^0$$
$$= d_{n-1}b^{n-1} + \cdots + d_1 b^1 + d_0 \qquad (2.1)$$

It now remains for us to determine the base-b digit symbols $d_{n-1}, \ldots, d_1, d_0$ that satisfy this equality. To do this, both sides of Eq. (2-1) can be divided by b. This division results in an integral quotient

$$N_I' = d_{n-1}b^{n-2} + \cdots + d_2 b^1 + d_1 b^0 \qquad (2.2)$$

and a remainder

$$\text{Remainder}\left(\frac{N_I}{b}\right) = d_0$$

Thus, the remainder is equal to the least-significant digit of the base-b number, i.e., d_0. As a result of this computation, the remainder can consist of more than a single digit when b is greater than 10. However, since the remainder will always be less than b, d_0 in the base-b number must be the digit symbol corresponding to the quantity indicated by the remainder.

If the division process is now repeated on the integral quotient of Eq. (2.2), the result is the integral quotient

$$N_I'' = d_{n-1}b^{n-3} + \cdots + d_2 b^0$$

and the remainder

$$\text{Remainder}\left(\frac{N_I'}{b}\right) = d_1$$

In this case the remainder corresponds to the next least-significant digit of the number in base b. Clearly, by repeating this process until the resulting quotient is 0, the digit symbols of Eq. (2.1) can be generated. (It should be kept in mind that the remainders are to be represented by the corresponding base-b digit symbols.) Furthermore, this procedure will terminate in a finite number of steps.

As an illustration of the above procedure, consider the conversion of the decimal number 52 into its equivalent binary form. The computation proceeds, using repeated divisions by 2, as follows:

	Remainder
2)52	
2)26	$0 = d_0$
2)13	$0 = d_1$
2)6	$1 = d_2$
2)3	$0 = d_3$
2)1	$1 = d_4$
0	$1 = d_5$

Therefore, $52_{10} = 110100_2$.

As a second illustration, consider the conversion of the decimal number 58506 into a hexadecimal number. Repeated divisions by 16 yield

	Remainder	Digit symbol equivalent to remainder
16)58506		
16)3656	10	$A = d_0$
16)228	8	$8 = d_1$
16)14	4	$4 = d_2$
0	14	$E = d_3$

Therefore, $58506_{10} = E48A_{16}$.

To convert a decimal fraction into a base-b fraction, a different procedure is necessary. To develop this procedure, let N_F be a decimal fraction having the equivalent polynomial

$$d_{-1}b^{-1} + d_{-2}b^{-2} + \cdots + d_{-m}b^{-m}$$

where $d_{-1}, d_{-2}, \ldots, d_{-m}$ are the base-b digits that must be determined. Since this polynomial denotes the same quantity as N_F, we have

$$N_F = d_{-1}b^{-1} + d_{-2}b^{-2} + \cdots + d_{-m}b^{-m} \qquad (2.3)$$

Multiplying both sides of this equation by b results in

$$bN_F = d_{-1}b^0 + d_{-2}b^{-1} + \cdots + d_{-m}b^{-m+1}$$
$$= d_{-1} + d_{-2}b^{-1} + \cdots + d_{-m}b^{-m+1}$$
$$= d_{-1} + N'_F \qquad (2.4)$$

The product consists of an integral portion d_{-1} and a fractional portion N'_F. The integral portion is equivalent to the most-significant fractional digit of the base-b number being determined. Again it should be realized that the integral quantity corresponding to d_{-1} can be anywhere in the range from 0 to $b - 1$. Hence, in dealing with base-b number systems where b is greater than 10, the appropriate alphabetic digit symbol must be used for d_{-1}.

If the fractional result of Eq. (2.4) is now manipulated in a similar manner, i.e., multiplied by b, the second most-significant digit of the fractional expansion given by Eq. (2.3) can be determined. In particular, since

$$bN'_F = d_{-2}b^0 + d_{-3}b^{-1} + \cdots + d_{-m}b^{-m+2}$$
$$= d_{-2} + d_{-3}b^{-1} + \cdots + d_{-m}b^{-m+2}$$
$$= d_{-2} + N''_F$$

the integral portion of the product corresponds to d_{-2}. Clearly, by repeating this process on the fractional portion of each product, the remaining digits of the base-b number can be established. This process should be continued until no product has a fractional portion. However, even though the conversion of a decimal integer into a base-b integer always terminates in a finite number of steps, this is not the case for decimal fractions. That is, a decimal fraction with a finite number of digits may have a base-b equivalent with an infinite number of digits. For this reason, the conversion process is terminated when the desired precision is obtained.

Two examples will illustrate the conversion of a decimal fraction into a base-b fraction. Consider first the conversion of the decimal number 0.6875 into binary form. The conversion proceeds as follows:

$$2 \times 0.6875 = 1.3750 \qquad \therefore d_{-1} = 1$$

$$2 \times 0.375 \; = 0.750 \qquad \therefore d_{-2} = 0$$

$$2 \times 0.75 \; \; = 1.50 \qquad \therefore d_{-3} = 1$$

$$2 \times 0.5 \; \; \; = 1.0 \qquad \therefore d_{-4} = 1$$

Collecting the generated digits, we have $0.6875_{10} = 0.1011_2$.

For a second example, consider the conversion of the decimal fraction 0.8435 into a hexadecimal fraction. The series of multiplications that must be performed are

$$16 \times 0.8435 = 13.496 \qquad \therefore d_{-1} = D \qquad \text{since D is the hexadecimal digit for the decimal number 13}$$

$$16 \times 0.496 \; = 7.936 \qquad \therefore d_{-2} = 7$$

$$16 \times 0.936 \; = 14.976 \qquad \therefore d_{-3} = E$$

$$16 \times 0.976 \; = 15.616 \qquad \therefore d_{-4} = F$$

Terminating at this point, we are left with the result that $0.8435_{10} = 0.D7EF \cdots_{16}$. It should be noted in this example that the conversion could not be carried to completion, since a 6 will always be obtained in the third fractional-digit position at each step.

For the case of a mixed decimal number, the integral and fractional portions are handled separately. In particular, the integral decimal portion is converted into a base-b integer by repeated divisions, and the fractional decimal portion is converted into a base-b fraction by repeated multiplications as indicated above. Then the mixed base-b number is formed by connecting the two portions with a radix point.

2.3 BINARY-OCTAL AND BINARY-HEXADECIMAL CONVERSIONS

By using the procedures of the previous section, it is possible to convert any number from base b_1 into base b_2 by first converting the base-b_1 number into a decimal number and then into base b_2. Generalizations of these procedures also exist that allow a direct conversion between two bases. In general, these direct procedures are difficult for human computation, since they involve nondecimal arithmetic. However, there are simple, direct conversion procedures between binary numbers and those numbers whose bases are a power of 2. Two such cases pertain to octal numbers, whose base is $8 = 2^3$, and hexadecimal numbers, whose base is $16 = 2^4$.

Consider a binary number

$$N = \cdots d_8 d_7 d_6 d_5 d_4 d_3 d_2 d_1 d_0 \,.\, d_{-1} d_{-2} d_{-3} \cdots$$

The decimal equivalent is obtained by writing the polynomial

$$\cdots d_8 2^8 + d_7 2^7 + d_6 2^6 + d_5 2^5 + d_4 2^4 + d_3 2^3 + d_2 2^2$$
$$+ d_1 2^1 + d_0 2^0 + d_{-1} 2^{-1} + d_{-2} 2^{-2} + d_{-3} 2^{-3} \cdots$$

By performing some simple factoring, the above expression can be manipulated into the form

$$\cdots + (d_8 2^2 + d_7 2^1 + d_6 2^0) 2^6$$
$$+ (d_5 2^2 + d_4 2^1 + d_3 2^0) 2^3$$
$$+ (d_2 2^2 + d_1 2^1 + d_0 2^0) 2^0$$
$$+ (d_{-1} 2^2 + d_{-2} 2^1 + d_{-3} 2^0) 2^{-3} + \cdots$$

$$= \cdots + (d_8 2^2 + d_7 2^1 + d_6 2^0) 8^2$$
$$+ (d_5 2^2 + d_4 2^1 + d_3 2^0) 8^1$$
$$+ (d_2 2^2 + d_1 2^1 + d_0 2^0) 8^0$$
$$+ (d_{-1} 2^2 + d_{-2} 2^1 + d_{-3} 2^0) 8^{-1} + \cdots$$

This expression, involving powers of 8, has the form of an octal number. Furthermore, within each pair of parentheses is the binary equivalent of a decimal number between 0 and 7. If the quantity within each pair of parentheses is replaced by its equivalent octal digit (which is the same as its equivalent decimal digit), the conversion from binary into octal form is completed.

In summary, to convert a binary number into its octal equivalent, the bits of the binary number are grouped into blocks of 3 bits by starting at the binary point and working both left and right. Additional leading and trailing 0s are included if needed. Then, each block of 3 bits is replaced by its octal equivalent. The result is the octal representation of the initial binary number. For example, the bits of the binary number 11011001.1011 can be grouped as follows:

$$011\,011\,001\,.\,101\,100_2$$

By replacing each block of 3 bits by its octal equivalent, the octal representation

$$331.54_8$$

is obtained.

The above procedure can also be reversed so as to convert an octal number into its binary form. For example, starting with the octal number 57.2, we have

$$57.2_8 = \underline{101}\,\underline{111}.\underline{010}_2$$

An analogous conversion procedure between binary and hexadecimal numbers can also be developed. In this case, blocks of four binary digits are related to a single hexadecimal digit. For example, to convert the binary number 1011100101.11_2 into a hexadecimal number, the bits are grouped into blocks of four by proceeding left and right from the binary point and including any needed leading and trailing 0s:

$$\underline{0010}\,\underline{1110}\,\underline{0101}.\underline{1100}_2$$

Replacing each block by its hexadecimal equivalent completes the conversion procedure:

$$001011100101.1100_2 = 2E5.C_{16}$$

Reversing this procedure provides a means of converting hexadecimal numbers into binary numbers.

As was mentioned in the previous chapter, computers normally use the binary number system. However, because of the simple conversion procedures just established and the need for fewer digits in a number, it is more convenient from the viewpoint of reading and writing numbers to regard all numbers as being octal or hexadecimal. This is the reason for their common usage in the computer industry.

2.4 BINARY ARITHMETIC

The four basic arithmetic operations, i.e., addition, subtraction, multiplication, and division, can be performed in any radix-weighted positional number system. Since computers normally use the binary number system, it is important to understand arithmetic in this number system. Although in the ensuing discussion only binary arithmetic will be emphasized, the reader should be able to generalize from these principles to other number systems.

Table 2.3 summarizes the rules for the binary addition of two digits. It should be noted that a carry bit is generated under the binary addition $1 + 1$ and that the sum bit is 0.†

In order to add two binary numbers, one applies the rules of Table 2.3 on an order-by-order basis, starting with the pair of least-significant digits, just as one does in the case of decimal addition. After the least-significant pair of digits is added, forming the least-significant sum digit, the next pair of least-significant digits is added along with the carry from the previous-order addition. This process

---

† In general, when the addition of two base-b digits is equal to or exceeds the base of the number system, the sum is formed modulo the base and a carry digit is generated.

**Table 2.3 Two-digit
binary addition table**

$a + b$ b

		0	1
	0	0	1
a	1	1	0 and carry 1

allows the generation of another sum digit and a possible carry. The process is then repeated. The following is an example:

$$
\begin{array}{rl}
111 \quad 1 & \text{Carries} \\
1011.101_2 & \text{Augend} \\
+ \quad 1110.001_2 & \text{Addend} \\
\hline
11001.110_2 & \text{Sum}
\end{array}
$$

Binary subtraction is the inverse of binary addition. The rules for this operation are summarized in Table 2.4. It can be seen that when a larger digit is to be subtracted from a smaller digit, it is necessary to "borrow" from the next-higher-order digit position. In decimal subtraction, when "borrowing" occurs at the nth-order position, 1 is subtracted from the $(n + 1)$th-order minuend digit, and the amount brought back to the nth-order position from the $(n + 1)$th-order position is 10 (i.e., the base of the number system). This very same principle applies to binary subtraction, with the slight variation that the amount brought back to the nth-order position from the $(n + 1)$th-order position is 2 (i.e., the base of the number system being used). Again, in borrowing, 1 is subtracted from the $(n + 1)$th-order minuend digit. Thus, as indicated by Table 2.4, when 1 is sub-

**Table 2.4 Two-digit
binary subtraction table**

$a - b$ b

		0	1
	0	0	1 and borrow 1
a	1	1	0

**Table 2.5 Two-digit
binary multiplication table**

$a \times b$	b	
	0	1
0	0	0
1	0	1

tracted from 0, the difference after borrowing is 1. The following example illustrates binary subtraction:

010	Modification of minuend resulting from borrowing
$1\not{0}10.11_2$	Minuend
$-\ \ 111.01_2$	Subtrahend
11.10_2	Difference

The rules for two-digit binary multiplication are shown in Table 2.5. Binary multiplication of two numbers follows the same procedure as decimal multiplication in that an array of partial products is formed, based on the multiplier and multiplicand, and then the partial products are added. However, the addition is now binary. The principle of binary multiplication is readily seen by the following example:

11.01_2	Multiplicand
$\times\ \ 101_2$	Multiplier
1101	
0000	Array of partial products
1101	
10000.01_2	Product

Finally, binary division is completely analogous to decimal division. A trial quotient digit is selected and multiplied by the divisor. The product is subtracted from the dividend to determine whether the trial quotient is correct. The multiplication and subtraction operations involved in binary division are the binary operations previously discussed. Although this trial-and-error procedure is a familiar process to us in performing decimal division, it is considerably simpler in binary division since there are only two possible quotient bits (0 or 1) for each order position that must be considered. The following is an example of binary division:

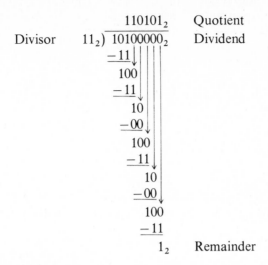

$$
\begin{array}{r}
110101_2 \quad \text{Quotient} \\
\text{Divisor} \quad 11_2)\ \overline{10100000_2} \quad \text{Dividend} \\
-11 \\
\hline
100 \\
-11 \\
\hline
10 \\
-00 \\
\hline
100 \\
-11 \\
\hline
10 \\
-00 \\
\hline
100 \\
-11 \\
\hline
1_2 \quad \text{Remainder}
\end{array}
$$

2.5 SIGNED BINARY NUMBERS

All the numbers that have been considered thus far were assumed to be unsigned or, equivalently, always positive. However, from our past experiences with numbers, we know that it is frequently of interest to deal with both positive and negative quantities. It should be realized immediately that an appropriate symbol could be simply appended to the number to handle the concept of signed numbers. However, with the computer in mind, it is frequently useful to consider signed numbers in a slightly different way.

Three representations of signed binary numbers have been of interest to computer people: the *sign-magnitude representation*, the *1's-complement representation*, and the *2's-complement representation*. This section will consider these three representations. Furthermore, since a radix point does not appear explicitly within a microcomputer data word, we shall use only integers in studying signed binary numbers.

Sign-Magnitude Representation

When a digital computer is required to manipulate numbers, the total number of bits that comprise the numbers is known and fixed. Furthermore, since computers represent all information by means of 0s and 1s, the concept of a sign must also be represented with these symbols. A straightforward approach is to reserve one bit of the number, say, the most-significant bit, as the sign bit, where 0 denotes positive and 1 denotes negative. The remaining bits are then used to denote a magnitude as a conventional binary number. This approach is known as the

Table 2.6 Three computer representations of signed binary numbers using 4 bits

The most-significant bit corresponds to the sign; the comma in a number appears only for emphasis and should not be regarded as part of the signed binary number

Signed decimal equivalent	Sign-magnitude representation	1's-complement representation	2's-complement representation
+7	0,111	0,111	0,111
+6	0,110	0,110	0,110
+5	0,101	0,101	0,101
+4	0,100	0,100	0,100
+3	0,011	0,011	0,011
+2	0,010	0,010	0,010
+1	0,001	0,001	0,001
0	$\begin{cases} 0{,}000 \\ 1{,}000 \end{cases}$	$\begin{cases} 0{,}000 \\ 1{,}111 \end{cases}$	0,000
−1	1,001	1,110	1,111
−2	1,010	1,101	1,110
−3	1,011	1,100	1,101
−4	1,100	1,011	1,100
−5	1,101	1,010	1,011
−6	1,110	1,001	1,010
−7	1,111	1,000	1,001
−8	—	—	1,000

sign-magnitude representation of signed binary numbers. Table 2.6 illustrates this concept by showing the signed decimal and the equivalent sign-magnitude representation of all 4-bit binary numbers. Here, the most-significant bit of the sign-magnitude representation serves as the sign bit, and the remaining 3 bits denote the magnitude in the binary number system. In this table, the comma in a number is to be regarded only as a demarcator to separate the sign bit from the magnitude bits for ease of reading. In a computer data word, of course, the comma will *not* actually appear. Furthermore, it should be noted that in this table, 0 has two different representations.

In the sign-magnitude representation, if the signed binary number consists of n bits and is denoted by $X = d_{n-1} d_{n-2} \cdots d_0$, where the most-significant bit corresponds to the sign, it can be seen that the decimal equivalent is given by the polynomial

$$(-1)^{d_{n-1}}(d_{n-2}2^{n-2} + d_{n-3}2^{n-3} + \cdots + d_0 2^0)$$

The range of the numbers in this representation is

$$1 - 2^{n-1} \le X_{10} \le 2^{n-1} - 1$$

where X_{10} is the signed decimal equivalent of X.

1's-Complement Representation

Although the sign-magnitude representation is commonly used by humans, computers usually denote signed numbers in a *complement representation*. In this representation, positive quantities appear exactly as in the sign-magnitude representation. The negative quantities, however, have a representation equivalent to that of displacing the magnitude by a constant. That is, if z denotes some positive quantity, then $-z$ is denoted by $K - z$, where K is such that the result of the subtraction is positive. The value of K selected depends upon which complement representation is used, the 1's-complement representation or the 2's-complement representation.

Let X_{10} denote a signed decimal number that is to be represented in the 1's-complement system with n bits, including the sign bit. Thus, $n - 1$ bits are available for the magnitude portion of the representation. If $X_{10} \geq 0$, the n-bit 1's-complement representation has a 0 in the most-significant-bit position, which is regarded as the sign bit, followed by the $(n - 1)$-bit conventional binary representation of X_{10}. Thus, positive numbers in the 1's-complement representation appear exactly as in their sign-magnitude representation. On the other hand, if $X_{10} \leq 0$, the n-bit 1's-complement representation has a 1 in the most-significant-bit position, which is regarded as the sign bit, followed by the $(n - 1)$-bit binary number whose decimal equivalent is

$$2^{n-1} - 1 - |X_{10}| \tag{2.5}$$

To illustrate the 1's-complement representation, consider the positive number $+13_{10}$. Assuming a 6-bit 1's-complement representation including a sign, i.e., $n = 6$, we have $0,01101_2$. It should be noted that 5 bits are used to denote the magnitude. Again the comma in the number is being used to indicate the sign bit. Within a computer this demarcator does not actually appear. Next consider the negative number -13_{10}. Again assume that a 6-bit 1's-complement representation including a sign, i.e., $n = 6$, is desired. Since $|-13_{10}| = 13_{10} = 01101_2$, expressed in 5 bits, and $(2^5 - 1)_{10} = 11111_2$, Eq. (2.5) yields

$$(2^{6-1} - 1 - 13)_{10} = (11111 - 01101)_2 = 10010_2$$

expressed in 5 bits. With the sign bit appended, the 6-bit 1's-complement representation of -13_{10} becomes $1,10010_2$. Additional examples of the 1's-complement representation are given in Table 2.6, which shows the signed decimal equivalent and the 1's-complement representation of all 4-bit binary numbers. It should be noted that in the table, there exist two representations for 0.

Actually, whenever a sequence of binary digits denoting a magnitude M is subjected to Eq. (2.5), where $n - 1$ is the number of bits in M, the result is known as the *1's-complement of M*. For signed 1's-complement binary numbers, the process of applying Eq. (2.5) to the magnitude portion of a signed 1's-complement binary number and reversing the sign bit is known as *taking the 1's-complement of a signed binary number* (or, more simply, *complementing the signed number*). Thus, regarding the above example, $1,10010_2$ is said to be the 1's-complement of $0,01101_2$.

To illustrate the process of taking the complement of a negative number, again consider the decimal number -13_{10}. The 1's-complement representation of this signed number was shown to be $1,10010_2$. Since the magnitude portion of the signed number, i.e., 10010_2, corresponds to 18_{10} and since the signed representation has 6 bits, by applying Eq. (2.5) we have

$$(2^{6-1} - 1 - 18)_{10} = (11111 - 10010)_2 = 01101_2$$

expressed in 5 bits. With the opposite sign bit appended, the 1's-complement of the signed binary number $1,10010_2$ is therefore $0,01101_2 = +13_{10}$. It can be seen that taking the complement of a signed number is equivalent to taking the negative of the number.

There is a very simple rule for complementing signed numbers in the 1's-complement system. In particular, if each 0 in the number is replaced by 1 and each 1 by 0, including the sign bit, the complement of the signed number is obtained. This property is readily seen in the above example, where $+13_{10}$ is represented by $0,01101_2$ and -13_{10} by $1,10010_2$.

In the 1's-complement representation, if $X = d_{n-1}d_{n-2} \cdots d_0$ is an n-bit signed binary number, it can be seen that its decimal equivalent is given by

$$(1 - 2^{n-1})d_{n-1} + d_{n-2}2^{n-2} + \cdots + d_0 2^0$$

The range of X is

$$1 - 2^{n-1} \leq X_{10} \leq 2^{n-1} - 1$$

where X_{10} is the signed decimal equivalent of X. It should be noted that the sign bit is associated with a negative weighting factor.

2's-Complement Representation

The most commonly used representation of signed binary numbers in microcomputers is the 2's-complement representation. Let X_{10} denote a signed decimal number that is to be represented in the 2's-complement system with n bits, i.e., 1 bit to denote the sign and $n - 1$ bits to denote a magnitude. As in the case of sign-magnitude and 1's-complement representations, if $X_{10} \geq 0$, the n-bit 2's-complement representation has a 0 in the most-significant-bit position, which is regarded as the sign bit, followed by the $(n - 1)$-bit conventional binary representation of X_{10}. On the other hand, if $X_{10} < 0$, the n-bit 2's-complement representation has a 1 in the most-significant-bit position, which is regarded as the sign bit, followed by the $(n - 1)$-bit binary number whose decimal equivalent is

$$2^{n-1} - |X_{10}| \tag{2.6}$$

To show the application of Eq. (2.6), consider again the negative number -13_{10}. Assume that a 6-bit 2's-complement representation including a sign, i.e., $n = 6$, is desired. Since $|-13_{10}| = 13_{10} = 01101_2$, expressed in 5 bits, and

$2_{10}^5 = 100000_2$, Eq. (2.6) yields

$$(2^{6-1} - 13)_{10} = (100000 - 01101)_{10} = 10011_2$$

expressed in 5 bits. With the sign bit appended, the 6-bit 2's-complement representation of -13_{10} becomes $1,10011_2$. The signed decimal equivalent and the 2's-complement representation of all 4-bit binary numbers is shown in Table 2.6. It should be noted that in the table, 0 has a single representation in the 2's-complement system.

Since 0 has a single representation, the range of integers is slightly larger in the 2's-complement system than in the other two systems previously discussed. Again the sign bit is weighted negatively, so that in the 2's-complement representation, if the n-bit signed binary number is $X = d_{n-1}d_{n-2} \cdots d_0$, its decimal equivalent is given by

$$-2^{n-1}d_{n-1} + d_{n-2}2^{n-2} + \cdots + d_0 2^0 \tag{2.7}$$

The range of X is

$$-2^{n-1} \leq X_{10} \leq 2^{n-1} - 1$$

where X_{10} is the signed decimal equivalent of X.

Whenever a sequence of binary digits denoting a magnitude M is subjected to Eq. (2.6), where $n - 1$ is the number of bits in M, the result is known as the *2's-complement of M*. For signed 2's-complement binary numbers, the process of applying Eq. (2.6) to the magnitude portion of the signed binary number and reversing the sign bit is known as *taking the 2's-complement of a signed binary number* (or, more simply, *complementing the signed number*). The effect of taking the 2's-complement of a signed binary number is equivalent to taking the negative of the number.

Recall that the 2's-complement representation of -13_{10} is $1,10011_2$. Since the magnitude portion of the signed number, i.e., 10011_2, corresponds to 19_{10} and since the signed representation has 6 bits, by applying Eq. (2.6) we have

$$(2^{6-1} - 19)_{10} = (100000 - 10011)_2 = 01101_2$$

expressed in 5 bits. With the opposite sign bit appended, the 2's-complement of the signed binary number $1,10011_2$ is therefore $0,01101_2 = +13_{10}$.

The close relationship between Eqs. (2.5) and (2.6) forms the basis for a common algorithm for taking the 2's-complement of a signed binary number. First the 1's-complement of the signed binary number is formed, as discussed previously, by replacing each 0 and 1 of the number by 1 and 0, respectively. Then 1 is added to the result. The sum is the 2's-complement.†

---

† Another common algorithm for taking the 2's-complement of a signed binary number is as follows: Proceeding left from the least-significant bit, all 0s up to the first 1 and the first 1 itself are retained unaltered. After the first 1, all the remaining 0s and 1s, including the sign bit, are replaced by 1s and 0s, respectively.

Two cases need attention in applying the above algorithm. First, since 0 has a single representation, if the above procedure is applied, starting with the number 0, the carry into the $(n + 1)$-bit position should be ignored. Second, the range of numbers is not the same in the 1's-complement representation and the 2's-complement representation. In particular, $+2^{n-1}$ does not exist in the 1's-complement representation. For this reason, -2^{n-1} in the 2's-complement representation cannot be obtained by the above algorithm. However, -2^{n-1} does have the unique 2's-complement representation

$$\underbrace{100 \cdots 0}_{n - 1 \ 0s}$$

as indicated by Eq. (2.7).

2.6 SIGNED BINARY ADDITION AND SUBTRACTION

Computers make extensive use of the complement representation of numbers. This representation allows simple realizations of signed addition and subtraction. It was noted in the preceding section that taking the complement of a signed number in a complement system has the effect of taking the negative of the number.† Thus, the signed subtraction process can be achieved by first performing complementation of the subtrahend and then performing signed addition. Furthermore, as will be seen in this section, signed addition is essentially achieved by simply performing conventional, unsigned binary addition, as discussed in Sec. 2.4, on all bits of the numbers, including the sign bits. The net result is that if the complement representation of signed numbers is used, there is no need for both adder and subtractor networks in a computer.

Addition and Subtraction with 2's-Complement Representation

Let us first consider signed binary addition when the 2's-complement number representation is used. Assume that the two numbers are both expressed with n bits. In this case, the two signed binary numbers are added according to the rules of binary addition developed in Sec. 2.4, bit position by bit position, including the sign bits. If a carry is generated from the sign-bit position, it is disregarded. Assuming that the algebraic sum can be adequately represented with n bits, i.e., if it is in the range $-2^{n-1} \leq \text{sum} \leq 2^{n-1} - 1$, the result of this addition will be algebraically correct and in the 2's-complement representation. The following examples illustrate this algorithm. The reader should carefully note that the 2's-complement representation with 5 bits is used in these examples.

---

† The single exception to this occurs when the n-bit number is the 2's-complement representation of -2^{n-1}.

Example

$$
\begin{array}{rlr}
\text{Augend} & (+6) = & 0,0110 \\
\text{Addend} & +(-4) = & +1,1100 \\
\hline
\text{Sum} & (+2) = & 1\rfloor 0,0010
\end{array}
$$

↑—— Carry disregarded

Example

$$
\begin{array}{rlr}
\text{Augend} & (+6) = & 0,0110 \\
\text{Addend} & +(-13) = & +1,0011 \\
\hline
\text{Sum} & (-7) = & 1,1001
\end{array}
$$

Example

$$
\begin{array}{rlr}
\text{Augend} & (-3) = & 1,1101 \\
\text{Addend} & +(-11) = & +1,0101 \\
\hline
\text{Sum} & (-14) = & 1\rfloor 1,0010
\end{array}
$$

↑——Carry disregarded

When the two n-bit numbers have the same sign, it is possible that their signed sum will not be within the range representable with n bits. This is known as an *overflow* condition and must be detected. In general, the overflow condition exists only when the two numbers have the same signs and the result of the addition has the opposite sign. Another common algorithm for the detection of the overflow condition involves the existence of a carry *into* the sign-bit position C_s and the existence of a carry *from* the sign-bit position C_{s+1}. In particular, there is an overflow if and only if (1) $C_s = 0$ and $C_{s+1} = 1$ or (2) $C_s = 1$ and $C_{s+1} = 0$.

As was stated previously, signed binary subtraction can be performed by first taking the complement of the subtrahend and then performing signed binary addition. The following examples illustrate this procedure.

Example

$$
\begin{array}{rll}
\text{Minuend} & (+12) = & 0,1100 \\
\text{Subtrahend} & -(+7) = & -0,0111 \\
\hline
\text{Difference} & (+5) = &
\end{array}
\xrightarrow{\text{Take 2's-comp.}}
\begin{array}{l}
0,1100 \\
+1,1001 \\
\hline
1\rfloor 0,0101
\end{array}
$$

↑——— Carry disregarded

Example

$$
\begin{array}{rll}
\text{Minuend} & (-14) = & 1,0010 \\
\text{Subtrahend} & -(-3) = & -1,1101 \\
\hline
\text{Difference} & (-11) = &
\end{array}
\xrightarrow{\text{Take 2's-comp.}}
\begin{array}{l}
1,0010 \\
+0,0011 \\
\hline
1,0101
\end{array}
$$

Addition and Subtraction with 1's-Complement Representation

Although most microprocessors utilize the 2's-complement representation for signed binary numbers, the 1's-complement representation can also be used. Furthermore, signed addition and subtraction can be performed with such a representation. The algorithm to perform signed addition with the 1's-complement representation is as follows: The two signed binary numbers are added, including the sign bits, according to the rules of unsigned binary addition. If a carry is generated from the addition of the sign bits, it is carried around to the least-significant-bit position of the sum and added to it. This is known as the *end-around carry*. The sum will be algebraically correct, including the sign, and in the 1's-complement number representation if the result does not indicate that an overflow condition exists. As in the case of numbers in 2's-complement representation, the overflow condition exists if and only if the two operands have the same signs and the result has the opposite sign. The existence of the carries into and from the sign-bit position, prior to the end-around carry operation, can also be used to detect an overflow as indicated previously.

It should be noted that the signed addition algorithm for numbers in the 1's-complement representation is the same as that for numbers in the 2's-complement representation, with the single change that if a carry is generated out of the sign-bit position, 1 must be added to the result. The following examples illustrate this algorithm. It should be noted that all numbers consist of 5 bits and are in the 1's-complement representation.

Example

$$
\begin{array}{rlr}
\text{Augend} & (+14) = & 0{,}1110 \\
\text{Addend} & +\ (-3) = & +1{,}1100 \\
\hline
& & 1\,|\,0{,}1010 \\
& + & \nearrow 1 = \text{End-around carry} \\
\hline
\text{Sum} & (+11) = & 0{,}1011
\end{array}
$$

Example

$$
\begin{array}{rlr}
\text{Augend} & (+9) = & 0{,}1001 \\
\text{Addend} & +(-14) = & +1{,}0001 \\
\hline
\text{Sum} & (-5) = & 1{,}1010
\end{array}
$$

Signed binary subtraction can also be done with the 1's-complement number representation by first taking the 1's-complement of the subtrahend and then performing signed addition. The following example illustrates the procedure for signed binary subtraction.

Example

Minuend	$(-6) =$	1,1001	1,1001
Subtrahend	$-(-13) =$	$-1,0010 \xrightarrow{\text{Take 1's-comp.}}$	$+0,1101$

$$1\,|\,0,0110$$

$+ \qquad \searrow 1 = \text{End-around carry}$

Difference	$(+7) =$	0,0111

2.7 BINARY-CODED DECIMAL NUMBERS AND DECIMAL ARITHMETIC

The popularity of the binary number system in computer technology can be attributed to the simplicity and reliability of circuits that can be used for handling numbers that have only two digit symbols. To humans, however, this number system is awkward. Thus, frequently a digital system is desired that will operate with the use of decimal numbers. To have the two advantages of using simple binary circuits and still have the convenience of the decimal number system, schemes are used in which the digits of the decimal system are coded by groups of binary digits. The computer then considers each code group as a single entity. Coding schemes in which each decimal digit is represented by a binary code group are called *binary-coded decimal schemes*.

Binary Codes for the Decimal Digits

Several schemes have been developed to code the decimal digits. The best known is the *8421 binary-coded decimal (8421 BCD) scheme*.† In this coding scheme, the first ten 4-bit binary numbers are used to denote the 10 decimal digits. This code is shown in Table 2.7. The name 8421 BCD comes from the fact that these are the weights associated with the 4 corresponding bits of the code group. For this reason such a coding scheme is called a *weighted code*.

By concatenating the code groups for the decimal digits, the 8421 BCD representation of larger decimal numbers can be formed. For example, the 8421 BCD representation of the decimal number 658 is simply 0110 0101 1000. It should be noted that to avoid any ambiguity, the number of bits within each code group must be fixed. Leading 0s are used for the code groups corresponding to the decimal digits 0 through 7.

Although the 8421 BCD scheme is the one most commonly encountered in computers when decimal representations are desired, other codes have been used. Some of these are also listed in Table 2.7. The *excess-3 code* is a nonweighted code.

---

† The 8421 BCD scheme is frequently called simply *BCD*.

Table 2.7 Binary codes for the decimal digits

Decimal digit	8421 binary code	Excess-3 code	2-out-of-5 code
0	0000	0011	11000
1	0001	0100	00011
2	0010	0101	00101
3	0011	0110	00110
4	0100	0111	01001
5	0101	1000	01010
6	0110	1001	01100
7	0111	1010	10001
8	1000	1011	10010
9	1001	1100	10100

It is derived by adding $0011_2 = 3_{10}$ to the 8421 BCD representation of each decimal digit. For example, the decimal digit 5 appears as 1000 (which is the binary representation of 8). The advantage offered by this code is that if each 0 is changed to 1 and each 1 to 0 in the code group for the decimal digit X, the code group for the decimal digit $9 - X$ results. Codes that have this property are said to be *self-complementing* and are useful when signed decimal arithmetic is performed with the aid of a complement number representation.

A third coding scheme shown in Table 2.7 is the *2-out-of-5 code*. This is a nonweighted code using 5 bits for each code group, of which exactly 2 of the bits are 1s and the remaining bits are 0s. An advantage of this code is that it has error-detecting properties. This property will be discussed further in Sec. 2.8.

Decimal Addition Using 8421 BCD

When decimal arithmetic is performed by a computer in which a coding scheme is used for the decimal digits, the rules of binary arithmetic have to be modified to accommodate the coding scheme. Because of the popularity of the 8421 BCD scheme in microprocessors, we will consider the addition and subtraction operations when this coding scheme is used.

Consider the two decimal numbers 27 and 36. If we were to add them using binary arithmetic, we would have

$$\begin{array}{rl} 27_{10} = & 0010\ 0111 \\ +36_{10} = & +0011\ 0110 \\ \hline & 0101\ 1101 \end{array}$$

Clearly the sum is not the 8421 BCD representation of 63. The difficulty lies in the fact that only ten of the possible sixteen 4-bit 0-1 combinations are used in the coding scheme. In the above addition, the 4-bit combination 1101 does not exist in the 8421 BCD scheme. It is easily seen that whenever any of the 4-bit binary combinations 1010, 1011, ..., 1111 occur in an addition, a carry must be propagated to the next-higher-order digit and a correction performed to skip over the six illegal combinations. These two conditions are easily satisfied by adding a correction factor of $6_{10} = 0110_2$ to each illegal code group of the resulting binary addition and allowing carries to be propagated. Thus, in the above example we have

$$
\begin{array}{rl}
27_{10} = & 0010\ 0111 \\
+36_{10} = & +0011\ 0110 \\
\hline
& 0101\ 1101 \\
\text{Correction} & +0000\ 0110 \\
\hline
\text{Sum} \quad 63_{10} = & 0110\ 0011
\end{array}
$$

There is still another condition in which it is necessary to introduce a correction. Consider the following addition:

$$
\begin{array}{rl}
& \text{carry} \\
28_{10} = & 0010\ \overset{\curvearrowleft}{}\ 1000 \\
+59_{10} = & +0101\ 1001 \\
\hline
& 1000\ 0001
\end{array}
$$

Again the binary addition of the two numbers leads to an incorrect result, although the two resulting code groups are legal. In particular, the code group for the least-significant sum digit is again 6 too small. The problem here stems from the fact that the sum of the least-significant digits of the two numbers is greater than 15. In such a case a legal code group results, but the sum digit is incorrect. This condition is easily detected by the fact that a carry is generated when the two code groups are added. Thus, returning to the above example, we have

$$
\begin{array}{rl}
& \text{carry} \\
28_{10} = & 0010\ \overset{\curvearrowleft}{}\ 1000 \\
+59_{10} = & +0101\ 1001 \\
\hline
& 1000\ 0001 \\
\text{Correction} & +0000\ 0110 \\
\hline
\text{Sum} \quad 87_{10} = & 1000\ 0111
\end{array}
$$

In summary, a correction of $6_{10} = 0110_2$ must be added to *each* code group in the sum of two 8421 BCD numbers in which (1) the resulting sum digit code group is illegal or (2) a carry is generated upon the addition of two code groups when the sum digit is formed. Several microprocessors have the capability of detecting these two conditions and performing the correction under command so that decimal arithmetic can be easily performed.

Decimal Subtraction Using 8421 BCD

Let us now turn our attention to decimal subtraction. Again assume that the 8421 BCD scheme is used to represent the decimal numbers. If we were to perform subtraction with the decimal numbers 61 and 38, using the rules of binary arithmetic, we would have

$$
\begin{array}{r}
\text{borrow} \\
61_{10} = \quad 0110\ \overset{\frown}{0001} \\
-38_{10} = -0011\ 1000 \\
\hline
0010\ 1001
\end{array}
$$

The digit represented by the least-significant code group in the difference is incorrect. The difficulty is caused by the borrow that is necessary between the code groups. In binary subtraction, this borrow is equivalent to 16_{10}; however, in decimal subtraction, the borrow should correspond to 10_{10}. To compensate for this "overborrow," a correction factor of $6_{10} = 0110_2$ should be subtracted from the code group in the difference that receives the borrow. Thus, the above subtraction becomes

$$
\begin{array}{r}
\text{borrow} \\
61_{10} = \quad 0110\ \overset{\frown}{0001} \\
-38_{10} = -0011\ 1000 \\
\hline
0010\ 1001 \\
\text{Correction} \qquad -0000\ 0110 \\
\hline
\text{Difference} \quad 23_{10} = \quad 0010\ 0011
\end{array}
$$

In summary, the only condition that must be detected for the purpose of making a correction when subtracting two 8421 BCD numbers is the occurrence of a borrow between code groups. The correction consists of subtracting $6_{10} = 0110_2$ from *each* code group in the difference that makes use of the detected borrow.

Signed Decimal Addition and Subtraction

The above decimal additions and subtractions concerned unsigned numbers. As in the case of binary numbers, when signed numbers must be represented, sign-magnitude or complement representations can be used. Again a binary digit, 0 or 1, serves as a sign indicator. Sign-magnitude representation simply involves appending the sign digit to the corresponding magnitude. The analogous concepts of the 1's-complement and the 2's-complement representations for binary numbers are the *9's-complement* and the *10's-complement representations*, respectively, of decimal numbers. In both of these complement representations, if $X_{10} \geq 0$, the sign digit is 0 and the remaining $n - 1$ decimal digits correspond to X_{10}. On the other hand, if $X_{10} \leq 0$, the 9's-complement representation has a 1 in the most-significant-digit position, which is regarded as the sign digit, followed by the $(n - 1)$-digit decimal number given by

$$
10^{n-1} - 1 - |X_{10}| \tag{2.8}
$$

Also, if $X_{10} < 0$, the 10's-complement representation has a 1 in the most-significant-digit position, which is regarded as the sign digit, followed by the $(n - 1)$-digit decimal number given by

$$10^{n-1} - |X_{10}| \qquad (2.9)$$

As an illustration of these definitions, the signed decimal number $+375$ becomes $0,375$ in all three signed decimal representations; -375 becomes $1,375$ in the sign-magnitude representation, $1,624$ in the 9's-complement representation, and $1,625$ in the 10's-complement representation. As in Sec. 2.5, the comma in the number has been included only as a demarcator of the sign digit.

Whenever a sequence of decimal digits denoting a magnitude M is subjected to Eq. (2.8), the result is known as the *9's-complement of M*. Similarly, the result of the application of Eq. (2.9) to a sequence of decimal digits denoting a magnitude M is known as the *10's-complement of M*. When dealing with signed decimal numbers, the process of applying Eqs. (2.8) and (2.9) along with reversing the sign digit (i.e., replacing the sign digit 0 by 1 or 1 by 0) is known as *taking the 9's-complement* and *taking the 10's-complement*, respectively, of a signed decimal number. In general, the 9's-complement of a signed decimal number is easily obtained by subtracting each magnitude digit of the signed number from 9 and reversing the sign digit.† The 10's-complement of a signed decimal number can be obtained by adding 1 to the 9's-complement. As in the binary case, taking the complement of a signed decimal number is equivalent to taking the negative of the number.

Signed decimal addition and subtraction can be easily performed by using complement representations. The processes parallel those discussed in Sec. 2.6. In the case of subtraction, the complement of the subtrahend is first taken. Then signed decimal addition is performed. In doing signed decimal addition, the magnitude digits in corresponding positions are added according to the rules of decimal arithmetic, and the sign digits are added according to the rules of binary arithmetic. When the 10's-complement representation is used, a carry from the addition of the sign digits is ignored. When the 9's-complement representation is used, the end-around carry operation must be performed. In both cases, the overflow condition must be detected.

The following examples illustrate signed decimal addition and subtraction using the 10's-complement representation with two magnitude decimal digits and a sign digit. The reader should note the use of binary arithmetic on the sign digits.

Example

Augend	$(+35) =$	$0,35$
Addend	$+(-74) =$	$+1,26$
Sum	$(-39) =$	$1,61$

---

† It should be noted that when a self-complementing binary-coded decimal scheme is used, e.g., the excess-3 code, taking the 9's-complement of the decimal number involves simply changing all 0s to 1s and 1s to 0s in the binary code.

Example

$$
\begin{array}{lll}
\text{Augend} & (+73) = & 0,73 \\
\text{Addend} & +(-42) = & +1,58 \\
\hline
\text{Sum} & (+31) = & 1\rfloor 0,31
\end{array}
$$

↑——Carry disregarded

Example

$$
\begin{array}{lll}
\text{Augend} & (-23) = & 1,77 \\
\text{Addend} & +(-46) = & +1,54 \\
\hline
\text{Sum} & (-69) = & 1\rfloor 1,31
\end{array}
$$

↑——Carry disregarded

Example

$$
\begin{array}{lll}
\text{Minuend} & (+37) = & 0,37 \qquad\qquad\qquad 0,37 \\
\text{Subtrahend} & -(+12) = & -0,12 \xrightarrow{\text{Take 10's-comp.}} +1,88 \\
\hline
\text{Difference} & (+25) = & \qquad\qquad\qquad\quad 1\rfloor 0,25
\end{array}
$$

↑——Carry disregarded

Example

$$
\begin{array}{lll}
\text{Minuend} & (-58) = & 1,42 \qquad\qquad\qquad 1,42 \\
\text{Subtrahend} & -(-6) = & -1,94 \xrightarrow{\text{Take 10's-comp.}} +0,06 \\
\hline
\text{Difference} & (-52) = & \qquad\qquad\qquad\quad 1,48
\end{array}
$$

Two examples of signed decimal addition using the 9's-complement representation are

Example

$$
\begin{array}{lll}
\text{Augend} & (+76) = & 0,76 \\
\text{Addend} & +(-34) = & +1,65 \\
\hline
& & 1\rfloor 0,41 \\
& & +\ \searrow 1 = \text{End-around carry} \\
\hline
\text{Sum} & (+42) = & 0,42
\end{array}
$$

Example

$$
\begin{array}{lll}
\text{Augend} & (+27) = & 0,27 \\
\text{Addend} & +(-84) = & +1,15 \\
\hline
\text{Sum} & (-57) = & 1,42
\end{array}
$$

The above examples illustrate signed decimal addition and subtraction using complements. Clearly, if these operations are to be performed by a computer, the decimal digits must be coded. In such a case, it is necessary to correct the results as discussed earlier.

2.8 ERROR DETECTION

When information is transferred between various parts of a computer system, it is possible for errors to be introduced. These errors take the form of transmitted 0s inadvertently becoming received 1s or transmitted 1s inadvertently becoming received 0s. For the purpose of system reliability, it is desirable that such situations be detected.

In Sec. 2.7 it was noted that decimal digits could be represented by a 2-out-of-5 coding scheme. In this case exactly 2 of the bits within a code group are 1s. Thus, if a single 0 should become a 1 during information transferal or a single 1 should become a 0 (but not both), there will no longer be exactly two 1s within the received code group. In this way, the determination of the number of 1s in a received code group can be used as a means for detecting the occurrence of a single error.

Not all codes have error-detecting capability, as is evident by the 8421 BCD scheme. Furthermore, when pure binary coding is used to represent numerical information, again there is no property within the string of 0s and 1s making up the numerical information that provides for detecting an error in transmission.

A very simple scheme has been developed that provides the single-error-detecting capability. This scheme involves appending an additional bit to the string of 0s and 1s, known as a *parity bit*. The appended bit is selected so that the total number of 1s in the string is always even or odd, depending upon the parity rule being employed. For example, in an odd-parity scheme, the parity bit is made a 1 if the remainder of the string has an even number of 1s within it, and the parity bit is made a 0 if the remainder of the string has an odd number of 1s within it. The net effect is that there will now be an odd number of 1s within the string. If, during the course of information transfer in this case, a single 0 or 1 should be accidentally changed, the total number of 1s within the received string of bits, including the parity bit, will no longer be odd. In this way single-error detection is readily accomplished. Clearly, an even-parity scheme, in which the parity bit is selected so that an even number of 1s must exist within the string, can be used instead.

The testing for an even or odd number of 1s within a string of bits can easily be done by digital circuitry. When an error is detected, the computer may request the retransmission of the string of bits or provide an indication that the error has occurred. It should be noted that although the parity scheme will detect the occurrence of a single error, it will not detect the occurrence of a double error. However, the scheme does detect any odd number of errors.

2.9 ALPHANUMERIC CODES

In Sec. 2.7 several schemes were introduced for coding the decimal digits. However, it is frequently desirable to represent both numeric and nonnumeric information within a computer. Thus, several codes have been proposed for this

Table 2.8 The 7-bit ASCII code

$(b_7)^\dagger b_6 b_5 b_4$

$b_3 b_2 b_1 b_0$	000	001	010	011	100	101	110	111
0 0 0 0	NUL	DLE	SP	0	@	P	`	p
0 0 0 1	SOH	DC1	!	1	A	Q	a	q
0 0 1 0	STX	DC2	"	2	B	R	b	r
0 0 1 1	ETX	DC3	#	3	C	S	c	s
0 1 0 0	EOT	DC4	$	4	D	T	d	t
0 1 0 1	ENQ	NAK	%	5	E	U	e	u
0 1 1 0	ACK	SYN	&	6	F	V	f	v
0 1 1 1	BEL	ETB	'	7	G	W	g	w
1 0 0 0	BS	CAN	(	8	H	X	h	x
1 0 0 1	HT	EM	)	9	I	Y	i	y
1 0 1 0	LF	SUB	*	:	J	Z	j	z
1 0 1 1	VT	ESC	+	;	K	[	k	{
1 1 0 0	FF	FS	,	<	L	\	l	|
1 1 0 1	CR	GS	-	=	M	]	m	}
1 1 1 0	SO	RS	.	>	N	^	n	~
1 1 1 1	SI	US	/	?	O	_	o	DEL

† b_7 is frequently used as a parity bit.

Control characters

NUL	Null	BS	Backspace
SOH	Start of Heading	HT	Horizontal Tab
STX	Start of Text	LF	Line Feed
ETX	End of Text	VT	Vertical Tab
EOT	End of Transmission	FF	Form Feed
ENQ	Enquiry	CR	Carriage Return
ACK	Acknowledge	SO	Shift Out
BEL	Bell	SI	Shift In

Table 2.8 (continued)

DLE	Data Link Escape	EM	End of Medium
DC1	Device Control 1	SUB	Substitute
DC2	Device Control 2	ESC	Escape
DC3	Device Control 3	FS	File Separator
DC4	Device Control 4	GS	Group Separator
NAK	Negative Acknowledge	RS	Record Separator
SYN	Synchronous Idle	US	Unit Separator
ETB	End of Transmission Block	SP	Space
CAN	Cancel	DEL	Delete

purpose. These codes allow the coding of the decimal digits; the letters of the alphabet; special symbols such as punctuation marks, $, +, and = ; and control operations such as End of Transmission and Carriage Return. Typically, alphabetic symbols, numeric symbols, special symbols, and certain control operations are referred to as *characters*; the codes for these characters are called *alphanumeric codes*.

The most commonly used alphanumeric code in microcomputer systems is the *American Standard Code for Information Interchange* (ASCII). The 7-bit version of this code is given in Table 2.8. An eighth bit is frequently appended as a parity bit. In this code, under an odd-parity scheme, the decimal digit 5 is coded by $b_7 b_6 \cdots b_0 = 10110101$ where b_7 is the odd-parity bit. It should be noted that a character in the ASCII code can be denoted conveniently by two hexadecimal digits. In regard to the above example, the decimal digit 5 can be written as $B5_{16}$. Alternatively, an even-parity scheme may be employed. In this case the decimal digit 5 is coded by $b_7 b_6 \cdots b_0 = 00110101$, where b_7 is the even-parity bit.

PROBLEMS

2.1 Convert each of the following numbers into its decimal equivalent.
- (a) 1101110.101_2
- (b) 2102.1_3
- (c) 3201.13_4
- (d) 2413.42_5
- (e) 735.6_8
- (f) $4B6.9_{12}$
- (g) $1FD.8_{16}$

2.2 Convert the decimal number 467.75 into its equivalent in each of the following bases.
- (a) Binary
- (b) Ternary
- (c) Quaternary
- (d) Quinary
- (e) Octal
- (f) Duodecimal
- (g) Hexadecimal

2.3 Convert each of the following binary numbers into its octal and hexadecimal equivalents.
- (a) 1111000010.01
- (b) 111100101011.110111
- (c) 10101111101.1
- (d) 1010101001.011

2.4 Convert each of the following octal numbers into its binary equivalent.

(a) 364.1   (b) 570.6

(c) 267.4   (d) 12.35

2.5 Convert each of the following hexadecimal numbers into its binary equivalent.

(a) 4B6.3   (b) 8F3.B

(c) 6A.C   (d) 4D5.65

2.6 Using the ideas of Sec. 2.3, write an algorithm for direct binary-quaternary number conversion.

2.7 Perform the following operations in the binary number system.

(a) 110110.11 + 11010.1   (b) 10110.01 − 1011.1

(c) 1011.1 × 1100.1   (d) 1000101 ÷ 110

2.8 Develop a set of addition, subtraction, and multiplication tables for performing ternary arithmetic. Then perform the following operations in the ternary number system.

(a) 1211.2 + 1102.1   (b) 2102.1 − 1021.2

(c) 120.1 × 2.1   (d) 22022 ÷ 12.1

2.9 Develop a set of addition, subtraction, and multiplication tables for performing octal arithmetic. Then perform the following operations in the octal number system.

(a) 673.56 + 572.43   (b) 7530.62 − 4271.71

(c) 73.4 × 16.2   (d) 10534 ÷ 13

2.10 Perform the following additions and subtractions in the hexadecimal number system.

(a) 9C52.6 + 3BF6.D   (b) E54F.7 + 86A0.3

(c) 7E30.42 − 2B9F.71   (d) CA41.3 − 1D22.F

2.11 Express each of the following signed decimal numbers as signed 8-bit binary numbers in the sign-magnitude, 1's-complement, and 2's-complement representations.

(a) +55   (b) +123

(c) −45   (d) −57

(e) −88   (f) −114

2.12 Perform the following additions of signed binary numbers in the 2's-complement number representation. (*Note:* The most-significant bit is the sign bit.)

(a) 0,10010 + 0,00111   (b) 0,10110 + 1,11100

(c) 0,00110 + 1,10100   (d) 1,01101 + 1,11001

2.13 Perform the following subtractions of signed binary numbers in the 2's-complement number representation by first taking the 2's-complement of the subtrahend and then performing signed addition. (*Note:* The most-significant bit is the sign bit.)

(a) 0,10010 − 0,00111   (b) 0,10110 − 1,11100

(c) 1,10100 − 0,00110   (d) 1,01101 − 1,11001

2.14 Perform the following additions of signed binary numbers in the 1's-complement number representation. (*Note:* The most-significant bit is the sign bit.)

(a) 0,00110 + 0,01011   (b) 0,11001 + 1,01100

(c) 0,10011 + 1,00101   (d) 1,10110 + 1,01101

2.15 Perform the following subtractions of signed binary numbers in the 1's-complement number representation by first taking the 1's-complement of the subtrahend and then performing signed addition. (*Note:* The most-significant bit is the sign bit.)

(a) 0,00110 − 0,01011   (b) 0,01001 − 1,01100

(c) 1,01101 − 0,00110   (d) 1,10110 − 1,01101

2.16 Give the coded representation of the decimal number 473 in each of the following coding schemes.

(a) 8421 BCD   (b) Excess-3 code

(c) 2-out-of-5 code

2.17 Write each of the following 8421 BCD numbers as decimal numbers.

(a) 1001 0000 0101   (b) 0111 0001 0010

(c) 0001 0110 0011   (d) 1000 0100 0000

2.18 Perform the following additions of 8421 BCD numbers. Indicate the necessary correction in each case.

(a)   0101 1000 0010
     +0010 0110 1001

(b)   0100 1001 0011
     +0001 0111 0010

(c)   0011 0101 1001
     +0100 0111 1001

2.19 Perform the following subtractions of 8421 BCD numbers. Indicate the necessary correction in each case.

(a)   0111 0011 1000
     −0010 0110 0100

(b)   0101 0010 0001
     −0001 0100 0110

(c)   0110 0000 0011
     −0010 0111 1000

2.20 Assume that the excess-3 code is being used to represent decimal digits. Develop a set of rules for the necessary corrections when decimal addition is performed with numbers in this coding scheme.

2.21 The signed decimal numbers given below are in sign-magnitude representation. After rewriting the signed numbers in the 10's-complement representation, perform the indicated signed additions and subtractions.

(a) $0,632 + 1,271$
(c) $1,140 + 1,326$
(e) $0,417 − 0,953$

(b) $0,408 + 1,835$
(d) $0,732 − 0,460$

2.22 The signed decimal numbers given below are in sign-magnitude representation. After rewriting the signed numbers in the 9's-complement representation, perform the indicated signed additions and subtractions.

(a) $0,548 + 1,321$
(c) $1,426 + 1,159$
(e) $0,379 − 0,895$

(b) $0,137 + 1,620$
(d) $0,806 − 0,321$

2.23 Assume that the odd-parity scheme is being employed in conjunction with the 7-bit ASCII code, where the most-significant bit is the parity bit. Represent each of the following character strings as a hexadecimal number.

(a) 57
(c) END

(b) X = 8

THREE

BOOLEAN ALGEBRA AND LOGIC NETWORKS

A simple algebra, called *Boolean algebra*, can be used to describe the behavior and structure of logic networks. Such a formal mathematical tool is convenient in discussing the internal workings of a microcomputer and as an aid in the design of logic systems. Furthermore, since one of the main applications of microprocessors is as a software replacement for hard-wired logic, the operations of Boolean algebra occur frequently in a microcomputer program.

This chapter will introduce a Boolean algebra for two-valued logic. The various mathematical operations will be defined and several types of Boolean algebraic expressions will be introduced. Manipulations of algebraic expressions will be illustrated. Finally, the association between the Boolean algebra expressions and logic diagrams will be established. In Chap. 5 extensive use will be made of Boolean algebra in the analysis of basic computer networks and as the mathematical tool for logic design.

3.1 BOOLEAN ALGEBRA AS A MATHEMATICAL SYSTEM

In general, a formal mathematical system consists of a set of elements, a set of operations, and a set of postulates. Boolean algebra, being a mathematical system, is also defined in terms of these three sets.

Some of the circuits in a microcomputer provide for manipulating binary symbols comprising numbers or other information. Other circuits are used for communication purposes by providing appropriate paths through a logic network for information to travel. Finally, still other circuits are intended for control purposes, such as the activation of particular functions and the indication of various conditions. In all three cases, the signals at the various points within a circuit are two-valued. That is, the signals can represent the binary symbols, or they can correspond to true-false conditions depending upon whether or not certain events are to be caused or have occurred. Thus, the Boolean algebra that

Table 3.1 Definition of the AND operation

x	y	$x \cdot y$

$0 \cdot 0 = 0$
$0 \cdot 1 = 0$
$1 \cdot 0 = 0$
$1 \cdot 1 = 1$

we will use needs two elements to correspond to the two values of the signals. In all our future discussions, this two-valued Boolean algebra will be assumed.† This algebra is also known as the *switching algebra*.

The two elements of the Boolean algebra are called its *constants*, and we will use the convention of denoting them by 0 and 1. To avoid confusion with the binary digits, these symbols frequently are called *logic-0* and *logic-1*. At times a correspondence will be established between logic-0 and logic-1 and the binary digits 0 and 1. At other times logic-1 will correspond to a certain affirmative condition and logic-0 to its negative counterpart. The power of an abstract algebra is that its results are valid regardless of the nature of its elements as long as they satisfy the postulates.

For the purpose of having an algebra that describes the behavior and structure of logic networks, the terminals and internal points of a network are associated with *Boolean variables* that are restricted to the two values logic-0 and logic-1. Formally, a variable x in a two-valued Boolean algebra is a symbol such that

$$x = 0 \qquad \text{if } x \neq 1$$

and

$$x = 1 \qquad \text{if } x \neq 0$$

The letters of the alphabet will be used to denote Boolean variables.

Now that the elements of the Boolean algebra have been defined, it is necessary to introduce a set of operations and a set of postulates that indicate the behavior of the operations. There are several Boolean operations. The most important are AND, OR, and NOT. Additional Boolean operations will be introduced in Sec. 3.7.

The AND operation is denoted by the dot product sign ($\cdot$) or simply by the juxtaposition of Boolean variables. Thus, the AND operation between two variables x and y is written as

$$x \cdot y \qquad \text{or} \qquad xy$$

This operation is often referred to as *logical multiplication*.

The postulates for the AND operation are given in Table 3.1. From this table

---

† Boolean algebras with more than two elements exist. However, their study is beyond the scope of this book.

Table 3.2 Definition of the OR operation

x	y	$x + y$

$$0 + 0 = 0$$
$$0 + 1 = 1$$
$$1 + 0 = 1$$
$$1 + 1 = 1$$

it can be seen that the value of $x \cdot y$ is logic-1 if and only if both x and y are logic-1; otherwise, $x \cdot y$ has the value of logic-0. Although Table 3.1 defines logical multiplication between only two variables, the concept of the AND operation can be generalized to any number of variables. Thus, $x_1 \cdot x_2 \cdots x_n$ is logic-1 if and only if $x_1, x_2, \ldots, x_n$ are each logic-1; otherwise, $x_1 \cdot x_2 \cdots x_n$ is logic-0.

As indicated above, the dot product symbol or juxtaposition will be used to denote the AND operation. Frequently in literature, however, the AND operation is denoted by the symbol $\wedge$. The AND operation between the two variables x and y is then written as $x \wedge y$.

The next Boolean operation to be introduced is the OR operation. This operation is denoted by a plus sign $(+)$. Thus, the OR operation between two variables x and y is written as

$$x + y$$

This operation is often referred to as *logical addition*.

The postulates for the OR operation are given in Table 3.2. From this table it can be seen that the value of $x + y$ is logic-0 if and only if both x and y are logic-0; otherwise, $x + y$ has the value of logic-1. This operation can also be generalized for the case of n variables. Thus, $x_1 + x_2 + \cdots + x_n$ is logic-1 if and only if at least one of the variables is logic-1; otherwise, $x_1 + x_2 + \cdots + x_n$ is logic-0.

Although the plus sign will always be used to indicate the OR operation in this book, the symbol $\vee$ frequently appears in computer literature. In this case the OR operation between the two variables x and y is written as $x \vee y$.

The final operation to be introduced at this time is the NOT operation. This operation is also known as *complementation, negation,* and *inversion.* An overbar $(^-)$ will be used to denote the NOT operation. Thus, the negation of the single variable x is written $\bar{x}$.

As indicated in Table 3.3, the postulates of the NOT operation are

$$\bar{x} = 1 \quad \text{if } x = 0$$

and

$$\bar{x} = 0 \quad \text{if } x = 1$$

or, equivalently,

$$\bar{0} = 1 \quad \text{and} \quad \bar{1} = 0$$

The prime symbol $(')$ is also used to indicate the NOT operation in computer literature. In this case the complementation of x is written as x'.

Table 3.3 Definition of the NOT operation

x	$\bar{x}$
0	1
1	0

A two-valued Boolean algebra can now be defined as a mathematical system with the elements logic-0 and logic-1 and the three operations AND, OR, and NOT, whose postulates are given by Tables 3.1 to 3.3.

3.2 TRUTH TABLES AND BOOLEAN EXPRESSIONS

Now that the constituents of a Boolean algebra have been defined, it is next necessary to show how they are used. The object of a Boolean algebra is to describe the behavior and structure of a logic network. Figure 3.1 shows a logic network as a black box. The inputs are the Boolean variables $x_1, x_2, \ldots, x_n$, and the output is f. To describe the terminal behavior of the black box, it is necessary to express the output f as a function of the input variables $x_1, x_2, \ldots, x_n$. This can be done by using a truth table (or table of combinations) or by using Boolean expressions.

Logic networks that are readily described by truth tables or Boolean expressions are said to be *combinational networks*. A combinational network is one in which the values of the input variables at any instant determine the values of the output variables. A second class of logic networks is that in which there is an internal memory. Such networks are said to be *sequential* and have the property that the past as well as the present input values determine the output values from the network. This chapter will concentrate on combinational networks.

As indicated earlier, each of the Boolean variables $x_1, x_2, \ldots, x_n$ is restricted to the two values logic-0 and logic-1. Furthermore, all points within the black box, including the output line, are also restricted to these values. A tabulation of all the possible input combinations of values and their corresponding output values, i.e., functional values, is known as a *truth table* (or *table of combinations*). If there are n input variables and one functional output, this table will consist of 2^n rows and $n + 1$ columns. The general form of a truth table is shown in Table 3.4. It should be noted that a simple way of including all possible input values in a truth table is

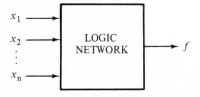

Figure 3.1 The logic network as a black box.

Table 3.4 The truth table

x_1	x_2	$\cdots$	x_{n-1}	x_n	f
0	0	$\cdots$	0	0	$f(0, 0, \ldots, 0, 0)$
0	0	$\cdots$	0	1	$f(0, 0, \ldots, 0, 1)$
0	0	$\cdots$	1	0	$f(0, 0, \ldots, 1, 0)$
0	0	$\cdots$	1	1	$f(0, 0, \ldots, 1, 1)$
$\cdots$	$\cdots$	$\cdots$	$\cdots$	$\cdots$	$\ldots\ldots\ldots\ldots$
1	1	$\cdots$	1	1	$f(1, 1, \ldots, 1, 1)$

to count in the binary number system from 0 to $2^n - 1$. The value of f will, of course, be 0 or 1 in each row, depending upon the specific function.

The second method of describing the terminal behavior of a combinational logic network uses a *Boolean expression*. This is a formula consisting of Boolean constants and variables connected by the Boolean operators AND, OR, and NOT. Parentheses may also be used as in regular algebra to indicate a hierarchical ordering of the operations. For example, a three-variable Boolean expression might be

$$f(x_1, x_2, x_3) = [(x_1 + \bar{x}_2)(\bar{x}_1 + x_3)] + (x_2 x_3)$$

In order to reduce the number of parentheses, however, it is usually assumed that the AND operation (i.e., logical multiplication) takes precedence over the OR operation (i.e., logical addition). Thus, the above expression is normally written as

$$f(x_1, x_2, x_3) = (x_1 + \bar{x}_2)(\bar{x}_1 + x_3) + x_2 x_3$$

Obtaining a Truth Table from a Boolean Expression

Both truth tables and Boolean expressions are useful tools for describing the terminal behavior of a logic network. Since they both can describe the same network, it is desirable at times to be able to convert each of these descriptions into the other. Clearly, by replacing each of the variables in a Boolean expression with its corresponding logic value and by evaluating the expression with the use of the definitions of the AND, OR, and NOT operations, a value for the expression can be obtained. This evaluation corresponds precisely to one row of the truth table. If this procedure is carried out for each input combination, the corresponding truth table can be readily obtained.

To illustrate the manner in which the truth table is obtained from a Boolean expression, again consider the formula

$$f(x_1, x_2, x_3) = (x_1 + \bar{x}_2)(\bar{x}_1 + x_3) + x_2 x_3 \tag{3.1}$$

Since this expression is a function of three variables, the truth table must consist of $2^3 = 8$ rows. In Table 3.5 the eight combinations of values for the three variables x_1, x_2, and x_3 are listed in the first three columns.

Table 3.5 Truth table for the Boolean expression
$$f(x_1, x_2, x_3) = (x_1 + \bar{x}_2)(\bar{x}_1 + x_3) + x_2 x_3$$

x_1	x_2	x_3	$\bar{x}_1$	$\bar{x}_2$	$x_1 + \bar{x}_2$	$\bar{x}_1 + x_3$	$(x_1 + \bar{x}_2)(\bar{x}_1 + x_3)$	$x_2 x_3$	f
0	0	0	1	1	1	1	1	0	1
0	0	1	1	1	1	1	1	0	1
0	1	0	1	0	0	1	0	0	0
0	1	1	1	0	0	1	0	1	1
1	0	0	0	1	1	0	0	0	0
1	0	1	0	1	1	1	1	0	1
1	1	0	0	0	1	0	0	0	0
1	1	1	0	0	1	1	1	1	1

To complete the construction of the truth table, we can evaluate Eq. (3.1) for each of the eight combinations of values. For example, when $x_1 = 0$, $x_2 = 1$, and $x_3 = 1$, we have

$$f(0, 1, 1) = (0 + \bar{1})(\bar{0} + 1) + 1 \cdot 1$$
$$= (0 + 0)(1 + 1) + 1$$
$$= 0 \cdot 1 + 1$$
$$= 0 + 1$$
$$= 1$$

The last column of Table 3.5, showing the functional values of the expression, is the result of the eight evaluations.

There is an alternate procedure for obtaining a truth table from a Boolean expression. This procedure involves carrying out the Boolean operations on the columns of the table in accordance with the expression to be evaluated. To illustrate this approach, again consider Eq. (3.1). Since both $\bar{x}_1$ and $\bar{x}_2$ appear in the expression, two columns are added to Table 3.5 such that the logic values in these columns are the complements of those in the first two columns. Next, the values of x_1 given in the first column are ORed with the values of $\bar{x}_2$ given in the fifth column. This operation results in the sixth column of Table 3.5, which shows the evaluation of $x_1 + \bar{x}_2$. In a similar manner the values of $\bar{x}_1$ and x_3 are used to obtain the evaluation of $\bar{x}_1 + x_3$ given in the seventh column. The results in the sixth and seventh columns are then ANDed to obtain the evaluation of $(x_1 + \bar{x}_2)(\bar{x}_1 + x_3)$ indicated in the eighth column. The evaluation of $x_2 x_3$, in the ninth column, is also easily obtained by the use of the second and third columns. Finally, the entries in the eighth and ninth columns are ORed. This operation produces the final column, giving the value of Eq. (3.1) for each possible combination of values for the variables x_1, x_2, and x_3.

Table 3.6 A truth table

x_1	x_2	x_3	f
0	0	0	0
0	0	1	1
0	1	0	1
0	1	1	0
1	0	0	0
1	0	1	1
1	1	0	0
1	1	1	0

The Minterm Canonical Form

It is also possible to write Boolean expressions from a truth table. One such expression is known as the minterm canonical form or standard sum-of-products.

To see how the minterm canonical form is obtained, consider Table 3.6. The first row of the table in which the functional value is logic-1 has the combination $x_1 = 0$, $x_2 = 0$, and $x_3 = 1$. Now consider the product term $\bar{x}_1 \bar{x}_2 x_3$. Substituting the logic values 0, 0, and 1 for x_1, x_2, and x_3 in the term $\bar{x}_1 \bar{x}_2 x_3$, we can see that the value of the term is logic-1. Furthermore, for any of the other seven combinations of logic values of x_1, x_2, and x_3, this term will have the value logic-0. In a sense, then, the product term $\bar{x}_1 \bar{x}_2 x_3$ can be used to describe the condition given by the second row of Table 3.6.

Proceeding further along these lines, we find that the next row in which Table 3.6 has a functional value of logic-1 is the third row, which corresponds to the combination $x_1 = 0$, $x_2 = 1$, and $x_3 = 0$. If this set of values is substituted into the product term $\bar{x}_1 x_2 \bar{x}_3$, the resulting value will be logic-1. Again the property holds that for only a single combination of values does this product term have the value logic-1. Thus, we can conclude that the third row of Table 3.6 can be described by the product term $\bar{x}_1 x_2 \bar{x}_3$. Finally, by similar reasoning, we find that the sixth row of Table 3.6, in which $x_1 = 1$, $x_2 = 0$, and $x_3 = 1$, can be described by the product term $x_1 \bar{x}_2 x_3$.

Combining the above results, we can see that the Boolean expression

$$f(x_1, x_2, x_3) = \bar{x}_1 \bar{x}_2 x_3 + \bar{x}_1 x_2 \bar{x}_3 + x_1 \bar{x}_2 x_3$$

precisely describes Table 3.6, since each product term in the expression corresponds to exactly one row in which the functional value is logic-1 and the sum corresponds to the collection of the three rows. For the remaining five combinations of values, the expression has the value logic-0. An expression of this type is called the *minterm canonical form* or *standard sum-of-products*. Such an expression is characterized as a sum of product terms in which every variable appears exactly once, either complemented or uncomplemented, in each product term. The product terms that comprise the expression are called *minterms*.

Table 3.7 Boolean algebra theorems

$1a$	$\bar{0} = 1$	$1b$	$\bar{1} = 0$	
$2a$	$x + 0 = x$	$2b$	$x \cdot 1 = x$	
$3a$	$x + 1 = 1$	$3b$	$x \cdot 0 = 0$	
$4a$	$x + x = x$	$4b$	$xx = x$	Idempotent law
$5a$	$x + \bar{x} = 1$	$5b$	$x\bar{x} = 0$	
6	$\overline{(\bar{x})} = x$			Involution law
$7a$	$x + y = y + x$	$7b$	$xy = yx$	Commutative law
$8a$	$x + xy = x$	$8b$	$x(x + y) = x$	Absorption law
$9a$	$x + \bar{x}y = x + y$	$9b$	$x(\bar{x} + y) = xy$	
$10a$	$\overline{(x + y)} = \bar{x}\bar{y}$	$10b$	$\overline{(xy)} = \bar{x} + \bar{y}$	DeMorgan's law
$11a$	$(x + y) + z = x + (y + z)$	$11b$	$(xy)z = x(yz)$	
	$\quad = x + y + z$		$\quad = xyz$	Associative law
$12a$	$x + yz = (x + y)(x + z)$	$12b$	$x(y + z) = xy + xz$	Distributive law

In general, each row of a truth table that has a functional value of logic-1 can be described by a minterm. The minterm, which is a product term, has a complemented variable if the value of that variable is logic-0 in the row in question and contains an uncomplemented variable if the value of the variable is logic-1. Connecting all the product terms constructed for rows that have a functional value of logic-1 by the Boolean OR operation results in the minterm canonical form for the given truth table.

3.3 BOOLEAN ALGEBRA THEOREMS

Several theorems can be developed that show the basic relationships in a Boolean algebra. The most important of these are listed in Table 3.7.

The first three theorems essentially reiterate the properties of the Boolean operations AND, OR, and NOT. Since the variables in these theorems are generic,† each variable can denote an entire Boolean expression. Thus, Theorem $3a$ states that ORing logic-1 with anything will always result in a logic-1. The fourth theorem, which is also known as the *idempotent law*, states that repetitions of variables in an expression are redundant and may be deleted. Thus, the concepts of raising a variable to a power and having coefficients other than logic-0 and logic-1 do not exist in this algebra. The fifth and sixth theorems emphasize the complementary nature of the Boolean variables. The *involution law* states that double complementation has a cancellation effect.

The next four theorems involve two generic variables. The first of these, the *commutative law*, states that the order in which an operation is performed on a pair of variables does not affect the result of the operation. Theorems 8 and 9

---

† A *generic variable* is one that can denote a single variable, the complement of a single variable, a Boolean expression, or the complement of a Boolean expression.

provide for the simplification of Boolean expressions. Theorem 10, *DeMorgan's law*, shows the effect of complementation on generic variables when connected by the AND and OR operations.

The final two theorems pertain to three generic variables. The *associative law* states that when ANDing variables or when ORing variables, they may be grouped in any order. The *distributive law* states that factoring is permissible in a Boolean algebra. Special attention should be given to the type of factoring possible by Theorem 12a.

It should be noted that a symmetrical property exists in the Boolean algebra theorems. In particular, each theorem in Table 3.7, except Theorem 6, appears in pairs. These pairs are related by interchanging each occurrence of the AND operation with an OR operation, each occurrence of the OR operation with an AND operation, each occurrence of a logic-0 with a logic-1, and each occurrence of a logic-1 with a logic-0. This symmetrical property is known as the *principle of duality*.

Many of the theorems given in Table 3.7 can be generalized for a larger number of variables. For example, the generalized form of DeMorgan's law can be written as

$$\overline{(x + y + \cdots + z)} = \bar{x}\bar{y} \cdots \bar{z}$$

and

$$\overline{(xy \cdots z)} = \bar{x} + \bar{y} + \cdots + \bar{z}$$

while the generalized form of the distributive law is

$$w + xy \cdots z = (w + x)(w + y) \cdots (w + z)$$

and

$$w(x + y + \cdots + z) = wx + wy + \cdots + wz$$

The theorems listed in Table 3.7 can readily be proved by the method of *perfect induction*. Perfect induction is proof by exhaustion. That is, the validity of the theorem can be established by substituting all possible combinations of values of the variables in both sides of the expression and verifying that the equality holds for every combination. Since the variables are limited to two values in our Boolean algebra, such a procedure is not prohibitive.

To illustrate a proof by perfect induction, consider the distributive law

$$x + yz = (x + y)(x + z)$$

A truth table can be constructed for $x + yz$ and $(x + y)(x + z)$ as explained in the preceding section. This has been done in Table 3.8. In the fifth column, the expression $x + yz$ is evaluated for the eight combinations of values of the three variables, and the expression $(x + y)(x + z)$ is evaluated in the eighth column. Since these two columns are identical, it can be concluded that the equality $x + yz = (x + y)(x + z)$ holds under all possible conditions. Thus, the validity of the theorem is established.

Table 3.8 Proof of the distributive law $x + yz = (x + y)(x + z)$
by perfect induction

x	y	z	yz	$x + yz$	$x + y$	$x + z$	$(x + y)(x + z)$
0	0	0	0	0	0	0	0
0	0	1	0	0	0	1	0
0	1	0	0	0	1	0	0
0	1	1	1	1	1	1	1
1	0	0	0	1	1	1	1
1	0	1	0	1	1	1	1
1	1	0	0	1	1	1	1
1	1	1	1	1	1	1	1

3.4 USING THE BOOLEAN ALGEBRA THEOREMS

There are many ways in which the Boolean algebra theorems can be used. In general, they provide rules for the manipulation of Boolean expressions. Thus, equivalent expressions can be derived. These derived expressions can be simpler or more complex than the original expressions, depending upon the objective of the manipulation. For example, the simplest expression, as measured by the number of symbols within the expression, may be desired; or the objective may be to obtain the minterm canonical form without having to construct the truth table first.

Equation Simplification

To illustrate the process of equation simplification, consider the following three examples.

Example 3.1 To simplify the expression

$$(x_1 + x_3)(x_1 + \bar{x}_3)(\bar{x}_2 + x_3)$$

we can proceed as follows:

$$(x_1 + x_3)(x_1 + \bar{x}_3)(\bar{x}_2 + x_3) = (x_1 + x_3 \bar{x}_3)(\bar{x}_2 + x_3) \qquad \text{by Theorem } 12a$$

$$= (x_1 + 0)(\bar{x}_2 + x_3) \qquad \text{by Theorem } 5b$$

$$= x_1(\bar{x}_2 + x_3) \qquad \text{by Theorem } 2a$$

Example 3.2 To simplify the expression

$$\bar{x}_1 \bar{x}_2 + x_1 \bar{x}_2 + x_1 x_2 + x_2 x_3$$

we can proceed as follows:

$\bar{x}_1 \bar{x}_2 + x_1 \bar{x}_2 + x_1 x_2 + x_2 x_3$

$$= \bar{x}_1 \bar{x}_2 + x_1 \bar{x}_2 + x_1 \bar{x}_2 + x_1 x_2 + x_2 x_3 \qquad \text{by Theorem } 4a$$

$$= \bar{x}_2 \bar{x}_1 + \bar{x}_2 x_1 + x_1 \bar{x}_2 + x_1 x_2 + x_2 x_3 \qquad \text{by Theorem } 7b$$

$$= \bar{x}_2 (\bar{x}_1 + x_1) + x_1 (\bar{x}_2 + x_2) + x_2 x_3 \qquad \text{by Theorem } 12b$$

$$= \bar{x}_2 (x_1 + \bar{x}_1) + x_1 (x_2 + \bar{x}_2) + x_2 x_3 \qquad \text{by Theorem } 7a$$

$$= \bar{x}_2 \cdot 1 + x_1 \cdot 1 + x_2 x_3 \qquad \text{by Theorem } 5a$$

$$= \bar{x}_2 + x_1 + x_2 x_3 \qquad \text{by Theorem } 2b$$

$$= x_1 + \bar{x}_2 + x_2 x_3 \qquad \text{by Theorem } 7a$$

$$= x_1 + \bar{x}_2 + x_3 \qquad \text{by Theorem } 9a$$

Example 3.3 To simplify the expression

$$x_1 x_2 + x_2 x_3 + \bar{x}_1 x_3$$

we can proceed as follows:

$x_1 x_2 + x_2 x_3 + \bar{x}_1 x_3$

$$= x_1 x_2 + x_2 x_3 \cdot 1 + \bar{x}_1 x_3 \qquad \text{by Theorem } 2b$$

$$= x_1 x_2 + x_2 x_3 (x_1 + \bar{x}_1) + \bar{x}_1 x_3 \qquad \text{by Theorem } 5a$$

$$= x_1 x_2 + x_2 x_3 x_1 + x_2 x_3 \bar{x}_1 + \bar{x}_1 x_3 \qquad \text{by Theorem } 12b$$

$$= x_1 x_2 + x_1 x_2 x_3 + \bar{x}_1 x_3 x_2 + \bar{x}_1 x_3 \qquad \text{by Theorem } 7b$$

$$= x_1 x_2 + x_1 x_2 x_3 + \bar{x}_1 x_3 + \bar{x}_1 x_3 x_2 \qquad \text{by Theorem } 7a$$

$$= x_1 x_2 + \bar{x}_1 x_3 \qquad \text{by Theorem } 8a$$

As can be seen from the above examples, the simplification of Boolean expressions is not algorithmic. Hence, it is not always obvious which theorem to apply at each step. Proficiency in this process comes from experience. For this reason, algorithmic techniques have been developed for the simplification of Boolean expressions. One such technique will be described in Sec. 3.5.

Equation Complementation

Frequently a Boolean expression must be complemented. This complementation is achieved by using DeMorgan's law. The following example illustrates how complementation of an expression is performed:

Example 3.4 To complement the expression

$$(\bar{x}_1 \bar{x}_2 + x_3) \bar{x}_1 x_4$$

we proceed as follows:

$$\overline{[(\bar{x}_1\bar{x}_2 + x_3)\bar{x}_1 x_4]} = \overline{(\bar{x}_1\bar{x}_2 + x_3)} + \overline{(\bar{x}_1)} + \bar{x}_4$$

$$= \overline{(\bar{x}_1\bar{x}_2 + x_3)} + x_1 + \bar{x}_4$$

$$= \overline{(\bar{x}_1\bar{x}_2)}\bar{x}_3 + x_1 + \bar{x}_4$$

$$= [\overline{(\bar{x}_1)} + \overline{(\bar{x}_2)}]\bar{x}_3 + x_1 + \bar{x}_4$$

$$= (x_1 + x_2)\bar{x}_3 + x_1 + \bar{x}_4$$

The Minterm Canonical Form

Another use of the Boolean algebra theorems is to obtain the minterm canonical form of a given expression. In Sec. 3.2 it was shown how the minterm canonical form can be obtained from a truth table. Clearly, given a Boolean expression, we can first construct its truth table and then write the minterm canonical form. However, by use of the theorem $x + \bar{x} = 1$ and the distributive law $x(y + z) = xy + xz$, it is possible for us to expand an equation directly into its minterm canonical form.

To illustrate the procedure, consider the expression

$$x + \bar{x}(z + y\bar{z})$$

To start the process, we apply the distributive law so that the expression consists of only a sum of product terms. In this case, we have

$$x + \bar{x}z + \bar{x}y\bar{z}$$

Next, the product terms that are not minterms must be modified to include the missing variables. The first term x is not a minterm, since it does not contain the y and z variables. These variables can be introduced by ANDing x with $(y + \bar{y})(z + \bar{z})$, which is equivalent to ANDing x with logic-1. By similar reasoning, the variable y can be introduced into the second term $\bar{x}z$ by ANDing it with $y + \bar{y}$. Finally, the last term is a minterm since all three variables appear. Combining our results, we can rewrite the given expression as

$$x(y + \bar{y})(z + \bar{z}) + \bar{x}(y + \bar{y})z + \bar{x}y\bar{z}$$

If the distributive law is now applied to this expression and duplicate terms are dropped when they appear, the minterm canonical form will result. In this case we have

$$xyz + xy\bar{z} + x\bar{y}z + x\bar{y}\bar{z} + \bar{x}yz + \bar{x}\bar{y}z + \bar{x}y\bar{z}$$

The Maxterm Canonical Form

In Sec. 3.2 the minterm canonical form was introduced as a Boolean expression obtained from a truth table. A canonical expression for a function is one that is

Table 3.9 The truth table for the complement of the function given in Table 3.6

x_1	x_2	x_3	f	$\bar{f}$
0	0	0	0	1
0	0	1	1	0
0	1	0	1	0
0	1	1	0	1
1	0	0	0	1
1	0	1	1	0
1	1	0	0	1
1	1	1	0	1

unique and has a standard form. It can therefore be of value in determining the equivalence of functions. That is, two functions are equivalent if their canonical expressions are the same. The minterm canonical form consists of a sum of product terms in which every variable appears within each product term. Another standard formula in Boolean algebra is known as the maxterm canonical form or standard product-of-sums. As in the case of the minterm canonical form, the maxterm canonical form can be obtained from the truth table or by expanding a given Boolean expression.

Again consider Table 3.6 in Sec. 3.2. This truth table denotes a Boolean function f. The truth table for the complement of this function, i.e., $\bar{f}$, is constructed by complementing each of the values in the last column, i.e., the functional values. The resulting truth table is shown in Table 3.9. Using the procedure of Sec. 3.2, we can now write the minterm canonical form for the complementary function $\bar{f}$ as

$$\bar{f}(x_1, x_2, x_3) = \bar{x}_1\bar{x}_2\bar{x}_3 + \bar{x}_1 x_2 x_3 + x_1\bar{x}_2\bar{x}_3 + x_1 x_2\bar{x}_3 + x_1 x_2 x_3$$

If both sides of the above equation are complemented with the use of DeMorgan's law, an equation for the function f will result:

$$\overline{[\bar{f}(x_1, x_2, x_3)]}$$

$$= f(x_1, x_2, x_3) = \overline{(\bar{x}_1\bar{x}_2\bar{x}_3 + \bar{x}_1 x_2 x_3 + x_1\bar{x}_2\bar{x}_3 + x_1 x_2\bar{x}_3 + x_1 x_2 x_3)}$$

$$= \overline{(\bar{x}_1\bar{x}_2\bar{x}_3)}\,\overline{(\bar{x}_1 x_2 x_3)}\,\overline{(x_1\bar{x}_2\bar{x}_3)}\,\overline{(x_1 x_2\bar{x}_3)}\,\overline{(x_1 x_2 x_3)}$$

$$= (x_1 + x_2 + x_3)(x_1 + \bar{x}_2 + \bar{x}_3)(\bar{x}_1 + x_2 + x_3)(\bar{x}_1 + \bar{x}_2 + x_3)(\bar{x}_1 + \bar{x}_2 + \bar{x}_3)$$

This last expression is the maxterm canonical form for the function f.

The *maxterm canonical form* or *standard product-of-sums* is characterized as a product of sum terms in which every variable of the function appears exactly once, either complemented or uncomplemented, in each sum term. The sum terms that comprise the expression are called *maxterms*.

In general, to obtain the maxterm canonical form from a truth table, the truth table of the complementary function is first written by changing each logic-1 functional value to logic-0 and vice versa. The minterm canonical form is then written for the complementary function. Finally, the resulting expression is complemented by DeMorgan's law to obtain the maxterm canonical form.†

The maxterm canonical form can also be arrived at algebraically if a Boolean expression is given. In this process, use is made of the theorem $x\bar{x} = 0$ and the distributive law $x + yz = (x + y)(x + z)$.

To illustrate the procedure, consider the expression

$$\bar{x}y + \bar{y}z$$

Since the maxterm canonical form consists of a product of sum terms, it is first necessary to rewrite the expression in this general form. This rewriting can be done by use of the distributive law. In this case,

$$
\begin{aligned}
\bar{x}y + \bar{y}z &= (\bar{x}y + \bar{y})(\bar{x}y + z) \\
&= (\bar{x} + \bar{y})(y + \bar{y})(\bar{x} + z)(y + z) \\
&= (\bar{x} + \bar{y}) \cdot 1 \cdot (\bar{x} + z)(y + z) \\
&= (\bar{x} + \bar{y})(\bar{x} + z)(y + z)
\end{aligned}
$$

Once an expression is obtained that consists of only a product of sum terms, it is next necessary to determine whether each sum term is a maxterm. If not, we can introduce the appropriate variables by using the theorem $x\bar{x} = 0$. Thus, for the above example, we get

$$
\begin{aligned}
(\bar{x} + \bar{y})(\bar{x} + z)(y + z) &= (\bar{x} + \bar{y} + 0)(\bar{x} + 0 + z)(0 + y + z) \\
&= (\bar{x} + \bar{y} + z\bar{z})(\bar{x} + y\bar{y} + z)(x\bar{x} + y + z)
\end{aligned}
$$

Finally, the distributive law is applied and duplicate terms are removed by the idempotent law. Thus, we have

$$
\begin{aligned}
(\bar{x} + \bar{y})(\bar{x} + z)(y + z) \\
= (\bar{x} + \bar{y} + z)(\bar{x} + \bar{y} + \bar{z})(\bar{x} + y + z)(\bar{x} + \bar{y} + z)(x + y + z)(\bar{x} + y + z) \\
= (\bar{x} + \bar{y} + z)(\bar{x} + \bar{y} + \bar{z})(\bar{x} + y + z)(x + y + z)
\end{aligned}
$$

3.5 THE KARNAUGH MAP METHOD OF BOOLEAN SIMPLIFICATION

In the previous section it was stated that the Boolean algebra theorems provide a means for the manipulation of Boolean expressions. Since the expressions resulting from such manipulation are equivalent, the combinational logic networks that they describe will be equivalent. It is therefore of interest to determine what is, in

---

† It should be noted that this procedure is really double complementation, which, by Theorem 6 in Table 3.7, results in an algebraic description of the given truth table.

x	y	$f(x, y)$
0	0	$f(0, 0)$
0	1	$f(0, 1)$
1	0	$f(1, 0)$
1	1	$f(1, 1)$

(a)

y

	0	1
0	$f(0,0)$	$f(0,1)$
1	$f(1,0)$	$f(1,1)$

x

(b)

Figure 3.2 A two-variable Boolean function. (a) Truth table. (b) Karnaugh map.

some sense, the "simplest" expression. Unfortunately, such an expression may be difficult to determine by algebraic manipulations. Several methods have been developed for deriving simple expressions. One such method, utilizing Karnaugh maps, will be presented in this section.

Karnaugh Maps

A *Karnaugh map* is a graphic representation of a truth table. The structure of the Karnaugh maps for two-, three-, and four-variable functions is shown in Figs. 3.2 to 3.4 along with the general form of the corresponding truth tables. It can be seen that for each row of a truth table, there is one cell in a Karnaugh map, and vice versa. Each cell in a map is located by a coordinate system according to its axis labelings, and the entry in the cell is the value of the function for the corresponding assignment of values associated with the cell. Figure 3.5 gives the truth table and Karnaugh map for the particular Boolean function

$$f(x, y, z) = \bar{x}(\bar{y} + \bar{z}) + xz$$

The truth table is arrived at by evaluating the expression for the eight combinations of values as described in Sec. 3.2, and the Karnaugh map is then constructed as indicated by the general form shown in Fig. 3.3.

When Karnaugh maps are used for simplifying Boolean expressions, rectangular groupings of cells are formed. In general, every $2^a \times 2^b$ rectangular grouping of cells corresponds to a product term with $n - a - b$ variables, where n is the total number of variables associated with the map and a and b are nonnegative

x	y	z	$f(x, y, z)$
0	0	0	$f(0, 0, 0)$
0	0	1	$f(0, 0, 1)$
0	1	0	$f(0, 1, 0)$
0	1	1	$f(0, 1, 1)$
1	0	0	$f(1, 0, 0)$
1	0	1	$f(1, 0, 1)$
1	1	0	$f(1, 1, 0)$
1	1	1	$f(1, 1, 1)$

(a)

yz

	00	01	11	10
0	$f(0,0,0)$	$f(0,0,1)$	$f(0,1,1)$	$f(0,1,0)$
1	$f(1,0,0)$	$f(1,0,1)$	$f(1,1,1)$	$f(1,1,0)$

x

(b)

Figure 3.3 A three-variable Boolean function. (a) Truth table. (b) Karnaugh map.

w	x	y	z	$f(w,x,y,z)$
0	0	0	0	$f(0, 0, 0, 0)$
0	0	0	1	$f(0, 0, 0, 1)$
0	0	1	0	$f(0, 0, 1, 0)$
0	0	1	1	$f(0, 0, 1, 1)$
0	1	0	0	$f(0, 1, 0, 0)$
0	1	0	1	$f(0, 1, 0, 1)$
0	1	1	0	$f(0, 1, 1, 0)$
0	1	1	1	$f(0, 1, 1, 1)$
1	0	0	0	$f(1, 0, 0, 0)$
1	0	0	1	$f(1, 0, 0, 1)$
1	0	1	0	$f(1, 0, 1, 0)$
1	0	1	1	$f(1, 0, 1, 1)$
1	1	0	0	$f(1, 1, 0, 0)$
1	1	0	1	$f(1, 1, 0, 1)$
1	1	1	0	$f(1, 1, 1, 0)$
1	1	1	1	$f(1, 1, 1, 1)$

(a)

yz

wx	00	01	11	10
00	$f(0,0,0,0)$	$f(0,0,0,1)$	$f(0,0,1,1)$	$f(0,0,1,0)$
01	$f(0,1,0,0)$	$f(0,1,0,1)$	$f(0,1,1,1)$	$f(0,1,1,0)$
11	$f(1,1,0,0)$	$f(1,1,0,1)$	$f(1,1,1,1)$	$f(1,1,1,0)$
10	$f(1,0,0,0)$	$f(1,0,0,1)$	$f(1,0,1,1)$	$f(1,0,1,0)$

(b)

Figure 3.4 A four-variable Boolean function. (a) Truth table. (b) Karnaugh map.

integers. Since the dimensions of these groupings are $2^a \times 2^b$, it follows that the total number of cells in a grouping must always be a power of 2. All future references to groupings will pertain only to those whose dimensions are $2^a \times 2^b$.

Minimal Sums

One method of obtaining a Boolean expression from a Karnaugh map is to consider only those cells that have a logic-1 entry. These are called *1-cells*. They correspond to the minterms of the canonical expression. Every $2^a \times 2^b$ grouping of 1-cells will correspond to a product term that can be used in describing part of the truth table. If a sufficient number of groupings are selected such that every 1-cell appears in at least one grouping, the ORing of these product terms will completely describe the function. By a judicious selection of groupings, simple Boolean expressions can be obtained. One measure of the degree of simplicity of a Boolean expression is a count of the number of occurrences of letters, i.e., variables and their complements, called *literals*, in the expression. Expressions consisting of a

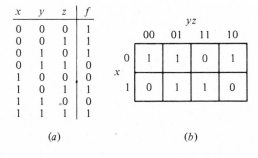

x	y	z	f
0	0	0	1
0	0	1	1
0	1	0	1
0	1	1	0
1	0	0	0
1	0	1	1
1	1	0	0
1	1	1	1

(a)

yz

x	00	01	11	10
0	1	1	0	1
1	0	1	1	0

(b)

Figure 3.5 The Boolean function $f(x, y, z) = \bar{x}(\bar{y} + \bar{z}) + xz$. (a) Truth table. (b) Karnaugh map.

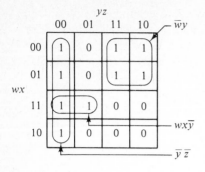

Figure 3.6 Groupings on a four-variable Karnaugh map.

sum of product terms and having a minimum number of literals are called *minimal sums*.

There are two guidelines for a judicious selection of groupings that will enable a minimal sum to be written. First, the groupings should be as large as possible. This guideline follows from the fact that the larger the grouping, the fewer will be the number of literals in its corresponding product term. Second, a minimum number of groupings should be used. This guideline stems from the fact that each grouping corresponds to a product term. By using a minimum number of groupings the number of product terms, and consequently the number of literals in the expression, can be kept to a minimum.

In Fig. 3.6 a four-variable Karnaugh map and the optimal groupings of 1-cells are shown. No larger groupings are possible on this map. Also, no fewer than three groupings will encompass all the 1-cells. The columnar grouping corresponds to the rectangle with dimensions $2^2 \times 2^0 = 4 \times 1$, the square grouping has dimensions $2^1 \times 2^1 = 2 \times 2$, and the small grouping of two cells has dimensions $2^1 \times 2^0 = 2 \times 1$. It should be noted that the rectangular groupings may overlap.

In order to write the Boolean expression from a Karnaugh map, reference must be made to the labels along the map's axes. It is necessary to determine which axis variables do not change value within each grouping. Those variables whose values are the same for each cell in the grouping will appear in the product term. A variable will be complemented if its value is always logic-0 in the grouping and will be uncomplemented if its value is always logic-1.

To illustrate the writing of a Boolean expression, again consider Fig. 3.6. Referring to the square grouping, we can see that the grouping appears in the first and second rows of the map. In these rows the variable w has the value of logic-0. Thus, the product term for this grouping must contain $\bar{w}$. Furthermore, since the x variable changes value in these two rows, this variable will not appear in the product term. When we now consider the two columns that contain the grouping, the y variable has the same value in these two columns, i.e., logic-1, and hence, the literal y must appear in the product term. Finally, we can see that the z variable changes value in these two columns and, hence, will not appear in the product term. Combining the results, we find that the square grouping corresponds to the product term $\bar{w}y$.

If this procedure is applied to the remaining two groupings in Fig. 3.6, their corresponding product terms can be determined. The columnar grouping corresponds to the term $\bar{y}\bar{z}$, since the variables y and z both have the value logic-0 associated with every cell in this grouping. Furthermore, since no row variables have the same logic value for every cell of the grouping, neither the w nor x variables appear in the product term. In a similar manner, the two-cell grouping corresponds to the product term $wx\bar{y}$. Thus, the minimal sum for this Karnaugh map is given by the expression

$$f(w, x, y, z) = \bar{w}y + \bar{y}\bar{z} + wx\bar{y}$$

Although the three- and four-variable Karnaugh maps are normally drawn as the two-dimensional configurations shown in Figs. 3.3 to 3.4, from the point of view of the permissible rectangular groupings that can be formed, it is necessary to regard them as three-dimensional configurations.

For the three-variable map of Fig. 3.3, it is necessary to regard the left and right edges of the map as being connected, thus forming a cylinder. It is on the surface of this cylinder that the rectangular groupings are formed. Hence, rectangular groupings may appear split when drawn. Figure 3.7 shows a split rectangular grouping. The corresponding product term is obtained as explained previously and is $\bar{x}\bar{z}$ for the case shown in Fig. 3.7.

Split rectangular groupings can also appear on four-variable maps. In general, the left and right edges of a four-variable map are connected as well as the top and bottom edges. Thus, the four-variable map of Fig. 3.4 should be regarded as appearing on the surface of a toroid. Figure 3.8 shows some examples of split rectangular groupings on a four-variable map. In Fig. 3.8a the grouping of the four cells corresponds to the term $x\bar{z}$ and the grouping of the two cells corresponds to $\bar{x}yz$. Special attention should be paid to the grouping illustrated in Fig. 3.8b. The four corners form a $2^1 \times 2^1$ rectangular grouping if the map is visualized as being a toroid. The corresponding product term is $\bar{x}\bar{z}$.

In summary, the basic approach to determining the optimal groupings on a Karnaugh map leading to a minimal sum is as follows. First a 1-cell is selected that can be placed in only one grouping that is not a subgrouping of some larger grouping. The largest grouping containing this 1-cell is then formed. Next, another 1-cell with the above property, not already grouped, is selected and its grouping formed. This process is repeated until all the 1-cells are in some grouping or there remain ungrouped 1-cells that can be grouped in more than one way. At this point, a minimum number of additional groupings are formed to account for

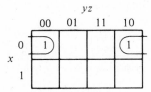

Figure 3.7 Split grouping on a three-variable Karnaugh map.

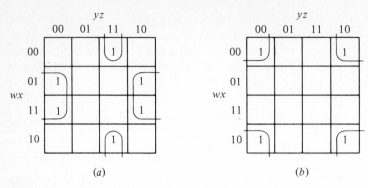

Figure 3.8 Examples of split groupings on a four-variable Karnaugh map.

the remaining 1-cells. The following examples illustrate this procedure for obtaining minimal sums from Karnaugh maps.

> **Example 3.5** Consider the Karnaugh map shown in Fig. 3.9. The 1-cell in the upper right-hand corner can be grouped with the 1-cells in the other three corners. Furthermore, this 1-cell can appear in no other groupings that are not subgroupings of these four cells. Thus, the term $\bar{x}\bar{z}$ must appear in the minimal sum. Next, it is noted that the 1-cell in the first row, second column, still is not in a grouping. It can be placed in a grouping of four cells to yield the term $\bar{x}\bar{y}$. Finally, the remaining ungrouped 1-cell can be grouped with the cell just below it to produce the term $wy\bar{z}$. The minimal sum is
>
> $$f(w, x, y, z) = \bar{x}\bar{z} + \bar{x}\bar{y} + wy\bar{z}$$
>
> which consists of seven literals.

> **Example 3.6** Consider the Karnaugh map shown in Fig. 3.10. The 1-cell in the upper left-hand corner can be grouped only with the 1-cell next to it. Similarly, the 1-cell in the lower right-hand corner can be grouped only with the 1-cell above it. The 1-cell in the second row, third column, can be grouped only by itself. At this point there still remain three 1-cells that have not been placed in some grouping. It should be noticed that these 1-cells, unlike the

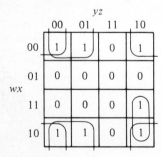

Figure 3.9 Example 3.5.

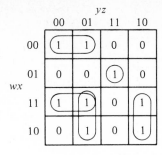

Figure 3.10 Example 3.6.

other cases, can be placed into more than one grouping. To complete the process, a minimum number of groupings must be selected to account for these remaining 1-cells. The groupings shown on the map correspond to the minimal sum

$$f(w, x, y, z) = \bar{w}\bar{x}\bar{y} + wy\bar{z} + \bar{w}xyz + wx\bar{y} + w\bar{y}z$$

which consists of 16 literals. There are two other equally good minimal sums that could have been formed:

$$f(w, x, y, z) = \bar{w}\bar{x}\bar{y} + wy\bar{z} + \bar{w}xyz + w\bar{y}z + wx\bar{z}$$

and $\qquad f(w, x, y, z) = \bar{w}\bar{x}\bar{y} + wy\bar{z} + \bar{w}xyz + wx\bar{y} + \bar{x}\bar{y}z$

It can be seen from this example that more than one minimal sum can exist for a given function.

Minimal Products

Thus far it has been shown how a minimal sum can be obtained from a Karnaugh map. Karnaugh maps can also be used to construct minimal expressions, as measured by a literal count, consisting of a product of sum terms. These expressions are called *minimal products*.

To obtain a minimal product, attention is given to those cells in the Karnaugh map that contain a logic-0. These are called *0-cells*. In this case a minimal sum is written for the complement of a given function by including every 0-cell, and only 0-cells, in at least one grouping while satisfying the requirements of using the largest and the fewest groupings possible. Again, the three-dimensional nature of the maps must be kept in mind. Then, DeMorgan's law is applied to the complement of the expression. This results in an expression for the Karnaugh map (and, hence, the truth table). Furthermore, it consists of a product of sum terms and a minimum number of literals.

Example 3.7 Consider the function in Example 3.5, whose Karnaugh map is given in Fig. 3.9. The map is redrawn in Fig. 3.11, where the 0-cells are

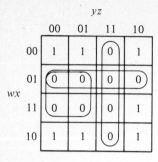

Figure 3.11 Example 3.7.

grouped to form a minimal sum for the complement of the function:

$$\bar{f}(w, x, y, z) = yz + \bar{w}x + x\bar{y}$$

or

$$f(w, x, y, z) = \overline{(yz + \bar{w}x + x\bar{y})}$$

By applying DeMorgan's law, we obtain the minimal product

$$f(w, x, y, z) = (\bar{y} + \bar{z})(w + \bar{x})(\bar{x} + y)$$

which consists of six literals. In this case the minimal product of the function has fewer literals than its minimal sum.

Example 3.8 Consider the function in Example 3.6, whose Karnaugh map is shown in Fig. 3.10 and is redrawn in Fig. 3.12. By grouping the 0-cells, there are three minimal products that can be formed. The minimal product corresponding to the groupings in Fig. 3.12 is

$$f(w, x, y, z) = (w + \bar{x} + y)(\bar{w} + \bar{y} + \bar{z})(\bar{w} + x + y + z)(w + \bar{y} + z)(w + x + \bar{y})$$

The two other minimal products are

$$f(w, x, y, z) = (w + \bar{x} + y)(\bar{w} + \bar{y} + \bar{z})(\bar{w} + x + y + z)(w + \bar{y} + z)(x + \bar{y} + \bar{z})$$

and

$$f(w, x, y, z) = (w + \bar{x} + y)(\bar{w} + \bar{y} + \bar{z})(\bar{w} + x + y + z)(w + x + \bar{y})(w + \bar{x} + z)$$

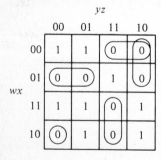

Figure 3.12 Example 3.8.

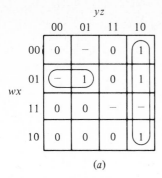
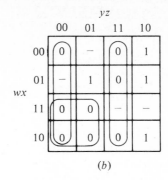

Figure 3.13 Karnaugh maps involving don't-care conditions.

In each of these expressions, 16 literals appear. Hence, the same number of literals appear in the minimal product descriptions of this function as in its minimal sum descriptions.

Don't-Care Conditions

Before we close this discussion on Karnaugh maps, one more situation must be considered. It should be recalled that Boolean expressions are used to describe the behavior and structure of logic networks. Each row of a truth table (or cell of a Karnaugh map) corresponds to the response (i.e., output) of the network as a result of a combination of logic values on its input terminals (i.e., the values of the input variables). Occasionally, a certain input combination is known never to occur, or if it does occur, the network response is not pertinent. In such cases, it is not necessary to specify the response of the network (i.e., the functional value in the truth table). These situations are known as *don't-care conditions*. When don't-care conditions exist, minimal sums and products can still be obtained with Karnaugh maps.

Don't-care conditions are indicated on the Karnaugh maps by dash entries. To obtain a minimal sum or product, the cells with dash entries, called *don't-care cells*, may be used optionally in order to form the best possible groupings. Any of the don't-care cells can be used when grouping the 1-cells or the 0-cells. Furthermore, it is not necessary that they be used at all or that they be used only for one particular type of grouping.

Figure 3.13 shows a Karnaugh map with don't-care conditions. The map of Fig. 3.13a can be used to obtain a minimal sum

$$f(w, x, y, z) = y\bar{z} + \bar{w}x\bar{y}$$

while the map of Fig. 3.13b can be used to obtain a minimal product

$$f(w, x, y, z) = (y + z)(\bar{y} + \bar{z})(\bar{w} + y)$$

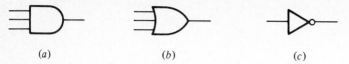

(a)   (b)   (c)

Figure 3.14 Gate symbols. (a) AND gate. (b) OR gate. (c) NOT gate (or inverter).

It should be noted that the cell corresponding to the values $w = 0$, $x = 1$, $y = 0$, and $z = 0$ is used for both a minimal sum and a minimal product; while the cell corresponding to the values $w = 0$, $x = 0$, $y = 0$, and $z = 1$ is not used at all.

Although the Karnaugh map method can be extended to more than four variables, the maps get increasingly difficult to analyze. To handle these larger problems, computer techniques have been developed.†

3.6 LOGIC NETWORKS

Boolean algebra serves to describe the logical aspects of the behavior and structure of logic networks. Thus far we have considered only its behavioral descriptive properties. That is, the algebraic expression or the truth table provides a mechanism for describing the output logic value of a network in terms of the logic values on its input lines. However, Boolean algebra expressions can also provide an indication of the structure of a logic network.

The Boolean algebra, as described in the preceding sections, includes the three logic operators: AND, OR, and NOT. If there are circuits whose terminal logic properties in some sense correspond to these three operators, then the interconnection of such circuits, as indicated by a Boolean expression, will provide a logic network. Furthermore, the terminal logic behavior of this network will be described by the expression. In the next chapter it will be seen that such circuits exist and are called *gates*. Of course, electrical signals really appear at the terminals of the gates. However, if these signals are classified as two-valued, then logic-0 can be associated with one of the signal values and logic-1 with the other. In this way, the actual signal values can be disregarded at the terminals of the gate circuits, and the logic values themselves can be assumed to appear.

The gate symbols for the three Boolean operations introduced thus far are shown in Fig. 3.14. Inasmuch as these symbols denote the Boolean operators, the terminal characteristics for these gates are described by the definitions previously stated in Tables 3.1 to 3.3. That is, the output from the AND gate will be logic-1 if and only if all its inputs are logic-1; the output from the OR gate will be logic-1 if

---

† The interested reader should consult books on switching circuit theory for further details, e.g., Donald D. Givone, *Introduction to Switching Circuit Theory*, McGraw-Hill Book Company, New York, 1970, and Fredrick J. Hill and Gerald R. Peterson, *Introduction to Switching Theory and Logical Design*, 2d ed., John Wiley & Sons, New York, 1974.

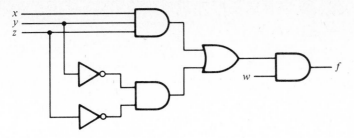

Figure 3.15 Logic diagram whose terminal behavior is described by the Boolean expression $f(w, x, y, z) = w(xyz + \bar{y}\bar{z})$.

and only if at least one of its inputs is logic-1; and the output from the NOT gate will be logic-1 if and only if its input is logic-0. NOT gates are also commonly called *inverters*.

A drawing that depicts the interconnection of the logic elements is called a *logic diagram*. In general, when a logic diagram consists only of gate elements with no feedback lines around them, the diagram is said to be of a *combinational network*. A combinational network is one that has no memory property and, thus, one in which the inputs to the network alone determine the outputs from the network.†

There is a correspondence between the logic diagram of a combinational network and a Boolean expression. Hence, Boolean expressions serve as descriptions of combinational networks. As an example, consider the logic diagram shown in Fig. 3.15. The two NOT gates are used to generate $\bar{y}$ and $\bar{z}$. The output from the upper-left-hand AND gate is described by xyz, and the output from the lower-left-hand AND gate is given by $\bar{y}\bar{z}$. These two outputs serve as inputs to the OR gate. Thus, the output from the OR gate is described by $xyz + \bar{y}\bar{z}$. Finally, the output from the OR gate enters the remaining AND gate along with a w input. Hence, the logic diagram of Fig. 3.15 is described by the equation

$$f(w, x, y, z) = w(xyz + \bar{y}\bar{z})$$

Clearly, it is just as easy to reverse the above process. That is, from a given Boolean expression, it is a simple matter to construct a corresponding logic diagram.

In order that the gate symbols can all be kept the same size in a logic diagram and in order to prevent the crowding of several inputs to AND gates or OR gates, the generalized symbols shown in Fig. 3.16 are frequently used when a single gate has a large number of input lines.

---

† Networks having the memory property are called *sequential networks*. These networks will be studied in Chap. 5.

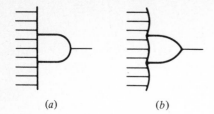

(a) (b)

Figure 3.16 Gate symbols to accommodate a large number of inputs. (a) AND gate. (b) OR gate.

3.7 ADDITIONAL LOGIC GATES

Three logic gates were introduced in the previous section. However, several additional ones frequently appear in logic diagrams. Figure 3.17 summarizes the commonly encountered gate symbols. First, it should be noted that several additional logic functions are symbolized. Second, two gate symbols are shown for each function. These symbols utilize the *inversion bubble notation*.

The Inversion Bubble Notation

As indicated in Fig. 3.17, a simple triangle denotes a *buffer amplifier*. These circuits are needed to provide isolation, amplification, signal restoration, and impedance matching in various parts of a logic network. Logically, its output is the same as its input; i.e., it performs the IDENTITY function.

With the inversion bubble notation, the appearance of a small circle on the input or output of a gate is simply regarded as the Boolean NOT operation. Thus, a triangle with a small circle on its input or output, but not both, becomes the NOT-gate symbol introduced previously; and an inversion bubble on both the input and output of a buffer amplifier is simply another symbol for a buffer amplifier, since $f = x = \overline{(\overline{x})}$.

Inversion bubbles can also be applied to the basic AND-gate and OR-gate symbols. For example, the Boolean expression $f = xy$ can be written as $f = \overline{(\overline{x} + \overline{y})}$. This expression serves as the basis for the second AND-gate symbol shown in Fig. 3.17. Similarly, $f = x + y$ can be written as $f = \overline{(\overline{x}\overline{y})}$. This expression implies a second OR-gate symbol.

The NAND Function

Figure 3.17 also introduces four new logic functions: NAND, NOR, EXCLUSIVE OR, and NOT EXCLUSIVE OR. Consider first the NAND operation. Table 3.10 gives the definition of this operation as performed on two variables x and y. Algebraically this operation can be written as $\overline{(xy)}$, and symbolically it can be regarded as an AND gate, with inputs x and y, followed by a NOT gate. Furthermore, since $\overline{(xy)} = \bar{x} + \bar{y}$, the NAND operation can also be regarded as an OR gate preceded by NOT gates at its inputs. These two interpretations suggest the gate symbols shown in Fig. 3.17.

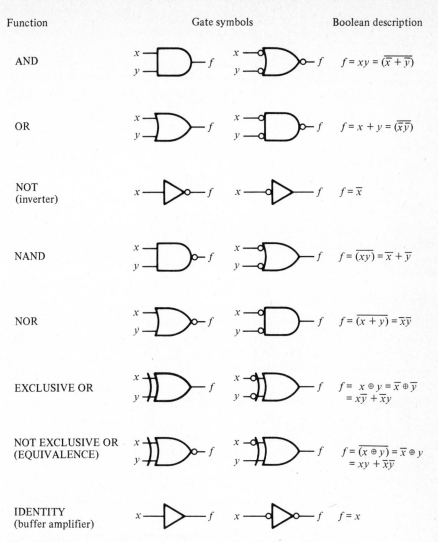

Function	Gate symbols	Boolean description

AND $\qquad$ $f = xy = (\overline{\overline{x} + \overline{y}})$

OR $\qquad$ $f = x + y = (\overline{\overline{x}\,\overline{y}})$

NOT (inverter) $\qquad$ $f = \overline{x}$

NAND $\qquad$ $f = \overline{(xy)} = \overline{x} + \overline{y}$

NOR $\qquad$ $f = \overline{(x + y)} = \overline{x}\overline{y}$

EXCLUSIVE OR $\qquad$ $f = x \oplus y = \overline{x} \oplus \overline{y}$
$\qquad\qquad = x\overline{y} + \overline{x}y$

NOT EXCLUSIVE OR (EQUIVALENCE) $\qquad$ $f = \overline{(x \oplus y)} = \overline{x} \oplus y$
$\qquad\qquad = xy + \overline{x}\overline{y}$

IDENTITY (buffer amplifier) $\qquad$ $f = x$

Figure 3.17 Summary of gate symbols frequently found in logic diagrams.

Table 3.10 Definition of the NAND operation

x	y	$f = \overline{(xy)}$
0	0	1
0	1	1
1	0	1
1	1	0

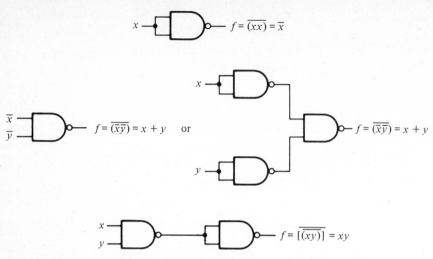

Figure 3.18 The universal property of NAND gates.

In general, the output of a NAND gate is defined as $\overline{(x_1 x_2 \cdots x_n)} = \bar{x}_1 + \bar{x}_2 + \cdots + \bar{x}_n$. Thus, the output is a logic-1 if and only if at least one of its inputs has the value of logic-0; otherwise, the output is logic-0.

One reason for the popularity of the NAND gate in logic networks stems from the fact that the NAND operation is a *universal operation*. A universal operation is one that can be used to implement the three basic Boolean operations AND, OR, and NOT. Figure 3.18 illustrates this universal property. As a consequence of the universal property, it follows that any combinational logic network can be realized by using only NAND gates.

One procedure for obtaining a logic diagram consisting of only NAND gates from a Boolean expression involves applying the algebraic definition of the NAND gate, i.e., $f(x_1, x_2, \ldots, x_n) = \overline{(x_1 x_2 \cdots x_n)}$. To illustrate this, consider the Boolean expression

$$f(w, x, y, z) = w + \bar{y}z + \bar{w}(x + y)$$

By applying DeMorgan's law, this expression can be written as

$$f(w, x, y, z) = \overline{\{\bar{w}(\overline{\bar{y}z})[\overline{\bar{w}(x + y)}]\}}$$

Since this is the general algebraic descriptive form for a NAND gate with inputs $\bar{w}$, $(\overline{\bar{y}z})$, and $[\overline{\bar{w}(x + y)}]$, the logic network shown in Fig. 3.19a can be constructed. Furthermore, the term $(\overline{\bar{y}z})$ is the algebraic form for a NAND gate with inputs $\bar{y}$ and z, and the term $[\overline{\bar{w}(x + y)}]$ is the algebraic form for a NAND gate with inputs $\bar{w}$ and $(x + y)$. The resulting network is shown in Fig. 3.19b. Finally, the term $x + y$ can be written as $(\overline{\bar{x}\bar{y}})$, which implies the network of Fig. 3.19c. Assuming that the complemented form of the input variables is available, the logic network of Fig. 3.19c is a NAND-gate realization of the Boolean function

$$f(w, x, y, z) = w + \bar{y}z + \bar{w}(x + y)$$

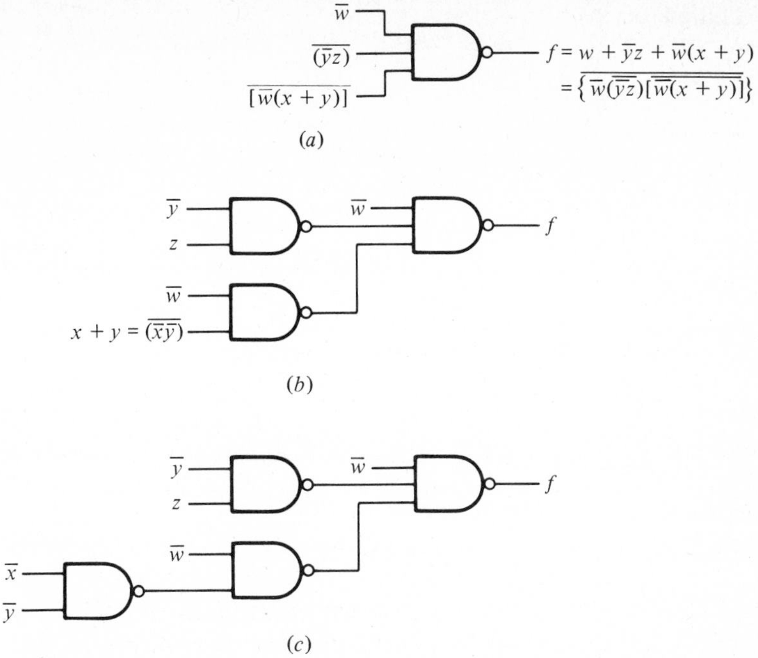

Figure 3.19 Procedure to obtain the logic diagram consisting only of NAND gates for the Boolean expression $f(w, x, y, z) = w + \bar{y}z + \bar{w}(x + y)$.

Clearly, if the complemented form of the input variables is not available, NOT gates can always be used.

In order to carry out the above procedure, it is necessary that the highest-order operation in the original Boolean expression be the OR operation. The highest-order operation is that operation which would be performed last if the logic diagram were to be constructed according to the hierarchical order of the original expression. When this condition is not satisfied because the highest-order operation is the AND operation, the expression is first complemented by DeMorgan's law. The result is that the highest-order operation is the OR operation. Then the logic diagram with NAND gates for the complemented expression is obtained by using the above procedure, and a NOT gate (or a NAND gate with its inputs tied together)† is placed at the output.

The NOR Function

Another gate that has the universal property is the NOR gate. The definition of the NOR operation as performed between two variables x and y is given in Table 3.11. Algebraically this operation can be written as $\overline{(x + y)}$, and symbolically it can be regarded as an OR gate, with inputs x and y, followed by a

† Occasionally a single-input NAND gate is regarded as a NOT gate.

Table 3.11 Definition of the NOR operation

x	y	$f = \overline{(x + y)}$
0	0	1
0	1	0
1	0	0
1	1	0

NOT gate. Since $\overline{(x + y)} = \bar{x}\bar{y}$, the NOR operation can also be regarded as an AND gate preceded by NOT gates at its inputs. These two interpretations suggest the gate symbols shown in Fig. 3.17.

In general, the output of a NOR gate is defined as $\overline{(x_1 + x_2 + \cdots + x_n)} = \bar{x}_1 \bar{x}_2 \cdots \bar{x}_n$. Thus, the output is logic-1 if and only if all its inputs have the value of logic-0; otherwise, the output is logic-0. The universal nature of NOR gates is illustrated in Fig. 3.20, where it is shown that by the use of these gates alone, the three basic Boolean operations can be realized.

As a consequence of the universal property of NOR gates, any combinational logic network can be realized by the use of just this one type of gate. One procedure for obtaining a logic diagram with NOR gates from a Boolean expression involves applying the algebraic definition of the NOR gate, i.e., $f(x_1, x_2, \ldots, x_n) = \overline{(x_1 + x_2 + \cdots + x_n)}$. The only restriction placed on the initial Boolean expression is that the highest-order operation must be the AND operation. When this condition is not satisfied because the highest-order operation is the OR operation, the logic diagram with NOR gates for the complement of the

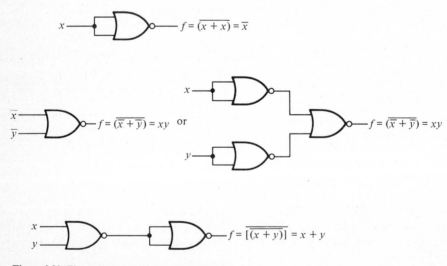

Figure 3.20 The universal property of NOR gates.

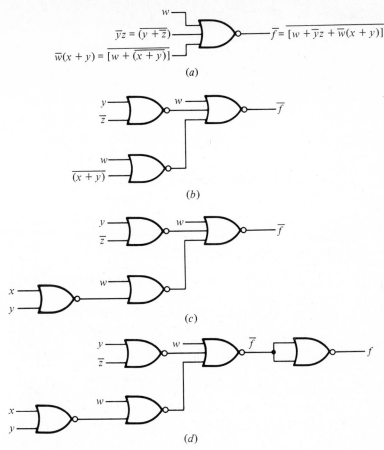

Figure 3.21 Procedure to obtain the logic diagram consisting only of NOR gates for the Boolean expression $f(w, x, y, z) = w + \bar{y}z + \bar{w}(x + y)$.

expression is first obtained. Then a NOT gate (or a NOR gate with its inputs tied together)† is placed at the output.

To illustrate the construction of a logic diagram, again consider the expression

$$f(w, x, y, z) = w + \bar{y}z + \bar{w}(x + y)$$

Since the highest-order operation in this expression is the OR operation, the expression is complemented:

$$\bar{f}(w, x, y, z) = \overline{[w + \bar{y}z + \bar{w}(x + y)]}$$

The logic diagram for the complemented expression is then constructed as indicated in Fig. 3.21*a–c*. The logic diagram is completed by placing a NOR gate with its inputs tied together at the output of the network, as shown in Fig. 3.21*d*.

† Occasionally a single-input NOR gate is regarded as a NOT gate.

Table 3.12 Definition of the EXCLUSIVE-OR operation

x	y	$x \oplus y$

$$0 \oplus 0 = 0$$
$$0 \oplus 1 = 1$$
$$1 \oplus 0 = 1$$
$$1 \oplus 1 = 0$$

The EXCLUSIVE-OR and NOT-EXCLUSIVE-OR Functions

The final two gate symbols introduced in Fig. 3.17 are the EXCLUSIVE-OR gate and the NOT-EXCLUSIVE-OR gate. The EXCLUSIVE-OR operation is denoted by the symbol $\oplus$ and is frequently called the *modulo-2-sum* operation. By definition, the value of $x \oplus y$ is logic-1 if and only if x or y, but not both x and y, has the value of logic-1; otherwise, $x \oplus y$ has the value of logic-0. This definition is tabulated in Table 3.12. From this table the following relationship can be seen to exist:

$$x \oplus y = \bar{x}y + x\bar{y}$$

The complement of the EXCLUSIVE-OR operation is the NOT-EXCLUSIVE-OR operation. Algebraically,

$$\overline{(x \oplus y)} = \overline{(\bar{x}y + x\bar{y})} = (x + \bar{y})(\bar{x} + y) = xy + \bar{x}\bar{y}$$

From this equation it can be seen that $\overline{(x \oplus y)}$ has the value of logic-1 if and only if the logic value of both x and y are the same; otherwise, $\overline{(x \oplus y)}$ has the value of logic-0. For this reason, the NOT-EXCLUSIVE-OR gate is also called the EQUIVALENCE gate.

Although NAND and NOR gates are available with several input lines, the EXCLUSIVE-OR and NOT-EXCLUSIVE-OR gates are typically available with only two input lines.

As with all the other functions described, two gate symbols are given in Fig. 3.17 for both the EXCLUSIVE-OR and the NOT-EXCLUSIVE-OR operations. It can easily be shown that by regarding the bubble symbol as a NOT gate, the alternate gate symbols shown each correspond to the indicated function.

PROBLEMS

3.1 Form the truth table for each of the following Boolean functions.
    (a) $f(x_1, x_2, x_3) = (\bar{x}_1 x_2 + x_3) + \bar{x}_1 x_3$
    (b) $f(x, y, z) = (x + \bar{y})(\bar{x}z + y)$
    (c) $f(x_1, x_2, x_3, x_4) = \overline{[x_1(x_2 x_3 + x_4) + \bar{x}_1 \bar{x}_2 x_3]}$

3.2 Write the minterm canonical form for each of the truth tables in Table P3.2.

3.3 Using the method of perfect induction, prove each of the following theorems.
    (a) $x(x + y) = x$ (b) $x + \bar{x}y = x + y$
    (c) $\overline{(x + y)} = \bar{x}\bar{y}$

Table P3.2

x_1	x_2	x_3	f
0	0	0	1
0	0	1	0
0	1	0	0
0	1	1	1
1	0	0	0
1	0	1	0
1	1	0	1
1	1	1	1

(a)

x	y	z	f
0	0	0	0
0	0	1	1
0	1	0	1
0	1	1	1
1	0	0	0
1	0	1	1
1	1	0	0
1	1	1	1

(b)

3.4 Using the Boolean algebra theorems, prove the following identities by going from the expression on the left side of the equals sign to the expression on the right side. State which theorem is applied at each step.

(a) $(x_1 + x_2)(\bar{x}_1 + x_3) = x_1 x_3 + \bar{x}_1 x_2$

(b) $\bar{x}_1 \bar{x}_3 x_4 + \bar{x}_1 x_3 x_4 + x_1 x_2 x_4 = \bar{x}_1 x_4 + x_2 x_4$

(c) $x_1 x_2 + x_3 x_4 = (x_1 + x_3)(x_1 + x_4)(x_2 + x_3)(x_2 + x_4)$

(d) $x_1 \bar{x}_2 + x_2 \bar{x}_3 + \bar{x}_1 x_3 = \bar{x}_1 x_2 + \bar{x}_2 x_3 + x_1 \bar{x}_3$

3.5 Using the Boolean algebra theorems, simplify each of the following expressions as much as possible.

(a) $\bar{x}_1 x_3 + \bar{x}_1 \bar{x}_3 + x_1 x_2$

(b) $\bar{x}_1 \bar{x}_2 x_3 + x_1 \bar{x}_2 x_3 + x_1 x_2 x_3$

(c) $\bar{x}_1 x_3 + \bar{x}_1 \bar{x}_2 \bar{x}_3 + x_1 x_2 x_3$

3.6 Form the complement of each of the following expressions.

(a) $(x_1 + \bar{x}_2 + x_3)(x_2 + \bar{x}_1 x_4) + \bar{x}_2 \bar{x}_4$

(b) $x_1 \bar{x}_2 (x_3 + \bar{x}_2 \bar{x}_4)$

(c) $x_1 \overline{(x_3 \bar{x}_4 + x_2 x_4)} + \bar{x}_1 (\bar{x}_3 + x_4)$

3.7 Rewrite the expression $\bar{y}(x + \bar{z}) + \bar{x} y$ in minterm canonical form without constructing the truth table first.

3.8 Write the maxterm canonical form for each of the truth tables in Table P3.8.

Table P3.8

x_1	x_2	x_3	f
0	0	0	0
0	0	1	1
0	1	0	1
0	1	1	0
1	0	0	0
1	0	1	1
1	1	0	1
1	1	1	1

(a)

x	y	z	f
0	0	0	0
0	0	1	1
0	1	0	0
0	1	1	1
1	0	0	0
1	0	1	0
1	1	0	1
1	1	1	0

(b)

3.9 Rewrite the expression $\bar{y}(x + \bar{z}) + \bar{x}y$ in maxterm canonical form without constructing the truth table first.

3.10 Using Karnaugh maps, determine a minimal sum and a minimal product for each of the truth tables in Table P3.10.

Table P3.10

x	y	z	f
0	0	0	1
0	0	1	0
0	1	0	1
0	1	1	0
1	0	0	0
1	0	1	0
1	1	0	1
1	1	1	0

(a)

x	y	z	f
0	0	0	0
0	0	1	1
0	1	0	1
0	1	1	1
1	0	0	1
1	0	1	1
1	1	0	0
1	1	1	0

(b)

3.11 Determine a minimal sum and a minimal product from each of the Karnaugh maps given in Fig. P3.11.

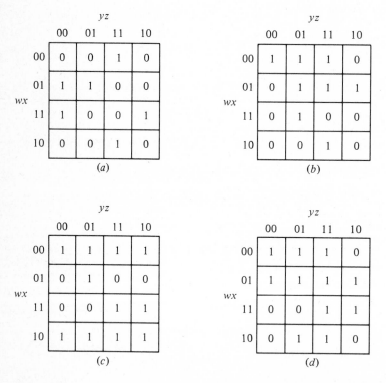

(a)

(b)

(c)

(d)

Figure P3.11

3.12 Using Karnaugh maps, determine a minimal sum and a minimal product for each of the following expressions.

(a) $f(w, x, y, z) = \bar{w}x\bar{y}\bar{z} + \bar{w}x\bar{y}z + \bar{w}xy\bar{z} + w\bar{x}yz + wxyz$

(b) $f(w, x, y, z) = (w + x + \bar{y} + \bar{z})(w + \bar{x} + y + \bar{z})(w + \bar{x} + \bar{y} + z)(w + \bar{x} + \bar{y} + \bar{z})(\bar{w} + \bar{x} + \bar{y} + \bar{z})$

(c) $f(w, x, y, z) = \bar{w}x\bar{y} + x\bar{y}z + w\bar{y}z + w\bar{x}\bar{z} + wxy\bar{z}$

3.13 Determine a minimal sum and a minimal product from each of the Karnaugh maps given in Fig. P3.13, where the dashes indicate don't-care conditions.

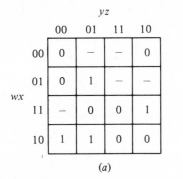

	yz			
wx	00	01	11	10
00	0	–	–	0
01	0	1	–	–
11	–	0	0	1
10	1	1	0	0

(a)

	yz			
wx	00	01	11	10
00	1	–	0	1
01	1	1	0	1
11	–	1	–	0
10	0	1	1	–

(b)

Figure P3.13

3.14 Write a Boolean expression for each of the logic diagrams shown in Fig. P3.14.

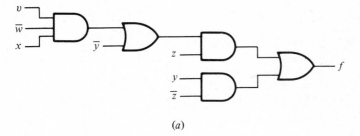

(a)

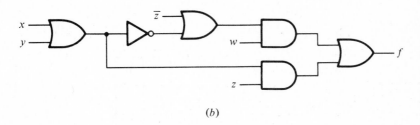

(b)

Figure P3.14

3.15 Draw a logic diagram with AND, OR, and NOT gates for each of the following Boolean expressions.

(a) $f(w, x, y, z) = w(\bar{x}y + \bar{y}z) + \bar{w}\bar{z}$

(b) $f(v, w, x, y, z) = [(w + x)(\bar{v} + \bar{x}y) + z](x + \bar{y})$

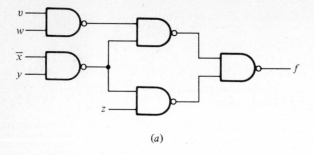

(a)

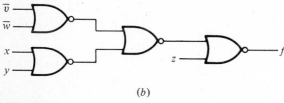

(b)

Figure P3.16

3.16 Write a Boolean expression for each of the logic diagrams shown in Fig. P3.16.

3.17 Draw a logic diagram with only NAND gates for each of the following Boolean expressions.

(a) $f(w, x, y, z) = (wx + \bar{y})z + \bar{x}y$

(b) $f(w, x, y, z) = [(\bar{x} + y)(x + z) + \bar{y}\bar{z}](x + y)$

3.18 Draw a logic diagram with only NOR gates for each of the Boolean expressions in Prob. 3.17.

3.19 Design a combinational logic network that will detect, by producing a logic-1 output, the invalid code groups of an 8421 BCD code by first forming a truth table and then obtaining a simple Boolean expression by using a Karnaugh map.

3.20 Design a combinational logic network that will convert the decimal digits in 8421 BCD code into their equivalent forms in excess-3 code. This network will have four output terminals. For each output terminal, first form a truth table and then obtain a simple Boolean expression by using a Karnaugh map.

FOUR

DIGITAL ELECTRONIC CIRCUITS

There is a wide variety in the types of electronic circuits that are used in the implementation of commercially available logic gates and components. Each of these types has certain features, with regard to switching speed, power drain, circuit density, flexibility, and other characteristics, that make it more suitable for some applications and less suitable for others. The purpose of this chapter is to investigate some of the common types of circuits that are used for basic logic gates. This should serve not only to point out the features of the different types for comparison but also to bring out nonlogical aspects of the gates, such as voltage levels, current flow, and timing, that are necessary to know in order to use them. These same concerns generally apply to logical components other than basic gates, including microprocessors, since they are constructed from the same types of circuits.

This chapter starts with a review of semiconductor devices, including the *pn* junction diode, the bipolar junction transistor, and the field-effect transistor, since these are the basic circuit components constituting the logic gates. This review will primarily be concerned with the large-signal, or switching, behavior of the devices rather than the small-signal, or amplification, characteristics. Two major categories of circuits are identified: those mainly composed of bipolar junction devices and those mainly composed of field-effect transistors. A number of logic families in each of these two categories will be discussed.

4.1 REVIEW OF SEMICONDUCTOR DEVICES

The conductive properties of a material depend primarily upon the availability of movable charged particles to convey current. The atoms making up any material are often viewed as consisting of a positively charged nucleus surrounded by negatively charged electrons. The electrons revolve in orbits of varying distances from the nucleus and therefore of varying energy levels. The level of energy possessed by an orbiting electron is attributed both to its potential energy due to charge attraction and to its kinetic energy due to its motion. It is known that the possible energy levels of orbiting electrons must lie within discrete energy bands. Each band has a certain maximum limit on the number of electrons that it may contain. The energy level of electrons in these bands increases with increasing distance from the nucleus. Electrons in the lower energy bands are strongly attracted to the nucleus and are therefore generally unable to move from atom to atom. The electrons in the outer bands, however, are less attracted to the nucleus, mainly because the inner electrons tend to cancel the attraction of the nucleus. Also, the outer electrons have a higher kinetic energy and therefore a greater momentum than the inner electrons. The electrons in the outer bands are, therefore, more able to move from one atom to another. There is generally a *conduction band* associated with the atoms of a given material. Any electrons appearing in this conduction band (or higher band) are able to move easily from atom to atom, whereas electrons in lower bands are more tightly bound to their individual atom and are not easily moved to another atom. The band just below the conduction band is referred to as the *valence band*. These two bands play the major role in the conduction properties of a material.

At normal temperatures, electrons associated with each atom tend to fill the energy bands from the lowest band up to the valence or conduction band. If electrons appear in the conduction band for a material, they will be available to convey a current, and the material thus behaves as a conductor. Most metals have this property. Electrons in the conduction band are referred to as *charge carriers*. More specifically, they are negative charge carriers. There also exists positive charge carriers called *holes*. Holes correspond to missing electrons in the valence band of individual atoms of a material in which most of the atoms have their valence band filled with electrons. Such vacancies in the valence band of some atoms allow electrons in the valence band of neighboring atoms to migrate and fill the vacancies. When a valence electron moves from one atom to fill the vacancy of another, it leaves a vacancy in the first. In this way, holes, which are the vacancies, move about from atom to atom carrying a positive charge with them.

A *semiconductor*, generally speaking, is a type of material in which the conductive properties are controlled by a limited number of charge carriers. Silicon, the most commonly used semiconductor material, normally has very few electrons or holes for conduction purposes. At ordinary temperatures, an individual silicon atom has four electrons in the valence band. In a crystalline structure, however, silicon atoms share valence electrons with neighboring atoms. Each atom shares one of its valence electrons with each of four neighbors and in turn partakes in the sharing of a valence electron belonging to each of the four neighbors. An electron shared between two atoms can be associated with both atoms. Thus, the atoms in crystalline silicon each have a total of eight valence electrons associated with it. This causes the valence band to be filled, since eight is the maximum number of electrons that can appear in the valence band for silicon. In this case, there are no holes or conduction electrons available as charge carriers.

This can be changed, however, by mixing a small amount of "doping" material with the silicon. Certain elements, such as boron and aluminum, when mixed with silicon, cause a drastic increase in the number of holes, since the atoms of these elements have one less electron in their valence band than those of silicon. The resulting semiconductor material is referred to as *p-type*, because the predominant charge carriers are holes (which are positively charged). Other elements, such as phosphorus and arsenic, when mixed with silicon, cause a drastic increase in the number of mobile electrons, since the atoms of these elements have one more electron in their valence band than those of silicon. The extra electrons are forced into the conduction band, where they become available as charge carriers. The resulting semiconductor material is referred to as *n-type* because the predominant charge carriers are electrons (which are negatively charged). For either type of semiconductor material, the predominant charge carriers are referred to as *majority* charge carriers, and the others are referred to as *minority* charge carriers.

The way in which charge carriers are made to interact in various semiconductor devices to yield a desired switching behavior is of prime interest to us. We are thus concerned with the large-signal characteristics of such devices rather than the small-signal characteristics, which are of importance in regard to nonswitching or analog circuits. One basic device having an important switching property is the *pn* junction diode, which will now be considered.

The *pn* Junction Diode

A *pn junction diode* is a two-terminal device formed by joining two pieces of semiconductor material, one *p*-type and the other *n*-type. The interaction of the charge carriers from each of the two types of material gives rise to the well-known rectifying property of diodes. This behavior is described more specifically as follows.

When the two types of semiconductor material are brought into contact to form a junction, there is a tendency for some of the predominant or majority charge carriers of each region to move into the other region. This tendency is due to the random motion that the carriers constantly follow. On the average, more electrons tend to move from the *n* region to the *p* region than the other way, simply because there are many more electrons in the *n* region that may move. Likewise, more holes will move from the *p* region to the *n* region than the other way. This average motion of each type of charge carrier, due to an unbalance in their distribution, is referred to as *diffusion*.

As carriers migrate across the junction, the two regions become more and more charged. The *n* region becomes positively charged because of both the missing electrons and the gained holes. The *p* region, on the other hand, becomes negatively charged because of the missing holes and the gained electrons. Consequently, an electric field E in the vicinity of the junction results, which is in the direction to oppose the diffusion of carriers. This field thus tends to limit the diffusion of majority carriers. Furthermore, the field exerts a force on all carriers that are in the vicinity of the junction. This force is in the direction away from the junction for majority carriers in each region, but in the direction toward the junction for minority carriers. The resulting flow of minority carriers across the junction opposes the flow of majority carriers due to diffusion. An equilibrium condition eventually reached in which the diffusion of majority carriers across the junction is limited to an amount that is exactly canceled by the flow of minority carriers due to the field. In this case, no net current flows across the junction.

When an external voltage V is applied across the diode, the equilibrium of carrier flow is upset, resulting in a nonzero net current. If the voltage is applied with plus to the p region and minus to the n region (*forward-biased*), the diffusion of majority carriers is enhanced. This happens because the applied voltage tends to remove electrons from the p region and holes from the n region, causing the internal field to be reduced, thereby allowing an increase in the rate of diffusion. Thus, a net current I flows through the diode, which increases very rapidly with an increase in the voltage. However, if the voltage is applied with plus to the n region and minus to the p region (*reverse-biased*), the diffusion of majority carriers is reduced. A net current then flows which is due to the movement of minority carriers across the junction under the influence of the internal field. This current is limited, however, to a rather small value since the number of minority carriers in each region is small.

The overall effect is characterized by the current-voltage relationship shown in Fig. 4.1. The direction of positive voltage and current is also indicated in the figure. To emphasize the switching behavior of a diode, the current-voltage relationship is often simplified to that of Fig. 4.2. The simplification assumes that zero current flows for voltages less than some positive threshold voltage V_T (approximately 0.7 V for silicon) and that the current becomes unlimited for voltages greater than V_T. This relationship corresponds to a voltage-sensitive switch that is open for voltages less than V_T and closed for voltages greater than V_T. When the diode is forward-biased with a voltage greater than V_T, it is said to be *conducting*. Conversely, when the applied voltage is less than V_T, it is said to be *nonconducting*. Figure 4.3 shows the conventional circuit symbol used to represent a diode. The

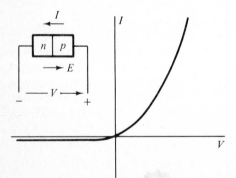

Figure 4.1 Current-voltage relationship for a *pn* junction.

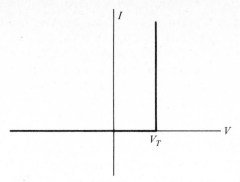

Figure 4.2 Simplification of the *I-V* relationship for a *pn* junction.

triangle points in the direction of current flow when the junction is forward-biased.

The switching speed of junction diodes is affected primarily by two mechanisms. One mechanism is the capacitance associated with the junction as a result of the internal field and the charges under its influence. This junction capacitance must be charged or discharged before the diode can be switched between conducting and nonconducting. The other mechanism is the storage of minority carriers in each region that occurs when a diode is forward-biased. These stored minority carriers must be removed before the diode can be switched from conducting to nonconducting.

The Bipolar Junction Transistor

A *bipolar junction transistor* is a three-terminal device formed from two *pn* junctions. There are three regions making up the two junctions, one of which is shared by the two junctions. There are two possible configurations: the *npn* configuration, having a *p*-type region in the center of two *n*-type regions, as shown in Fig. 4.4; and the *pnp* configuration, having an *n*-type region in the center of two *p*-type regions. In either case, the regions are labeled, in order, as *emitter*, *base*, and *collector*.

In normal operation the two junctions interact in such a way that the current component flowing through both the base-emitter and base-collector junctions can be controlled by a smaller current component flowing through just the base-emitter junction. This so-called *transistor action* is accomplished by applying an external voltage to the base-collector junction in the direction that makes it reverse-biased. Then only a small current composed of minority carriers from each region normally flows through the base-collector junction. This can be altered, however, by forward-biasing the base-emitter junction. With the base-emitter junction forward-biased, a sizable current flows through it. This current is

Figure 4.3 Circuit symbol for a *pn* junction diode.

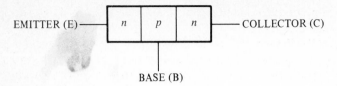

EMITTER (E) —— [n | p | n] —— COLLECTOR (C)

BASE (B)

Figure 4.4 *npn* bipolar transistor.

composed primarily of majority carriers from the emitter. Once across the base-emitter junction, these carriers are minority carriers in the base region, where they become available to contribute to the otherwise small (minority-carrier) current through the base-collector junction. Since these minority carriers in the base have the correct charge to be drawn by the base-collector voltage and since the base region is made purposely thin, most of them indeed continue on across the base-collector junction and contribute to the collector current. Those carriers that do not cross the base-collector junction give rise to a relatively small base current. The emitter current is approximately equal to the collector current, since the difference between them is the relatively small base current. The transistor is then said to be *conducting* or *on*. On the other hand, if the base-emitter junction is not forward-biased, then the current flowing through the reverse-biased base-collector junction remains small. The transistor is then said to be *nonconducting* or *off*.

For a further illustration of this behavior of a bipolar junction transistor, consider the circuit of Fig. 4.5. Besides an *npn* transistor, there is an input subcircuit, composed of V_i, R_i, and a switch; and an output subcircuit, composed of V_o and R_o. The input circuit is connected between the base and emitter, and the output circuit is connected between the collector and emitter. Such a configuration is referred to as a *common-emitter circuit*. The base current I_B can be identified as the current flowing in the input circuit, and the collector current I_C can be identified as the current flowing in the output circuit. When the switch of the circuit is placed in the grounded (lower) position, the voltage across the base-emitter junction is nearly 0, so that almost no charge carriers (i.e., electrons) enter the base region from the emitter. In this case, since the base-collector junction is reversed-biased, the collector current I_C is nearly 0. This condition is

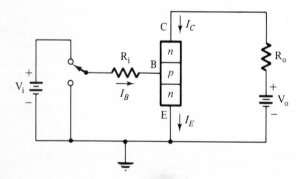

Figure 4.5 Common-emitter transistor circuit.

referred to as *cutoff*. In this condition there is almost no voltage drop across R_o, and thus the collector voltage is almost V_o.

When the switch is placed in the V_i (upper) position, the base-emitter junction is forward-biased, causing a significant flow of electrons from the emitter to the base region. Transistor action then causes a collector current to flow, which depends upon the values of R_o and V_o as well as upon the amount of base current. This collector current flowing through R_o causes a voltage drop, which reduces the collector voltage from that of the power supply V_o.

A condition referred to as *saturation* arises when the forward bias of the base-emitter junction is brought to a value around the threshold voltage V_T associated with the junction (approximately 0.7 V for silicon). In this situation a large flow of electrons across the base-emitter junction occurs, which gives rise to a large collector current limited only by the external components R_o and V_o. The collector voltage is thereby reduced to a few tenths of a volt, which is less than the voltage that is assumed to appear across the base-emitter junction. This fact implies that the base-collector junction must actually be forward-biased.

The two extreme conditions of transistor operation, cutoff and saturation, are often used in switching circuits to correspond to the two logic levels, 0 and 1, since they are obtained for a wide range of input conditions and are relatively insensitive to parameter variations. The potential switching speed of a circuit, however, is considerably reduced if the transistors are allowed to reach saturation. When a transistor is in saturation, both junctions contribute to the storage of minority carriers in the base region, since they are both forward-biased. These stored minority carriers must be removed in order to switch the transistor to cutoff. On the other hand, when a transistor is conducting but not in saturation, only the forward-biased base-emitter junction contributes to the storage of minority carriers in the base region; the reverse-biased base-collector junction actually removes many of the minority carriers. There are several methods to avoid saturation that are used in circuits when high switching speed is important. Two such methods will be discussed in later sections in regard to particular types of circuits.

The conventional circuit symbols for the two types of bipolar junction transistors, *npn* and *pnp*, are shown in Fig. 4.6. An arrow on the emitter lead distinguishes the two types. It points in the direction in which current normally flows in the emitter lead, which is toward the *n* region of the base-emitter junction.

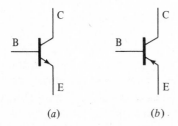

(a)

(b)

Figure 4.6 Bipolar junction transistor symbols. (a) *npn* transistor. (b) *pnp* transistor.

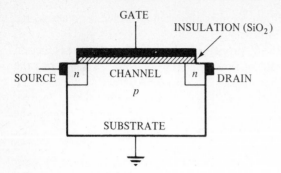

Figure 4.7 *n*-channel normally-off (enhancement mode) metal oxide semiconductor field-effect transistor.

The Field-Effect Transistor (FET)

A *field-effect transistor* (FET) is a semiconductor device in which the resistance between two terminals is controlled by the voltage on a third terminal. One form of field-effect transistor, referred to as a *metal oxide semiconductor field-effect transistor* (MOSFET), is shown in Fig. 4.7. It is constructed from a piece of lightly doped semiconductor material, called a *substrate*, upon which are formed two regions of the opposite type of semiconductor material. One of these regions is referred to as the *source*, since charge carriers originate from it; the other region is referred to as the *drain*, since charge carriers terminate at it. The region of semiconductor material lying between the source and drain is referred to as the *channel*. Above the channel is a metal electrode, called the *gate*, lying along the entire length of the channel, but separated from it by a layer of insulation (usually silicon dioxide). The name for this type of field-effect transistor comes from the metal gate, oxide insulation, and semiconductor substrate.

In operation, a current flows through the channel from the source to the drain. This current consists of the flow of charge carriers of the type that is the majority in the source and drain regions. Thus, for the field-effect transistor shown in Fig. 4.7, the current through the channel consists of the flow of electrons. Normally, the channel is lacking in electrons, since its material is *p*-type. This gives rise to a very high resistance. This situation is altered, however, when a positive voltage is applied to the gate with respect to the grounded substrate. The positive voltage deposits positive charges on the gate electrode. This causes electrons to be attracted from the bulk of the substrate and accumulate in the channel region. These electrons have the effect of lowering the resistance of the channel. There is usually a threshold value for the gate voltage that causes a drastic reduction in the channel resistance. When the gate voltage is less than the threshold value, the transistor is said to be *off*. When the gate voltage exceeds the threshold value, the transistor is said to be *on*.

The type of field-effect transistor described above is said to operate in the *enhancement mode*, since an applied voltage enhances the number of charge carriers in the channel. It is also referred to as a *normally-off* field-effect transistor, since it corresponds to an open switch when a zero voltage is applied to the gate.

There also exists a *normally-on* field-effect transistor, which has a relatively low channel resistance for a zero gate voltage. Such a field-effect transistor is similar to the type just discussed, except that the substrate is made of the same type of semiconductor material as the source and drain, which is *n*-type for the transistor shown in Fig. 4.7. In this case, the electrons normally available for conduction in the channel can be driven away by applying a negative voltage to the gate. This type of field-effect transistor is said to operate in the *depletion mode*, since the application of a nonzero gate voltage depletes the charge carriers in the channel.

Field-effect transistors of the type shown in Fig. 4.7, whether normally on or normally off, are classified as *n-channel* devices, since the charge carriers that provide conduction in the channel are electrons. They are usually operated with a drain voltage that is positive with respect to the source. There are also *p-channel* field-effect transistors, which utilize holes as the mechanism for conduction in the channel. Their operation is similar to that of *n*-channel devices, except that all voltages are of the opposite polarity.

There are four types of MOSFETs, corresponding to the possible combinations of channel type, *n* or *p*, and conduction type, normally off or normally on. These types are distinguished by the circuit symbols that are used to represent them, as shown in Fig. 4.8. The normally-off types have a symbol with a broken line connecting the drain and source, whereas the normally-on types have a solid line. An arrow on the substrate lead indicates the channel type. The arrow points toward the channel in the case of *n*-type and away from the channel in the case of *p*-type. The substrate lead is very often connected internally to the source, resulting in a three-terminal device. In this case all voltages are usually referred to the source.

The switching speed of circuits using MOS field-effect transistors is affected primarily by the capacitance encountered between the gate and the other electrodes as a result of the geometrical arrangement of the gate. This capacitance, which is usually appreciable, must be charged or discharged before a field-effect transistor can be switched between on and off. This is compounded by the fact that field-effect transistors tend to have an on resistance that is rather high in comparison with that of bipolar junction transistors. Since a field-effect transistor

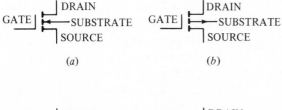

(a) (b)

(c) (d)

Figure 4.8 Circuit symbols for different types of MOSFETs. (*a*) *n*-channel normally off (enhancement mode). (*b*) *p*-channel normally off (enhancement mode). (*c*) *n*-channel normally on (depletion mode). (*d*) *p*-channel normally on (depletion mode).

in a circuit is generally driven by another field-effect transistor, a considerable time constant results from the combination of the on resistance of the driving transistor with the gate capacitance of the driven transistor. There is therefore an overall tendency for circuits based on MOS field-effect transistors to be significantly slower than circuits based on bipolar junction transistors and diodes.

4.2 LOGIC GATES

A *logic gate* is a component that is designed to carry out a basic logical operation. In the rest of this chapter, we will be concerned with various types of semiconductor circuits that make up logic gates, especially those that are commercially available in integrated-circuit form.

To illustrate some of the concepts that are involved in gate circuits, it might help to start with what is perhaps the simplest form, namely, diode gates. One diode gate, consisting of two diodes and a resistor, is shown in Fig. 4.9.† For this circuit, the logic levels 0 and 1 will be represented, respectively, by 0 V and $+V$ V. The circuit has two input lines A and B. If both input lines are placed at $+V$ V (logic-1), then the resistor will pull the output line up to $+V$ V. If, however, either input line is placed at 0 V (logic-0), that input line will pull the output line to almost 0 V, because the interconnecting diode will be forward-biased and therefore conducting. The behavior of this circuit corresponds to the logical operation AND, since the output is logic-1 if and only if both input lines are at logic-1.

This diode gate is useful for some applications, but it has two major limitations that hinder its general-purpose use. One limitation is that its output is sensitive to input voltage variations. This is especially noticeable for logic-0 at one input line. In this case, any deviation of the input voltage from the ideal value of 0

---

† It should be pointed out that whenever a ground symbol is shown in a circuit diagram, it is conventional to use that point as the reference for all circuit voltages unless otherwise indicated. Thus, any voltage specified for a circuit node, such as for power supplies and logic signals, corresponds to the voltage difference between that node and ground.

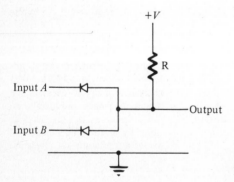

Figure 4.9 A diode gate.

Figure 4.10 Three parts of a gate circuit.

contributes the same deviation to the output voltage, in addition to that caused by the nonzero voltage drop across the forward-biased diode. Such output sensitivity to input variations would become serious if a number of diode gates were cascaded, since deviations could then accumulate from one gate to the next. The second limitation is that the performance of the gate is adversely affected by loading on the output line. For a high output level, the load generally draws a current from the output line, which must flow through the pull-up resistor in the gate. This causes a voltage drop across the resistor, resulting in a reduced voltage at the output. This reduction in output voltage will be significant since the value of the pull-up resistor must be made relatively large to avoid greatly loading the input lines when they are low. For a low output level, on the other hand, the load generally supplies a current into the output line of the diode gate. This current must flow out of those input lines that are at a low voltage level. This could lead to a situation in which one input line must absorb current from many other gates, which may not be practical.

These two limitations can be attributed to the fact that diodes are passive devices. Transistors, on the other hand, are active devices in the sense that a low-power signal can control a higher-power signal. The two limitations of diode gates can be alleviated by connecting transistors to the diodes. One additional piece of circuitry could serve to restore the voltage levels of the gate output to values that are close to the ideal values and thereby reduce the sensitivity to input voltage variations. Another circuit addition could serve to isolate the output load current from the input lines and also to provide current sufficient to drive a number of input lines of other gates. These two circuit additions might be referred to, respectively, as a *restorer* and a *buffer*. The original diode circuit might be referred to as a *combiner*, since it combines the input signals. A modified gate obtained by the interconnection of these three parts has the general configuration shown in Fig. 4.10. The particular overall circuit under discussion is called a *diode-transistor-logic* (DTL) gate, since diodes are used in the front portion of the circuit and transistors in the rest.

We will use the conceptual representation of Fig. 4.10 to analyze certain other types of logic gates. This partitioning will allow us to deal with the function of each part separately. In particular, the buffer circuit portion of a gate can be varied to serve different purposes without affecting the treatment of the rest of the gate circuit. As will be seen, however, some types of gates cannot be broken into the three parts. In particular, certain types of gates are constructed in a form referred to as *direct-coupled logic*, in which the transistors in a single circuit part accomplish all three functions.

The following sections in this chapter will each deal with a specific type of gate circuit. In each case, the gate can be thought of as part of a logic family, which includes several gates that have the same basic design concept but perform different logic operations. Generally, one logic operation is the most prevalent for a logic family, and a gate for this operation will be emphasized in the presentation. The prevalent operation is always one that is universal (such as NAND or NOR), so that it alone is sufficient to implement all logic functions. The logic families can be divided between two major categories: those based on bipolar junction devices, referred to as *bipolar logic*; and those based on MOSFETs, referred to as *MOS logic*.

In the preceding discussion of the diode gate, the more positive of the two voltages was assigned to logic-1, and the more negative voltage was assigned to logic-0. This convention is known as *positive logic*. The alternate convention, in which the assignment is reversed, is known as *negative logic*. The logic operation corresponding to a particular gate depends upon the logic convention that is used. To avoid confusion without loss of generality, this book will utilize only the positive-logic convention.

Before we close this general discussion on logic gates, certain performance aspects of gates, such as fan-out, fan-in, propagation delay, noise immunity, and power dissipation, should be introduced. The term *fan-out* refers to the maximum number of input lines that can be driven by the output line of a given gate. Usually, the fan-out of a gate is determined by the amount of current that can be conveyed by the output line while maintaining specified voltage levels associated with the two logic values. The term *fan-in* refers to the largest number of input lines that can be incorporated into, or that are available for, a gate of a certain type. The *propagation delay* of a gate is the amount of time that elapses between the application of an input combination to the input lines and the time in which the appropriate output value is available on the output line. The load placed on the output line of a gate, especially capacitive components, very often affects the propagation delay. *Noise immunity* refers to the general ability of a network of gates to tolerate disturbances to the signals that represent the two logic values. A logic family generally includes a margin between output and input voltage levels corresponding to each logic value to allow for variations due to noise disturbances. Finally, *power dissipation* refers to the amount of power consumed by a logic gate in operation. Generally, this consumed power comes primarily from the power supply and therefore should be kept to a minimum, especially for applications using batteries. Moreover, the power dissipated in a circuit must be physically removed in the form of heat. However, the rate in which heat can be removed from an integrated circuit is limited. Consequently, the rated power dissipation for a gate often acts as a limitation to the attainable density of gates in an integrated circuit.

4.3 TRANSISTOR-TRANSISTOR LOGIC (TTL)

Transistor-transistor logic (TTL) is a very prominent logic family. Its name refers to the use of bipolar junction transistors throughout the circuit for a gate. One

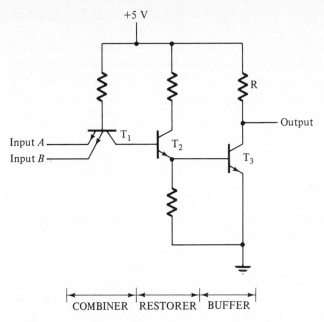

Figure 4.11 A TTL gate with resistor pull-up.

circuit for a TTL gate is shown in Fig. 4.11. The logic values 0 and 1 are represented, respectively, by the nominal voltages 0 V and +5 V. As indicated in the figure, the circuit can be broken into the three parts mentioned in the preceding section: combiner, restorer, and buffer. The function of each of these parts will now be treated individually.

The combiner consists of a multiple-emitter transistor T_1. Two emitters are shown, but the number can be increased. The input signals to the gate are each connected to a separate emitter. Each of these emitters forms a junction with the base. It is assumed that if any base-emitter junction is sufficiently forward-biased, then the transistor will be in the conductive state; i.e., current will tend to flow in the collector lead. Since the base is connected through a resistor to the positive voltage supply, a particular base-emitter junction will be forward-biased whenever the emitter is close to ground. Thus, the transistor will be in the conductive state whenever any emitter has a voltage that is low (logic-0). In such a case, a significant amount of current flows out of the emitters that have a low voltage, which is primarily due to the base current. When all emitters are high (logic-1), the transistor will be in cutoff. In such a case, very little current flows in any of the emitters.

The restorer consists of the transistor T_2 and two resistors. The base of T_2 is connected to the collector of T_1, so that the current in both these leads is the same. When the transistor T_1 of the combiner is on, current flows into its collector and out of the emitter or emitters that are low. This current is in the direction opposite to that of the current that flows into the base of transistor T_2 when its base-emitter junction is forward-biased. Thus, when T_1 is on, it is assured that T_2 is in cutoff. Actually, appreciable current flows out of the base of T_2 into the collector of T_1 only during the brief time that it takes T_2 to switch from saturation to cutoff. This current is due to the removal of excess charges in the base region of T_2 that accumulate when T_2 is in saturation. Once T_2 is in cutoff, very little current flows in its base. If, on the other hand, T_1 is in cutoff, its base-collector junction will be forward-biased because of the $+5$ V that is applied to the base resistor. The base-collector junction of T_1, as for any forward-biased diode, will therefore be conductive. This in turn will cause the base-emitter junction of T_2 to be forward-biased, so that T_2 will be in saturation (a conductive state). The two conditions for T_2, cutoff and saturation, each occur for a range of input conditions. In this sense, the circuit involving T_2 acts as a signal restorer.

The buffer part of the gate circuit consists of transistor T_3 and a resistor. The base of T_3 is driven by the emitter of transistor T_2 in the restorer. When transistor T_2 becomes conductive, it causes both its emitter and collector to obtain a voltage between ground and $+5$ V that is determined by the two resistors in the restorer. This, in turn, causes the base-emitter junction of the buffer transistor T_3 to be forward-biased, so that T_3 will then be in the conductive state. In this situation, the output line of the gate is forced to near ground level. On the other hand, when T_2 of the restorer is not conducting, its emitter will be at ground. This, in turn, causes the base-emitter junction of T_3 not to be forward-biased, so that T_3 will then be in cutoff. In this situation, the resistor of the buffer pulls up the output line to near the power-supply voltage of $+5$ V. The actual voltage at the output line, in this case, depends upon the voltage drop across the resistor due to the load current that flows through it. The overall operation of the TTL gate is summarized in Table 4.1. If 0 V and 5 V are replaced with the respective logic values of 0 and 1, it can be seen that Table 4.1 corresponds to the logic operation NAND. In the case of just one input emitter, the gate is an inverter.

Let us further consider the function of the buffer part of a gate. Its task is primarily to fulfill the drive requirements imposed on the gate output line by circuits to which it is connected, specifically the input lines of other gates. For a TTL gate, appreciable current flows in an input line only when that input line is driven low. The current then flows out of the input line and into the output line of the driving gate. The previously described buffer circuit can meet the drive require-

Table 4.1 Summary of the operation of the TTL gate of Fig. 4.11

A	B	State of T_1	State of T_2	State of T_3	Output
0 V	0 V	On	Off	Off	~ 5 V
0 V	5 V	On	Off	Off	~ 5 V
5 V	0 V	On	Off	Off	~ 5 V
5 V	5 V	Off	On	On	~ 0 V

ments of the gate provided that the driving transistor is capable of sinking the current from all driven inputs plus the current through the pull-up resistor. The switching speed of such a gate, however, is somewhat restricted by the use of a resistor to pull the output line high when the output transistor is off. There is always a considerable amount of stray capacitance that is encountered between the output line of a gate and ground. This capacitance is due to, among other things, the wiring that interconnects the gates as well as the junction capacitances associated with the transistors. This stray capacitance must be charged whenever the output makes a low-to-high transition. The charging current must come primarily from the pull-up resistor. The output voltage therefore rises exponentially with a time constant determined by the pull-up resistor and the amount of stray capacitance. High-to-low transitions are accomplished much faster, however, since the output transistor effectively serves as a low-resistance path to ground, which quickly discharges the capacitance.

Totem-Pole Output

It is common to use a transistor in place of the output pull-up resistor in a TTL buffer in order to enhance the switching speed. This pull-up transistor is turned on when the output is to be high, thereby providing an effective low-resistance path to charge the stray capacitance. A circuit for a TTL gate with such a modified buffer is shown in Fig. 4.12. Such a buffer circuit is frequently called a *totem-pole*

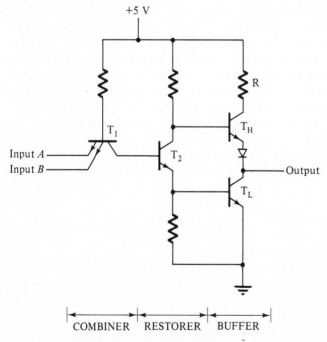

Figure 4.12 A TTL gate with transistor pull-up.

output. In this case, there are two transistors in the buffer, T_H and T_L. T_H serves to pull the output line high, whereas T_L serves to pull it low. The restorer transistor T_2 drives these two output transistors in a complementary fashion. When T_2 is in cutoff, the base of T_L is at ground level, and the base of T_H is high. This causes T_H to conduct and T_L to be in cutoff. On the other hand, when T_2 is conducting, the bases of both T_L and T_H are brought to an intermediate voltage, which is high enough to cause T_L to conduct, but not high enough for T_H to conduct. The diode that is shown in series with T_H is included to raise the emitter voltage of T_H by about 0.7 V to ensure that its base-emitter junction will not be forward-biased in the latter situation. A small-valued resistor in series with the two transistors T_H and T_L is included to limit the current that flows through them during the switching transition, when they both are partially conducting.

Using TTL Gates to Drive Other Components

It is often necessary to have TTL gates drive components other than input lines of other TTL gates, e.g., in any situation involving an interface between TTL gates and nonlogic output devices such as indicator lamps, control circuits, and digital-to-analog converters. In such cases, it is important to note that a TTL gate primarily sinks current for a low output. However, it is normally not capable of supplying sufficient current for a high output. Components should be interfaced to TTL gates with this fact in mind. For example, suppose it is desirable to connect a lamp to indicate the output level of a TTL inverter or other TTL gate. A way to do this is to connect the lamp from the output line to V_{CC} as shown in Fig. 4.13. Of course, the lamp must be rated at about 5 V, and it must not draw current that exceeds the maximum sinking current of the gate. The lamp will light when the output is low (logic-0). If the opposite of this lighting condition is desired, the lamp can be connected from the output line to ground and a pull-up resistor supplied as shown in Fig. 4.14. In this case, the resistor will supply most of the lamp current when the gate output is high. When the gate output is low, it will shunt current away from the lamp. R should be sufficiently low to supply the rated lamp current, but never so low as to exceed the current sinking capability of the gate-output line.

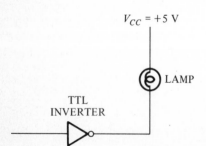

$V_{CC} = +5\text{ V}$

LAMP

TTL
INVERTER

Figure 4.13 Driving a lamp with a TTL gate. Lamp is on for low output.

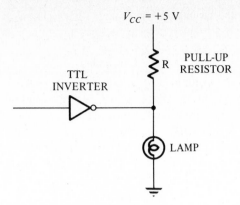

Figure 4.14 Alternative connection for driving a lamp with a TTL gate. Lamp is on for high output.

4.4 WIRED LOGIC

TTL gates that have an output pull-up resistor (as in Fig. 4.11) can be used to implement what is called *wired logic*. This term refers to the fact that a certain logic operation can be performed upon the output signals of several gates by simply connecting their output lines together. Figure 4.15 shows two TTL NAND

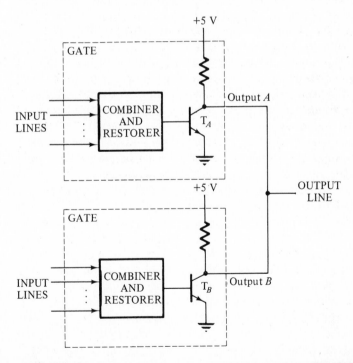

Figure 4.15 Wired-AND formed from the output lines of two TTL NAND gates having pull-up resistors.

Table 4.2 Results of the wired AND for the circuit of Fig. 4.15

| T_A | T_B | Without common connection | | Common output |
		Output A	Output B	
On	On	Low	Low	Low
On	Off	Low	High	Low
Off	On	High	Low	Low
Off	Off	High	High	High

gates having output pull-up resistors with their output lines connected together. If either buffer transistor is on, then the common output will be forced to a voltage near ground. Otherwise, the common output will be pulled high by both pull-up resistors. This behavior is summarized in Table 4.2. For positive logic the common output is equal to the AND of the logic values that would correspond to the individual outputs if the lines were not connected together. The overall logic operation from the gate inputs to the common output corresponds to an AND of NANDs. Thus, two levels of logic are realized with the use of only one level of gates. Of course, the logic values corresponding to the individual gate outputs are no longer available.

Wired logic offers advantages other than a means for achieving a gate at no cost. The AND operation corresponding to the connected gate outputs is performed without incurring any additional propagation delay. Also, since there is essentially no limitation on the number of gates that can be connected, wired logic is valuable for situations that require a large fan-in (number of input variables).

Perhaps the most important advantage of wired logic within the context of microcomputers is the potential that it offers for the implementation of logic buses. A bus is a line or set of lines that interconnects a number of logic devices and allows one of the devices to send information to one or more of the other devices. The bus may be unidirectional, in which case a specific device is always the sender; or it may be bidirectional, in which case any one of the devices may be the sender at a particular time. Figure 4.16 illustrates a bidirectional bus consisting of a single line that connects several devices. In this example, only one device is designated to be the sender at any given time. All the other devices are set in such a way that the buffer transistor in the gate connected to the bus is off (corresponding to logic-1 for positive logic). The logic value of the common bus line is thus determined by the state of the buffer transistor of the sending device. If that transistor is off (logic-1), then the bus line will be pulled high (logic-1) by all the resistors. If the buffer transistor of the sending device is on (logic-0), then it will force the bus line to be low (logic-0). The bus line is connected to the input lines of logic circuits located at each device, which receive the information that is conveyed by the bus. It is thus apparent that a single connection may be time-shared among many devices so that any one of them can originate a signal that is

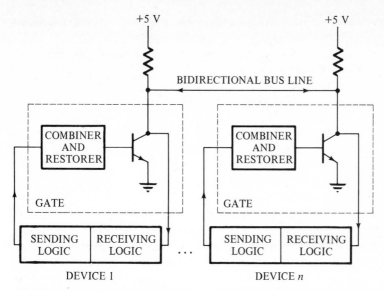

Figure 4.16 Example of a bidirectional bus using gates with pull-up resistors.

to be sent to the other devices. Chapter 5 will develop the concept of a bus more extensively.

At this point let us take notice of the many pull-up resistors that appear when the buffer outputs are tied together. Clearly, all of them together are not desired since they combine in parallel, resulting in a rather low equivalent resistance. This causes an unduly large current to be conducted by the transistors that are on, an effect which is especially undesirable in the worst case, when only one transistor is on. The situation can be simply remedied by replacing all the pull-up resistors with just one that has the proper value. This is done by using gates having no pull-up device in the buffer portion of the gate and then adding a single external pull-up resistor. TTL gates that have no output pull-up device are available especially for wired logic and are referred to as *open-collector* gates. The label "o.c." is often used next to a gate symbol to indicate an open-collector gate.

Three-State Outputs

It would be nice if wired logic could be used with TTL gates that have pull-up transistors in their buffer section, since such gates do have a fast low-to-high switching speed. However, if the outputs of two such gates were connected together, a conflict would arise whenever the output signals differed. The upper transistor in the buffer portion of one of the gates would be on, forcing the common output to be high; the lower transistor in the buffer portion of the other gate would be on, forcing the common output to be low. The net result is that a large current would flow through the two conducting transistors, which could cause damage to the transistors. However, even if damage did not occur, the output voltage would have a value somewhere between the acceptable values for logic-0 and for logic-1, thereby causing undefined behavior.

There is a way, however, of using wired logic and achieving the advantage of the fast switching speed that is associated with gates having output pull-up transistors. In particular, the logical behavior of TTL gates can be modified by introducing a third output state, which is neither a high nor a low voltage. These gates are said to have *three-state outputs*. The third state is actually the absence of the other two states and is frequently referred to as the *high-impedance* or *high-Z* state. Physically, the third state corresponds to a condition in which the output line of the gate is floating or undriven. This state is achieved in a TTL gate by means of a buffer section having an upper and a lower transistor both of which can be off at the same time. Figure 4.17a shows a circuit for a TTL NAND gate having three-state outputs. A supplementary input line, labeled "Enable," is provided to control the two output transistors T_L and T_H. The Enable line is connected through a diode to the base of the upper output transistor and is also connected to an

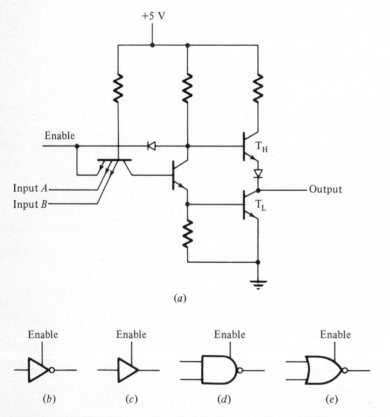

(a)

(b)   (c)   (d)   (e)

Figure 4.17 Logic gates with three-state outputs. (a) Circuit for TTL three-state-output NAND gate. (b) Symbol for three-state-output inverter. (c) Symbol for three-state-output driver. (d) Symbol for three-state-output NAND gate. (e) Symbol for three-state-output NOR gate.

Table 4.3 Results of connecting output lines of two three-state-output gates together

X_1	E_1	X_2	E_2	Y
0	0	0	0	Undefined
0	0	0	1	0
0	0	1	0	Undefined
0	0	1	1	1
0	1	0	0	0
0	1	0	1	Not allowed
0	1	1	0	0
0	1	1	1	Not allowed
1	0	0	0	Undefined
1	0	0	1	0
1	0	1	0	Undefined
1	0	1	1	1
1	1	0	0	1
1	1	0	1	Not allowed
1	1	1	0	1
1	1	1	1	Not allowed

emitter of the input transistor. When the Enable line is low (logic-0), both output transistors will be off. The upper output transistor will be off because its base is forced to be low by the Enable line passing through the forward-biased diode. The lower output transistor will be off because of the logic-0 applied to an emitter of the input transistor. On the other hand, when the Enable line is high (logic-1), the diode to the base of the upper transistor will not be forward-biased, so that the upper transistor will be allowed to behave as in an ordinary TTL gate. Furthermore, the logic-1 from Enable on an emitter of the input transistor will make that emitter ineffective. Thus, when Enable is logic-1, the gate will operate upon the other inputs in the manner of an ordinary TTL NAND gate. Logic diagram symbols for gates having three-state outputs are shown in Fig. 4.17b–e.

The output lines of two or more TTL gates with three-state outputs may be connected together with the restriction that only one gate may be enabled at any given time. The result is a restricted form of wired logic, which is logically described in a somewhat more complicated manner than ordinary wired logic. To illustrate this kind of logic, assume that n three-state-output gates have their output lines connected. Let X_i represent the output value that gate G_i has when enabled. Let E_i represent the value of the Enable input to gate G_i. For $n = 2$ the overall output Y may be tabulated as shown in Table 4.3. There are two entries in the column for Y other than 0 or 1. A "not allowed" entry is shown in each row for which both Enable inputs are 1. Also, an "undefined" entry is shown in each row for which both Enable inputs are 0, since in that case neither gate is driving the common output line.

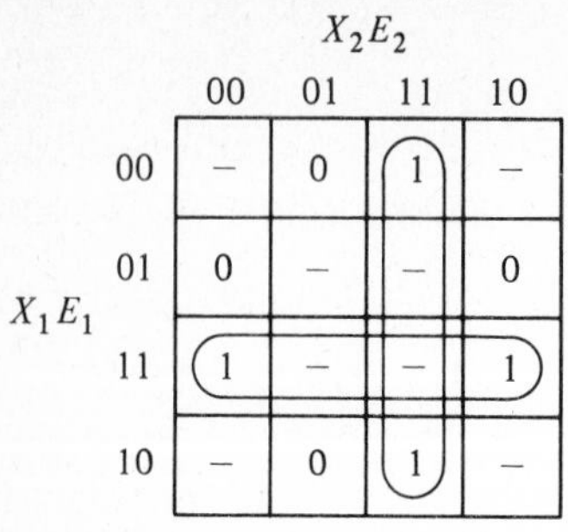

Figure 4.18 Karnaugh map for the function $Y(X_1, E_1, X_2, E_2)$ of Table 4.3.

The result of plotting the incompletely specified function $Y(X_1, E_1, X_2, E_2)$ in Table 4.3 on a Karnaugh map is shown in Fig. 4.18. The "not allowed" and "undefined" entries in Table 4.3 are both treated as don't-cares in the Karnaugh map. This classification is based on the assumption that exactly one gate is enabled. A sum-of-products expression can be obtained for $Y(X_1, E_1, X_2, E_2)$ by forming the two groupings as shown in the Karnaugh map. The corresponding expression is

$$Y = X_1 E_1 + X_2 E_2$$

It should be noted that in the expression, there is a term for each gate. If a gate G_i is enabled, then the corresponding term is equal to X_i and the other term is logic-0 (since only one gate may be enabled). Thus, Y takes on the logic value of the output of the enabled gate. It is apparent that additional gates would add corresponding terms into the sum-of-products expression for Y. In general, then,

$$Y = X_1 E_1 + X_2 E_2 + \cdots + X_n E_n$$

Alternatively, a product-of-sums expression can be found for $Y(X_1, E_1, X_2, E_2)$ by grouping the 0s in the Karnaugh map in Fig. 4.18. Two groupings, the second row from the top and the second column from the left, cover all 0s. The resulting product-of-sums expression is

$$Y = (X_1 + \bar{E}_1)(X_2 + \bar{E}_2)$$

This expression generalizes for an arbitrary n to

$$Y = (X_1 + \bar{E}_1)(X_2 + \bar{E}_2) \cdots (X_n + \bar{E}_n)$$

As a consequence of the two expressions derived above, it appears that we have a choice in logically interpreting three-state-output wired logic. It may be thought of as corresponding to *wired OR* or *wired AND*. The variables that are ORed or ANDed, however, do not correspond to just the usual gate-output signals. Rather, they are conditioned by the state of the Enable input line. If the interpretation is wired OR, then each usual gate output X_i is conditioned by ANDing it with E_i. On the other hand, if the interpretation is wired AND, then each usual gate output X_i is conditioned by ORing it with $\bar{E}_i$.

4.5 TTL FAMILY VARIATIONS

There are several subfamilies of transistor-transistor logic based on two basic circuit variations. One variation involves power levels, and the other involves the use of Schottky devices.

Standard and Low-Power TTL

TTL in integrated-circuit form is widely used and is made according to specifications that are uniform among manufacturers. One set of specifications for TTL is referred to as *standard TTL*, and another is referred to as *low-power TTL*. Both types generally have the same voltage levels representing the two logic values, which for outputs are a maximum of 0.4 V for logic-0 and a minimum of 2.4 V for logic-1. Also, the two types have the same power-supply voltage requirement of +5 V. The two types, however, differ in their input current requirement, output current capability, and power dissipation. Appreciable current flows only at the low-voltage level (logic-0) for either type. This current flows out of the input line of a gate and into the output line of its predecessor gate. At logic-0, the input lines of standard TTL require nominally 1.6 mA of current, and the output lines are capable of producing 16 mA. The fan-out (i.e., the maximum number of input lines that may be driven by an output line) of standard TTL is thus equal to 10. For low-power TTL, on the other hand, the logic-0 input current requirement is 0.36 mA, and the output current capability is 8 mA. The fan-out of low-power TTL is thus approximately 22. The most significant characteristic in this comparison is the lower input current requirement of low-power TTL as compared with standard TTL (less than one-fourth). This is important in connecting TTL components to microprocessors, which usually have a low current capability in their output lines.

Another difference between the two types of TTL is the power that is dissipated by each gate. The power dissipation for low-power TTL is about one-tenth of that for standard TTL. A disadvantage of low-power TTL is that it is slower than standard TTL (about one-third the speed). This is primarily due to the fact that the lower operating currents of low-power TTL result in a longer time needed to charge or discharge various capacitances in the circuit for a gate.

Schottky TTL

A variation of transistor-transistor logic, which is available in integrated-circuit form, makes use of Schottky diodes and Schottky transistors to achieve an appreciable improvement in switching speed. A *Schottky diode* is formed from a junction between a metal and an n-type semiconductor material, as shown in Fig. 4.19. The majority charge carriers in both the metal and semiconductor are electrons. However, the electrons in the semiconductor occupy higher energy states than those in the metal. Consequently, electrons from the semiconductor are able to diffuse across the junction and to occupy energy states in the metal by dissipat-

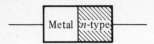

Figure 4.19 Schottky diode formed from a junction between a metal and an *n*-type semiconductor.

ing some of their energy. However, electrons in the metal are inhibited from crossing the junction because of the higher energy states in the semiconductor. The diffusion of electrons from the semiconductor to the metal results in the development of a potential across the junction that retards this diffusion. This internal potential can be counteracted by applying an external voltage to the diode that makes the metal positive with respect to the semiconductor. In such a case, a current will flow as a result of the increase in the diffusion of electrons. On the other hand, if an external voltage is applied in the opposite direction, very little current will flow. A Schottky diode therefore exhibits a rectifying property similar to that of *pn* junction diodes. However, the switching speed of a Schottky diode does not suffer from the storage of minority carriers, as does a *pn* junction diode. The reason is that only electrons are involved, which are majority carriers in both regions. A distinctive circuit symbol is conventionally used for a Schottky diode, as shown in Fig. 4.20.

In addition to having an improved switching speed, Schottky diodes demonstrate a lower forward voltage drop than *pn* junction diodes, about 0.2 to 0.3 V. This leads to the use of Schottky diodes with bipolar junction transistors to enhance their switching speed. If a Schottky diode is connected across the base-collector junction of a transistor oriented with the same polarity, as shown in Fig. 4.21, it will prevent the forward bias of the junction from reaching its usual value of about 0.7 V. Consequently, the transistor will be kept from going deeply into saturation. As a result, the on-to-off switching speed of the transistor will be improved, since the storage of minority carriers in the base will be alleviated. Such a configuration is called a *Schottky transistor* and has the circuit symbol shown in Fig. 4.22.

Schottky TTL is available in both standard and low-power form. Standard and low-power Schottky TTL show an improvement in switching speed of about 3 to 4 times over their respective non-Schottky forms. It may be observed that the switching speed of low-power Schottky TTL is, therefore, about the same as that of standard non-Schottky TTL.

Actually, some liberty is taken by manufacturers in the implementation of low-power Schottky TTL. One such circuit, shown in Fig. 4.23, actually corresponds to diode-transistor logic, since the combination of input signals is done with diodes. However, the voltage levels, current levels, and current direction are the same as if an input transistor were used.

Figure 4.20 Circuit symbol for a Schottky diode.

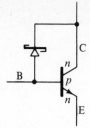
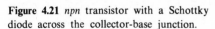

Figure 4.21 *npn* transistor with a Schottky diode across the collector-base junction.

Figure 4.22 Circuit symbol for an *npn* Schottky transistor.

4.6 EMITTER-COUPLED LOGIC (ECL)

It was noted before that for logic circuits that use bipolar junction transistors, the switching speed can be increased by avoiding saturation. Recall that saturation refers to the condition of a transistor in which both junctions are forward-biased. Consequently, when a transistor is in saturation, minority charge carriers are injected into the base region from both junctions. This results in an excess of

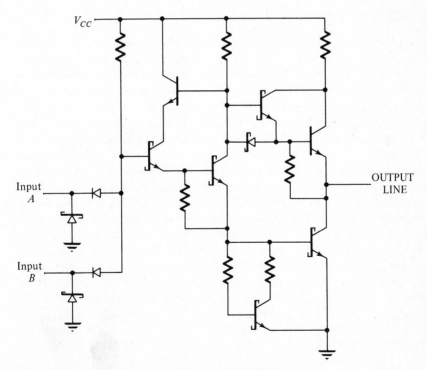

Figure 4.23 A two-input low-power Schottky TTL NAND gate.

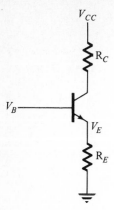

Figure 4.24 Transistor circuit with emitter resistor to control collector current.

minority carriers stored in the base region, which must be removed before the transistor can be switched to cutoff. The family of logic gates referred to as *emitter-coupled logic* (ECL) avoids saturation of each transistor through the careful control of collector current.

Control of Collector Current

The collector current of a transistor in an ECL gate is controlled by the use of a resistor in series with the emitter, as shown in Fig. 4.24. Ordinarily, with the resistor not in series with the emitter (i.e., with the emitter grounded), it is difficult to cause the transistor to avoid saturation while conducting. The reason for this difficulty is that there is a difference of only about 0.2 to 0.3 V between the values of the base-emitter voltage corresponding to the onset of transistor conduction and that of transistor saturation. Consequently, if a voltage is applied to the base of the transistor to cause it to conduct, any signal noise or transistor-parameter variation can cause the transistor to go into saturation. However, with a resistor in series with the emitter, the current through the emitter can be limited to a value that does not result in transistor saturation. In particular, suppose a positive voltage V_B relative to ground is applied to the base of the transistor in Fig. 4.24. When an emitter current flows, it produces a voltage drop across the emitter resistor R_E, resulting in a positive voltage V_E on the emitter. The voltage V_{BE} across the base-emitter junction is therefore reduced from the base voltage V_B by the amount V_E. Furthermore, as V_B increases, the emitter current increases, causing a higher emitter voltage. This higher emitter voltage tends to counteract the increase in base voltage. Thus, the net increase in the base-emitter voltage V_{BE} is considerably less than the increase in base voltage with respect to ground. In other words, the emitter resistor causes a negative feedback effect that reduces the sensitivity of the transistor to changes in the applied base voltage. This negative feedback also makes the collector current less sensitive to variations in the parameters of the transistor.

To avoid saturating the transistor in Fig. 4.24, the emitter current must be kept below a value that would cause the collector-to-emitter voltage V_{CE} to be less than the base-to-emitter voltage V_{BE} (otherwise the collector-base junction would be forward-biased). V_{CE} is seen to be equal to the supply voltage V_{CC} minus the voltage drops across the two resistors R_C and R_E. Thus, assuming that the collector current is approximately equal to the emitter current, i.e., $I_C \approx I_E$, the collector-to-emitter voltage is given by

$$V_{CE} = V_{CC} - I_E R_C - I_E R_E = V_{CC} - I_E (R_C + R_E)$$

Now, to avoid saturation,

$$V_{BE} < V_{CE} = V_{CC} - I_E (R_C + R_E)$$

or $\qquad\qquad$ Maximum $I_E = \dfrac{V_{CC} - V_{BE}}{R_C + R_E}$

This limit on the emitter current I_E can be used to find a limit on the base voltage V_B to avoid saturation. Notice that the base voltage is equal to the voltage drop across R_E plus the base-emitter voltage V_{BE}. That is,

$$V_B = I_E R_E + V_{BE}$$

Thus, to avoid saturation,

$$\text{Maximum } V_B = \left(\frac{V_{CC} - V_{BE}}{R_C + R_E} \right) R_E + V_{BE}$$

$$= \frac{R_E V_{CC}}{R_C + R_E} + \frac{R_C V_{BE}}{R_C + R_E}$$

The second term in this last expression is generally small compared with the first term, since R_C is usually made considerably less than R_E for ECL and since V_{BE} is considerably less than V_{CC}. Thus,

$$\text{Maximum } V_B \approx \frac{R_E V_{CC}}{R_C + R_E}$$

Since R_C is considerably less than R_E, the last expression indicates that the base voltage can be brought close (but not equal) to the supply voltage V_{CC} and still avoid saturation. There is, however, a definite region between V_{CC} and the maximum V_B to avoid saturation.

Differential Circuit

As just seen, the use of a resistor in series with the emitter of a transistor helps avoid saturation, but as a result the base voltage must be changed over a wide range to achieve a desired change in the emitter current. It is undesirable, however, to require a large separation in the voltages corresponding to the two logic values at the input of a gate. Consequently, in an ECL gate, input signals are

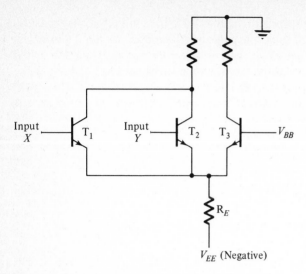

Figure 4.25 Two-input combiner circuit for an ECL gate.

V_{EE} (Negative)

combined by a circuit, such as shown in Fig. 4.25, that operates in a differential manner. Such a circuit requires a relatively small separation in the input voltages that correspond to the two logic values. The circuit includes several transistors with emitters that are tied together and share a common emitter resistor. The transistors appear on two sides of the circuit. The bases of the transistors on the left side are connected to input lines. These input transistors have their collectors tied to a common collector resistor. The one transistor on the right side (T_3) has its base connected to a fixed reference voltage V_{BB} and its collector connected to a separate collector resistor. Note that ground is placed at the top of the collector resistors and that a negative voltage V_{EE} is supplied to the bottom of the emitter resistor.

The voltage V_{BB}, applied to the base of T_3, serves as a threshold value for the input voltages. The voltage on all emitters is pulled up by transistor T_3 to a value that is at least equal to $V_{BB} - V_{BE}$. Consequently, if any input transistor on the left side has a base voltage somewhat less than V_{BB}, then that transistor will not conduct, since its base-emitter junction will not be sufficiently forward-biased. On the other hand, if any input transistor on the left has a base voltage somewhat greater than V_{BB}, then the emitter voltage will be pulled up higher than $V_{BB} - V_{BE}$. In such a case, the right-hand transistor T_3 will not conduct, since its base-emitter junction will no longer be sufficiently forward-biased. Thus, current flows through the transistor or transistors on just one side of the circuit depending upon the input voltages.

Actually, the input voltages are kept fairly close to the value V_{BB}, so that the emitter voltage is relatively constant. Consequently, the current I flowing through the emitter resistor, which is the current that flows through the conducting transistors, is also relatively constant. The value of V_{BB} is chosen to ensure that this current I does not result in the saturation of a conducting transistor.

The collector resistor on the side in which the current I is flowing has a resulting voltage drop. Consequently, the collector voltage on the side that is conducting is pulled to a negative value $-V_{CL}$, and the collector voltage on the nonconducting side is 0. Specifically, if any input voltage is high relative to V_{BB} (less negative), then a transistor on the left side will be conducting, causing the collector voltage on the left side to be the negative value $-V_{CL}$ and the collector voltage on the right to be 0. On the other hand, if all input voltages are low relative to V_{BB}, then all transistors on the left side will be in cutoff, causing the collector voltage on the left side to be 0 and the collector voltage on the right to be $-V_{CL}$. Thus, the circuit acts as a combiner for the input signals. It also acts as a restorer, since the collector voltages are relatively insensitive to the input signal variations, provided that these variations are small.

ECL Buffer Circuit

In addition to the previous circuit, an ECL gate includes a buffer circuit, such as shown in Fig. 4.26. The base of the transistor in the buffer is connected to the collector node on either side of the combiner circuit. The output of the overall gate is the emitter of the transistor in the buffer. Since the emitter of the buffer transistor is in series with a resistor that is connected to the negative supply voltage, the base-emitter junction is forward-biased. Consequently, the buffer transistor will always be conducting. However, because of the emitter resistor, the transistor will not be saturated. The emitter voltage of the buffer transistor is lower (more negative) than the base voltage by the relatively constant amount of V_{BE}. When the base voltage changes, the emitter voltage changes with it. In this sense, the emitter voltage follows the base voltage. Therefore, such a circuit is referred to, in general, as an *emitter follower*. The buffer circuit serves two purposes in an ECL gate. It serves to isolate the collector voltage in the combiner from the effects of load current at the gate output. The buffer circuit also serves to shift the output voltage values by the amount $-V_{BE}$ from the corresponding values, 0 and $-V_{CL}$, of collector voltage in the combiner circuit. Thus, the low output voltage from a gate is $-(V_{CL} + V_{BE})$, which corresponds to logic-0, and the high output voltage is

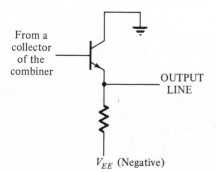

From a collector of the combiner

OUTPUT LINE

V_{EE} (Negative)

Figure 4.26 Output buffer circuit for an ECL gate.

$-V_{BE}$, which corresponds to logic-1. This voltage shift is necessary, since otherwise an output value of 0, when applied to an input line of another ECL gate, would certainly cause the input transistor to saturate.

Since the output voltage values from an ECL gate are $-V_{BE}$ for logic-1 and $-(V_{CL} + V_{BE})$ for logic-0, the combiner circuit of the gate should be adjusted to accommodate these same values on the input lines. This can be done by setting the reference voltage V_{BB} at a value midway between the two input values. Thus, the value for V_{BB} should be near $-(V_{CL}/2 + V_{BE})$.

Overall ECL Circuit

Figure 4.27 shows the overall circuit for an ECL gate that is commercially available in integrated-circuit form. A nominal value of -5.2 V is specified for the supply voltage V_{EE}. The gate includes two buffer circuits, each connected to opposite collector nodes in the combiner. Thus, there are two output lines, which are complementary to each other. The values of the resistors in the combiner circuit are such that $-V_{CL}$, i.e., the low value for collector voltage on either side of the combiner, is -0.85 V. Also, the value for V_{BE} for each conducting transistor is about 0.75 V. Thus, the output voltage for logic-0 is $-(0.85 + 0.75) = -1.6$ V and for logic-1 is -0.75 V.

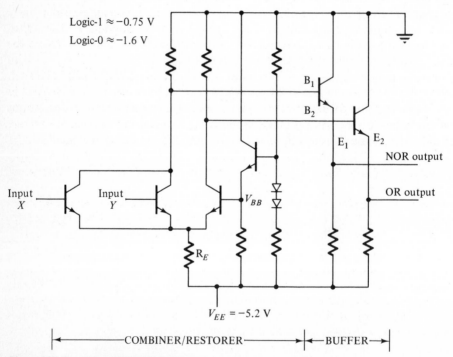

Figure 4.27 Two-input OR/NOR ECL gate.

Table 4.4 Operation of the ECL gate in Fig. 4.27

(a) Voltage relationship (b) Logic relationship

X	Y	B_1	B_2	E_1	E_2
-1.6	-1.6	0	-0.85	-0.75	-1.6
-1.6	-0.75	-0.85	0	-1.6	-0.75
-0.75	-1.6	-0.85	0	-1.6	-0.75
-0.75	-0.75	-0.85	0	-1.6	-0.75

(a)

X	Y	E_1	E_2
0	0	1	0
0	1	0	1
1	0	0	1
1	1	0	1

(b)

The reference voltage V_{BB} is set at the value -1.175 V, which is midway between the two logic levels. V_{BB} is produced by a circuit that consists of a transistor operating as an emitter follower connected to a voltage divider. Two diodes are included in the voltage divider to provide for temperature compensation. As temperature varies, the change in the voltage drop across the two diodes tends to offset a similar change in V_{BE} for the transistor.

The operation of the ECL gate in Fig. 4.27 is summarized in Table 4.4. Table 4.4a shows the effect of each input voltage combination upon the voltage at each of the two output-transistor bases B_1 and B_2, and at each of the two output-transistor emitters E_1 and E_2. Noting the previous assignment of logic values, we can derive the logic relationship between the gate inputs and outputs as shown in Table 4.4b. It is apparent that the gate output at E_1 corresponds to the logic operation NOR and that the gate output at E_2 corresponds to the logic operation OR.

These ECL gates may be connected to perform wired logic, since the pull-down component for each output is a resistor. Suppose output lines from two or more ECL gates are connected together. The common output line can then be pulled up (logic-1) by any output transistor involved in the connection. Otherwise, the common output line is pulled low (logic-0) by the resistors at all the gate outputs. It is apparent, then, that wired logic for these ECL gates corresponds to the logic operation OR. To facilitate wired logic, some forms of ECL gates have pull-down resistors on the input lines to the gates rather than the output lines. In this way, many gate-output lines can be involved in a wired-logic connection without incurring the effect of many parallel pull-down resistors.

The fan-out of these ECL gates is very high, since the input lines have a very high impedance. Also, as mentioned before, the speed of these ECL gates is very high, approximately 2 ns. A disadvantage of ECL is its rather stringent requirements for proper circuit-board layout and lead placement to avoid signal-transmission difficulties due to its high switching speeds. The voltage levels for ECL are notably different from those of TTL, so that the two logic families are not directly compatible.

4.7 INTEGRATED INJECTION LOGIC (IIL)

The number of gates that can be included in a monolithic integrated circuit is an important consideration in the implementation of microprocessors and related components. A high gate density must be achieved if a microprocessor is to fit on a single chip. One bipolar family of gates, referred to as *integrated injection logic* (IIL or I^2L), has such a simple circuit structure that high densities can be obtained.

The circuits for IIL gates can be broken down to a two-transistor circuit, shown in Fig. 4.28, which acts as an inverter. The *pnp* transistor T_1 with the resistor R acts as a current source, which is connected to the base of the *npn* transistor T_2. The base of T_1 is grounded and the base-emitter junction of T_1 is forward-biased. The voltage at the emitter of T_1 is therefore fairly constant and small, about 0.7 V. This causes the resistor R to have a relatively fixed voltage drop of approximately $V_S - 0.7$ V. As a result, the current through the resistor, which is the same as the emitter current of T_1, is fixed at $(V_S - 0.7)/R$. This current is also approximately the same as the collector current of T_1, since the difference between the two is just the usually small base current.

This collector current from T_1 will flow into the base of T_2 provided that the input line is not drawing any current. The current is said to be "injected" into the base, an expression which suggests the name for this logic family. In such a case, the base-emitter junction of T_2 will be sufficiently forward-biased to make T_2

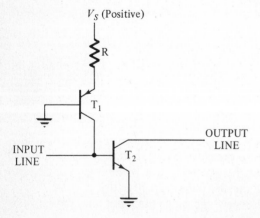

Figure 4.28 IIL inverter circuit.

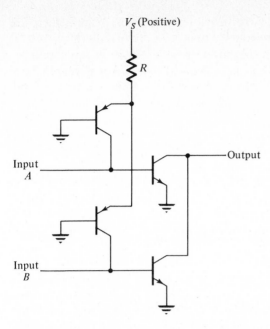

Figure 4.29 Two-input IIL NOR gate.

conducting. On the other hand, if the input line is brought close to ground, the current from T_1 will be diverted from the base of T_2, causing T_2 to be in cutoff. Thus, if the input line is connected to an open circuit, the output line will become grounded; if the input line is grounded, the output line will be open-circuited. By letting an open circuit and a short circuit to ground represent the two logic values, the circuit of Fig. 4.28 can be regarded as an inverter.

The fabrication of an IIL inverter is even simpler than the circuit indicates. Since the collector of T_1 and the base of T_2 are connected and are both p-type material, they are made to correspond to the same region on an integrated-circuit chip. Likewise, the base of T_1 and the emitter of T_2 are made to correspond to a single region. For this reason IIL is also referred to as *merged-transistor logic* (MTL).

Gates having several input lines can be built up from the basic inverter circuit by using wired logic. A two-input gate, for example, can be formed from two inverter circuits by tying their output lines together, as shown in Fig. 4.29. In such a case, if either input line is open-circuited, the corresponding *npn* transistor will conduct, causing the common output line to be short-circuited to ground. By letting an open circuit correspond to logic-1 and a short circuit to logic-0, the circuit can be seen to perform the NOR operation.

It should be noted that only a single emitter resistor is included in the two-input circuit, which is shared by both current-source transistors. Generally, only one resistor is included for an entire integrated circuit, to be used in common by all current sources on the chip. Consequently, the total current is fixed. This total current is split up among the many individual current sources in a way that depends upon the parameters of the individual *pnp* transistors. Care is therefore taken in the manufacture of the integrated circuits to achieve uniform characteristics for the *pnp* transistors so that the current is split in a fairly equal manner. The resistor R is not included within the integrated circuit, but is supplied externally. In this way, its value can be chosen in order to obtain a desired value for the injection currents for a given supply voltage V_S. There is a trade-off between power dissipation and switching speed that influences the choice for the value of R. The greater the value of the injection current, the faster will be the switching speed (since it is the injection current that must charge the capacitance associated with the base of the transistor in the gate and the collector of the assumed transistor driving the input line). On the other hand, the lower the value of the injection current, the lower will be the power dissipation of each gate and the lower will be the current drive requirements for a gate output line for a given fan-out (since the injection current must be sunk to ground by the driving gate). In practice, a value for V_S is first chosen (say, $+5$ V), and then a value for R is chosen to optimize the trade-off between power dissipation and switching speed.

Wired logic plays an important role in the application of IIL gates. Tying the output lines of any two or more gates together corresponds to the ANDing of the signals that would otherwise appear on those output lines. Of course, these individual output signals are no longer available after the connection has been made. To enhance the ability of performing wired logic, transistors having more than one collector are often used in the inverter circuits. The collectors of each transistor are all controlled by the base-emitter junction, but are isolated from one another so that they may be used in different wired-logic connections. Figure 4.30 shows an example of an IIL inverter with two collectors, each of which is involved in a wired-AND connection with other collectors. Thus, output 1 is described by the Boolean expression $\overline{(A + B)} = \overline{A}\overline{B}$ and output 2 by $\overline{(B + C)} = \overline{B}\overline{C}$.

The switching transistors in an IIL gate go into saturation when they are conducting. This, of course, limits the speed of operation, as in the other saturation bipolar logic families. To enhance switching speed, a form of Schottky IIL has been developed which has an improvement in speed of about 2 times over non-Schottky IIL.

4.8 MOSFET LOGIC

There are several logic families that are based on the field-effect transistor. Two well-known families are NMOS, which denotes that *n*-channel MOSFETs are used, and PMOS, which denotes that *p*-channel MOSFETs are used. A third family, called CMOS, utilizes both *n*-channel and *p*-channel MOSFETs within the same circuit. The CMOS logic family will be discussed in the next section.

The NMOS and PMOS logic circuits are generally in the form of direct-coupled logic. This term refers to circuits that implement various logic functions by a corresponding series-parallel connection of transistors that act as switches. For example, a two-input NOR gate can be formed from a parallel connection of

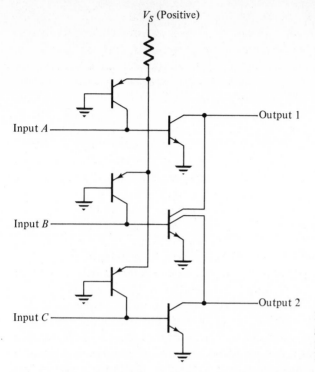

V_S (Positive)

Input A

Input B

Output 1

Input C

Output 2

Figure 4.30 Example of an IIL gate with a multiple-collector output transistor involved in wired logic with other IIL gates.

two *n*-channel normally-off (enhancement mode) MOSFETs as shown in Fig. 4.31. If a positive voltage is applied to either transistor, it will turn on and thereby establish a low-resistance path between the output line and ground. This will result in a low voltage at the output. If, on the other hand, ground is applied to both input transistors, they will turn off. In such a case, the resistor R will pull the output up to approximately V_{DD}, since the FETs act as large impedances. For positive logic the logic gate of Fig. 4.31 corresponds to the NOR operation since the output is low if and only if at least one input is high.

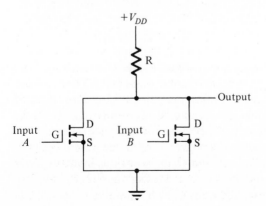

$+V_{DD}$

R

Output

Input A   G   D   S

Input B   G   D   S

Figure 4.31 A two-input NOR gate using *n*-channel normally-off MOSFETS.

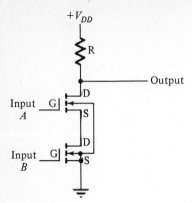

Figure **4.32** A two-input NAND gate using n-channel normally-off MOSFETs.

If the n-channel normally-off MOSFETs are connected in series instead of parallel, as shown in Fig. 4.32, then a NAND gate will result. In this case, only when both input lines are high will a relatively low impedance path be created between the output line and ground through the series connection. If either input is low, the output will approach V_{DD}. Since impedances add up when placed in series, there is a limitation to the number of FETs that can be placed in series.

By arranging n-channel MOSFETs in a more general series-parallel configuration, a logic gate can be directly implemented for a Boolean expression that has an overall complementation and for which no other complements appear, except possibly on individual variables. For example, the expression

$$f(A, B, C, D) = \overline{(A + B)C + D}$$

can be implemented with the NMOS logic gate shown in Fig. 4.33. It should be noted that the OR operation is achieved by a parallel connection, that the AND operation is achieved by a series connection, and that the output is the complement of the indicated structure.

In practice, resistors are awkward to produce in integrated circuits since they tend to be rather large compared to the other components. Consequently, the pull-up resistor in a MOS logic gate is usually replaced with a field-effect transistor connected in such a manner that it acts as a nonlinear resistor. Very often a depletion-mode FET is used for this purpose. In this case, the gate of the FET is connected to the source and no connection is made to the substrate, as shown in the inverter circuit of Fig. 4.34. When the input signal to the inverter is low, the lower transistor is nonconducting. In this case, only the small current drawn from the output line flows through the pull-up FET. This pull-up FET is conducting since it is of the depletion mode. Thus, only a small voltage drop appears across the pull-up FET, causing the output signal to be high. On the other hand, when the input signal is high, the lower transistor conducts, forcing the source and gate of the pull-up FET as well as the output line to be low (i.e., approximately ground). In this case, the gate is negative with respect to points in the channel near the drain. As a result, the resistance of the pull-up FET increases sharply. This

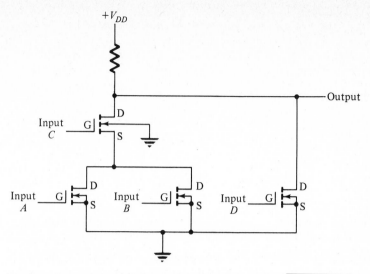

Figure 4.33 An NMOS gate for the function $f(A, B, C, D) = \overline{(A + B)C + D}$.

pull-up transistor thus behaves like a nonlinear resistor, which is actually prefer-able to a linear resistor.

It should be noted that **MOS** circuits using n-channel FETs (NMOS) have a positive voltage for V_{DD}. By designing for a power-supply voltage of $+5$ V and by controlling the gate threshold voltage V_T for the FETs, manufacturers can pro-duce NMOS circuits compatible with TTL.

Circuits for PMOS logic gates are similar in form to those for NMOS. However, p-channel FETs normally operate with negative voltages on their drain and gate leads with respect to their source. Consequently, PMOS logic gates, such as the inverter shown in Fig. 4.35, have a negative supply voltage V_{DD} and work with negative logic levels.

MOSFETs have an extremely high resistance to current flowing into the gate. Consequently, MOS logic gates draw almost no steady-state current from

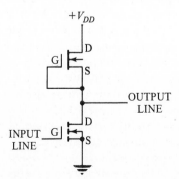

Figure 4.34 An NMOS inverter with a depletion-mode FET for pull-up.

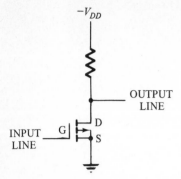

Figure 4.35 A PMOS inverter.

whatever is driving their input lines. This implies that they are capable of a large fan-out. Also, a relatively high logic-gate density can be achieved for MOSFET integrated circuits. The capacitance from the gate of a MOSFET to the source, substrate, and drain is, on the other hand, quite large. Consequently, MOS logic gates tend to be rather slow in comparison with bipolar logic, since these capacitances must be charged before the input signal can effectively switch. Also, the current to charge these capacitances must come from the driving logic gate, resulting in a significant increase in power dissipated at high switching frequencies.

4.9 CMOS LOGIC

CMOS is a family of logic that has a widely used standard form with specifications that are uniform among manufacturers. It stands for *complementary metal oxide semiconductor* logic, a term which refers to the fact that both *p*-channel and *n*-channel MOSFETs appear in the same circuit. All MOSFETs used in the family are normally off. A CMOS logic gate consists of two portions, one of which pulls down the gate output for appropriate input conditions and the other of which pulls up the gate output for other input conditions. Both portions have a direct-coupled-logic structure.

Figure 4.36 shows a CMOS inverter. The pull-down portion of the inverter consists of an *n*-channel normally-off MOSFET, which is connected with its drain to the output line and with its source to ground. The pull-up portion consists of a *p*-channel normally-off MOSFET, which is connected with its drain to the output line and with its source to the positive supply voltage V_{DD}. The input line of the inverter is connected to the gates of both transistors. The *n*-channel transistor turns on whenever the input voltage exceeds the gate threshold voltage V_T, thereby causing the output line to be pulled low. Otherwise, this pull-down transistor acts as a high resistance and does not influence the voltage on the output line. The *p*-channel transistor is operated with its source more positive than its drain. It turns on whenever its gate is sufficiently more negative (i.e., less positive) than its source, which is at V_{DD}. Thus, whenever the input voltage falls below V_{DD} by an amount that exceeds the gate threshold voltage V_T, this pull-up transistor turns

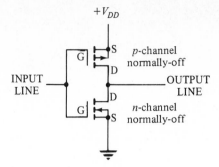

$+V_{DD}$

INPUT
LINE

OUTPUT
LINE

p-channel
normally-off

n-channel
normally-off

Figure 4.36 A CMOS inverter.

on, causing the output line to be pulled high. Otherwise, the pull-up transistor acts as a large resistance and does not influence the voltage on the output line. It can therefore be seen that for positive logic, a logic-1 on the input line of the inverter causes the output line to be pulled to logic-0 by the lower transistor, whereas a logic-0 on the input line causes the output line to be pulled to logic-1 by the upper transistor.

As a further illustration of CMOS logic, a two-input CMOS NOR gate is shown in Fig. 4.37. The pull-down portion of the logic gate consists of two n-channel MOSFETs, which are connected in parallel with their sources grounded. The gate of each of these two transistors is connected to one of the two input lines. Whenever either input voltage exceeds the gate threshold voltage V_T, the corresponding transistor turns on, causing the output line to be pulled low. Otherwise, these two transistors act as high resistances and do not influence the voltage on the output line.

The pull-up portion of the logic gate consists of two p-channel MOSFETs, which are connected in series. The gate of each of these two transistors is connected to one of the two input lines. Whenever both input voltages fall below V_{DD} by an amount that exceeds the gate threshold voltage V_T, both these pull-up transistors turn on, causing the output line to be pulled high. Otherwise, the two transistors act as large resistances and do not influence the output line.

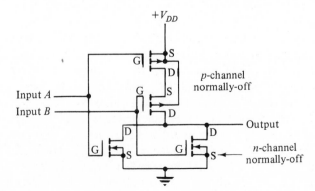

$+V_{DD}$

Input A

Input B

p-channel
normally-off

Output

n-channel
normally-off

Figure 4.37 A two-input
CMOS NOR gate.

Table 4.5 The operation of a two-input CMOS NOR gate

A	B	Output from lower portion	Output from upper portion	Output
0	0	—	1	1
0	1	0	—	0
1	0	0	—	0
1	1	0	—	0

For positive logic, a logic-1 on either input line causes the output to be pulled to logic-0 by the lower portion of the circuit, whereas a logic-0 on both input lines causes the output to be pulled to logic-1 by the upper portion of the circuit. This is precisely the NOR operation. Table 4.5 summarizes this behavior. As can be seen from the table, the lower portion of the gate determines when the output will be logic-0, and the upper portion determines when the output will be logic-1.

CMOS NAND gates are formed by connecting the n-channel transistors of the pull-down portion in series and the p-channel transistors of the pull-up portion in parallel. This kind of gate is illustrated in Fig. 4.38.

In general, a CMOS gate can be formed for any Boolean expression that is in the same form as that assumed for NMOS. The pull-down portion of the gate is first formed as a series-parallel configuration of n-channel transistors, in which OR corresponds to a parallel connection and AND corresponds to a series connection. The pull-up portion is then formed in the opposite manner by placing the p-channel transistors in series for OR and in parallel for AND. The output, then, is the complement of the structure. To illustrate this concept, Fig. 4.39 shows a CMOS gate for the expression

$$f(A, B, C) = \overline{AB + C}$$

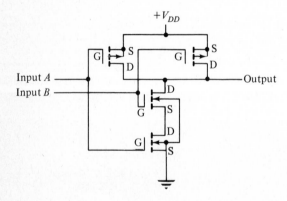

Figure 4.38 A two-input CMOS NAND gate.

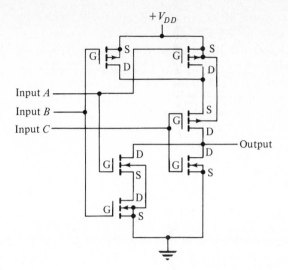

Figure 4.39 CMOS gate for the function $f(A, B, C) = \overline{AB + C}$.

The pull-down portion of the gate has two transistors in series for inputs A and B. This series connection is placed in parallel with a transistor for C. The pull-up portion consists of a parallel connection of transistors for A and B which is in series with a transistor for C.

CMOS logic is somewhat more complex than NMOS or PMOS and is therefore not capable of achieving gate densities as high as those of the other two. However, its structure does offer a particular advantage over all other common forms of logic. There is never a conductive path in the steady state between ground and the power-supply voltage V_{DD}. Consequently, no discernible power is consumed during times in which the inputs are constant. This is of great importance for applications that involve power supplied from batteries. Power is consumed during switching, however, for two reasons. One reason is the existence of capacitances throughout the circuit, which primarily occur between the electrodes of the MOSFETs. These capacitances must be charged each time a gate is switched. The second reason is the fact that during the transition of input signals, both the pull-up and pull-down portions of a logic gate are partially on. As a result, current momentarily flows from V_{DD} to ground. The average dissipated power increases with switching frequency.

The fan-out for CMOS logic gates is very high, as it is for NMOS and PMOS, since MOSFETs have an extremely high gate-input resistance. However, the amount of capacitance on the output line of a CMOS gate significantly affects its switching speed. The reason is that MOSFETs have an appreciable resistance when they are turned on, which limits the amount of current that can be supplied to charge or discharge the capacitance of the output line.

A CMOS logic gate is capable of operating over a wide range of supply voltages. In particular, V_{DD} can be set at any value between 3 and 15 V for the standard form of CMOS because the output swings from almost 0 V for logic-0 to almost V_{DD} for logic-1. For this reason CMOS can be made compatible with TTL by setting V_{DD} at +5 V. In this case, a CMOS logic gate can drive two standard TTL input lines. On the other hand, the TTL output voltage for logic-1 is not quite high enough to drive a CMOS input line. This can be remedied by connecting a pull-up resistor of approximately 2 kΩ from the TTL output line to a supply of +5 V, which will cause the logic-1 voltage level of the TTL gate to become almost +5 V. The TTL gate will then be able to drive a large number of CMOS input lines.

PROBLEMS

4.1 An *npn* bipolar transistor is connected in a circuit as shown in Fig. P4.1. It is given that the transistor is in a state of saturation and that the voltage across the base-emitter junction is 0.7 V.
    (*a*) Determine the base current I_B.
    (*b*) Determine an approximate value for the collector current I_C.
    (*c*) Determine an approximate value for the current gain I_C/I_B.

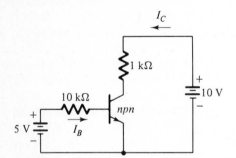

Figure P4.1

4.2 An *n*-channel normally-off (enhancement mode) MOS field-effect transistor is connected in the circuit shown in Fig. P4.2. Assume that when the gate-to-source voltage V_{GS} is 3 V, the resistance from the drain-to-source will be 800 Ω. Assume also that when the gate-to-source voltage is near 0, the drain-to-source resistance will be nearly infinite. Determine the output voltage swing when the switch is closed.

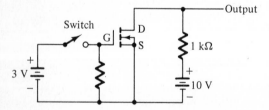

Figure P4.2

4.3 Figure P4.3 shows two circuits for diode-logic gates. Assuming positive logic and logic-signal voltages of 0 V and 5 V, what operation is performed by each gate?

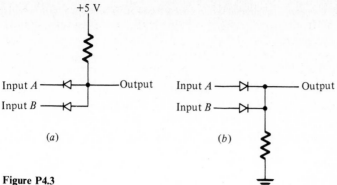

(a)   (b)

Figure P4.3

4.4 Suppose that the combiner portion of a TTL gate, shown in Fig. P4.4, is used by itself as a logic gate. Assuming positive logic, determine the operation that it would perform.

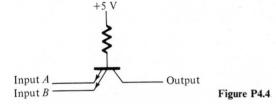

Figure P4.4

4.5 The outputs of two TTL NAND gates are combined with a diode-logic gate, as shown in Fig. P4.5. Will this arrangement operate properly? Explain.

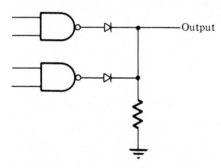

Figure P4.5

4.6 Two open-collector TTL NAND gates are connected as shown in Fig. P4.6. Determine a Boolean expression for the function $f(w, x, y, z)$ corresponding to the common output line.

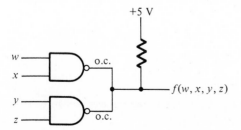

Figure P4.6

4.7 Implement the following function in a minimal fashion using AND gates with three-state outputs and an inverter:

$$f(w, x, y, z) = wxy + \bar{w}yz$$

4.8 Use the information given in Sec. 4.5.

(a) Determine the number of low-power TTL gate input lines that may be driven by a standard TTL gate.

(b) Determine the number of standard TTL gate input lines that may be driven by a low-power TTL gate.

4.9 Two ECL NOR gates are connected as shown in Fig. P4.9. Determine a Boolean expression for the function $f(w, x, y, z)$ corresponding to the common output line.

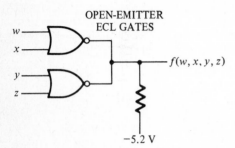

Figure P4.9

4.10 A light-bulb indicator is to be connected to the output of an ECL OR gate. Show how this connection could be made to work properly. For what logical conditions on the input lines of the gate will the indicator light?

4.11 As mentioned in Sec. 4.7, IIL inverters often have multiple collectors on the output transistor to allow for multiple wired-logic combinations. In such a case, the collectors are isolated but are controlled together. The circuit of Fig. P4.11 involves several IIL inverters, one with multiple collectors,

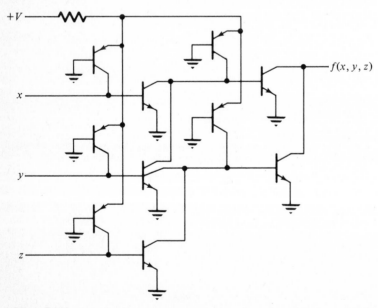

Figure P4.11

that are connected by using wired logic. Determine the logic function $f(x, y, z)$ that describes the operation of the circuit.

4.12 Circuits for two PMOS logic gates using p-channel normally-off MOSFETs are shown in Fig. P4.12. Assuming positive logic, what operation does each circuit perform?

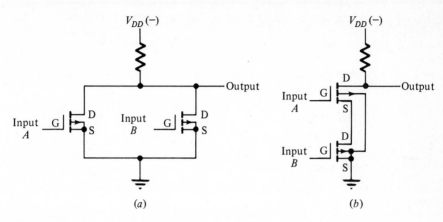

Figure P4.12

4.13 Making use of direct-coupled logic, design an NMOS gate for the function

$$f(A, B, C) = \overline{AB + AC + BC}$$

4.14 Making use of direct-coupled logic, design a CMOS gate for the function

$$f(A, B, C) = \overline{(A + B)C}$$

CHAPTER
FIVE

LOGIC COMPONENTS

Logic gates, which were discussed in the preceding chapter, are the basic devices used in the implementation of logic systems. Complex logic systems, including microcomputers, are generally made up from basic components that correspond to networks composed of logic gates. It is the purpose of this chapter to develop the basic component networks that play an important role in microcomputer systems. The components to be developed in this chapter are flip-flops, registers, counters, decoders, data selectors, arithmetic networks, and bus systems. Memory systems are treated separately in the next chapter.

5.1 FLIP-FLOPS

A property of many logic networks and systems is that their output values depend not only upon their current input values but also upon those of the past. Such logic networks are said to have a memory property and are called *sequential circuits*. Computers in general, and microcomputers in particular, are a prime example of logic systems whose behavior depends upon past events. The condition of a sequential circuit at any given time relating the total effect of past input values upon the circuit's behavior is referred to as the *state* of the sequential circuit. In other words, the state of a sequential circuit represents all the information concerning its past input values that is necessary in the determination of its present and future output values.

   In the design of a sequential circuit, some means must be provided to save the information related to the past input values, i.e., the state, so that it will be available to produce present and future output values. The most basic element for this purpose is the *flip-flop*. A flip-flop is itself a sequential circuit having two states, each of which is self-sustaining (i.e., stable) under certain input conditions. Each of the two states corresponds to a logic value (i.e., logic-0 or logic-1) stored in the flip-flop. Thus, in a sequential circuit, a separate flip-flop can be used to represent the value of each variable that is to be stored for present or future use. The overall state of a sequential circuit whose memory property is based on the use of flip-flops is just the combination of the individual states of all the flip-flops that make up the circuit.

   In general, a flip-flop has at least one output line that produces the logic value corresponding to the present state of the flip-flop. When the output corresponds to the logic-1 state, the flip-flop is said to be *set*. When the output corresponds to the logic-0 state, on the other hand, the flip-flop is said to be *reset*. A flip-flop also has a number of input lines that will, in conjunction with the present state, determine the next state of the flip-flop. The nature of the operation of these input lines specifies the type of the flip-flop.

The SR Flip-Flop

One particular type of flip-flop has two input lines, referred to as S and R, that are used to force the flip-flop to become, respectively, set and reset. The specific operation of this SR *flip-flop* is described by Table 5.1. Notice that the state of the flip-flop becomes logic-1 (i.e., set) when logic-1 is placed on S but not R and that the state becomes logic-0 (i.e., reset) when logic-1 is placed on R but not S. No change in state occurs when S and R are both logic-0. For this reason the input combination $S = 0$ and $R = 0$ is referred to as the *null input*. Finally, the state behavior of the SR flip-flop is not defined for the input combination $S = 1$ and $R = 1$.

   A simple form for an SR flip-flop can be constructed by interconnecting two NAND gates in a cross-coupled fashion as shown in Fig. 5.1. The NAND gates

Table 5.1 Behavior of an SR flip-flop

The current state of the flip-flop is denoted by Q and the resulting state due to the input combination is denoted by Q^*

S	R	Q^*
0	0	Q
0	1	0
1	0	1
1	1	Not defined

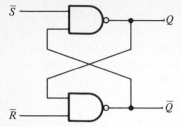

Figure 5.1 A simple SR flip-flop.

may be from any logic family, such as TTL, CMOS, etc. The state of this flip-flop corresponds to the value of the output variable Q appearing at the output line of the upper NAND gate. It will be seen that the output variable $\bar{Q}$ appearing at the output line of the lower NAND gate is the complement of Q. The two input lines to the flip-flop are denoted by $\bar{S}$ and $\bar{R}$, since the flip-flop is set when $\bar{S} = 0$ and reset when $\bar{R} = 0$.

To verify that the circuit does behave according to the definition of an SR flip-flop, first consider the input combination $\bar{S} = 1$ and $\bar{R} = 1$, which corresponds to the null input. In this case, the cross-coupling between the two NAND gates will cause either possible state to sustain itself. In particular, if the output line Q is at logic-1, then both input lines to the lower NAND gate will be at logic-1, causing its output $\bar{Q}$ to be logic-0. This logic-0 of $\bar{Q}$ is applied to an input line of the upper gate, causing its output Q to be logic-1, which was initially assumed. On the other hand, if Q is equal to logic-0, the lower gate has this logic-0 as an input, causing its output $\bar{Q}$ to be 1. Both inputs of the upper gate are then logic-1, resulting in logic-0 for the output Q, as assumed. Thus, it can be concluded that either of the two possible states for this flip-flop is stable when the input combination is $\bar{S} = 1$ and $\bar{R} = 1$.

Let us now consider the other two input combinations for which the state behavior of the flip-flop is defined. For each of these two input combinations only one of the two possible states is stable. In particular, let the input combination be $\bar{S} = 0$ and $\bar{R} = 1$. With the $\bar{S}$ input line to the upper NAND gate equal to logic-0, its output Q is forced to logic-1. Now with both inputs of the lower gate equal to logic-1, the output of the lower gate, $\bar{Q}$, will be logic-0. This logic-0 is applied to an input line of the upper gate, which will maintain the output Q at logic-1 even after $\bar{S}$ returns to 1. Thus, the input combination $\bar{S} = 0$ and $\bar{R} = 1$ causes the flip-flop to be set in accordance with the definition. Likewise, due to symmetry, it is immediately seen that the input combination $\bar{S} = 1$ and $\bar{R} = 0$ forces the output $\bar{Q}$ to logic-1 and therefore Q to logic-0. As before, the outputs will not change when $\bar{R}$ is returned to 1. Thus, the input combination $\bar{S} = 1$ and $\bar{R} = 0$ causes the flip-flop to be reset, which is also in accordance with the definition.

Finally, notice that the remaining input combination $\bar{S} = 0$ and $\bar{R} = 0$ forces both gate output lines to logic-1. This will lead to unpredictable results when the input combination is changed to the null input since the resulting state will depend upon such factors as thermal noise, component tolerances, etc. Thus, the

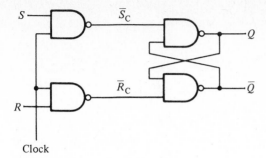

Figure 5.2 Clocked SR flip-flop.

combination $\bar{S} = 0$ and $\bar{R} = 0$ is considered to be an invalid input condition. It should be observed in the above discussion that the output $\bar{Q}$ from the flip-flop, except for the invalid input, was always the complement of the output Q.

Clocked Flip-Flops

Flip-flops are most often used for implementing sequential circuits that are *synchronous*. In synchronous circuits the information that is stored in the flip-flops may change only with the occurrence of a pulse on a designated line. Many of the components of microcomputer systems are primarily of this nature. To facilitate the implementation of synchronous sequential circuits, flip-flops of a form referred to as *clocked flip-flops* have a special input line, called the *clock line*, that is used to synchronize changes in state. The state of clocked flip-flops may change only in response to a pulse occurring on the clock line.

A clocked SR flip-flop can be formed from a simple SR flip-flop by adding two more NAND gates as shown in Fig. 5.2. The two additional NAND gates provide a means for blocking the overall S and R input signals when the clock line is at logic-0. During the time that the clock is logic-0, the input lines $\bar{S}_C$ and $\bar{R}_C$ to the unclocked flip-flop are both forced to logic-1. This corresponds to the null input, and thus, no change in the flip-flop state occurs. However, when the clock line is at logic-1, the S and R signals are inverted and passed to the input lines of the unclocked flip-flop. The resulting state of the flip-flop is then determined by the S and R values as indicated by Table 5.1.

During the time when the clock is at logic-1, the flip-flop is said to be *enabled*. If the S and R signals are changed while the flip-flop is enabled, the state will be updated to reflect these new values. The time that elapses before the state responds to changes on the input lines is determined by the propagation delay of the logic gates comprising the flip-flop. This amount of time, referred to as the *data setup time*, must be allowed between the last change in the input signals and the time the clock becomes logic-0 in order that the flip-flop can respond to the input signal. When the clock is at logic-0, the output state of the flip-flop is latched in and will not follow input changes. Such a flip-flop is therefore often called a *clocked latch*.

Figure 5.3 shows a symbol that is often used in logic diagrams to represent a clocked latch. As in the case of logic gate symbols, a bubble indicating inversion at

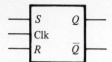

Figure 5.3 Symbol for a clocked latch.

a line is often used with this clocked-latch symbol. In particular, a bubble shown at the clock line indicates that the clocked latch is enabled when the clock line is at logic-0, rather than logic-1.

Master-Slave Flip-Flops

In many applications, e.g., counters, it is necessary to sense the state of a flip-flop while simultaneously causing a new state to be entered. A difficulty that can be encountered in such a situation is that the new flip-flop state may be logically dependent on itself. If a clocked latch is used in this case, it is possible that an oscillation will be set up causing the flip-flop to continually change state during the time period in which the clock is equal to logic-1. Thus, indeterminate network behavior is possible.

As an example, consider the network of Fig. 5.4, which involves an SR clocked latch. It is desired that when the input signal A to the network is logic-1, the state of the flip-flop changes exactly once per clock pulse. However, it appears that as long as the clock is at logic-1, the state will continually change between logic-0 and logic-1. This is due to the fact that the state of the clocked latch will follow changes in S and R when the clock is logic-1 and that S and R are dependent upon the state through the external AND gates.

One way to circumvent the effects of this logical dependency problem is to incorporate a certain amount of time delay at the output of each clocked latch.

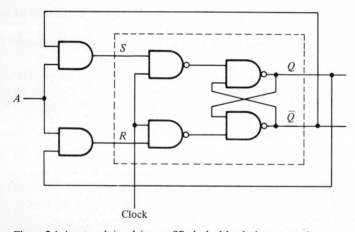

Clock

Figure 5.4 A network involving an SR clocked latch that can cycle.

MASTER   SLAVE

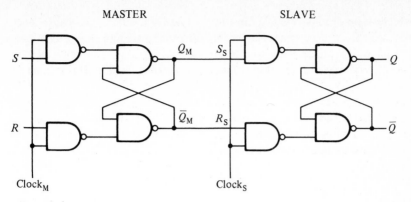

Figure 5.5 A master-slave flip-flop.

The flip-flop will then operate as desired if care is taken to make the duration time of the clock pulse less than the output delay time for the flip-flop. In that case there would only be enough time for the flip-flop to make one transition in state per clock pulse.

The provision of time delay at the output of a flip-flop to handle this logical dependency problem has several undesirable effects. One obvious effect is that the switching speed obtainable with the flip-flop is reduced. Moreover, it places a stringent requirement on the characteristics of the clock source. The clock pulse duration time must be carefully controlled so that it is less than the output delay but greater than the data setup time for each flip-flop in a network.

A better way of handling the effects of the logical dependency problem just described is to use *master-slave* flip-flops. A master-slave flip-flop consists of two sections, each a clocked latch, that are coupled together in cascade fashion as shown in Fig. 5.5. The first section, i.e., the master, accepts information from the overall input lines S and R. The output state of the master is then supplied to the second section, i.e., the slave. The two sections are shown with separate clock lines that are activated during mutually exclusive times, so that the state of only one section can change at a time. Specifically, the operation of the master-slave flip-flop occurs in a *clock cycle* of two steps. First, the clock line (Clock$_M$) of the master is brought to logic-1, causing the state of the master section to take on the value that is specified by the input lines S and R. After Clock$_M$ is returned to logic-0, the clock line (Clock$_S$) of the slave is brought to logic-1. At this time the state of the slave section becomes the same as the state of the master Q_M, since the set and reset signals of the slave are equal to Q_M and $\bar{Q}_M$, respectively. Finally, Clock$_S$ is returned to logic-0, causing the output to be latched. It is the information stored in the slave section that is presented at the overall output lines Q and $\bar{Q}$. It should be noted that this two-step operation of a master-slave flip-flop prevents a second change in the output signals from occurring during a clock cycle even though the input signals might be dependent externally upon the output signals.

The above type of master-slave flip-flop can be used with a *two-phase* clock source to provide the proper time relationship for the master and slave clock lines. Generally, such a two-phase clock source consists of two lines, each referred to as a *phase*, upon which pulses alternately appear in a periodic fashion. It is important that pulses for the two phases do not overlap, i.e., both phases may not be simultaneously equal to logic-1. Furthermore, a period of time is generally provided between pulses of the two phases in which neither phase is equal to logic-1. This period of time allows for variations in pulse arrival time, called *clock skew*, that might occur when a number of master-slave flip-flops are controlled by the same clock source. Also, the amount of time that each phase is equal to logic-1 must be at least equal to the data setup time for that section, i.e., the time required for the section to latch in the value of its next state.

To make master-slave flip-flops more convenient to use, a *phase splitter* that derives the two phases from a single clock line is commonly incorporated into each flip-flop. This is the usual arrangement for master-slave flip-flops that are fabricated under small-scale integration, especially TTL. The phase splitter determines the time relationship for the two phases by comparing the voltage on the incoming clock line with two threshold values, T_H and T_L, as shown in Fig. 5.6. The two threshold values T_H and T_L (with $T_H > T_L$) are placed between the two voltages V_0 and V_1, which are respectively the maximum voltage for logic-0 and the minimum voltage for logic-1 (assuming positive logic). The voltage of the incoming clock line is assumed to vary with nonzero rise and fall times as shown in Fig. 5.6. The phase splitter produces a logic-1 level on one phase line, Phase$_M$, when the voltage of the incoming clock line lies above T_H and a logic-1 level on the other phase line, Phase$_S$, when the voltage of the incoming clock line falls beneath T_L. In this way, pulses will appear on the two phase lines at mutually exclusive times, with no pulse on either line for a time determined by the rise and fall times of the incoming clock line.

A single-clock master-slave flip-flop using a phase splitter is illustrated in Fig. 5.7. Two threshold circuits are shown to perform the function of the phase splitter.

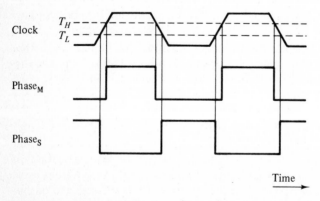

Figure 5.6 Timing relationship for a phase splitter.

MASTER   SLAVE

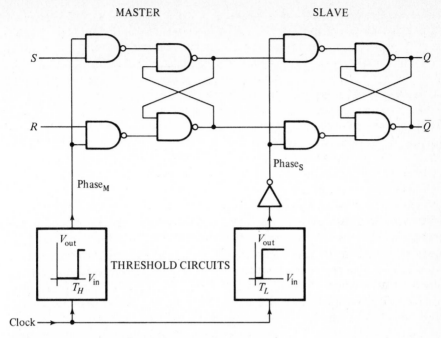

Figure 5.7 A master-slave flip-flop with a single clock line.

Each threshold circuit produces a logic-1 on its output line only when the voltage on its input line exceeds the indicated threshold value, T_H or T_L. Although these threshold circuits are explicitly shown, they may be encompassed in the logic gates to which they are connected. In particular, if the switching threshold of the inverter is made lower than the switching threshold for the master's input NAND gates, then the threshold circuits do not need to appear explicitly.

The operation of the master-slave flip-flop of Fig. 5.7 has the following sequence. Starting with the incoming clock line low, the master section is coupled to the slave, since Phase$_S$ is logic-1. However, the overall input lines S and R are decoupled from the master, since Phase$_M$ is logic-0. As the voltage of the incoming clock line increases past T_L, Phase$_S$ is brought to logic-0 due to the inverter, decoupling the slave from the master. Then as the voltage of the incoming clock line continues to increase and passes T_H, Phase$_M$ is brought to logic-1, coupling the overall input lines S and R to the master. At this time the values of S and R determine the state of the master. Eventually, the voltage of the incoming clock line begins to decrease. As the voltage passes T_H, Phase$_M$ is brought to logic-0, which decouples the S and R lines from the master. Finally, as the voltage passes T_L, Phase$_S$ is brought to logic-1, which recouples the master to the slave. At this time the state of the master is transferred to the slave, which is reflected at the overall output lines Q and $\bar{Q}$. This sequence is summarized in Fig. 5.8.

The symbol used in logic diagrams for a master-slave flip-flop is often distinguished from that for a clocked latch with the use of a triangle at the clock line as

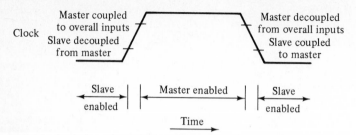

Clock — Master coupled to overall inputs / Slave decoupled from master

Master decoupled from overall inputs / Slave coupled to master

Slave enabled | Master enabled | Slave enabled

Time

Figure 5.8 Summary of timing sequence of a single-clock master-slave flip-flop.

shown in Fig. 5.9. The triangle indicates that the output of the master-slave flip-flop is allowed to change only at an edge of the clock pulse. In the case of the master-slave flip-flop just described, the output changes at the negative edge of the clock (i.e., the logic-1-to-logic-0 transition of the clock). However, there are other forms of master-slave flip-flops in which the output changes at the positive edge of the clock (i.e., the logic-0-to-logic-1 transition of the clock). To distinguish these two cases, an inversion bubble is usually shown at the clock line if the output changes at the negative clock edge.

JK, D, **and** T **Flip-Flops**

Several flip-flops having characteristics different than those of the SR type are also commonly used. These other types of flip-flops can be derived from the SR master-slave flip-flop by modifying the circuit with additional gates. Figure 5.10 illustrates how this modification might be done for three common types of clocked flip-flops: the JK, the D, and the T.

The JK flip-flop is a generalized version of the SR flip-flop. The J input terminal has an effect similar to that of the S terminal of an SR flip-flop (i.e., it sets the flip-flop), and the K input terminal has an effect similar to that of the R terminal (i.e., it resets the flip-flop). However, a difference in the behavior of the two types appears when both input terminals of each flip-flop are at logic-1. Whereas the state behavior of an SR flip-flop is undefined for the input combination $S = 1$ and $R = 1$, the state behavior of a JK flip-flop is defined for this input combination. Specifically, a JK flip-flop changes state in response to a pulse on its clock line for the input combination $J = 1$ and $K = 1$.

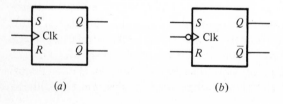

(a)

(b)

Figure 5.9 Symbols for master-slave flip-flops. (a) Output changes at the positive clock edge. (b) Output changes at the negative clock edge.

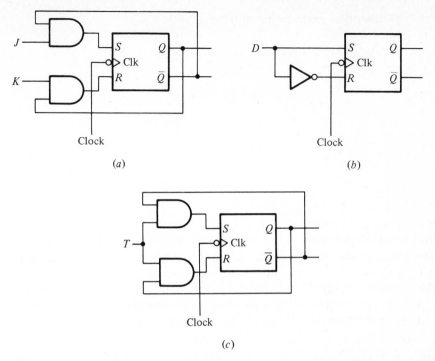

Figure 5.10 Common flip-flop types implemented from an *SR* master-slave flip-flop. (*a*) *JK* flip-flop. (*b*) *D* flip-flop. (*c*) *T* flip-flop.

An implementation of a *JK* master-slave flip-flop is the network in Fig. 5.10*a*. It includes two AND gates that are connected to the *S* and *R* terminals of the *SR* master-slave flip-flop. These AND gates serve to block the effect of one of the input lines, *J* or *K*, depending upon the state of the flip-flop. The input line that would otherwise cause no change in state to occur is the one that is blocked. In particular, *J* is blocked if the state *Q* is at logic-1, and *K* is blocked if *Q* is at logic-0. Thus, *J* is ANDed with $\bar{Q}$, and *K* is ANDed with *Q*. Consequently, when both *J* and *K* are equal to logic-1, only the input line that causes a change in state is effective, so that indeed the flip-flop will change its state upon the occurrence of a clock pulse.

The *D* flip-flop has the simplest relationship between its next state and the input line. In response to a pulse on the clock line, the state of a *D* flip-flop will take on the value appearing on the input line *D*.

As shown in Fig. 5.10*b*, a *D* flip-flop can be implemented by connecting the input terminal *S* of an *SR* master-slave flip-flop directly to the overall input line *D* and the terminal *R* to the complement of *D*. With these connections, if *D* is equal to logic-1, then *S* will also equal logic-1 and the flip-flop is set upon the occurrence of a clock pulse. On the other hand, if *D* is equal to logic-0, then *R* will equal logic-1 and the flip-flop is reset upon the occurrence of a clock pulse.

Table 5.2 The terminal relationship of three types of clocked flip-flops

In each case, the state prior to the clock pulse is denoted by Q and the state after the clock pulse is denoted by Q^*: (a) JK flip-flop, (b) D flip-flop, (c) T flip-flop.

J	K	Q^*	D	Q^*	T	Q^*
0	0	Q	0	0	0	Q
0	1	0	1	1	1	$\bar{Q}$
1	0	1				
1	1	$\bar{Q}$				

(a)	(b)	(c)

The T flip-flop has an interesting relationship between its state and the input terminal that proves to be useful for certain applications, notably counters, as will be seen. If the input line T is at logic-1, the state of the flip-flop becomes the complement of its previous state in response to a pulse. Otherwise, its state remains unchanged. It is called a *toggle* flip-flop, which suggests the name T for the input terminal.

Figure 5.10c is one way of implementing a T flip-flop from a SR master-slave flip-flop. It resembles the network for a JK flip-flop of Fig. 5.10a with the J and K terminals tied to form the overall input line T.

The terminal relationships for the three flip-flops of Fig. 5.10 are summarized by Table 5.2.

Edge-Triggered Flip-Flops

A property of the D master-slave flip-flop in Fig. 5.10b is that the input signals have effect and the output signal is updated both essentially at the time of a particular edge (say the negative edge) of the clock pulse. For this flip-flop the state of the master section will follow changes in the input signal as long as the clock is at logic-1. Whatever value appears on the D input line at the time just before the negative edge of the clock determines the final value of the state for the master section. It is this final state of the master that is transferred to the slave just after the negative clock edge. Thus the input signal must be correct only for a small time span (equal to the required data setup time of the master section) prior to the negative clock edge. Flip-flops having this property are said to be *edge-triggered*.

The SR, JK, and T master-slave flip-flops previously described (i.e., those shown in Figs. 5.7 and 5.10) are not edge-triggered, since the final state of the master flip-flop will depend on the values of the input signals during the entire time that the clock is at logic-1. In the case of the SR flip-flop the final state of the master section depends on whichever input line, S or R, was last at logic-1 during the time the clock is at logic-1.

In the case of the JK flip-flop the final state of the master section depends on only the input line, J or K, that is not blocked by the state of the slave. In particular, when the state of the flip-flop is logic-1, only K can effect a change in state. If K goes to logic-1 at any time while the clock is at logic-1, then the state of the master section will change to logic-0. During this time the J terminal remains blocked by the state of the slave (which is still logic-1). Thus, once the master is in the 0 state, it cannot be changed back until the next clock pulse. This is referred to as the *0s catching* property of such JK flip-flops. Similarly, such JK flip-flops demonstrate a *1s catching* property when initially in the 0 state. The T flip-flop has similar 0s and 1s catching properties, since its network is related to that of the JK flip-flop.

Because these SR, JK, and T master-slave flip-flops are not edge-triggered, the values of their input lines must be carefully controlled during the entire clock pulse time. For applications where this requirement on the input signals is too stringent, alternative networks are available for SR, JK, and T flip-flops that are edge-triggered. Such alternative networks can be derived from a D edge-triggered master-slave flip-flop by modifying it with additional gates. For this purpose, a function for the input line D is determined in terms of the specified input signals and the output state of the flip-flop. In particular, a JK flip-flop can be derived by using the function of Table 5.3. In the table, D is equal to the desired next state for each combination of J, K, and the present state Q. The function described by this table may be expressed as $D = J\bar{Q} + \bar{K}Q$. The network for an edge-triggered JK flip-flop using this function is shown in Fig. 5.11. Now, since the values of J and K just prior to the negative clock edge determine the value for D and since the D flip-flop is edge-triggered, then so is the overall JK flip-flop.

Flip-Flops with Data Lockout

In systems with many flip-flops that depend on each other, a problem owing to *clock skew* is possible. To be specific, consider a system comprising several

Table 5.3 Logic function for converting a D edge-triggered flip-flop into a JK edge-triggered flip-flop

J	K	Q	D
0	0	0	0
0	0	1	1
0	1	0	0
0	1	1	0
1	0	0	1
1	0	1	1
1	1	0	1
1	1	1	0

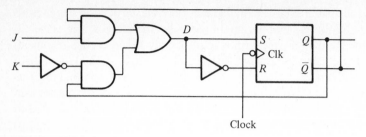

Figure 5.11 Edge-triggered *JK* flip-flop.

flip-flops that are connected to a common clock line. If such a system is to operate as a synchronous circuit, the next state of each flip-flop in response to a clock pulse should be logically determined from the *present* states of the flip-flops. However, this desired behavior might not be achieved if, for some reason, all the flip-flops in the system do not encounter the effect of the clock pulse at the same time. In such cases, a change in the states of the first flip-flops to encounter a clock pulse could affect the determination of the next states of those flip-flops that later encounter the clock pulse.

To more clearly illustrate this problem due to clock skew, consider a simple example. Figure 5.12*a* shows two negative-edge-triggered *D* master-slave flip-flops, A and B, interconnected in a cross-coupled fashion. It is intended that the two flip-flops exchange states in response to a clock pulse. Suppose, however, that flip-flop B encounters the negative edge of the clock pulse somewhat later than flip-flop A. It is then possible that the sequence of operation will lead to undesired behavior, as shown in the timing diagram of Fig. 5.12*b*. Starting at a time when the clock lines to both flip-flops are logic-1, it is seen that the output state of B determines the content of the master section of A. As the voltage on the clock line to A falls below the lower threshold, the content of the master section of A is transferred to the slave of A. At this point the previous output state of A is replaced by the output state of B. Since it is assumed that the clock line of B is still equal to logic-1 at this time, the new output state of A determines the content of the master section of B. Finally, as the voltage on the clock line to B falls below the upper threshold, this content of the master section of B is latched in. Consequently, the final output state of B will be the same as its previous state, rather than the previous state of A as intended.

Notice that if the time at which the clock line of A crosses the lower threshold does not precede the time at which the clock line of B crosses the upper threshold, then no problem occurs due to clock skew. Thus, master-slave flip-flops do have some tolerance to clock skew. Actually, the tolerance is somewhat greater than the time for the clock to make a transition between the two thresholds, because of the propagation delays associated with both the master and slave sections.

There are various reasons for clock skew among flip-flops in a system. For example, clock skew can result when several clock-line drivers having different

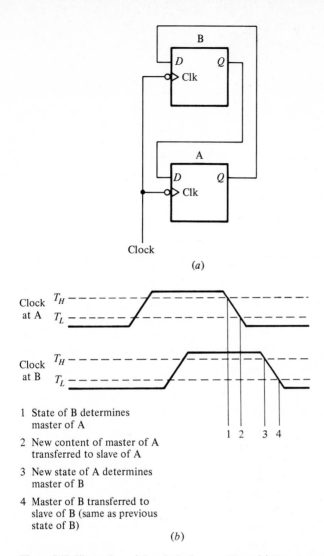

Figure 5.12 Illustration of the clock-skew problem. (*a*) Two interconnected master-slave flip-flops. (*b*) Timing diagram.

propagation delays are used. Another cause of clock skew might be due to differences in the propagation of the clock signal in the gates comprising the flip-flops themselves. Finally, for high-speed logic, another cause of clock skew might be due to the propagation time for a clock pulse to travel over different lengths of wire. Most often, however, the amount of clock skew that arises in a system is within the tolerance of master-slave flip-flops. For situations in which clock skew is so severe that it exceeds the tolerance of master-slave flip-flops, a special type of flip-flop having what is called *data lockout* may be used.

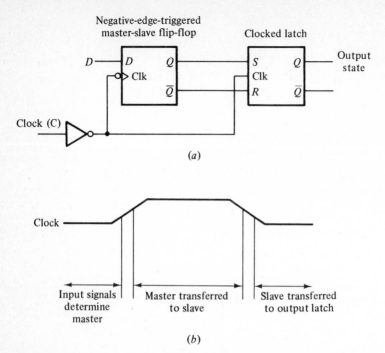

Figure 5.13 A flip-flop with data lockout. (a) Diagram. (b) Timing.

Flip-flops with data lockout can be formed from master-slave flip-flops by adding a third flip-flop section at the output as shown in Fig. 5.13a. The third section is a clocked latch that serves to hold the present output state of the flip-flop after the master-slave portion is updated. In the figure, it is assumed that the master-slave flip-flop is negative-edge-triggered and that the output latch is enabled when its clock line is logic-1. The master-slave portion is updated by the positive edge of the overall clock line C and the output latch is enabled after the negative edge.

The sequence of events for the overall flip-flop is shown by the timing diagram of Fig. 5.13b. Starting with the incoming clock at logic-0, its complement is at logic-1. At this time the master section is enabled and the value of the input line D determines the state of the master section. When the clock line changes to logic-1, first the master and output latch become disabled and then the slave becomes enabled. At this time the state of the master is transferred to the slave, but the output latch, still being disabled, retains the previous output state of the flip-flop. When the incoming clock eventually changes back to logic-0, the state of the slave is transferred to the output latch. As a consequence of this operation, any problem owing to clock skew can be avoided in a system by using these flip-flops and making the clock pulse duration longer than the worst-case time variation in the clock signals.

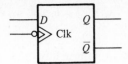

Figure 5.14 Symbol for master-slave flip-flop with data lockout.

The logic symbol for a master-slave flip-flop with data lockout is often distinguished from that for other clocked flip-flops with the use of a double triangle at the clock line as shown in Fig. 5.14. The two triangles indicate that the input values are sensed at one clock edge and the output is updated at the other clock edge. An inversion bubble, if placed at the clock line, indicates that the output is updated at the negative clock edge. Otherwise, with no inversion bubble the output is updated at the positive clock edge.

Asynchronous Inputs

Master-slave flip-flops often occur in an extended form that makes them more convenient to use. The extension involves auxiliary input terminals that function independently from the clock line. In particular, two terminals, Preset and Clear, frequently are provided to force a flip-flop into a known state regardless of the values appearing at the other input terminals, including the clock line. Since they operate independently from the clock they are often referred to as *asynchronous inputs*. Preset and Clear resemble the S and R terminals, respectively, of an unclocked SR flip-flop. When neither the Preset nor Clear lines are activated, the ordinary input signals and clock line determine the behavior of the flip-flop. However, when either the Preset or the Clear line is activated, but not both, the flip-flop is forced into its 1 or 0 state, respectively. Finally, as with the SR flip-flop, undefined behavior results when both Preset and Clear are activated simultaneously.

Figure 5.15 illustrates a logic-diagram symbol for a clocked JK master-slave flip-flop with the asynchronous input terminals Preset and Clear. The inversion bubbles at the asynchronous input terminals indicate that the activation state for those signals is logic-0, which is most common for TTL.

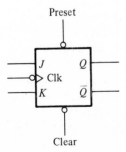

Figure 5.15 JK master-slave flip-flop with Preset and Clear inputs.

5.2 REGISTERS

In general, a *register* is a collection of flip-flops that operate in unison to perform some coordinated function. In this section we will consider two common functions that registers are designed to perform; namely, storage and shifting. Registers for counting will be discussed in the next section.

Actually, all registers perform the function of storage among other possible functions. A *storage register* will be taken here to be any register that does not have a more particular common function. This will allow us to treat some of the general properties of registers.

A storage register will be assumed to consist of clocked flip-flops with the clock lines tied together. In this way, the state behavior of all flip-flops is synchronized with pulses on the clock line. In many situations, the input signals to the flip-flops in a register will logically depend upon the output signals of these flip-flops as well as flip-flops of other registers. In order to ensure synchronous behavior for such situations, master-slave flip-flops can be used as was discussed in the preceding section. There are other situations, however, in which this logical dependence does not exist and in which the output signals of the flip-flops in a register are unimportant during the time of a clock pulse. Clocked latches are sufficient for this second situation. This leads to the consideration of two forms for storage registers, corresponding to the two situations just mentioned. It will be seen that both of these forms for storage registers are important in microcomputer systems.

Consider first a storage register with master-slave flip-flops. The flip-flops can be of any type, including JK, SR, D, and T. Figure 5.16 shows an arrangement of JK master-slave flip-flops forming a storage register. In order to synchronize the behavior of such a storage register with other components in a system, the clock lines of all registers and individual flip-flops are generally connected in common to a central clock source. In this way, information can be transferred into the registers for each clock pulse while their outputs are sensed.

Since the primary function of a storage register is to accept and retain information, some means is usually desired for transferring information into a storage register on a selective basis. For this purpose a *register-loading network* can be

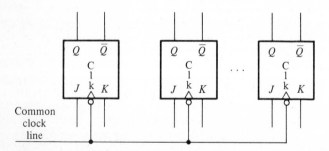

Figure 5.16 Storage register comprising JK master-slave flip-flops.

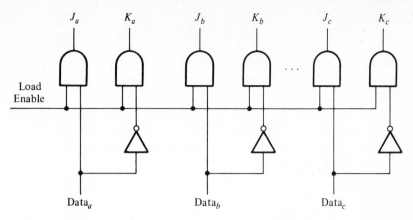

Figure 5.17 Loading network for register comprising JK flip-flops.

provided that will appropriately couple the input terminals of each flip-flop in a register to a data source. Figure 5.17 shows a register-loading network for use with a register consisting of JK flip-flops. The network consists of two AND gates and an inverter for each bit position in a register. These gates couple the logic signals from a data source, indicated by Data$_i$, to the J and K terminals of the flip-flops. A control line, referred to as *Load Enable*, is connected to an input of each AND gate. As can be seen, when the Load Enable line is placed at logic-1, each signal from the data source is passed to the J terminal of the corresponding flip-flop and the inversion of each signal is passed to the K terminal. This will cause each flip-flop in the register to take on the appropriate state in response to a clock pulse. On the other hand, when the Load Enable line is placed at logic-0, the J and K terminals of all flip-flops in the register are forced to logic-0. In this case, the register will retain the information it presently contains.

In many situations information from more than one data source is to be transferred into a storage register. For such situations, a register-loading network can be provided for each source. Corresponding outputs from the different networks can then be ORed as shown in Fig. 5.18. In operation, the Load Enable lines to the individual loading networks are used to select from which source, if any for a given clock pulse, that data will be transferred.

Consider now a storage register based on clocked latches. Such storage registers are generally used in situations where the output values of a register are not important at the time information is entered into the register. As will be seen, input and output ports of microcomputers, for example, are usually of this nature. It should be apparent that in such situations the timing of pulses on the clock line to the register is not critical relative to clock pulses to other components. Therefore, rather than have the clock line of the storage register connected to a central clock source of a system, the clock line can be driven by appropriate logic to selectively load data into the register. This can lead to a simplification in the overall circuitry. In particular, if the clocked latches are D type, the data-source

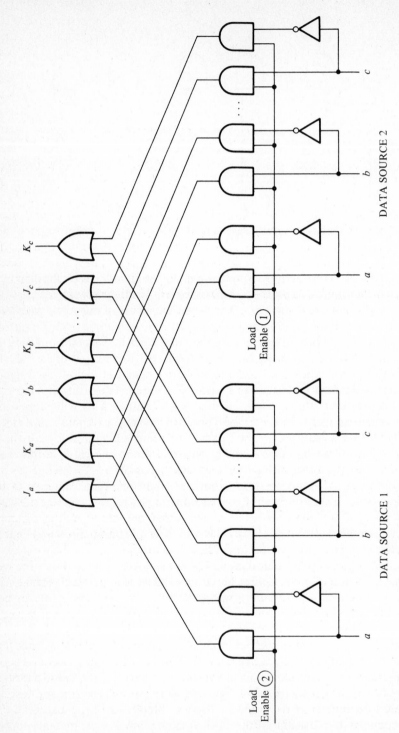

Figure 5.18 Two interconnected loading networks for one register.

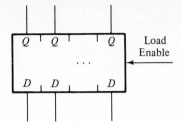

Figure 5.19 Symbol for register comprising clocked D latches.

lines can be connected directly to the D terminals of the corresponding clocked latches. Information will then be transferred into the register whenever the clock line is activated.

Since storage registers comprising clocked latches will be extensively used later in this book, especially for input/output ports, a logic symbol to represent such registers is shown in Fig. 5.19. In the figure, the terminals labeled D and Q represent the corresponding terminals of the individual clocked latches. The clock lines of the latches are assumed to be tied together to form a single overall clock line. This overall clock line is labeled "Load Enable" in the symbol to emphasize the fact that it is not usually connected to the central clock source of the system in which the register is used.

Shift Registers

The general function of shifting data in a register is very basic in digital systems and is used to accomplish various tasks such as serial-to-parallel and parallel-to-serial data conversion, multiplication and division by a power of two, bit positioning, and serial data storage. A shift register implemented from D master-slave flip-flops is shown in Fig. 5.20. As for a storage register, the clock lines of the flip-flops are tied to an overall clock line. Except for the leftmost flip-flop, the input terminal D of each flip-flop is connected to the output terminal Q of the flip-flop on its left. Consequently, for each clock pulse the state of each flip-flop will become equal to the present state of the flip-flop on its left, except, of course, for the state of the leftmost flip-flop. The state of the leftmost flip-flop is determined by the value on the line labeled "Serial data in."

It should be noted that the content of the rightmost flip-flop in Fig. 5.20 is lost upon the occurrence of each clock pulse. An important variation of this register is to connect the output line of the rightmost flip-flop to the D input line of the leftmost flip-flop. The resulting configuration is known as a *circular shift register*.

Serial data, consisting of a series of bits displaced in time, may be converted to parallel form with the shift register of Fig. 5.20. To perform such a conversion, the serial data is presented one bit at a time to the Serial data in line in synchronization with pulses on the clock line. Each bit is transferred to the leftmost flip-flop while its content and the content of all other flip-flops are shifted to the right. After the appropriate number of clock pulses, the data will be available in parallel form on the output lines of the flip-flops.

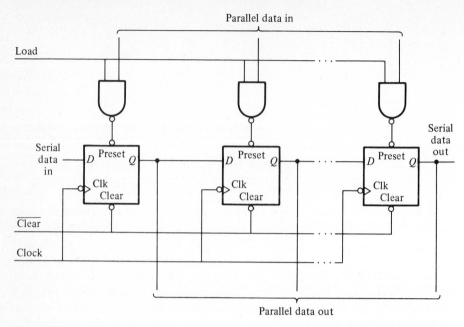

Figure 5.20 A unidirectional shift register consisting of D master-slave flip-flops.

The opposite conversion, i.e., parallel to serial, can also be accomplished with the shift register of Fig. 5.20. To perform such a conversion, data is first loaded into the register in parallel form. This is done independently of the clock line in two steps. The first step clears all flip-flops (i.e., forces their states to logic-0) by momentarily placing the Clear line to logic-0. The second step sets each flip-flop that corresponds to a logic-1 in the parallel input data. This is done by momentarily placing a logic-1 on the line labeled "Load" while applying the parallel input data. Both steps are done in the absence of clock pulses. Once the parallel data is loaded into the register, a serial form of the data is obtained at the output terminal of the rightmost flip-flop if a series of clock pulses is applied.

The shift register of Fig. 5.20 shifts data in only one direction, which is toward the right for the orientation shown. Of course, the same register could be used to shift data toward the left by simply reversing its orientation. A more general register that allows data to be shifted in either direction is shown in Fig. 5.21. Two separate control lines are provided, one for each direction of shift. It is assumed that both control lines will not be equal to logic-1 simultaneously, but if either control line is at logic-1, a one-bit shift in the corresponding direction will occur for each clock pulse. If neither line is at logic-1, then no shift will occur. To accomplish this, the circuit includes two register-loading networks. One network is controlled by the *Shift Right* control line. The input lines to this network for each bit position is connected to the output lines of the flip-flop to the left of that bit position. The other network is controlled by the *Shift Left* control lines. The

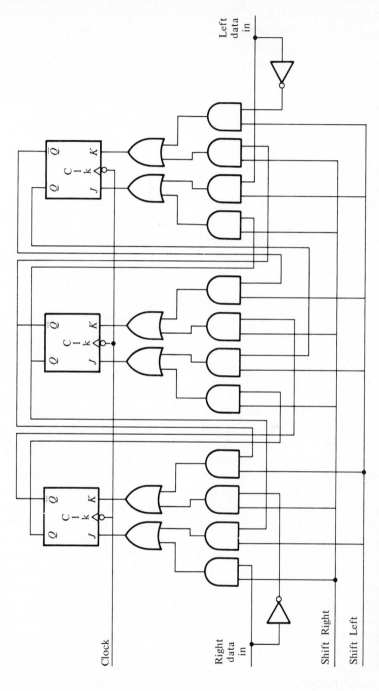

Figure 5.21 Bidirectional shift register.

143

input lines to this second network for each bit position is connected to the output lines of the flip-flop to the right of that bit position.

Bidirectional shift registers are useful components within the arithmetic-logic portion of digital processors. Also, they play a particularly important role in the implementation of stack-organized memories, as will be seen in Chap. 6.

5.3 COUNTERS

A *counter*, in general, is a sequential circuit in the form of a register that follows a prescribed sequence of states in response to pulses on a designated line. Since the number of states for any sequential circuit is finite, the prescribed sequence of states for a particular counter must either terminate with a certain state or else consist of a continually repeating subsequence of states. A counter having a state sequence that terminates is sometimes called a *saturating counter*. Saturating counters might be used, for example, to initiate some event after a certain number of pulses have been encountered on a line. Of course, some means of resetting such counters would be necessary if they are to be used more than once. In this section we will concentrate on counters having a repeating state sequence, which are called *modulus counters*. The term *modulus* is also used to refer to the number of different states that make up the counting sequence for modulus counters. Modulus counters are characterized both by the modulus and by the type of sequence involved, such as binary, binary coded decimal, Gray code, etc.

Binary Counters

A binary counter consists of a collection of flip-flops each of which is associated with a bit position in the binary representation for numbers. If there are n flip-flops in a binary counter, the number of possible states, and thus the modulus, is equal to 2^n. The counting sequence for a binary up counter is from zero to its maximum count, i.e., $2^n - 1$, at which point it reverts back to zero and the counting sequence is repeated. The counting sequence for a binary down counter, on the other hand, will follow the binary number sequence in reverse order, where the maximum number follows zero when the counting sequence is repeated.

Let us now consider the design of a binary up counter. Table 5.4 gives the sequence for the first few binary numbers. It should be noticed that the value of a particular bit position changes each time the current values of the bit positions to its right are each 1. Furthermore, this is the only time that a bit changes value. Using T master-slave flip-flops, this observation specifies the condition for when the T terminal of each flip-flop should be at logic-1. Recall that T master-slave flip-flops change state in response to a clock pulse if and only if T is equal to logic-1. Specifically, the T terminal of each flip-flop in a binary up counter should be equal to the AND of the Q outputs of all the flip-flops to its right.

Figure 5.22a illustrates a network for a 4-bit binary up counter. The counter comprises T master-slave flip-flops having their clock lines tied together. Each

Table 5.4 Binary number sequence

b_3	b_2	b_1	b_0
0	0	0	0
0	0	0	1
0	0	1	0
0	0	1	1
0	1	0	0
0	1	0	1
0	1	1	0
0	1	1	1
1	0	0	0
1	0	0	1
1	0	1	0
1	0	1	1
1	1	0	0
1	1	0	1
1	1	1	0
1	1	1	1

pulse on the common clock line will cause the counter to change to the next state in its counting sequence. The timing diagram depicting this behavior is shown in Fig. 5.22b. In this circuit, the functions needed for the T terminals are formed from a chain of two-input AND gates. The chain operates in an iterative fashion to generate the function for T_{i+1} by ANDing the function for T_i with Q_i, where T_i and Q_i are the terminals of the flip-flop corresponding to b_i. The function for T_0 is an exception, since T_0 belongs to the rightmost flip-flop. The terminal T_0 is connected to a control line referred to as *Count Enable*. When Count Enable is at logic-1, all the T terminals will have the appropriate values for the counter to go to its next state. When Count Enable is at logic-0, all the T terminals are forced to logic-0, so that no flip-flop in the counter will change state. Expansion of the counter in Fig. 5.22 to any number of bits can be done simply by including an additional two-input AND gate in the chain for each additional flip-flop.

The use of a chain of AND gates in a binary counter to generate the desired T-terminal functions is convenient, but acts to limit the overall counting speed. After one clock pulse has been applied to such a counter, a second clock pulse cannot be applied until all T-terminal values are determined. The value for the T terminal of the leftmost flip-flop will not be determined, however, until the effects of all flip-flop state changes owing to the first pulse have propagated through the entire AND-gate chain. This requires a time equal to $n - 1$ units of gate delay for a counter having n flip-flops.

An improvement in the counting speed of a binary counter can be obtained by replacing the chain of AND gates with a separate AND gate for each T terminal as shown in Fig. 5.23. In this case, the input lines of each AND gate are connected

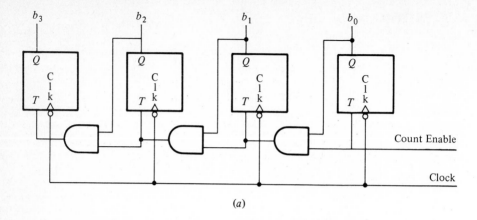

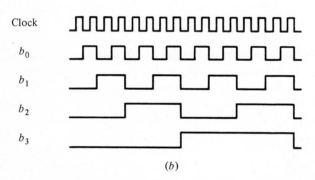

Figure 5.22 A synchronous binary up counter. (a) Network. (b) Timing diagram.

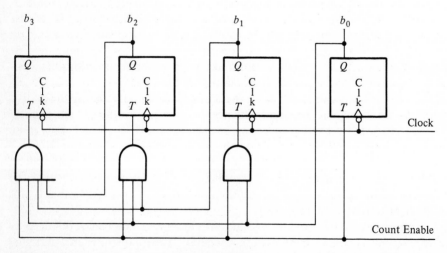

Figure 5.23 A parallel synchronous binary up counter.

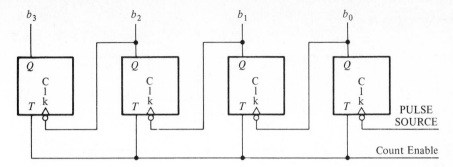

Figure 5.24 An asynchronous or ripple binary up counter.

directly to the appropriate flip-flop output lines. Consequently, there will be only one unit of gate delay (rather than $n - 1$) between the time the flip-flops change in response to a clock pulse and the time that all T-terminal values are ready for the next clock pulse. This improvement in counting speed is achieved, however, at the expense of requiring AND gates with many input lines rather than just two.

Since the flip-flops in either of the above counters are controlled by a common clock line their state behavior is synchronized; that is, those flip-flops that are going to change state in response to a clock pulse do so at the same time. Such counters are referred to as *synchronous*. A binary counter that does not have such synchronous behavior is illustrated in Fig. 5.24. As can be seen in the figure, the clock line of each flip-flop, excluding the rightmost, is connected to the output line of an adjacent flip-flop rather than to a common clock line. Consequently, the flip-flops will change state in response to certain state changes of the adjacent flip-flops rather than directly to clock pulses. It can be noticed in the binary counting sequence that the value of a particular bit position changes whenever the value of the bit to its right changes from 1 to 0. This is accomplished in the counter of Fig. 5.24 by using negative-edge-triggered T master-slave flip-flops with the clock line of each connected to the Q output line of the flip-flop to its right. The T terminal of each flip-flop is connected to a Count Enable line. The pulse source is applied to the T terminal of the rightmost flip-flop, causing it to change state with each negative edge of a source pulse provided that the Count Enable line is at logic-1. Each negative transition in state of the rightmost flip-flop will, in turn, cause a change in state of the second rightmost flip-flop and so on. In other words, a progression of state transitions occurs among the flip-flops from right to left terminating with the first flip-flop that makes a positive transition. This progression of state transitions suggests the name *ripple counter*. Such counters are also referred to as *asynchronous*.

Synchronous counters are generally required in systems that behave in a synchronous fashion. The sequential components in such systems are normally interdependent and controlled by a common clock source. In this case it is important that all flip-flops in the various components change state simultaneously in response to a clock pulse, so that the present states of the flip-flops can be used in

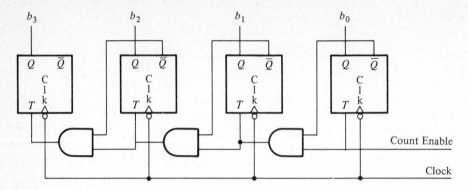

Figure 5.25 Synchronous binary down counter.

the determination of their next states. Thus, a ripple counter is not appropriate for such situations.

Ripple counters are, however, applicable for situations in which their outputs are not used to determine the states of other sequential components. For example, the output lines of a ripple counter might be used to only drive a visual display, such as for an event counter or a digital watch. A notable application for ripple binary counters is frequency division. Specifically, each stage of a ripple binary counter may be thought of as a divide-by-2 counter. This is true, since only half of the transitions of the signal at its input terminal cause a transition of the signal at its output terminal. Frequency division by any integral power of 2 may be accomplished by a ripple binary counter having an appropriate number of stages.

Synchronous counters may also be used for frequency division as well as for other situations in which ripple counters are applicable. However, ripple counters are generally capable of a higher speed of operation. This is true because as soon as the effect of one clock pulse passes the rightmost flip-flop of a ripple counter, a second clock pulse can be applied. There is no need to wait until the effect of a pulse ripples through the entire counter. In other words, the time between clock pulses for a ripple counter may be as little as the time necessary for one flip-flop to change state. In comparison, the minimum allowable time between clock pulses for a synchronous counter is equal to the amount of time necessary for one flip-flop to change state plus the amount of time required to determine new values for the T terminals of all flip-flops.

Thus far, only binary up counters have been discussed. Let us now consider the design of binary counters that count down. Both synchronous and ripple down counters can be designed. Notice that in going backward through the binary sequence (indicated in Table 5.4), the value of a particular bit position changes each time the current values of the bit positions to its right are each 0 (or, equivalently, the complements are each 1). This observation serves as a basis for the design of a synchronous binary down counter. Notice also that in going backward through the binary sequence, the value of a particular bit position changes whenever the value of the bit to its right changes from 0 to 1 (or, equivalently, the complement of the bit to its right changes from 1 to 0). This second observation serves as a basis for the design of a ripple binary down counter. In both cases, the conditions for the flip-flops to make a transition in a down counter are similar to those for an up counter, except that they are based on the complemented outputs rather than on the direct outputs of the flip-flops. Consequently, the synchronous binary up counter of Fig. 5.22 can be modified to a down counter by simply changing the AND-gate connections from the output line Q of each flip-flop to the complemented output line $\bar{Q}$, as shown in Fig. 5.25. The synchronous up counter of Fig. 5.23 can also be modified in a similar manner. Likewise, the ripple binary up counter of Fig. 5.24 can be modified to a down counter by redirecting the clock line of each flip-flop from the Q output terminal of the adjacent flip-flop to the $\bar{Q}$ terminal.

Decimal Counters

A decimal counter consists of a number of subcounters, each of which corresponds to one digit position. Each subcounter has a counting modulus equal to ten and is referred to as a *decade counter*. The counting sequence for a decade counter depends, of course, upon the way the decimal numbers are to be represented. Most often the 8421 binary-coded decimal (8421 BCD) representation is used, in which case each decimal digit is represented by its corresponding 4-bit binary number. The sequence for a decade up counter, in this case, is just the binary sequence from 0000 to 1001, back to 0000, and then repeating the binary sequence.

A network for a synchronous 8421 BCD decade up counter is shown in Fig. 5.26. The network has been formed by modifying a binary up counter so that its normal sequence is interrupted after a count of nine. Instead of continuing on to ten with the next clock pulse after a count of nine, the counter returns to zero. For this purpose a nine-detector circuit is provided, which consists of an AND gate

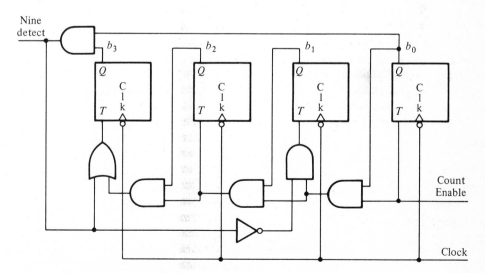

Figure 5.26 Synchronous 8421 BCD decade up counter.

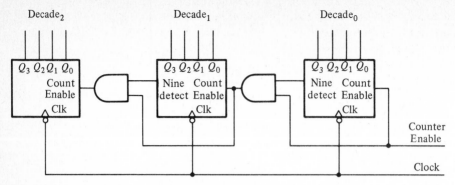

Figure 5.27 Three-decade synchronous 8421 BCD up counter.

connected to the output lines of the leftmost and rightmost flip-flops. The nine detector is used to change the values that appear at the T terminals of certain flip-flops when nine is present. In particular, the T terminal of the flip-flop for b_3 is forced to logic-1 with an OR gate when nine is present, so that the next clock pulse will cause b_3 to change to 0. Also, the T terminal of the flip-flop for b_1 is forced to logic-0 with an AND gate when nine is present, so that b_1 will remain 0 with the next clock pulse. The other two flip-flops are left unaltered, since the corresponding bits, b_2 and b_0, are 0 for both ten and zero.

The manner of interconnecting a number of such decade counters to form a synchronous 8421 BCD up counter is shown in Fig. 5.27. The clock lines of all the decade counters are connected together. The signal on the Count Enable line of each decade is determined by a chain of AND gates having as inputs the nine-detect signals from the decade counters. In this way, each decade is enabled to count only if all decades to its right are at nine.

Mod-B Counters

The scheme used to form a decade counter from a binary up counter can be generalized to form a synchronous counter having an arbitrary modulus B (i.e., a *mod-B counter*). To do this, the number of flip-flops n is chosen so that $2^n \leq B < 2^{n+1}$. A $(B-1)$-detector circuit is provided to interrupt the normal binary sequence at $B-1$, in a fashion similar to that of the nine-detector circuit in a decade counter. In particular, the $B-1$ detector is used when the counter reaches $B-1$ to force logic-1 on the T terminals of all flip-flops that would otherwise remain at logic-1 upon the next clock pulse and to force logic-0 on the T terminals of all flip-flops that would otherwise change from logic-0 to logic-1. In this way, the next clock pulse will cause the counter to go to zero rather than to B.

Gray-Code Counters

As a final example of a counter, let us consider the design of a Gray-code counter. The Gray code is a binary representation for positive integers having a sequence

Table 5.5 Four-bit Gray-code and binary sequences

Gray code				Binary			
g_3	g_2	g_1	g_0	b_3	b_2	b_1	b_0
0	0	0	0	0	0	0	0
0	0	0	1	0	0	0	1
0	0	1	1	0	0	1	0
0	0	1	0	0	0	1	1
0	1	1	0	0	1	0	0
0	1	1	1	0	1	0	1
0	1	0	1	0	1	1	0
0	1	0	0	0	1	1	1
1	1	0	0	1	0	0	0
1	1	0	1	1	0	0	1
1	1	1	1	1	0	1	0
1	1	1	0	1	0	1	1
1	0	1	0	1	1	0	0
1	0	1	1	1	1	0	1
1	0	0	1	1	1	1	0
1	0	0	0	1	1	1	1

with a special property. In going from any number in the Gray-code sequence to the next number, only one bit position changes value. This is in contrast to the binary sequence in which any number of bits can change. The sequence for 4-bit Gray-code numbers along with the corresponding binary numbers is shown in Table 5.5.

If two or more bits are to change value for a transition between two consecutive numbers in a sequence, it is unlikely that the bits will change at precisely the same instant. Therefore, during the transition between various pairs of consecutive numbers in the binary sequence, it is likely that combinations of bit values other than the two sequential numbers will momentarily occur. Such momentary occurrence of intermediate combinations is avoided with the Gray-code sequence, since only one bit changes during a transition. This is important for certain applications.

The general pattern for the Gray-code sequence can be stated in an inductive fashion. The sequence for the Gray code consisting of a single bit g_0 is 0, 1. Given the Gray-code sequence for n bits $g_{n-1} \cdots g_1 g_0$, the Gray-code sequence for $n + 1$ bits $g_n \cdots g_1 g_0$ is formed by first going through the n-bit sequence with $g_n = 0$ and then going through the n-bit sequence in reverse with $g_n = 1$. This property is readily seen in Table 5.5

Conversion between a binary number $b_{n-1} \cdots b_1 b_0$ and the corresponding Gray-code number $g_{n-1} \cdots g_1 g_0$ is easily accomplished. It can be shown that given a binary number, the bits of the corresponding Gray-code number can be obtained from the expressions

$$g_i = b_i \oplus b_{i+1} \qquad \text{for } i = 0, 1, \ldots, n-2$$

$$g_{n-1} = b_{n-1}$$

In these expressions, the symbol $\oplus$ denotes the mod-2-sum operation performed on binary digits, which is equivalent to the EXCLUSIVE-OR operation performed on logic variables. Also, given a Gray-code number, the bits of the corresponding binary number can be obtained from the expressions

$$b_{n-1} = g_{n-1}$$

$$b_i = g_i \oplus b_{i+1} \qquad \text{for } i = n-2, n-3, \ldots, 0$$

The above expressions are applied recursively. Starting with b_{n-1}, each computed b_{i+1} is used in the computation of b_i.

A Gray-code counter using D flip-flops can be designed by finding the appropriate function for each D terminal. Given a present state of the counter, the D terminal of each flip-flop should be made equal to the value in the same bit position of the next number in the Gray-code sequence. Referring to the Gray-code sequence in Table 5.5, the specific functions for the D terminals in a 4-bit counter are obtained for each row by using the values in the next row. Table 5.6 is a truth table specifying these four D functions in terms of the Q output values from the flip-flops. This truth table can be used to find a corresponding expression for

Table 5.6 Functions used for the D terminals of D-type flip-flops for a 4-bit Gray-code counter

Q_3	Q_2	Q_1	Q_0	D_3	D_2	D_1	D_0
0	0	0	0	0	0	0	1
0	0	0	1	0	0	1	1
0	0	1	1	0	0	1	0
0	0	1	0	0	1	1	0
0	1	1	0	0	1	1	1
0	1	1	1	0	1	0	1
0	1	0	1	0	1	0	0
0	1	0	0	1	1	0	0
1	1	0	0	1	1	0	1
1	1	0	1	1	1	1	1
1	1	1	1	1	1	1	0
1	1	1	0	1	0	1	0
1	0	1	0	1	0	1	1
1	0	1	1	1	0	0	1
1	0	0	1	1	0	0	0
1	0	0	0	0	0	0	0

each D_i in terms of the flip-flop outputs Q_i. The following is one set of such expressions:

$$D_0 = Q_3 \oplus \bar{Q}_2 \oplus Q_1$$

$$D_1 = Q_1 \bar{Q}_0 + (Q_3 \oplus \bar{Q}_2)Q_0$$

$$D_2 = Q_2 \overline{(Q_1 \bar{Q}_0)} + \bar{Q}_3 Q_1 \bar{Q}_0$$

$$D_3 = Q_3 \overline{(\bar{Q}_1 \bar{Q}_0)} + Q_2 \bar{Q}_1 \bar{Q}_0$$

Figure 5.28 shows a 4-bit synchronous Gray-code counter based on the above expressions for the D terminals.

5.4 DECODERS AND DATA SELECTORS

Often information does not appear in the appropriate form for its immediate use. A logic component that frequently provides the necessary information conversion

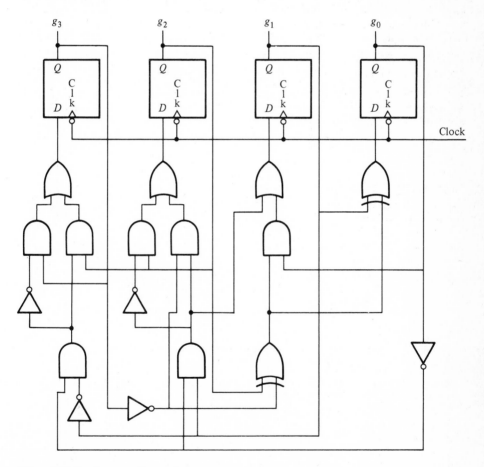

Figure 5.28 Synchronous Gray-code counter.

is the decoder. Decoders of various types play an important role in micro-computer systems.

One-Out-of-2^n Decoders

A basic type of decoder, referred to as a 1-*out-of-*2^n *decoder*, consists of a combinational circuit having n input lines and 2^n output lines. Each of the output lines corresponds uniquely to one of the 2^n possible input combinations. For a given input combination, the output line corresponding to that input combination will have a certain value, say logic-1, exclusive of all other output lines. In other words, the function describing each output line of a 1-out-of-2^n decoder is just a single minterm (or its complement) of the n input variables.

The most direct way of implementing a 1-out-of-2^n decoder is to use an n-input AND gate for each output line of the decoder. The input lines of each AND gate are connected to the appropriate combination of input variables and their complements. Such an implementation is shown in Fig. 5.29 for $n = 3$. This implementation involves the fewest AND gates of all implementations and is also the fastest. However, the AND gates need to have n input lines, which might not be feasible for large n.

As an alternative, a 1-out-of-2^n decoder for n inputs can be formed by combining the outputs of two or more smaller decoders, which involve AND gates with fewer than n input lines. In particular, an n-input decoder can be formed from two $n/2$-input decoders, each of which is connected to one-half of the overall input lines. Figure 5.30 shows the implementation of a 1-out-of-16 decoder using two

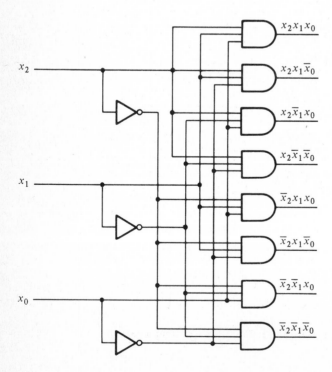

Figure 5.29 One-out-of-eight decoder.

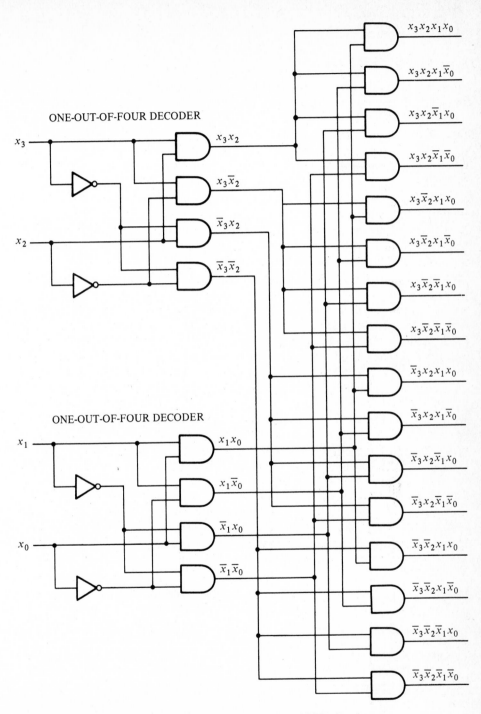

Figure 5.30 One-out-of-16 decoder formed from two one-out-of-four decoders.

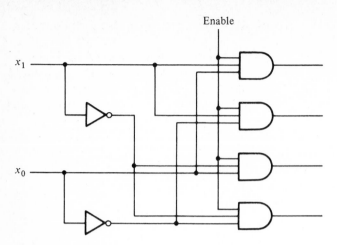

Figure 5.31 One-out-of-four decoder with Enable line.

1-out-of-4 decoders. In addition to the two smaller decoders, a two-input AND gate is provided for each of the 2^n output lines. These AND gates are connected to form each of the $2^{n/2} \times 2^{n/2} = 2^n$ possible combinations involving one output line from each of the two smaller decoders. As can be seen, more AND gates are needed for this alternative approach than for the direct approach, as well as an additional level of logic. However, the AND gates require fewer input lines.

To provide more flexibility, 1-out-of-2^n decoders often have an additional input line, Enable, that controls all output lines. When the Enable line is placed at logic-0, all output lines are forced to logic-0; otherwise, the decoder operates as usual. This can be accomplished, as shown in Fig. 5.31, by connecting the Enable line to an additional input line of each output AND gate.

One-out-of-2^n decoders are useful for any application that involves the selection of one alternative from many. The alternatives might, for example, correspond to commands, control signals, operation steps, data sources, or data destinations. The selection of data sources and destinations, in particular, is an important part of random-access memory systems and input/output systems. As will be seen, a decoder is used in a memory system to select a word location for reading or writing. Also, in an input/output system a decoder might be used to select which of several ports is to send or receive data.

Data Selector

To facilitate selecting data from one of several sources, devices called *data selectors* are made available in modular form. Basically, a data selector is a combinational circuit having one data output line, 2^n data input lines, and n input control lines. Each of the 2^n data input lines corresponds uniquely to one of the 2^n possible input combinations on the n control lines. For a given input combination on the n

control lines, the value of the corresponding data input line is placed onto the data output line.

A network for a data selector having eight data input lines is shown in Fig. 5.32. In the network, AND gates connected to one OR gate are used to couple each data input line to the output line. One input of each AND gate is connected to an output line of a 1-out-of-8 decoder. In this way, just one AND gate is selected by the decoder to pass data from a data input line to the output line.

The network for a data selector can be extended to data words having more than one bit position by providing additional AND and OR gates for each additional bit position. Just one decoder is needed for all bit positions. This allows an entire word to be selected rather than just 1 bit.

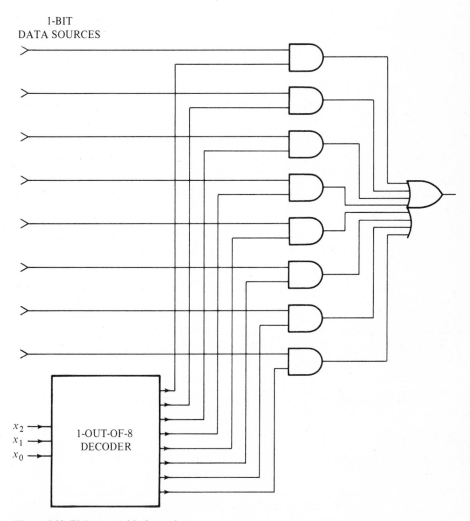

Figure 5.32 Eight-way 1-bit data selector.

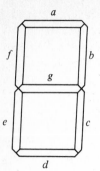

Figure 5.33 Seven-segment readout.

Other Decoders

In addition to the 1-out-of-2^n decoders, there are commonly available many special-purpose decoders. Such decoders convert a code word or number into a form that is convenient for a particular application.

An *8421 BCD-to-seven-segment decoder* is a notable example of a special-purpose decoder. Such a decoder accepts the 4 bits of the 8421 binary-coded-decimal (BCD) representation of a decimal digit and produces logic values on seven output lines to be used to control corresponding light segments of a display device. Figure 5.33 shows the arrangement of the seven segments making up a display device, such as a light-emitting diode (LED) readout. The decoder must select the appropriate segments of the display in order to form the decimal digit that corresponds to the 8421 BCD code on the input lines of the decoder. The functions for the seven output lines a, b, c, d, e, f, g of the decoder are shown in Table 5.7. In this table, a logic-1 output for each function denotes the correspond-

Table 5.7 Truth table for an 8421-BCD-to-seven-segment decoder

BCD				Segments						
x_3	x_2	x_1	x_0	a	b	c	d	e	f	g
0	0	0	0	1	1	1	1	1	1	0
0	0	0	1	0	1	1	0	0	0	0
0	0	1	0	1	1	0	1	1	0	1
0	0	1	1	1	1	1	1	0	0	1
0	1	0	0	0	1	1	0	0	1	1
0	1	0	1	1	0	1	1	0	1	1
0	1	1	0	1	0	1	1	1	1	1
0	1	1	1	1	1	1	0	0	0	0
1	0	0	0	1	1	1	1	1	1	1
1	0	0	1	1	1	1	1	0	1	1

ing segment is to be lit. The decoder basically consists of the circuit implementation of this table. In practice, however, additional components are often provided within the decoder for purposes of supplying the proper voltage levels for driving a seven-segment readout and for auxiliary functions such as leading-zero blanking and lamp testing.

5.5 ADDERS AND SUBTRACTORS

Addition and subtraction are, of course, basic arithmetic operations that are performed on numbers. This section is concerned with addition and subtraction as they apply to binary integers either in unsigned or in 2's-complement form. As discussed in Chap. 2, the addition or subtraction process is the same for either form. By interpreting the bits as logic variables, logic networks, called *adders* and *subtractors*, can be designed to perform these two operations.

An adder for two *n*-bit binary numbers can be designed as a combinational circuit having $2n + 1$ input lines, corresponding to the bits of the two operands and an input carry, and $n + 1$ output lines, corresponding to the bits of the result. The most direct approach of designing such a combinational circuit is to determine a minimal set of two-level Boolean expressions for the $n + 1$ output lines. The resulting network is referred to as a *parallel adder*. A *parallel subtractor* can be designed in a similar fashion. Parallel adders and subtractors have the highest speed of operation of all implementations of addition and subtraction, since they involve only two levels of logic. However, the complexity of the two-level networks for parallel adders and subtractors increases rapidly with the number of input bits and tends to become unfeasible for reasonable *n*.

Humans add and subtract numbers a digit position at a time. Interdependence of the digit positions is accommodated with the concept of carrying and borrowing from one digit position to the next. This same process can also serve as a design basis for adder and subtractor networks that are quite feasible to implement.

Ripple-Carry Adder

Consider now the design of an adder for binary numbers based on the digit-by-digit process. Let the two binary numbers to be added be represented as $A = a_{n-1} a_{n-2} \cdots a_1 a_0$ and $B = b_{n-1} b_{n-2} \cdots b_1 b_0$. It was pointed out in Chap. 2 that in adding two binary numbers the values in each bit position are added along with any carry from the previous position. If the result for any bit position exceeds the capacity of 1 bit, then a carry is produced for the next bit position. In a logic network, the carry information into each position i can be represented by a carry bit c_i that is equal to 1 if there is a carry from the previous position and 0 otherwise. The operation to be performed at each position i will then consist of adding the 3 bits a_i, b_i, and c_i to produce values for the sum bit for that position s_i and the carry bit for the next position c_{i+1}. Actually, c_{i+1} and s_i are just the

Table 5.8 Determination of the sum bit s_i and next carry bit c_{i+1} from a_i, b_i, and c_i for addition

a_i	b_i	c_i	Sum of a_i, b_i, c_i	c_{i+1}	s_i
0	0	0	00	0	0
0	0	1	01	0	1
0	1	0	01	0	1
0	1	1	10	1	0
1	0	0	01	0	1
1	0	1	10	1	0
1	1	0	10	1	0
1	1	1	11	1	1

most-significant and least-significant bits, respectively, of the 2-bit sum of the 3 bits a_i, b_i, and c_i, as shown in Table 5.8.

The functions defined in Table 5.8 for s_i and c_{i+1} can be used to find corresponding logic expressions. One possible logic expression for s_i is the minterm canonical formula, i.e.,

$$s_i = \bar{a}_i \bar{b}_i c_i + \bar{a}_i b_i \bar{c}_i + a_i \bar{b}_i \bar{c}_i + a_i b_i c_i$$

This expression can be manipulated as follows:

$$s_i = \bar{a}_i(\bar{b}_i c_i + b_i \bar{c}_i) + a_i(\bar{b}_i \bar{c}_i + b_i c_i)$$
$$= \bar{a}_i(b_i \oplus c_i) + a_i(\overline{b_i \oplus c_i})$$
$$= a_i \oplus (b_i \oplus c_i)$$
$$= a_i \oplus b_i \oplus c_i$$

Similarly, the minterm canonical formula for c_{i+1} is

$$c_{i+1} = \bar{a}_i b_i c_i + a_i \bar{b}_i c_i + a_i b_i \bar{c}_i + a_i b_i c_i$$

By using a Karnaugh map or by algebraic manipulation, the following expression can be determined for c_{i+1}:

$$c_{i+1} = a_i b_i + a_i c_i + b_i c_i$$

Figure 5.34 shows a logic network corresponding to the expressions for s_i and c_{i+1}. Such a network is referred to as a *full adder*, since at a bit position it performs the addition of all 3 bits including the carry bit. A network to perform the addition of two n-bit numbers can now be formed by cascading n full adders as shown in Fig. 5.35. The two numbers to be added are presented to the a_i and b_i input lines and the result is produced at the s_i output lines. The final carry bit c_n is the most-significant bit of the $(n + 1)$-bit sum. The input carry line c_0 into the right-

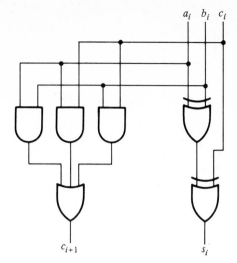

$$a_i \quad b_i \quad c_i$$

$$c_{i+1} \qquad\qquad s_i$$

Figure 5.34 Full adder.

most full adder serves as an overall input line to the network. This input line allows an initial carry value to be specified to provide for multiprecision addition.

The network of Fig. 5.35 is referred to as a *ripple-carry adder* owing to the chain of dependence that exists for the carry bits. Each full adder contributes two levels of logic in the determination of all succeeding carry bits. The final carry c_n therefore depends upon the rightmost bits a_0, b_0, and c_0 through $2n$ levels of logic. Consequently, a ripple-carry adder is considerably slower in operation than a parallel adder, which involves only two levels of logic.

Ripple-Carry Subtractor

A *ripple-carry subtractor* can be derived in a fashion similar to a ripple-carry adder. Let $A = a_{n-1} a_{n-2} \cdots a_1 a_0$ be the minuend and $B = b_{n-1} b_{n-2} \cdots b_1 b_0$ be the subtrahend; i.e., the subtractor computes $A - B$. The concept of a borrow

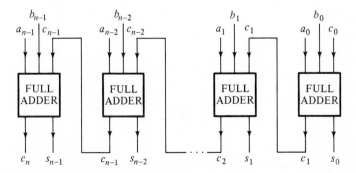

Figure 5.35 A ripple-carry binary adder.

Table 5.9 Determination of the difference bit s_i and next carry c_{i+1} from a_i, b_i, and c_i for subtraction

a_i	b_i	c_i	c_{i+1}	s_i
0	0	0	0	0
0	0	1	1	1
0	1	0	1	1
0	1	1	1	0
1	0	0	0	1
1	0	1	0	0
1	1	0	0	0
1	1	1	1	1

from one bit position to the next can be thought of as a negative carry. Thus, in subtraction, a carry bit c_i can be used for each bit position i to represent the presence of a borrow condition from the preceding bit position. The operation to be performed at each bit position in subtracting is specified by Table 5.9. In the table, the difference bit is represented by s_i to keep the notation similar to that for an adder.

Comparing Table 5.9 for subtraction with Table 5.8 for addition, we see that the s_i columns are identical. Thus the expression for s_i of a subtractor is the same as that for an adder. To obtain an equation for c_i of a subtractor, the minterm canonical formula can be written and then simplified. The resulting expression is

$$c_{i+1} = \bar{a}_i b_i + \bar{a}_i c_i + b_i c_i$$

It should be noted that the equation for c_{i+1} of a subtractor becomes the same as that of an adder if $\bar{a}_i$ is replaced by a_i.

Figure 5.36 shows a network, called a *full subtractor*, implementing the expressions for s_i and c_{i+1} for subtraction. A ripple-carry subtractor for two n-bit numbers can be formed by cascading n full subtractors in a fashion similar to that for a ripple-carry adder.

Adder/Subtractors

Because of the similarity in the Boolean expressions for adders and subtractors, it is relatively easy to combine the two operations in a network that adds or subtracts. This just involves using a control line to selectively complement the a_i bit in the network depending upon which operation is desired. Specifically, let the control line K be logic-1 for subtraction and logic-0 for addition. An EXCLUSIVE-OR gate may now be used to selectively complement each a_i. To see this, consider the Boolean expression

$$K \oplus a_i = K\bar{a}_i + \bar{K}a_i$$

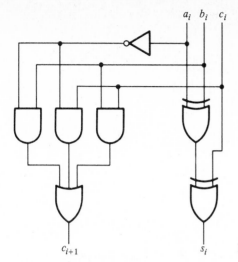

$$a_i \quad b_i \quad c_i$$

$$c_{i+1} \qquad\qquad\qquad s_i$$

Figure 5.36 Full subtractor.

If $K = 0$, the first term on the right side of this expression is 0 and the second term is a_i. If $K = 1$, then the second term is 0 and the first term is $\bar{a}_i$. Thus, $K \oplus a_i$ corresponds to the desired logic for selectively complementing a_i. Figure 5.37 shows a network for an n-bit adder/subtractor based on this scheme of selectively complementing a_i for each c_{i+1}.

An alternative scheme for an adder/subtractor accomplishes subtraction by adding the 2's-complement of the subtrahend to the minuend. Compared to the first scheme, this alternative scheme has the advantage of using full-adder modules without any internal modification. It was shown in Chap. 2 that the 2's-complement of the subtrahend can be obtained by adding 1 to the 1's-complement of the subtrahend. Taking the 1's-complement of a number is equivalent to logically complementing each bit of the number. EXCLUSIVE-OR gates may be used to selectively complement the b_i bits, based on a control line. Furthermore, 1 can be effectively added to the 1's-complement of the subtrahend simply by letting the input carry bit c_0 be 1.

A network based on this alternative scheme for an adder/subtractor is shown in Fig. 5.38. The control line K is EXCLUSIVE ORed with each b_i bit as well as being tied to the line c_0. Thus, when K is equal to logic-1, the 2's-complement of B is effectively taken, which causes the network to subtract B from A.

It should be pointed out that the two adder/subtractor networks differ in the way that the c_i bits behave during subtraction. For the first network (Fig. 5.37) the c_i bit for each position will directly indicate the presence of a borrow condition during subtraction; i.e., c_i is 1 when there is a borrow by position i. For the network of Fig. 5.38, on the other hand, the c_i bit for each position will inversely indicate the presence of a borrow condition during subtraction; i.e., c_i is 0 when there is a borrow by position i. A particular microprocessor might use

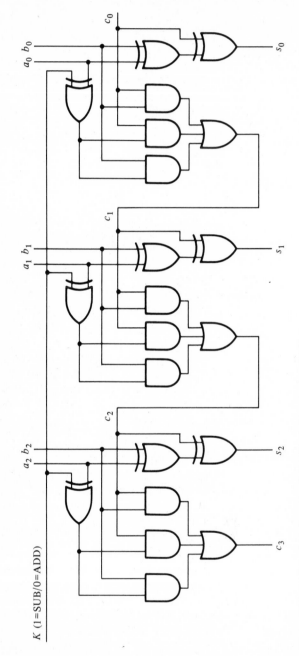

Figure 5.37 Adder/subtractor using full adder/subtractor modules.

164

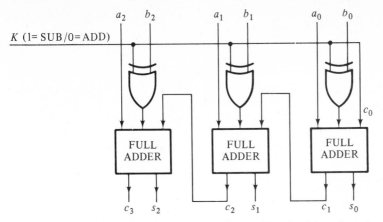

K (1= SUB/0= ADD)

Figure 5.38 Adder/subtractor using 2's-complement of subtrahend for subtraction.

either of these schemes. Therefore, it is important to note the difference between the two schemes, especially in regard to the end carry bit c_n.

Range and Overflow

Each of the networks for addition and/or subtraction just discussed can be used with operands that are in either unsigned form or signed 2's-complement form. In the case of unsigned operands, a representation for the correct result can be obtained from any of the networks and any combination of operands if the end carry bit c_n is retained with the n s_i-bits. In particular, for the addition of two n-bit unsigned numbers the carry bit c_n will correspond to the most-significant bit of the $(n + 1)$-bit unsigned sum. For the subtraction of two n-bit unsigned numbers, the carry bit c_n will correspond to the sign of the $(n + 1)$-bit result expressed in signed 2's-complement form. If subtraction is performed by adding the 2's-complement of the subtrahend to the minuend, as in Fig. 5.38, the carry bit c_n will actually be the logical complement of the sign bit of the result.

In a computer, the end carry bit is not usually retained when the results of arithmetic are transferred, since data words in a computer are generally restricted to a fixed length. In this situation an *overflow* condition is said to occur whenever the results exceed the capacity of the n s_i-bits. In particular, for the addition of two unsigned numbers an overflow occurs if c_n is 1 and for the subtraction of two unsigned numbers an overflow occurs if the difference is negative.

In the case of addition or subtraction of operands in signed 2's-complement form with any of the networks discussed, only the n s_i-bits can be used to represent the result. In this case s_{n-1} will be the sign bit of the n-bit result. As mentioned in Chap. 2, it can be shown that with this interpretation an overflow exists if the two carry bits c_{n-1} and c_n differ in value. This overflow condition for signed numbers can be expressed logically with the EXCLUSIVE-OR operation as follows:

$$\text{Overflow} = c_{n-1} \oplus c_n$$

5.6 HIGH-SPEED ADDITION AND SUBTRACTION

A considerable amount of delay is encountered in the operation of ripple-carry adders and subtractors owing to the propagation of carry information. As mentioned in the preceding section, for an n-bit adder or subtractor the final carry bit c_n depends on $2n$ levels of logic. To alleviate this delay in the determination of the carry bits, each carry bit could be determined directly from the a_i and b_i bits of the input numbers and the input carry bit c_0. In other words, the network that generates each carry bit c_i could look beyond the intermediate carry bits and work directly with the input bits a_i, b_i, and c_0. The term *look-ahead carry* is used to describe adders and subtractors that are based on such a scheme for generating the carry bits.

Let us consider the design of a *look-ahead-carry adder* for two binary numbers $A = a_{n-1} a_{n-2} \cdots a_0$ and $B = b_{n-1} b_{n-2} \cdots b_0$. It is desired to find Boolean expressions for the carry bits that involve only the direct inputs to the adder, i.e., the a_i's, b_i's, and c_0. Furthermore, it is desired that these Boolean expressions be in a sum-of-products form, so that the corresponding logic networks have a small number of logic levels. Consider the Boolean equation for the carry output at the ith stage of a ripple-carry adder

$$c_{i+1} = a_i b_i + a_i c_i + b_i c_i$$

$$= a_i b_i + (a_i + b_i) c_i$$

$$= g_i + p_i c_i \tag{5.1}$$

where $g_i = a_i b_i$ and $p_i = a_i + b_i$. In Eq. (5.1) g_i represents a generated carry from position i; i.e., if $g_i = 1$, then $c_{i+1} = 1$ independent of c_i. The term $p_i c_i$ represents a propagated carry past position i to position $i + 1$; i.e., if $p_i = 1$, then c_i will propagate to c_{i+1}.

Equation (5.1) for c_{i+1} involves c_i, which is not a direct input bit to the adder. However, this expression for c_{i+1} can be expanded until it involves only the direct input bits to the adder. This expansion is done by repeated substitutions of Eq. (5.1) for decreasing values of the index i as follows:

$$c_{i+1} = g_i + p_i(g_{i-1} + p_{i-1} c_{i-1})$$

$$= g_i + p_i g_{i-1} + p_i p_{i-1} c_{i-1}$$

$$= g_i + p_i g_{i-1} + p_i p_{i-1}(g_{i-2} + p_{i-2} c_{i-2})$$

$$= g_i + p_i g_{i-1} + p_i p_{i-1} g_{i-2} + p_i p_{i-1} p_{i-2} c_{i-2}$$

$$\cdots\cdots\cdots\cdots\cdots\cdots\cdots\cdots\cdots\cdots\cdots\cdots\cdots\cdots\cdots\cdots$$

$$= g_i + p_i g_{i-1} + p_i p_{i-1} g_{i-2} + \cdots + p_i p_{i-1} \cdots p_1 p_0 c_0 \tag{5.2}$$

Now, if each c_{i+1} expression is implemented according to the form of Eq. (5.2), then only three gate delays (as compared with $2n$ gate delays for a ripple-carry adder) are encountered between the time that the a_i and b_i bits are presented to the adder and the time that all carry bits become valid. In particular, one gate delay is caused by the formation of each g_i and p_i, a second gate delay is caused by the AND gate needed to form each product term in the c_{i+1} expression, and a third gate delay is caused by the OR gate needed to complete the implementation of Eq. (5.2).

To illustrate the above scheme more clearly, the necessary carry equations for a 4-bit look-ahead-carry adder are

$$g_0 = a_0 b_0 \qquad p_0 = a_0 + b_0$$
$$g_1 = a_1 b_1 \qquad p_1 = a_1 + b_1$$
$$g_2 = a_2 b_2 \qquad p_2 = a_2 + b_2$$
$$g_3 = a_3 b_3 \qquad p_3 = a_3 + b_3$$
$$c_1 = g_0 + p_0 c_0$$
$$c_2 = g_1 + p_1 g_0 + p_1 p_0 c_0$$
$$c_3 = g_2 + p_2 g_1 + p_2 p_1 g_0 + p_2 p_1 p_0 c_0$$
$$c_4 = g_3 + p_3 g_2 + p_3 p_2 g_1 + p_3 p_2 p_1 g_0 + p_3 p_2 p_1 p_0 c_0 \qquad (5.3)$$

These equations for the carry bits along with the equations for the sum bits can be used to implement a 4-bit look-ahead-carry adder, as shown in Fig. 5.39.

As can be appreciated by looking at the network of Fig. 5.39, the look-ahead-carry scheme is quite costly as far as the number of gates and the number of inputs to some gates are concerned. The general form for the carry equation indicates that the cost accelerates with an increase in the number of bits. For this reason, a modification of this look-ahead-carry scheme is often made for the design of adders that exceed a small number of bits (typically 4). This modification involves grouping the n bit positions of an adder into k-bit blocks, where n is assumed to be a multiple of k. The addition of the bits associated with each block is then implemented with a k-bit look-ahead-carry adder. Of course, each block will require an input carry bit corresponding to the block's position. This input carry information to each block is generally supplied by a logic network referred to as a *look-ahead-carry generator*. The general form of this approach is shown in Fig. 5.40.

A look-ahead-carry generator is patterned after the carry logic in a look-ahead-carry adder. It uses information from each block concerning whether a carry is generated in the block and whether a carry would be propagated through the block. Based on this information, the generator produces the input carry bit required by each block.

To be more specific, let us consider the design of a 16-bit adder comprising four 4-bit look-ahead-carry adder blocks. Let the adder blocks be labeled as T_0, T_1, T_2, T_3 from right to left. Let G_j represent the conditions for a carry from the T_j adder block to be generated in that block. Also, let P_j represent the conditions for a carry to be propagated through the T_j adder block. Now consider the determination of the input carry bit required by each of the four adder blocks. The carry bit into the T_0 adder block is just the overall input carry bit c_0. The carry bit

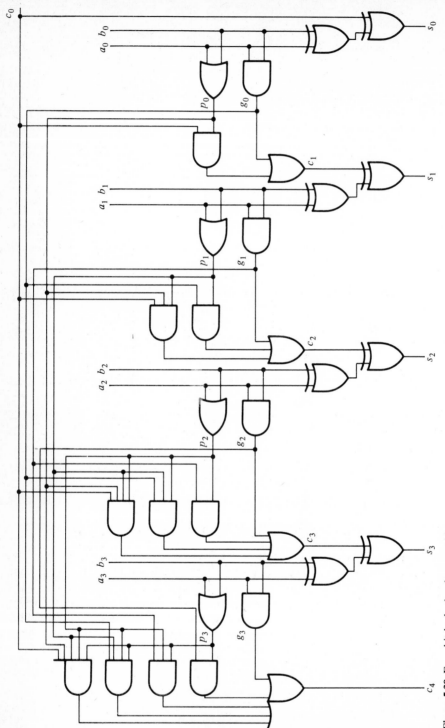

Figure 5.39 Four-bit look-ahead-carry adder.

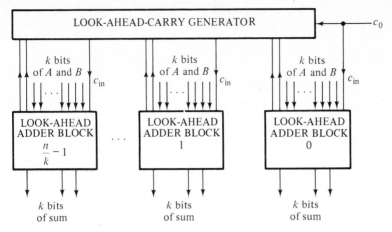

Figure 5.40 Modification of look-ahead carry scheme involving grouping bits into blocks.

into the T_1 adder block is c_4, which is 1 if a carry is generated in the T_0 adder block (i.e., $G_0 = 1$) or if a carry is propagated through the T_0 adder block (i.e., $P_0 c_0 = 1$). Thus c_4 is given by the Boolean expression

$$c_4 = G_0 + P_0 c_0 \qquad (5.4)$$

The carry bit into the T_2 adder block is c_8, which is 1 if a carry is generated in the T_1 adder block (i.e., $G_1 = 1$) or if a carry is generated in the T_0 adder block and propagated through the T_1 adder block (i.e., $P_1 G_0 = 1$) or if an overall input carry is propagated through both the T_0 and T_1 adder blocks (i.e., $P_1 P_0 c_0 = 1$). Thus, the expression for c_8 is

$$c_8 = G_1 + P_1 G_0 + P_1 P_0 c_0$$

Likewise, c_{12}, the carry bit into the T_3 adder block, is given by

$$c_{12} = G_2 + P_2 G_1 + P_2 P_1 G_0 + P_2 P_1 P_0 c_0$$

It is apparent that these carry expressions for a look-ahead-carry generator have the same form as the carry expressions for a look-ahead-carry adder. Consequently, the same type of logic network can be used for either purpose.

It now remains to find expressions for the conditions that determine G_j and P_j in each adder block. Equation (5.3) derived earlier indicates that for a 4-bit look-ahead-carry adder, c_4 is given by the expression

$$c_4 = g_3 + p_3 g_2 + p_3 p_2 g_1 + p_3 p_2 p_1 g_0 + p_3 p_2 p_1 p_0 c_0$$

For the look-ahead-carry generator, c_4 is given by Eq. (5.4), i.e.,

$$c_4 = G_0 + P_0 c_0$$

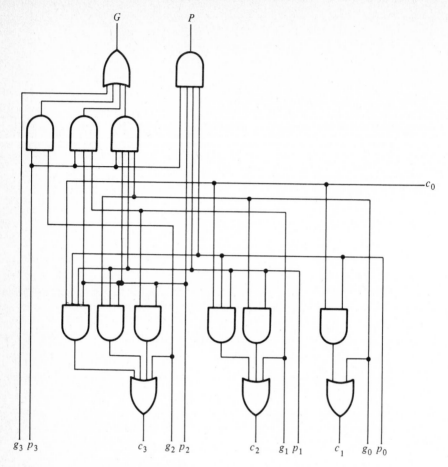

Figure 5.41 Look-ahead-carry generator.

Comparing these two results, it becomes apparent that

$$G_0 = g_3 + p_3 g_2 + p_3 p_2 g_1 + p_3 p_2 p_1 g_0$$

and $\qquad P_0 = p_3 p_2 p_1 p_0$

Similar expressions will also apply to the other G_j's and P_j's.

Figure 5.41 shows a network for a 4-bit look-ahead-carry generator that can be used to generate the carry bits inside an adder block or those outside the adder blocks. It includes the necessary gates to produce 3 carry bits from p_i and g_i. It also includes gates to produce values for P and G, which serve as propagate-carry and generate-carry variables for a higher level look-ahead-carry generator.

Figure 5.42 shows a 16-bit adder divided into four blocks. One layer of look-ahead-carry generators is used for the intrablock carry bits and a second

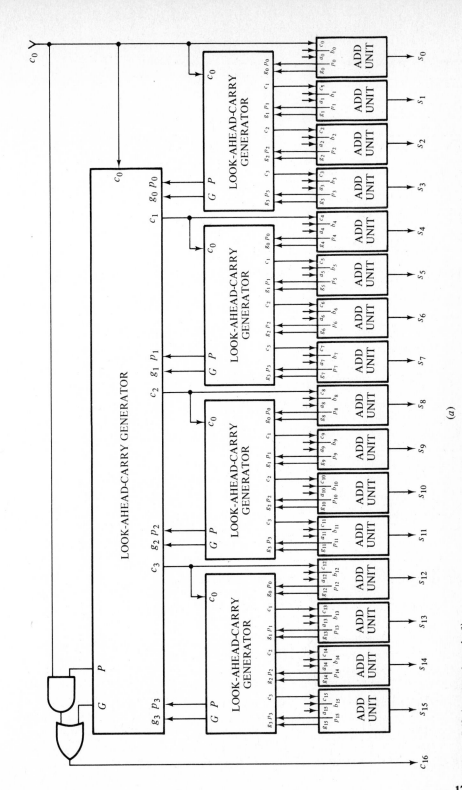

Figure 5.42 (*continued overleaf*)

(a)

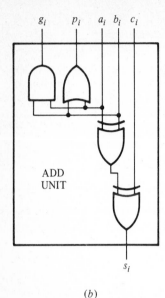

g_i p_i a_i b_i c_i

ADD
UNIT

s_i

(b)

Figure 5.42 Sixteen-bit modified look-ahead-carry adder. (a) General structure using the look-ahead-carry generator of Fig. 5.41. (b) The add unit.

layer is used for the interblock carry bits. Altogether, there are seven levels of logic involved in the generation of all carry bits. Two more levels of logic are involved in the production of the sum bits, resulting in an overall total of nine logic levels for the adder. This compares with 32 logic levels for a 16-bit ripple-carry adder.

This scheme of grouping the bits of a look-ahead-carry adder can be extended to additional layers. Thus, for example, a 64-bit adder could be arranged as four groups of four blocks of 4 bits. In this case, three layers of look-ahead-carry generators are used, for a total of 21 generators. The interconnections between layers are similar to those for the two layers of Fig. 5.42. In continuing with this scheme, it can be seen that each additional layer of look-ahead-carry generators contributes three levels of logic. Thus for the 64-bit adder, 12 levels of logic are involved.

5.7 BUSES

Complex digital systems typically comprise various functional units, each of which performs a part of the overall task for the system. A functional unit in such a system will generally interact with many of the other units in the system. The number of interconnections between the functional units can be quite large in order to accommodate all the ways in which they interact. As a practical matter, however, the number of connections that can be made to a particular unit is often limited by the way it is packaged, such as an integrated circuit or a printed-circuit board. Moreover, it is generally desirable to keep the number of interconnections in a system to a minimum, since they represent a major part in the manufacturing cost. The use of buses is an important way of reducing the required number of interconnections in digital systems.

A bus is an information pathway that is shared by many units of a system. Generally, information is conveyed over a bus in the form of words consisting of a group of bits. A bus might have a separate line to accommodate each bit of a word or it might have a single line that is shared in time by all bits of a word. The former is referred to as a *word-parallel*, or simply, *parallel*, bus, while the latter is referred to as a *word-serial*, or simply, *serial*, bus. This section will concentrate on word-parallel buses.

Word-Parallel Buses

In order to discuss word-parallel buses, consider a system comprising a number of modules interconnected by a single parallel bus. One such arrangement is shown in Fig. 5.43. The bus, consisting of n lines, is shared in time to convey information between pairs of modules. A special control module is provided that designates at any given time which module is to send information and which module is to receive information. Included in each module is an n-bit storage register that is used to both send and receive information. The flip-flops comprising each register may be clocked latches rather than master-slave flip-flops, since their outputs need not be sensed while information is entered into them. Furthermore, for simplicity of discussion, the flip-flops are assumed to be D type.

The input lines of the register in each module are tied directly to the corresponding lines of the bus. Thus, the content of the bus will be transferred into a register when its Load Enable line is activated. In the scheme of Fig. 5.43, the Load Enable line of each register is connected to a separate control line coming from the control module. In this way, the control module can designate the register that is to receive information conveyed on the bus.

The output lines of each register are coupled to the corresponding bus lines with logic gates capable of wired logic. In the scheme of Fig. 5.43, these coupling gates are shown as 3-state drivers, but other forms of gates may also be used, as will be shown shortly. In any case, the coupling gates for each register are controlled by a separate line from the control module. In this way, the control module can designate the register that is to send information over the bus.

It is assumed that only one register will be designated to send information at any given time. In the case where 3-state drivers are used as the coupling gates, only those 3-state drivers corresponding to the designated register will be enabled. The 3-state drivers for all other registers will be disabled. When disabled, a 3-state driver, as discussed in Chap. 4, will have a high-impedance output state, which is similar to no connection. Consequently, the 3-state gates for the designated register will be free to determine the logic values on the bus lines in accordance with the content of the designated register.

Logic gates capable of wired logic other than 3-state gates can also be used to couple the output lines of the registers to the bus. TTL gates with open-collector outputs, for example, are capable of wired logic. As discussed in Chap. 4,

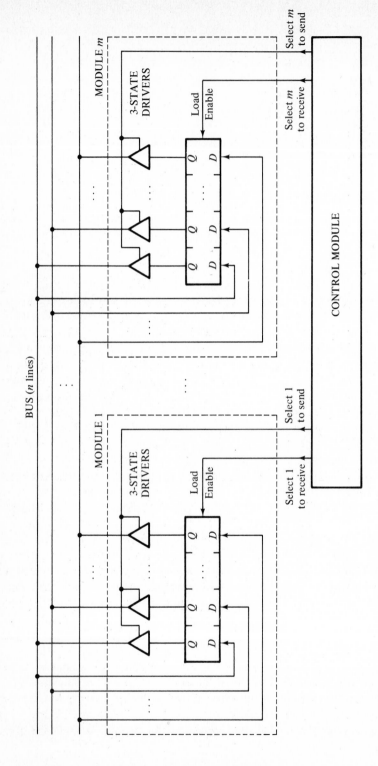

Figure 5.43 General word-parallel bus system.

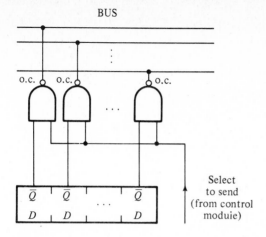

Figure 5.44 The use of open-collector TTL NAND gates to couple a register to a bus.

when the output lines of two open-collector TTL gates are connected together, either gate can force the common output line to logic-0. In other words, logic-1 at the output of one gate can be overridden by logic-0 at the output of the other gate. Consequently, if open-collector TTL gates are used to couple a register to a bus, proper operation can be achieved by having all gates that correspond to un-designated registers produce logic-1 at their outputs. Then the gates for the designated register can override all the other gates in order to establish the logic values on the bus lines. Figure 5.44 shows how this can be accomplished with open-collector NAND gates. Recall that the output of a NAND gate with inputs x and y can be described by the Boolean expression $\bar{x} + \bar{y}$. In Fig. 5.44, one input line, say x, of each NAND gate for a register is connected to a control line from the control module. The other input line, say y, is connected to the $\bar{Q}$ output of a flip-flop in the register. In this way, the control module can designate a register to send information by placing the control line for that register at logic-1 and the control line for all the other registers at logic-0. In this case, the flip-flops contain-ing logic-0 of the designated register will force the corresponding bus lines to logic-0.

Some types of gates capable of wired logic, such as open-emitter ECL gates, have logic-0 as the output state that can be overridden. When such gates are used to couple a register to a bus, the gates for all undesignated registers should have logic-0 as their output. This can be accomplished in an obvious way with the use of NOR gates.

In summary, the control module causes a word to be transferred between two modules as follows:

1. The control line that designates the sending module is first activated. This allows the coupling gates in that module to place the content of the module's register onto the bus.
2. The control line that designates the receiving module is then activated. This

causes the content of the bus to be loaded into the register of the receiving module.

Address Buses

In the bus scheme just discussed, each module connected to the bus requires two control lines from the control module. Thus, if there are m modules, a total of $2m$ control lines are needed in addition to the n bus lines. The required number of control lines can be reduced by assigning to each module an identifying code word. The minimum number of bits required to represent each code word for m modules is the smallest integer k such that $2^k \geq m$. The control module can then designate the module that is to send information on the bus and the module that is to receive information from the bus by specifying their code words. Figure 5.45 shows how this can be done using two *address buses*, one to specify the sending module and the other to specify the receiving module. Each address bus consists of k lines coming from the control module and going to all the other modules. An additional line from the control module, referred to as the *Strobe line*, indicates when an information transfer is to take place. The bus that conveys information between modules is now referred to as the *data bus* to distinguish it from the address buses.

It is the responsibility of each module to recognize its assigned code word when present on either address bus. This is done, as shown in Fig. 5.45, with an AND gate in each module for each address bus. The input lines of the AND gate in each case are directly connected to some of the bus lines and to the inversion of the other bus lines according to the bits of the assigned code word. Consequently, the output line, referred to as *Send-Select* or *Receive-Select* (whichever is appropriate), of each such AND gate in a module will be at logic-1 if and only if the code word for the module is present on the address bus to which the AND gate is connected.

As shown in Fig. 5.45, the Send-Select line of a module is used to enable the 3-state drivers that couple the output lines of the module's register to the data bus. Thus, at any given time, the data bus will convey the content of the register designated by the control module as the sender. On the other hand, the Receive-Select line of a module is used in conjunction with the Strobe line to load information into a module's register. Specifically, in each module the Load Enable line of the register is controlled by the AND of the Receive-Select line with the Strobe line. Thus, the information conveyed by the data bus will be transferred at the time determined by the Strobe line into the register designated by the control module as the receiver.

In summary, the control module in Fig. 5.45 causes a word to be transferred between two modules as follows:

1. The code words of the sending and receiving modules are first placed onto the respective address buses to all modules. This causes the content of the register in the designated sending module to be placed onto the data bus.

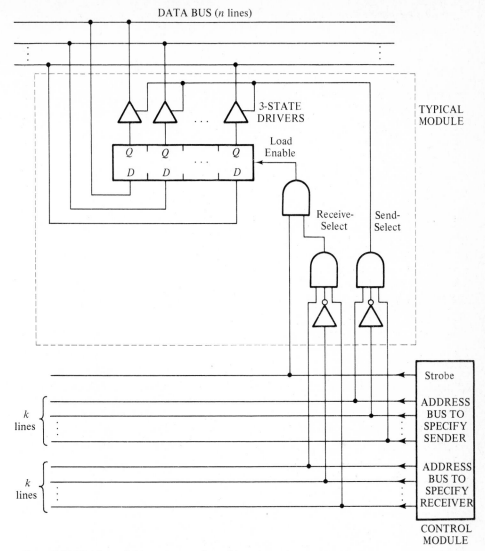

Figure 5.45 Word-parallel bus system using address buses for module selection.

2. The Strobe line is next momentarily placed at logic-1. This causes the content of the data bus to be transferred into the receiving register.

Single Bus for Addresses and Data

The number of lines in a bus system can be further reduced by conveying address information over the same bus lines as the data. In this case, the code words for the sending and receiving modules can be placed onto the data bus before a data transfer takes place. Each of the two code words can be placed separately on half of the bus lines or, alternatively, the two code words can be placed one at a time on the entire data bus. The two modules corresponding to these code words are then responsible for remembering that they were designated for either sending or receiving data. Finally, by the use of a Strobe line, any number of data words can be then transferred over the data bus between the two designated modules.

Figure 5.46 indicates how this single-bus scheme might be implemented. The single bus interconnects all modules including the control module. In addition, three strobe lines, referred to as the *Sender strobe*, *Receiver strobe*, and *Data strobe*, come from the control module and go to all the other modules. These

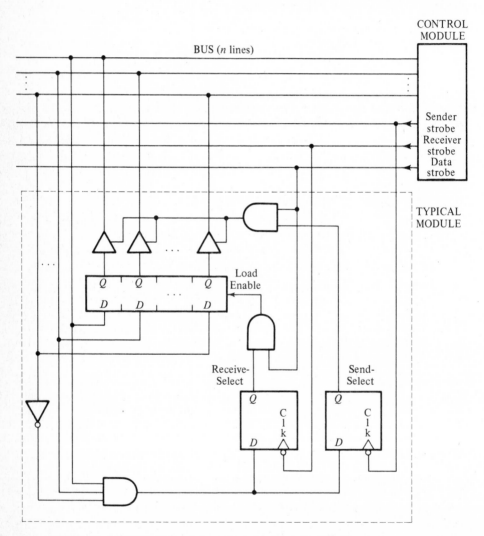

Figure 5.46 Word-parallel bus system using a single bus for data and addresses.

strobe lines respectively indicate the presence on the bus of the code word designating the sending module, the code word designating the receiving module, and a data word to be transferred.

Within each module, two D flip-flops, whose output lines are labeled "Send-Select" and "Receive-Select," are used to record whether the module has been designated for sending or receiving, respectively. The D input to both of these flip-flops is determined by an AND gate, which is connected to the bus with the appropriate lines inverted in accordance to the module's assigned code word. The clock line of each flip-flop is connected ·to the appropriate strobe line, Sender strobe or Receiver strobe. In this way, the Send-Select flip-flop in the module designated to send will be set to logic-1 when the Sender strobe line is activated. The Send-Select flip-flop in all the other modules will be reset. Likewise, the Receive-Select flip-flop in the module designated to receive will be set to logic-1 when the Receiver strobe line is activated.

The 3-state drivers coupling the register in a module to the bus are controlled by the AND of the Send-Select signal from the module's flip-flop and the Data strobe signal from the control module. Also, the Load Enable line of the register in a module is controlled by the AND of the Receive-Select signal and the Data strobe signal. In this way the content of the register designated to send is transferred to the register designated to receive when the Data strobe line is activated.

The overall operation of the bus system of Fig. 5.46 is as follows:

1. The control module places the code word of the sending module onto the bus and then activates the Sender strobe line. This causes the module whose code word is on the bus to record that it is the sender.
2. The control module then places the code word of the receiving module onto the bus and activates the Receiver strobe line. This causes the module whose code word is on the bus to record that it is the receiver.
3. The control module then activates the Data strobe line, which causes the content of the sender's register to be transferred to the receiver's register. This step can be repeated for any additional data words to be transferred between the same two modules.

Bidirectional Buses

In the previous bus schemes, data transfers were permitted between any pair of modules. For some situations, however, one of the pair is always the same module, which is generally the control module. This is the usual situation for the bus system of a microcomputer. This leads to a simplification for such bus systems, since then only one module involved in a data transfer needs to be specified. In a restricted sense, the data bus in such a system is referred to as *bidirectional*, since data can be transferred just from the fixed module to the specified module and vice versa.

Consider such a bidirectional bus system in which the fixed module for data transfers is the control module. The other module that is to partake in a data transfer can be designated in either manner previously discussed, i.e., by sending the corresponding code word over an address bus separate from the data bus or by sending the corresponding code word over the data bus. The direction of data transfer, whether to or from the control module, also needs to be specified. This can be done with the use of two strobe lines from the control module. One of these strobe lines is used to cause the content of the register in the designated module to be placed onto the data bus. This information on the bus is accepted into the control module. The other strobe line is used to transfer information placed onto the data bus from the control module into the register of the designated module. As a variation, one control line to specify direction and one strobe line to specify the time of a transfer could be provided rather than the two strobe lines.

Asynchronous Buses

The bus systems discussed so far involve the transfer of information over a data bus in a synchronous fashion. In particular, data is transferred between a sender and receiver module in response to a pulse on the appropriate strobe line from the control module. This requires that at the time of the strobe pulse, the sender module has data available and the receiver module is in a condition to accept the data. If the data transfer directly involves only registers in the two modules or other simple digital circuitry, then synchronous operation of the bus is generally feasible. In such cases the controller can predict times in which both modules are ready to partake in a data transfer. In many situations, however, either one or both of the sender and receiver modules must interact with external components having variable or unknown timing. For example, the sender module might obtain its data from a measuring instrument (such as a digital voltmeter) that operates in response to certain external events. Also, the receiver module might supply data to a control device (such as a motor speed controller) that accepts new data only under certain conditions. In such cases synchronous bus operation is not feasible, since the controller module cannot predict a time that each data-transfer strobe pulse should be issued.

The bus could be operated, however, in an asynchronous fashion. Rather than have a strobe line from the controller module, the transfer of data between a sender and receiver module could be coordinated with the use of status lines that reflect the condition of the two modules. One such scheme is depicted in Fig. 5.47. Two status lines are included, Sender ready and Receiver ready. Also, included are an n-line information bus and two strobe lines, Sender strobe and Receiver strobe. As before, the control module designates a module to be the sender by placing its assigned address onto the information bus and issuing a pulse on the Sender strobe line. Likewise, the control module designates the receiver by plac- ing its assigned address onto the information bus and pulsing the Receiver strobe line. Once a sender is designated, it controls the Sender ready line, indicating when it has data available. The designated receiver controls the Receiver ready line, indicating when it can accept data.

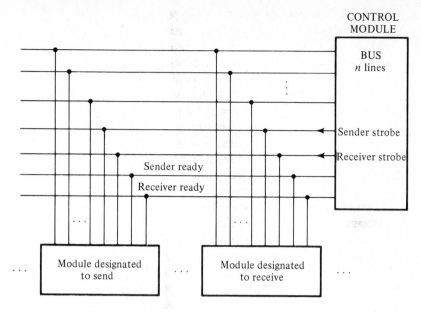

Figure 5.47 Parallel asynchronous bus system.

There are two objectives to be met in the coordination of data transfer between the designated modules.

1. The transfer of a data word should occur as soon as both sender and receiver are ready.
2. Each data word should be transferred no more than once.

To ensure that both of these objectives are met, a sequence is prescribed for transitions of the signals on the two status lines. This, in general, is referred to as *handshaking*. The following is one sequence that will work, although there are several other alternatives. As shown in Fig. 5.48, starting at a time in which the sender does not have data available, the Sender ready line is held at logic-0. At this time, the receiver holds the Receiver ready line at logic-0 whether or not it can accept data. When the sender eventually obtains data to be transferred, it changes the Sender ready line to logic-1. In response to this transition the receiver will change its ready line to logic-1 as soon as it can accept data (which might be immediately if the receiver had been ready). When both ready lines are logic-1, a data word is transferred from the sender to the receiver. As soon as the receiver has the data word, it brings its ready line back to logic-0. In response to this transition of the Receiver ready line, the sender brings its ready line to logic-0. Until the occurrence of this last transition of the Sender ready line to logic-0, the receiver is prevented from responding to a logic-1 on the Sender ready line.

With such handshaking the receiver is informed when a new word is available

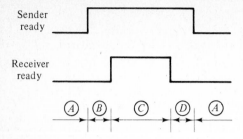

Sender
ready

Receiver
ready

(A) Sender obtains next word.

(B) Sender has new word but waits
       for receiver to use previous word.

(C) Data word is transferred over bus.

(D) Transfer is complete, receiver utilizes data word.

Figure 5.48 Handshaking for asynchronous
bus system of Fig. 5.47.

at the sender and the sender is informed when a data word has been accepted by
the receiver. Furthermore, as indicated in Fig. 5.48, the state of the two ready lines
at any point in time determines the appropriate action to be taken by each of the
two modules.

PROBLEMS

5.1 Two NOR gates are connected in a cross-coupled fashion as shown in Fig. P5.1. Can this circuit
serve as a flip-flop? Explain. If so, identify the terminals.

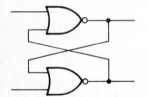

Figure P5.1

5.2 Construct a master-slave D flip-flop using the circuit of Fig. P5.1 for each section.

5.3 Convert a T master-slave flip-flop into a D flip-flop by adding whatever gates are necessary.
Perform the following two conversions in a similar fashion: T type to JK type; D type to SR type.

5.4 For each of the following applications is a master-slave flip-flop required rather than a clocked
latch? Explain.
   (a) Synchronous binary counter
   (b) Shift register
   (c) Storage register to hold output data from a system for display only
   (d) Storage register to hold input data to a system
   (e) Storage register to hold intermediate results in a synchronous system

5.5 Design a loading network (as discussed in Sec. 5.2) for a storage register that consists of T-type
flip-flops.

5.6 Design a 4-bit synchronous binary down counter using T master-slave flip-flops.

5.7 Design a 4-bit ripple binary down counter.

5.8 Design a synchronous binary-coded mod-12 counter using T master-slave flip-flops.

5.9 Design a 1-out-of-8 decoder using only inverters and two-input AND gates.

5.10 Form a 1-out-of-16 decoder using only 1-out-of-4 decoders with Enable lines.

5.11 Determine a set of minimal sum-of-products Boolean expressions for controlling the seven-segment readout discussed in Sec. 5.4. Use Table 5.7 assuming that the missing six input combinations will never occur.

5.12 Design a decoder for a seven-segment readout so as to produce some recognizable symbol for each of the 16 hexadecimal digits.

5.13 Design a network for a decade adder module that may be cascaded to form a decimal adder. The module, as shown in Fig. P5.13, is to have a set of four input lines for each of two 8421 binary-coded-decimal operands and a set of four output lines for the 8421 binary-coded-decimal sum. Furthermore, there is to be an input carry line and an output carry line. The network specifically should place on the sum output lines the modulo-10 results of adding the two operands along with the input carry. The output carry line should be set at 1 whenever the sum of the two operands exceeds 9.

It is suggested that the design follow the procedure discussed in Sec. 2.7. Specifically, a 4-bit ripple-carry binary adder is used to first form the binary sum of the operands. The binary adder is then followed by a corrector network that adjusts the results whenever the sum exceeds 9.

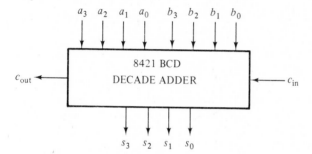

Figure P5.13

5.14 Determine an expression for c_5 in the look-ahead-carry adder described in Sec. 5.6.

5.15 Design a general bus system to interconnect four modules. Each module is to contain a 4-bit storage register that may receive information from the bus as well as send information. An additional central module is to specify the receiving and the sending module using separate control lines. For this purpose, two 1-out-of-4 decoders are to be included in the central module with the output lines running to the individual modules. The inputs to the decoders are to be externally specified corresponding to the modules that are selected.

5.16 In Sec. 5.7 on buses it was shown how open-collector TTL NAND gates can be used to couple the output lines of a register to the lines of a bus. In that case, the $\bar{Q}$ register outputs were used to compensate for signal inversion caused by the NAND gates. Furthermore, the NAND gates were connected to a control line which if at logic-1 caused the NAND gates to pass the content of the register to the bus.

(a) Determine a basic logic operation other than NAND in which open-collector TTL gates can be used to couple a register to a bus. Show how such gates can be connected and operated for this purpose.

(b) Show how open-emitter ECL NOR gates can be used to couple a register to a bus.

(c) Determine a second basic logic operation for open-emitter ECL gates. Show how such gates can be used to couple a register to a bus.

SIX

MEMORY CIRCUITS

Memory is the means by which information is transferred through time. The direction of transfer, of course, is always in the same direction for real time, specifically forward. A memory system is therefore a channel that allows information generated in the present to be transferred to the future. All sequential circuits, including computers, have a memory property, which allows their output at a given time to depend upon the input at previous times. In general, this memory property is due to the use of *memory elements*, such as flip-flops. In this chapter we are specifically interested in organized memory systems, which consist of memory elements that are arranged in some certain manner.

The organization of a memory system primarily affects the manner in which information is transferred to or from the memory elements. Information is generally transferred in units of a fixed number of bits, which are referred to as *words*. A memory system can be thought of as a storage space comprising a collection of identifiable *word positions*. For some memory systems, a fixed set of memory elements is assigned to each such word position. In this case the location of the memory elements identifies the word position, which is therefore called a *word location*. In other memory systems, the word positions move among the sets of memory elements while maintaining a certain relative order. In this case, a word position is identified by both the time and location of memory elements that it occupies. In either case, when a word of information is transferred into a memory system, it will occupy a particular word position. This process is referred to as a *memory write* operation. On the other hand, when information is transferred out of a memory system, it is obtained from a specified word position (usually the information is also left in the memory intact). This process is referred to as a *memory read* operation.

184

There are various ways in which a word position in a memory system is selected for either a memory write or read operation. The means for selecting a word position and for transferring information to or from that word position is referred to as *access*. There are two major types of access for memory systems, *random access* and *sequential access*. Random access refers to a type of memory system in which every word position may be selected or accessed in approximately the same amount of time. That is, the selection of a word position can be made at random without affecting the access time. Sequential access, on the other hand, refers to a type of memory system in which the word positions become available for access in some certain order. Each of these two types of memory systems will be discussed in the following sections.

6.1 RANDOM-ACCESS MEMORY ORGANIZATION

A random-access memory system is one in which units of information are stored in word locations that may be directly selected. In this way, the time needed to select any word location is approximately the same as for any other location. Each word location consists of a fixed number of memory elements and is assigned an identifier. This identifier, consisting of a fixed number of bits, is known as the *address* of the word location. The address allows each word location to be distinguished from the others for the purpose of performing either a read or a write operation.

A random-access memory system generally comprises a number of modular memory units having random access. In the case of electronic memory, generally these memory units are each in the form of an integrated circuit. The lines conveying the external signals of such memory units are generally arranged so as to facilitate their use within a bus-oriented system. Included for the external signals are usually lines to specify the address of the word to be accessed, lines to convey data into or from the unit, and several control lines to enable a read or a write operation to occur. There are variations in the exact nature of these external signals to accommodate various types of bus systems; however, most memory units can be characterized by one of the two models depicted in Fig. 6.1. The two models differ only in the arrangement of their data lines. In the model of Fig. 6.1*a* there is just one set of data lines, which is used to convey both incoming data in the case of a write operation and outgoing data in the case of a read operation. The model of Fig. 6.1*b*, on the other hand, has separate sets of data lines for incoming and outgoing data.

Both models have a set of address lines whose signals designate the word location to be accessed for either a read or a write operation. Also both models have a Write control line, which is used to place the unit into either a mode for writing (Write = 1) or a mode for reading (Write = 0). Finally, a control line, Chip Enable, is provided in both models to either allow the specified memory operation, i.e., write or read, to take place (when Chip Enable = 1) or to disable the unit (when Chip Enable = 0).

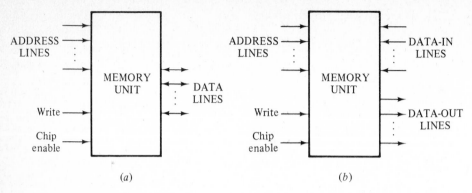

Figure 6.1 Arrangement of lines for external signals of a random-access memory unit. (*a*) Unit with bidirectional data lines. (*b*) Unit with separate lines for input and output data.

So that memory units described by either model can be incorporated into a bus-oriented memory system, logic gates that are capable of wired logic are used to drive the outgoing data lines (i.e., the data lines for Fig. 6.1*a* and the data-out lines for Fig. 6.1*b*). Information from the memory unit is present at the outgoing data lines of either model only during a read operation; otherwise, the lines are free to be driven by any other memory unit or device connected to the lines. This is especially important in the case of Fig. 6.1*a*, since the same data lines must be used to convey information into the unit during a write operation.

The actual condition of the outgoing data lines when a memory unit is not performing a read operation depends, of course, on the type of wired logic that is used. In the case of wired AND, with open-collector TTL gates for example, the condition allowing the lines to be free is logic-1, since this state can then be overridden by some other connected memory unit or device. For wired OR the free condition is logic-0. In the case of three-state wired logic, the free condition is, of course, the third state, which is a high impedance having the effect of no connection made to the line. In each case, this free condition of the outgoing data lines will occur if either the Write line is logic-1 or the Chip Enable line is logic-0.

Basic Internal Organization of Random-Access Memory

Now that the external characteristics of typical random-access memory units have been discussed, let us consider their internal organization. One organization that provides for the specification of a word location and for the transferring of information into or from that location is illustrated by the network of Fig. 6.2. This network uses memory elements based on unclocked *SR* flip-flops to store each bit of a word. Besides the flip-flop, each memory element includes gates that provide for the transfer of data between the flip-flop and common internal data lines. One of the two memory operations, read or write, may be performed with all memory elements in a row simultaneously. Each row corresponds to a word location and has an assigned address.

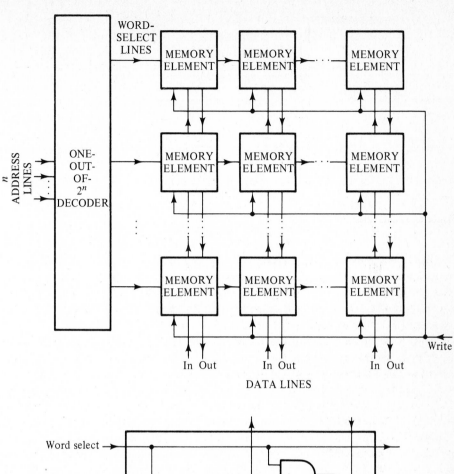

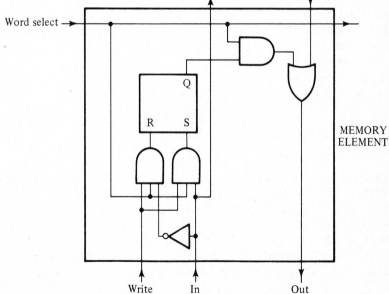

Figure 6.2 Basic internal organization of a random-access memory unit.

A 1-out-of-2^n decoder is used to select the word location that is designated by a given address. The decoder has n input lines; so there are 2^n input combinations. The address of the desired word location is placed onto these input lines. The decoder has 2^n output lines called the *word-select* lines. Depending upon the input combination, one word-select line is equal to logic-1 and the rest are equal to logic-0. Each word-select line is used to enable all memory elements in a row for reading or writing. Each column has two internal data lines, one for data in and the other for data out. The data-out line for each column takes on the value of the memory element that is in the selected row. This is accomplished by ANDing the output of every memory element with its word-select line and ORing the results onto the data-out line. A word in memory is thus read by presenting the address of the word to the decoder and observing the data-out lines.

The data-in line for each column is used to transfer information into the memory element of the selected row whenever a write command is issued. This is accomplished with two AND gates within each memory element that, when enabled by the word-select line and the internal control line Write, transfer the value of the data-in line and its complement to S and R, respectively. Thus, a word is written into a memory location by presenting the corresponding address to the decoder and the word to the data-in lines, and then setting the Write control line to logic-1.

It should be pointed out that in the above description the data-in, data-out, and Write signals appear on lines internal to the memory unit. These signals are related to the external signals of the memory unit through appropriate gates and buffer circuits. This is done in various ways depending upon the external characteristics specified for a particular memory unit. For example, the external characteristics depicted in Fig. 6.1a can be achieved by the arrangement of Fig. 6.3. Shown in Fig. 6.3 are the external lines Write, Chip Enable, and data. The internal Write line is derived by ANDing the external Write signal with Chip Enable. Also, the two internal data lines for one bit position in a word are connected as shown to the external data line with an input buffer circuit and a three-state output driver. The three-state driver is controlled by the AND of Chip Enable and the complement of the external Write signal. In this way the external data line will operate bidirectionally to supply information to the internal data-in line for a write operation and to accept information from the internal data-out line for a read operation.

Two-Dimensional Addressing

A disadvantage of the basic internal organization of the random-access memory just described is the required size of the address decoder. For example, with $n = 10$ the address decoder has $2^{10} = 1024$ output lines. Each output line has to be connected to each memory element in a row. This large number of wires can be reduced by allowing the memory elements themselves to participate in the decoding.

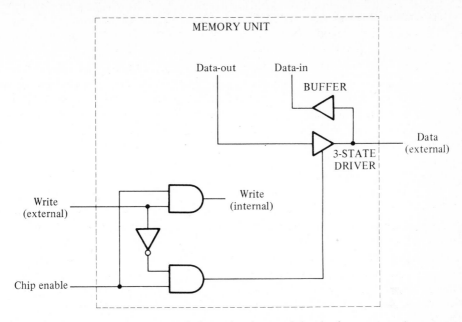

Figure 6.3 Relationship between certain internal and external signals of a memory unit.

To see how this can be done, let us take a single column of the random-access memory organization shown in Fig. 6.2 and arrange it into a rectangular array. For $n = 10$ there are 2^{10} memory elements involved. These can be put into an array of dimensions $2^5 \times 2^5$, or generally $2^m \times 2^{n-m}$, as shown in Fig. 6.4. Each memory element of the original column now lies at the intersection of a row and a column of the rectangular array. Two address decoders are now used, each having $n/2$ input lines and $2^{n/2}$ output lines (assuming n is even and the array is square). For $n = 10$ the number $2^{n/2}$ is equal to $2^5 = 32$. The output lines of one decoder are used to select a row and the output lines of the other decoder are used to select a column. The total number of decoder output lines with this method is $2^{n/2} + 2^{n/2} = 2^{n/2+1}$, which is a considerable reduction from 2^n for a single address decoder.

Each memory element must now perform the AND operation on the row-select and column-select lines. The memory element at the intersection of the selected row and the selected column produces logic-1 as a result of the AND operation, whereas all other memory elements produce logic-0, since either their row-select line or column-select line is logic-0. The output signal of the AND gate serves as a bit-select line that enables the memory element for reading or writing.

A similar two-dimensional array is needed for each of the bit positions in a memory word, which correspond to the columns in Fig. 6.2. Each array may be considered to lie in a plane parallel to one another. The different planes share the two address decoders, so that all bits in a word location are addressed together. It

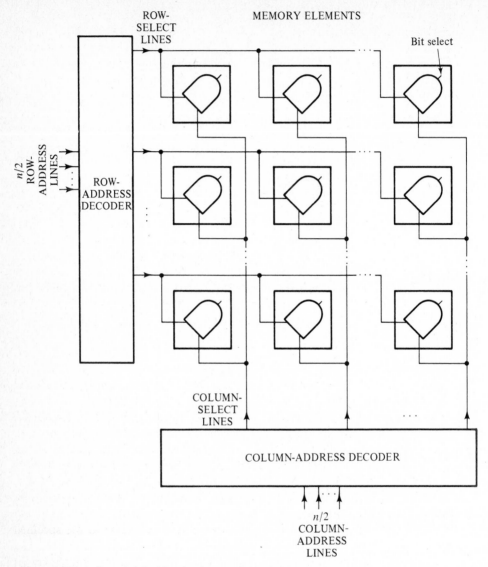

Figure 6.4 Two-dimensional addressing in a random-access memory.

should be noted that this will not cause an increase in the number of decoder output lines.

Memory with Internal Bidirectional Data Lines

Further reduction in the number of interconnections in a random-access memory unit can be achieved by combining the internal data-in lines with the data-out lines of Fig. 6.2. This is done by replacing both data lines for each bit position with a single bidirectional line. During a write operation, information to be entered into the memory is sent over this bidirectional line into the selected location. During a read operation, information from the selected location is sent over this line to the outside. For this purpose wired logic is used in a manner similar to that for data buses as discussed in Chap. 5. The use of wired logic has the additional advantage of eliminating the OR gate that was included in each memory element of Fig. 6.2 to allow the data in the element to be coupled onto the data-out line.

This scheme for a random-access memory unit is illustrated by Fig. 6.5. Included in the figure is the logic network for a memory element, which is modified to allow for two-dimensional addressing and a single bidirectional Data line. In this network the Write line is used to control the direction of data flow on the Data line. When the Write line is at logic-1, it allows the content of the Data line to be transferred into the memory element of the selected location, as before. When the Write line is at logic-0, it allows the content of the selected memory element to be placed onto the Data line. This is done by ANDing the complement of Write with the bit-select line and the output of the flip-flop in each memory element. In this case, a special AND gate is used that is capable of wired OR. The output line of this AND gate is connected to the Data line which effectively ORs its output with that of other such AND gates.

Column Selection with a Data Selector

A variation to this last scheme is very often used for memory units. As can be seen in Fig. 6.6, the variation still involves two-dimensional addressing for each memory element of a word location. However, rather than distinguishing the selected column within the memory elements, the column distinction is made at an edge of the memory array with the use of a special data-selector circuit having bidirectional capability. The row is selected as before. A separate bidirectional line is provided for each column to convey data between the elements of the column and the data selector. For a read operation, the content of each element in the selected row is sent over the respective column line to the data selector. The data selector then selects the bit position of one column according to the specified column address and places the value of this bit onto the output line. For a write operation, on the other hand, the data selector will force the one column line that corresponds to the specified column address to the value appearing on the input line. This forced value overrides the value that would otherwise be placed there by the element in the selected row. Special circuitry in the memory elements allows for this and furthermore to cause the flip-flop in the selected row to take on the forced value as its new state. As a result of using a data selector to access the columns in this way, a further reduction in the number of interconnections is realized, since one line for each column both selects the column and transfers the data.

These schemes just discussed indicate in a general way the manner in which random-access memory units can be made to operate. They include provision for

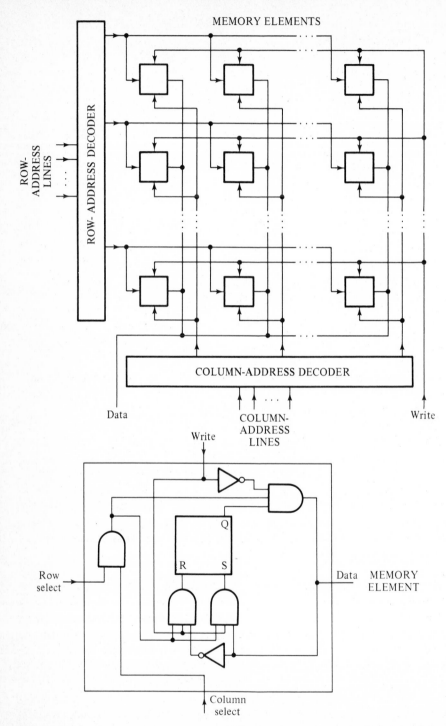

Figure 6.5 Random-access memory using two-dimensional addressing and a bidirectional data line. Plane for one bit position shown.

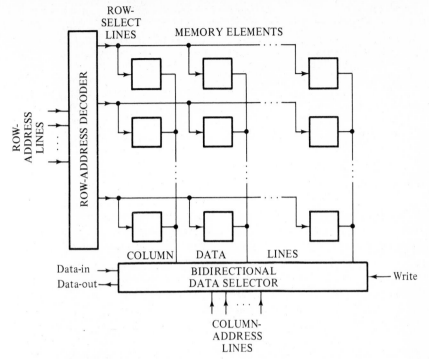

Figure 6.6 Two-dimensional memory array for a single-bit random-access memory, using a data selector to determine the column.

both storing information into a selected location and for receiving information from a selected location. Such memory units are said to be *read/write*. In many situations it is desirable to have only the provision for receiving information from a selected location and not the ability to alter the content of any location. Such units are referred to as *read-only memory*. The implementation of read-only memory will be considered in Sec. 6.3. Let us now consider some particular electronic circuits for the implementation of read/write memory units.

6.2 READ/WRITE MEMORY IMPLEMENTATION

There are two basic categories of circuits used to implement electronic memory units, static and dynamic. A *static* memory circuit is one that is capable of storing information indefinitely as long as power is applied. The flip-flop discussed previously has this property. A *dynamic* memory circuit, on the other hand, is only capable of storing information for a short time. It must, therefore, be periodically *refreshed* to retain information. A charged capacitor can be used as a dynamic memory element. The use of dynamic memory elements such as capacitors leads to a simpler circuit, reduced power drain, and sometimes faster switching speed.

For each of the two read/write memory categories there are many different circuits that are presently used and many more will probably be adopted in the future. The variety of such circuits reflects not only the various technologies (TTL, MOS, CMOS, ECL, etc.) and the way they are developing but also differing requirements for memory units involving such things as speed, density, and power dissipation. For illustration, three particular memory circuits have been chosen as typical examples in this section, but, of course, the details of other particular memory circuits will have to be ascertained from the manufacturers' literature. The examples consist of one each of the three types static TTL, static MOS, and dynamic MOS.

A Static TTL Memory Circuit

Figure 6.7 depicts a particular configuration for a static TTL memory unit. Shown in the figure is the electronic circuit that is used for each memory element. The circuit consists of two transistor stages that are cross-coupled to operate in a bistable manner. Each transistor has two emitters in order to provide for both storage and access. Such a transistor will conduct if either base-emitter junction is sufficiently forward-biased. As a consequence, the state of either transistor is dependent upon which emitter of the two emitters is at the lower potential.

When the row in which a memory element appears is not selected, the corresponding select line is low causing the bottom emitters of the two transistors to be at the lower potential. In this case, the circuit behaves as a bistable device and retains whatever state into which it was last placed. Specifically, if transistor T_1 is conducting, then its collector is pulled low causing the base of transistor T_2 to also be pulled low. T_2 is thus in cutoff, so that its collector, and the base of T_1, is high. The fact that the base of T_1 is high causes T_1 to conduct, as was assumed. Thus this assumed state is stable, i.e., it is self-sustaining. By symmetry, the opposite state, i.e., T_2 conducting and T_1 cutoff, is also stable. It should be seen that this circuit is similar to that of a simple flip-flop composed of two cross-coupled NAND gates. As a matter of fact, each transistor stage of this circuit does perform the function of a two-input NAND gate.

Now if, on the other hand, the row in which the memory element appears is selected, then the corresponding select line is high, causing the emitters on the bottom of each transistor to also be high. Consequently, the conducting state of each transistor will then depend upon its upper emitter. The upper emitter of transistor T_2 is fixed at 1.5 V. Thus the state of the circuit can be altered by adjusting the potential of the upper emitter of transistor T_1 relative to 1.5 V. Specifically, if the Data line, which is connected to the upper emitter of T_1, is pulled low, then T_1 becomes conducting. This is true since the collector voltage of T_2, which is the same as the base voltage of T_1, must be greater than 1.5 V, insuring that the upper base-emitter junction of T_1 is sufficiently forward-biased for T_1 to conduct. When T_1 conducts, it pulls the base of T_2 low, so that T_2 does not conduct. This circuit state is associated with logic-1. The opposite circuit state can be brought about by letting the upper emitter of T_1 be undriven. In that

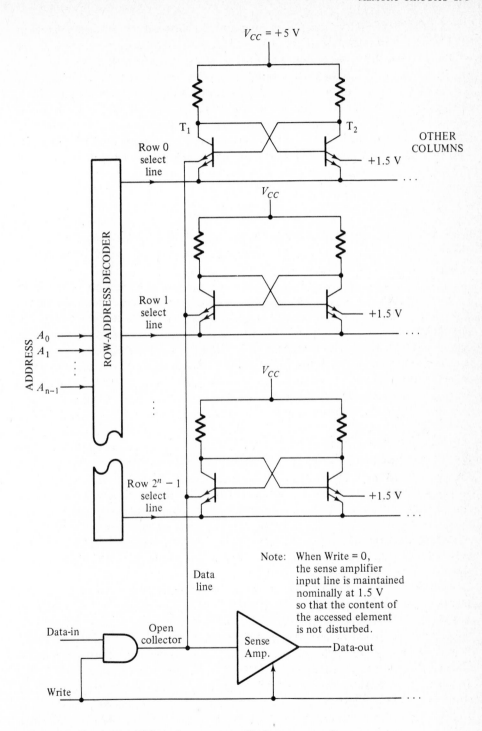

Figure 6.7 Circuit for a TTL random-access read/write memory unit.

case, T_1 does not conduct causing its collector and the base of T_2 to become high. This in turn causes T_2 to conduct. This state is associated with logic-0.

An open-collector NAND gate is provided for each column to drive the Data line that is connected to the upper emitter of all T_1 transistors in the column. One input line of the NAND gate, Data-in, serves as a source of input data for that column, while the other input line of the NAND gate is connected to a Write control line. When Write is at logic-1, then a logic-1 at the Data-in line causes the output of the NAND gate to be low, which will force the selected memory element to go into the 1 state; whereas a logic-0 at the Data-in line causes the output of the open-collector NAND gate to be undriven, which causes the selected memory element to go into the 0 state.

Now if the Write line is placed at logic-0, then a write operation is not to occur, and thus no memory element should change state. Furthermore, when Write is at logic-0, a read operation is to occur. For these two purposes a special current sense amplifier is provided for each column. This sense amplifier is enabled when the Write line is logic-0. When enabled, the sense amplifier maintains the Data line for the elements in its column at a potential close to 1.5 V. This prevents the element in the selected row from changing state, since then both upper emitters will be at the same voltage. Furthermore, the sense amplifier will respond to a current flowing in the Data line and produces a corresponding voltage at the Data-out line. If transistor T_1 of the selected element is conducting, corresponding to a stored 1, the current flows out of its upper emitter, since its bottom emitter is at a higher potential. This current flows through the Data line and into the sense amplifier, which then produces a logic-1 on the Data-out line. For a stored 0 in the selected element, T_1 is not conducting, so no current flows into the sense amplifier. In this case the Data-out line is placed at logic-0.

In summary, a write operation is performed with this memory unit by first specifying an address to select a row. The Write line is then set to logic-1 and the data to be stored is placed onto the Data-in line. The element in the selected row is then forced to the state corresponding to the input data. The elements in the nonselected rows are not affected. A read operation is performed by keeping the Write line at logic-0 and specifying an address to select a row. Only the element in the selected row responds. The state of this element is determined by sensing the current of its transistor T_1. The logic value corresponding to the state of the element appears on the Data-out line.

The columns of such a memory configuration might be connected in two different manners. In one manner they could be made to correspond to different bit positions of a memory word. In this case, the columns behave independently as shown in Fig. 6.7. Alternatively, the columns could be interconnected so that they all correspond to the same bit position of different memory words. For this purpose a bidirectional data selector is used to specify a column for access based on a column address, as was shown in Fig. 6.6.

A Static MOS Memory Circuit

Figure 6.8 depicts a particular configuration for a static MOS memory unit. The circuit for each memory element, like that for the previous example, has the form

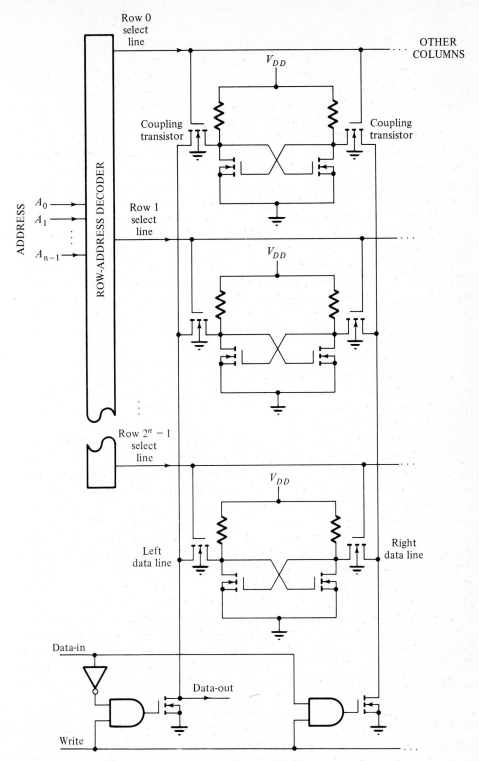

Figure 6.8 Circuit for a static MOS random-access read/write memory unit.

of a bistable device or flip-flop. It involves two cross-coupled transistor stages, which are of course based on MOSFETs rather than bipolar transistors. In the figure, the MOS transistors are of the n-channel normally-off (enhancement-mode) type. However, memory circuits are made that use other types of MOS transistors. The pull-up resistors shown in the circuit are generally implemented as MOS transistors in a fashion similar to that for MOS logic gates.

The major difference between the circuits of Figs. 6.7 and 6.8, in addition to the type of transistor used, is the manner in which the memory elements are accessed. In this MOS memory two complementary data lines are provided for each column to convey information to or from the element in the selected row. The memory elements in each column are coupled to the data lines with n-channel normally off MOS transistors. These coupling transistors act as bilateral switches in the sense that current as well as information can flow in either direction. This is possible since their substrates are connected to ground rather than to the sources. When the gate of such a transistor is made sufficiently positive, it becomes conductive between the source and drain. The transistor conducts in either direction in this case, since the symmetry of such a transistor allows the source and drain to change roles if need be.

The gates of the coupling transistors for each row of memory elements are connected to a corresponding row-select line. The row-select lines are the output lines of an address decoder, as before. Therefore, only those coupling transistors in the selected row, as determined by the specified address to the decoder, are turned on. In this way, information is channeled between the data lines and the selected element in each column.

A write operation is performed by driving low one of the two complementary data lines for each column according to the value of the Data-in input line. This will force the memory element in the selected row to take on the corresponding state. The data lines are driven with MOS transistors. The gate of each driving transistor is connected to the output line of an AND gate, which determines the conditions for when the transistor is to be turned on. The Write control line provides a condition for both driving transistors of each column, whereas the Data-in line provides a condition for the right transistor and the complement of the Data-in line provides a condition for the left transistor. Thus, when Write is logic-1, if Data-in is logic-1, then the gate of the right transistor is high and the right transistor is turned on. This forces the right side of the memory element in the selected row to go low, which, in turn, causes the left side of that element to go high. This stable state corresponds to a stored logic-1. If, on the other hand, Data-in is logic-0 when Write is logic-1, then the left transistor is turned on, causing the selected element to take on the stable state that corresponds to a stored logic-0.

If the Write line is placed at logic-0, then neither driving transistor is turned on and no change in state of the memory elements occurs. The data lines then take on values that correspond to the state of the element in the selected row, since the coupling transistors of that element are turned on. In particular, the left data line has the value that is stored in the selected element. A read operation, therefore, involves just using the value of the left data line when the Write line is placed at logic-0.

A Dynamic MOS Memory Circuit

Figure 6.9 depicts a particular configuration for a dynamic MOS memory unit. The memory elements are based on a storage device comprising a capacitor and one MOS transistor (T_2). This capacitor, shown connected between the gate and source of transistor T_2, is actually the gate-to-substrate capacitance that exists for any MOS transistor because of the parallel alignment of the gate electrode with the substrate. Storage of data in such a memory element is related to the conductive states of T_2, which are determined by the amount of charge of the capacitor. If the capacitor has a charge that causes the voltage on the gate of T_2 to be sufficiently positive, then T_2 is conductive. This state, which is not self-sustaining, since the capacitor will tend to discharge, is associated with logic-0. Otherwise, if the capacitor has a small or no charge, then T_2 is not conductive. This state, which is self-sustaining, is associated with logic-1.

Besides the capacitor and transistor T_2, each memory element has two MOS transistors for coupling the element to data lines. Each column has two data lines, one for writing data into the selected element and the other for reading data from the selected element. Transistor T_1 serves as a bilateral switch to couple the line for writing data (Data-write) to the capacitor of the element. When T_1 is activated, the capacitor may be charged or discharged through the Data-write line. Transistor T_3, on the other hand, couples the line for reading data (Data-read) to the drain of T_2. When T_3 is activated, the state of the element can be sensed with the Data-read line. Both T_1 and T_3 are controlled by the appropriate row-select line from the row-address decoder.

In operation, data is transferred to the capacitor of an element whenever either type of access is made, read or write. For a memory write operation, the data to be transferred to the capacitor comes from the Data-in line. In this case the data replaces whatever information was previously stored. For a memory read operation, the data to be transferred to the capacitor comes from the element itself, which is obtained from the Data-read line. That is, as can be seen in Fig. 6.9, the stored data is fed back whenever a read operation is performed.

For the purpose of selecting the appropriate data to be sent to the capacitor, a data-selector network, comprising four gates, is connected to the Data-write line. This data selector uses the Write line as a control to select either the Data-in line or the Data-read line. An inversion occurs for either source of data, since a high voltage on the capacitor has been defined to correspond to logic-0, which is the opposite of the assumed convention for all data lines.

The conductive state of T_2 of the selected element is converted to a voltage on the Data-read line with the use of a pull-up resistor. When T_2 is conducting, corresponding to a stored logic-0, the Data-read line is forced low. Otherwise, the line is pulled high by the pull-up resistor.

As noted before, the state of an element corresponding to a stored logic-0 is

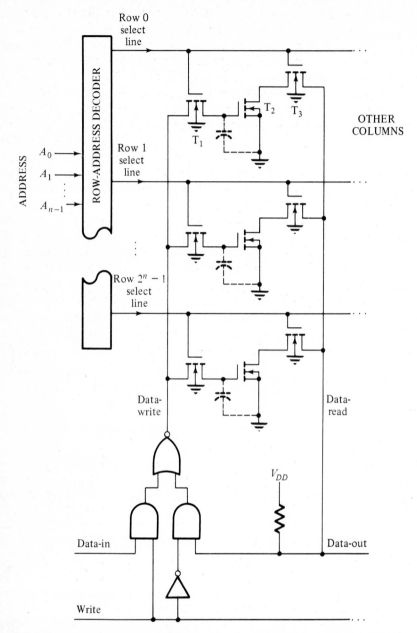

Figure 6.9 Circuit for a dynamic MOS random-access read/write memory unit.

not self-sustaining, since it involves a charged capacitor, which will tend to discharge owing to leakage. After some time the charge of the capacitor reaches a level that can no longer be distinguished from that for a stored logic-1. Before this happens the element should be refreshed, which is done by performing a read operation. Consequently, the use of such dynamic memory units necessitates repetitively refreshing each row within a specified period of time. This period of time is generally on the order of several milliseconds. To keep the number of rows small, dynamic memory units are usually organized with a two-dimensional addressing scheme using a bidirectional data selector to select columns for different words. In this way, fewer refresh operations are necessary, since all words in a row can be refreshed together.

In practice, the refreshing is generally done by a special logic network that is provided in a system consisting of many memory units. The logic network sequences through the rows of all memory units and periodically performs a refresh operation. This usually involves suspending access to the memory units by the computer during the time that a refresh operation is taking place.

It is apparent that the operation of dynamic memory units is more involved and requires considerably more outside circuitry than static memory units. However, they do offer several advantages for some applications that justify this inconvenience. A major advantage is a greater achievable density (bits per unit) owing to the fewer components needed, in general, for a dynamic memory element than for a static memory element. Another advantage is that dynamic memory elements draw no current from the power supply except during the relatively small fraction of time when they are being accessed. This leads to a greatly reduced dissipation of power for the whole memory unit. Quite often the maximum allowable power dissipation is the limiting factor on memory density; so in such cases an even greater density can be achieved with dynamic memory elements.

6.3 READ-ONLY MEMORY

In computer and other digital systems, memory units are often used as a source of information that remains fixed. Examples of such fixed information include lists of constants, tables for data conversion, and fixed computer programs. For such situations, the memory units that are used need not have a provision for altering the stored information by the system in which they are used. Such memory units are available and are referred to as *read-only memory* (ROM). The use of read-only memory units for applications in which the information is not to be altered offers a considerable convenience, since the information will remain unchanged even when the power is removed from the system. In addition to this convenience, much greater memory density can be achieved with read-only memory units, since the memory element circuits can be made much simpler.

The basic structure of a read-only memory unit that has random access may be viewed as consisting of an address decoder connected to a number of OR gates, as depicted by Fig. 6.10. The decoder output lines correspond one-to-one with

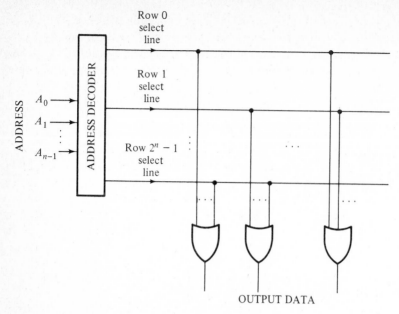

Figure 6.10 Basic structure of a random-access read-only memory unit.

memory locations, as is the case with read/write memory units. Each OR gate corresponds to a bit position of the memory words. The value of a bit of a memory word is specified to be 1 by connecting the corresponding decoder output line to an input line of the corresponding OR gate, otherwise the value is 0. Thus, for example, Fig. 6.10 indicates that the first, second, and last bits of the word in location 0 (i.e., row 0) is $10 \cdots 1$. Similarly, the first, second, and last bits of the words in location 1 and location $2^n - 1$ are $01 \cdots 1$ and $11 \cdots 0$, respectively.

It is interesting to note that since the decoder output lines correspond to the minterms formed from the address bits, the structure of such a read-only memory unit corresponds to the implementation of a multiple-output function in sum-of-minterm form. Consequently, any combinational function or set of functions can be realized with a read-only memory unit.

A read-only memory unit generally has some flexible means for establishing the connections between the row-select lines and the OR gates, so that the unit can be made to contain desired information. The act of putting information into a read-only memory unit is referred to as *programming*. In regard to the means of programming, commercially available electronic read-only memories may generally be categorized into the following three major types:

1. Programmed during manufacture
2. One-time programmable after manufacture by the user
3. Programmable after manufacture with provision for erasing and reprogramming

Provision for programming any of these three types commonly involves some sort of *link*, which may be opened or closed, between each row-select line and an input line of each OR gate. These links are then specified according to the information pattern that is to be programmed into the unit in a manner that depends upon the unit's type.

Manufacturer-Programmed Read-Only Memory

Read-only memory units of the first type are usually programmed as one of the final steps of their manufacture. The links are simply gaps that may be bridged by a final metalization pattern that is placed onto the circuit according to the desired information to be programmed. This is done with a mask that determines the precise pattern, which is custom-made for a particular application. The mask is rather expensive to make but may be used to program any number of units. Consequently, this type of read-only memory is best suited for mass production.

An example of this first type of read-only memory unit using *pn* junction devices is shown in Fig. 6.11. In this example the function of the OR gates is actually performed by diode AND gates on the inversion of the decoder output lines, which according to DeMorgan's law is equivalent to the operation NOR upon the noninverted decoder output lines. A diode is provided for each bit location in the unit. As can be seen a gap occurs in each path between a diode and the common line for a column. A value of 0 is programmed into a particular bit

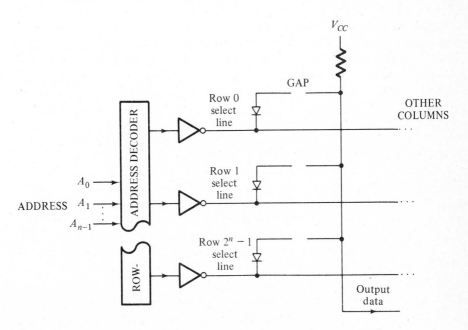

Figure 6.11 Circuit for a mask-programmed *pn* junction read-only memory unit.

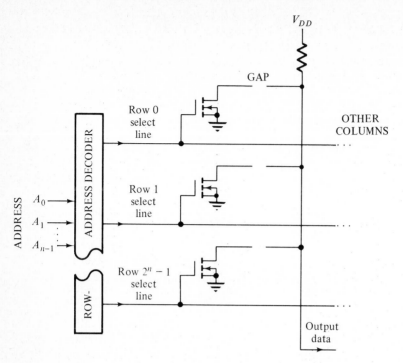

Figure 6.12 Circuit for a mask-programmed NMOS read-only memory unit.

position by bridging the corresponding gap; otherwise, the value of that bit is 1. To see this, notice that the common line of a column is normally pulled high by a resistor and that only the select line corresponding to the specified address can pull it low. If the gap to the diode connected to that select line is left open, then the common line remains high, corresponding to an output of 1. If the gap is closed on the other hand, then the common line is pulled low by the select line, corresponding to an output of 0.

Another example of the first type of read-only memory unit using **MOS** devices is shown in Fig. 6.12. In this example n-channel normally-off MOS transistors are used to perform the operation of NOR upon the decoder output lines. A gap is placed in series with the drain of each transistor. If a particular gap is bridged, the corresponding bit location will contain 0; otherwise, it will contain 1, which is similar to the previous example.

Programmable Read-Only Memory

Read-only memory units of the second type, which can be programmed one time by the user, are usually referred to as *programmable read-only memory* (**PROM**). They generally have a link that after manufacture can be altered one way, either from closed to open or vice versa. The most common way of doing this is to make the link from a fusible metal, such as nickel-chromium, which may be selectively "blown" (i.e., open-circuited) by supplying an external current of sufficient magnitude. An example of such a read-only memory unit is shown in Fig. 6.13. The unit is similar to the previous example of a *pn* junction read-only memory unit, except that nickel-chromium fuses are placed across the gaps and that there is provision

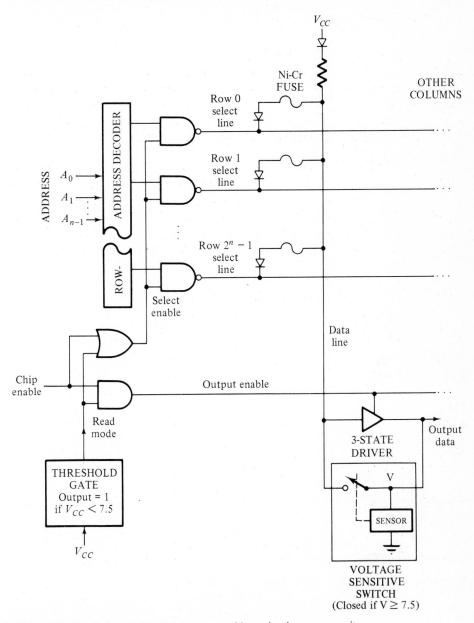

Figure 6.13 Circuit for a fusible-link programmable read-only memory unit.

for each of these fuses to be blown. There are two modes of operation for this unit, *read* and *program*. The mode at any time is determined by the value of the power-supply voltage V_{CC}. For the read mode, V_{CC} is placed at its normal value of 5 V; for the program mode, V_{CC} is raised to 10 V. A threshold circuit is connected to V_{CC} to generate the signal labeled "Read Mode," which is logic-1 when the unit is in the read mode of operation ($V_{CC} < 7.5$). This signal, Read Mode, is used in conjunction with an external signal, Chip Enable, to affect both the enabling of the row-select lines and the enabling of the output data lines.

In the read mode the row-select lines behave precisely the same as in the preceding example of a *pn* junction ROM. As can be seen in the figure, NAND gates are inserted into the row-select lines. The second input line of each of these NAND gates, which is driven by the OR of Chip Enable and the signal Read Mode, will be at logic-1, since Read Mode is at logic-1. In this case, the NAND gates simply invert the decoder outputs. The row-select line corresponding to the specified address is at logic-0, and all other row-select lines are at logic-1.

If the fuse is intact for a column and the selected row, then the data line for that column is forced low (logic-0); otherwise, the data line is pulled high (logic-1) by the pull-up resistor. A 3-state driver is used to couple each column data line to an overall output line labeled "Output Data." These 3-state drivers are controlled by a signal shown labeled " Output Enable," which is the AND of Chip Enable and the signal Read Mode.

For the program mode of operation, V_{CC} is raised to 10 V. This affects the circuit in several ways. It causes the signal Read Mode to go to logic-0, which has two effects. First, the signal Select Enable is made to depend upon the external signal Chip Enable. Thus, the row-select line corresponding to the specified address is logic-0 only if Chip Enable is logic-1. Second, it causes the signal Output Enable to be logic-0, which disables the 3-state output drivers independent of the value of Chip Enable. In addition and most important, the row-select lines that do not correspond to the specified address are raised to approximately 10 V, since the gates that drive them use the power-supply voltage V_{CC} to determine the logic-1 voltage level.

To cause a fuse to be blown, the desired address is specified, the Chip Enable line is then activated to enable the row-select lines, and then a specified current (say 65 mA) is applied from a current source to the appropriate Output Data line. This current passes through a voltage-sensitive switch to the data line of the corresponding column. The switch is a special circuit that closes when the voltage V applied by the current source exceeds a value somewhat higher than the maximum logic-1 level of 5 V. The applied voltage will be sufficiently high if the specified current is made to flow. Once past the switch, the applied current flows through the fuse and diode that are connected to the row-select line that is low (at logic-0). All other row-select lines are at approximately 10 V and therefore draw an insignificant amount of the applied current. This is the reason that V_{CC} was raised to 10 V, to ensure that the other row-select lines do not draw significant current. After a short time the current causes the fuse to melt away. When a sufficient amount of time has passed to allow for this, the Chip Enable line is deactivated. The process may then be repeated for other fuses that are to be blown in the same row and then for other rows.

It is interesting to note that no additional external lines are needed to provide for programming the PROM unit other than the lines that are normally used for reading.

Erasable Programmable Read-Only Memory

The third type of read-only memory unit, which can be programmed, erased, and reprogrammed, is referred to as *erasable programmable read-only memory* (EPROM). This type of unit generally makes use of a link that can be placed into one condition (say closed) on a selective basis and into the other condition (say opened) on a collective basis. Programming such a unit consists of first placing all links collectively into a specific condition, which amounts to erasing any previous information content, and then placing desired links into the opposite state, one at a time.

A notable example of a link that is used in EPROM units consists of a special type of MOS transistor having what is called a *floating gate*. A specific form of such a transistor is that of a *p*-channel normally-off (enhancement-mode) MOS transistor with its gate electrode surrounded by insulation, as shown in Fig. 6.14. The gate has no lead attached to it but may, however, be made to acquire a negative charge, as will be seen. When charged negatively, the gate induces a positive charge into the channel, just as it would if a negative potential with respect to the substrate were applied to the gate. With a positive charge in the channel the transistor is conductive. On the other hand, if the gate has no negative charge, then no positive charge is induced into the channel and the transistor is not conductive.

Negative charge is supplied to the gate by injecting electrons from the drain through the insulation to the gate. This is done by applying a relatively high positive voltage to the source with respect to the drain. The resulting electric field

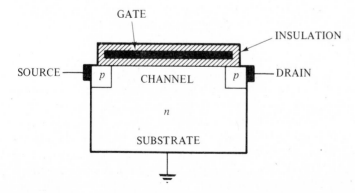

Figure 6.14 Floating-gate PMOS enhancement-mode transistor for EPROM units.

induces a relatively high positive voltage on the gate with respect to the drain. Roughly speaking, this voltage causes a breakdown to occur at the junction between the drain and the insulation, resulting in a flow of rather energetic electrons from the drain into the insulation. Owing to their energetic state, the electrons are able to drift through the insulation to the gate electrode. This electron charge on the gate will remain there almost indefinitely unless specifically removed. Charge is removed from the gate by irradiating the area with ultraviolet light, which imparts sufficient energy to each electron to bring it into a conductive energy band in the insulation. The electrons are then able to flow away from the gate owing to their mutual repulsion.

A read-only memory unit using these special transistors can be structured in a manner similar to the previous example of a MOS ROM, which was shown in Fig. 6.12. In this case, each gap in the unit is bridged with one of these floating-gate transistors. In addition, circuitry is included that allows each floating-gate transistor to be selected for application of the necessary voltage to charge the gate. This selection process involves the address and output-data lines.

To program the resulting EPROM, all links are first opened (corresponding to logic-1) by irradiating the unit with ultraviolet light of sufficient intensity and duration. Then, for those bit positions that are to contain logic-0, the corresponding links are closed one at a time.

6.4 SEQUENTIAL-ACCESS MEMORY

The term sequential access is used to refer to a type of memory system in which the word positions become available for reading or writing only in a certain order. For sequential-access memory, each stored word is not necessarily associated with specific memory elements, but rather with a position that is relative to other stored words. For example, the words may move among the memory elements, but must keep their order while doing so. In this case provision is made for reading the memory elements at one word location. A particular stored word is read by moving stored words through the system until the particular one reaches the set of memory elements that may be read. Likewise, information is written into a particular word position by moving words until the desired word position is at the memory elements that allow writing. Another form of sequential-access memory has the memory elements themselves in motion and the position of the reading and writing mechanism is fixed.

Consider the form of sequential-access memory in which words move among the memory elements. There are two basic types of this form based on the manner in which the words move through the memory elements. In one type, the memory words move in just one direction along a line of memory element sets (each set accommodating one word). Information is written into the set of elements at the upstream end of the line, whereas information is read from the set of elements at the downstream end. Thus, with this type, words become available for reading in the same order that they are written. In the other type of sequential-access

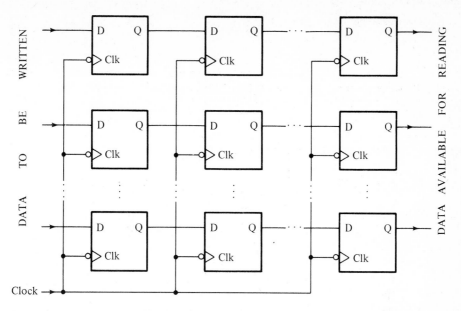

Figure 6.15 Shift-register model for sequential-access memory.

memory, words may move in either direction along a line of memory element sets, and information is written into and read from the same set of elements. Thus, with this second type, words are read in the opposite order in which they were written. Memory systems of this second type are referred to as *stacks* and will be treated in the next section.

A shift register, as discussed in the previous chapter, is a prime example of the first type of sequential-access memory system. As a matter of fact, a group of *m* shift registers operating in unison serve as a useful model for such memory systems having *m*-bit words. As shown in Fig. 6.15, the shift registers consist of interconnected clocked *D* flip-flops with their clock lines tied together. Information to be written is presented to the *D* terminals of the flip-flops at the left end, whereas information is read from the flip-flops at the right end. Each pulse applied to the clock line causes each stored word to move one place to the right, while the information to be written is entered into the left flip-flops. As can be seen, the word in the read position at the right end is lost when a clock pulse occurs.

To make such memory systems more useful for many applications, provision can be made to bring information from the right end around to be stored in the flip-flops at the left whenever outside information is not to be written. This might be accomplished in the manner depicted in Fig. 6.16, which shows the network for one shift register. The network uses a data selector comprising two AND gates and one OR gate, to choose either the content of the right flip-flop or an outside data bit as the data that enters the left flip-flop. The data selector is controlled by a signal labeled "Write." When Write is at logic-1, the outside data is selected

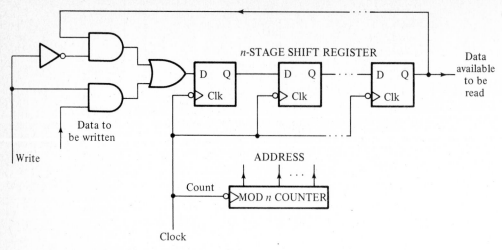

Figure 6.16 Recirculating sequential-access memory.

corresponding to a memory write operation; whereas recirculation occurs when Write is at logic-0.

Some means is generally needed to keep track of the position of each word in the memory. This can be accomplished, as shown in Fig. 6.16, with a counter connected to the clock line. The counter is made to count modulo n, where n is the number of flip-flops in each shift register. The content of the counter is therefore always the same each time a particular word occupies a particular location. Consequently, the content of the counter at any time can be associated with the word that is at the read location. In this way, a particular word to be read can be selected by waiting until its reference number appears in the counter. Furthermore, the content of that word position can then be changed to information from the outside by placing the Write line at logic-1 for the next clock pulse. Thus, the content of the counter serves as an address to be used for either reading or writing.

It is quite apparent that the access of a particular word in a sequential-access memory system requires considerably more time on the average than in a random-access system. Sequential-access memory still plays an important role in microcomputer applications, since its simpler structure leads to higher-density memory units and lower cost per bit.

Sequential-access memory units are available that use flip-flops of just about every common logic family, such as TTL, ECL, MOS, CMOS, etc. There are two notable forms of sequential-access memory units not based, however, on the use of flip-flops that we will now discuss, which show great promise in microcomputer applications. These are *charge-coupled* and *magnetic-bubble* memory devices.

Charge-Coupled Devices

A charge-coupled device (CCD) resembles a shift register except that it is based on the presence or absence of electric charge to represent stored information rather

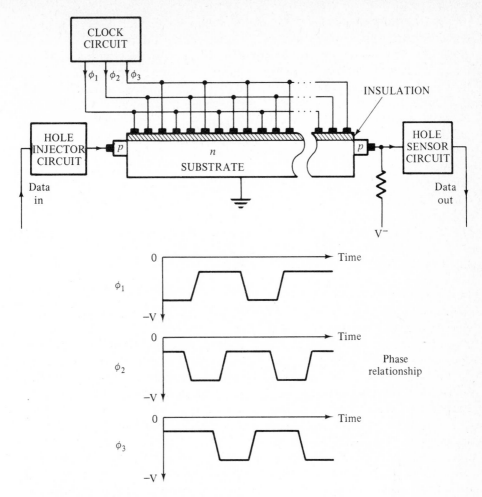

Figure 6.17 Scheme for a charge-coupled device.

than the state of a flip-flop. Charge, in the form of holes or electrons, is made to move along a line from one location to another with the use of electrodes placed at each location. Figure 6.17 depicts one possible arrangement for a charge-coupled device. It consists of a substrate of n-type semiconductor material covered with a layer of insulation upon which are placed many electrodes. The electrodes are connected to three lines such that every third electrode is connected to the same line. Each such line is driven by one phase of a three-phase clock.

In operation, the three phase lines are each biased with a negative voltage with respect to the substrate. This negative voltage causes electrons to be repelled from the region of the n-type semiconductor material adjacent to the insulation surface. Since electrons are the majority charge carrier in n-type semiconductor material, the region will be depleted of charge carriers. Holes (positive charge carriers) representing logic-1 are introduced into the depleted region at the left end. These holes remain in the depleted region rather than disperse into the semiconductor substrate, since they are attracted by the negative bias on the electrodes. At the time holes are introduced, the phase of the electrode closest to that end (phase-1) is made more negative than the other two phases. This causes the positively charged holes to be attracted to that electrode and will therefore stay in position beneath the electrode. These holes are made to move to the second electrode by making its phase the more negative and to move again to the third electrode by making its phase the more negative. This phase sequence is continually repeated causing holes to move step by step along the electrodes. The use of three phases instead of two insures that holes move in the desired direction. Some overlap of the phases is provided to allow time for the migration of the holes. Information is written into the device each time that phase-1 is the more negative, by introducing holes for logic-1 or no holes for logic-0. As information proceeds through the device, the stored bits occur at three-electrode intervals.

Holes are introduced into the device by means of a forward-biased *pn* junction. The junction is formed from a region of *p*-type material placed in contact with the *n*-type substrate. At the other end, holes are detected with a reversed-biased *pn* junction. Any holes present under the last electrode are drawn across the junction to the *p* region because the *p*-type region of the reverse-biased *pn* junction is more negative than the *n*-type region. These holes cause a current to flow through a resistor connected to the *p* region resulting in a corresponding voltage drop across the resistor.

The apparent simplicity in the structure of charge-coupled devices leads to the potential of high density and low cost per bit, making them quite attractive for use in applications of computers, especially microcomputers.

Magnetic-Bubble Memory Devices

Magnetic-bubble memory devices store information by the means of magnetic domains that move within a sheet of magnetic material. Magnetic domains are localized regions of magnetic flux that normally occur in any ferromagnetic material owing to alignment of the magnetized molecules. The presence of such domains is what gives rise to the magnetic field of a permanent magnet. The domains in a thin sheet of ferromagnetic material can be shaped into so-called bubbles by applying an external magnetic field in a direction perpendicular to the sheet. This causes the otherwise randomly shaped domains to constrict into cylinders with a small circular cross section having their axes aligned perpendicular to the sheet. These bubbles are easily moved about with the use of other magnetic fields.

Figure 6.18 depicts a possible configuration for a magnetic-bubble memory device. It includes a thin sheet of magnetic material with a perpendicular field applied from a separate permanent magnet (not shown). Above the surface of the sheet is an array of small *I*- and *T*-shaped pieces of magnetic material of thickness considerably greater than that of the sheet. These *I*- and *T*-shapes are magnetized in a changing manner by magnetic fields applied in a direction parallel to the sheet from two coils. One coil is aligned to produce a field along the axis labeled X, and

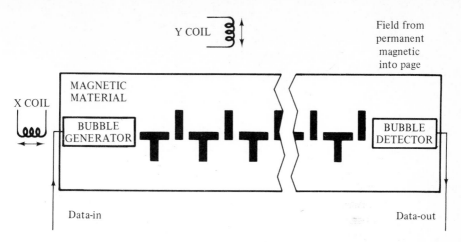

Figure 6.18 Scheme for a magnetic-bubble memory device.

the other coil is aligned to produce a field along the axis labeled Y. In this way, by changing the energization of the two coils, a rotating magnetic field can be produced. If the field produced by either coil is in a direction along an elongated segment of either shape, the segment becomes magnetized with a north pole at the end furthest in the field direction and a south pole at the other end. If it is assumed that each bubble is magnetized with a south pole at the top surface, then a bubble will be attracted to a north pole.

The device is operated in the following manner. Information is written at the left side by forming a magnetic bubble to correspond to logic-1 or no bubble to correspond to logic-0. At this time a magnetic field towards the left is produced by the X coil, causing a north pole to appear at the left end of the top bar of each T. If a bubble was formed during writing, it positions itself at the north pole of the closest T. The Y coil is then gradually energized to produce an upwards field, while the X coil is de-energized. This causes the north pole to move to the center of the top bar of the T pulling the bubble with it. The X coil is then gradually energized in the opposite direction from before, while the Y coil is de-energized. This causes the north pole to move to the right end of the T, and the bubble continues its motion to the right. The Y coil is then gradually energized in the opposite direction from before, while the X coil is de-energized. This causes a north pole to appear at the bottom of each I, which pulls the bubble from the T and onto the adjacent I. This cycle is continually repeated causing bubbles to move among the T- and I-shapes from left to right. Information is read at the right end by detecting the presence or absence of a bubble at appropriate times.

So that information is not lost when it reaches the right, the path is usually made in the form of a loop. Information then circulates around the loop and is read and written at some point in the loop.

Magnetic-bubble memory devices are only economical if they are made to store a relatively large number of bits. However, this would normally lead to an

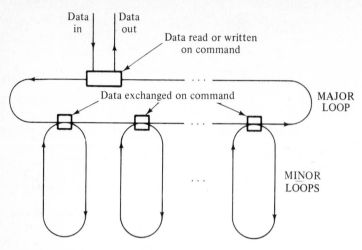

Figure 6.19 Illustration of major and minor loops in a magnetic-bubble memory device.

excessively long average access time. To alleviate this, the single loop can be replaced with many smaller loops in the same unit. In one method, these smaller loops, referred to as *minor loops*, are interconnected with a single loop, referred to as the *major loop*. This is shown schematically in Fig. 6.19.

The major loop serves to convey information between the minor loops and the outside. This is done with a provision that allows information to be exchanged between the major loop and each minor loop at the points where they intersect. Thus, information can be stored into the minor loops by first entering it into the major loop, a bit at a time. Then, when the bits are positioned at the desired minor loops, an exchange is made. Likewise, information stored in the minor loops can be obtained by first waiting until the desired bit of each minor loop is positioned at the major loop and then causing an exchange. The information can then be read from the major loop, a bit at a time.

The use of such magnetic-bubble devices requires an extensive amount of external circuitry to keep track of the position of information and to control the various functions that are involved. They do, however, have an important advantage over the other types of read/write memory discussed so far in that they are nonvolatile; i.e., stored information is not lost when power is removed. This is true, because the bubbles remain intact without power and their position is fixed, since the T- and I-shapes will remain magnetized. However, to be able to use the information when power is reapplied, it is necessary to know the arrangement of the information. This can be accomplished by always arranging the information in a specific way before power is removed from the device.

Queue Memories

The transfer of information between components of a microcomputer or other digital system is an important concern. Situations often arise in which information is sent at varying rates from one component to another component that can only accept such information at or below a prescribed rate. To reconcile such differences in data rate for the two components, a storage device known as a *queue memory* may be used. A queue memory is a form of sequential-access memory in which words are written and read in the same order but at rates independent of each other. They are sometimes commercially referred to as *first-in first-out* (FIFO) memories.

A general scheme for a queue memory is depicted in Fig. 6.20. It consists of a number of registers connected together in a line. Each register is capable of storing one memory word. Each register has an associated flag that indicates with logic-1 when that register is full (i.e., contains a stored word). Separate strobe lines are provided for entering and removing words. As a word is entered into the queue at the left, it moves toward the right until it reaches the last empty register. At this point the word remains in the register and the flag for the register is changed to logic-1. The flag for the leftmost register serves to indicate when the entire queue is filled, in which case no more words may be entered until some are removed. When a word is removed from the queue, it vacates the rightmost register. The flag of the rightmost register is then reset to indicate that the register is empty. This causes the content of the next register and subsequently of all other full registers to move towards the right to fill up the vacancy. If the flag of the rightmost register remains reset, it indicates that the entire queue is empty. In this case, no more words may be removed until some are entered.

A queue memory is often useful as a storage buffer between a computer and a peripheral device. In the case of an output device the computer can then output information as it is determined without concern for the rate in which the device can accept the information, provided that the capacity of the queue is not exceeded.

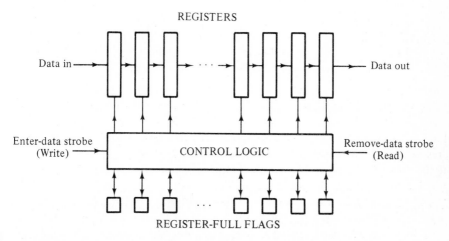

Figure 6.20 Scheme for a queue memory (FIFO).

Magnetic-Surface Memory Systems

An important class of memory systems is the *magnetic-surface* memory systems. These include magnetic drums, magnetic disk drives, and magnetic tape units. Information is stored in each of these by altering the magnetization at locations on the surface of some magnetic material. Reading or writing at a particular location is done by mechanically moving the surface past read and write heads. In some cases, a form of *saturation recording* is used in which extremes of magnetization represent the two logic values. In other cases, a form of *waveform modulation*, including frequency and phase modulation, of the magnetization is used to represent the two logic values. Of the two, saturation recording leads to the greater storage density. However, saturation recording is more subject to errors owing to surface imperfections and consequently requires greater control in the manufacture of the particular magnetic medium.

Although all magnetic-surface memory systems are classified generally as sequential-access memories, their individual means of access vary considerably. Magnetic tape units, in particular, have several different accessing methods. Cassette tape units store bits at locations along a single track on the tape. Words are formed as fixed-length bit sequences. The bit locations are encountered one at a time as the tape is moved past read and write heads. Thus, a cassette tape unit has access that is both bit-sequential and word-sequential. On the other hand, an industrial standard form of tape has seven or nine parallel tracks to store bits. Separate read and write heads are provided for each track. Thus, a 7- or 9-bit word can be accessed at one time with such tape units.

Magnetic drums and disks are similar to each other in that they both have many concentric tracks on a magnetic surface. The surface of a drum is the outside of a cylinder, and the surface of a disk is its face. In some cases, each track has a read/write head. In other cases, just one read/write head is provided that can be moved from one track to another. The surface is rotated past the head or heads at a constant speed. Thus, the information on each track, which is generally grouped into many words, is accessed sequentially. To access a particular word, both the location of the word on a track and the track itself must be accessed. If a read/write head is provided for each track, then the system has random access to the different tracks. If, on the other hand, just one read/write head is provided, then the system has sequential access to the different tracks.

6.5 MEMORY STACKS

A stack is a type of sequential-access memory system in which words are read in the reverse order than which they were written, i.e., last-in first-out. It may be thought of as a vertical array of word-storage locations, as shown in Fig. 6.21. All access is done through the top location. When a word is written into the top location, the word that occupied that location and the words of all other locations are each moved down one (the content of the bottom location is lost). This is referred to as *pushing* the stack. The reverse of this, in which the word at each

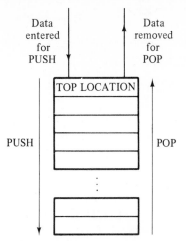

Figure 6.21 Scheme of a memory stack.

location is moved up one, can also be performed and is referred to as *popping* the stack. Popping the stack removes the word occupying the top location and replaces it with the word in the second top location, which may then be read.

The structure of a memory stack may be represented by a group of bidirectional shift registers, one for each bit column of Fig. 6.21, operating in unison. One such shift register is shown in Fig. 6.22. It consists of a number of flip-flops controlled by two lines, Clock and Shift direction. Each time a pulse occurs on the Clock line the content of each flip-flop is transferred to an adjacent flip-flop in the direction determined by the Shift-direction line. A stack push operation corresponds to a shift in one direction, whereas a stack pop operation corresponds to a shift in the other direction.

There are a number of applications for which memory stacks play a natural role. These generally include any use of memory in which words are not to be selected on the basis of an assigned address but rather on their relative order. For example, operands to be used at different points in a calculation could be entered into a stack in the opposite order in which they are to be used. Popping the stack then causes the operands to appear in their proper order.

Memory stacks play an especially important role for microcomputers in keeping track of return addresses and saving data for subroutines. Their use for this purpose leads to a considerable simplification when one subroutine calls another that might call another and so on. In this situation, each time a subroutine is called, the return address and any data to be saved are pushed into the stack. All such information will then be in the proper order to be used as needed in returning from the subroutines.

Simulated Stacks

Many microprocessors simulate the behavior of a memory stack with the use of random-access memory, rather than use a shift-register stack. The random-access

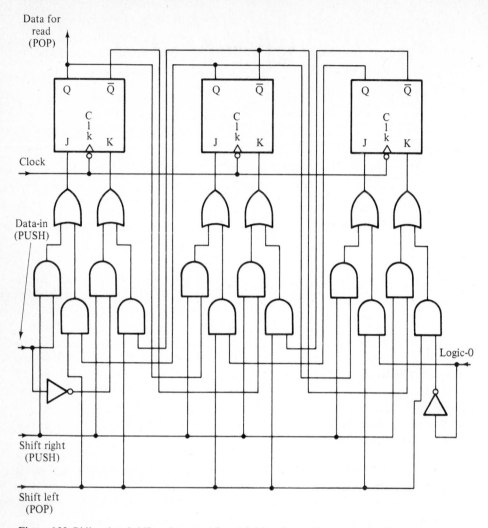

Figure 6.22 Bidirectional shift register used for each bit column of a memory stack.

memory that is used is generally a portion of the main memory. This offers additional flexibility, since the portion of main memory that is used as the stack can be varied as information is pushed into the stack. In this way, the capacity of the stack is only limited by the size of the main memory. Furthermore, this eliminates the need for providing space for a stack within the microprocessor itself.

To simulate a stack in random-access memory, a binary up-down counter is used. This counter is referred to as the *stack pointer*. The content of the stack pointer at any time is assumed to be an address of a location in the random-access memory that is associated with the top of the stack. The stack pointer is initially set at the address of a specific memory location. When a word is to be pushed into the stack, it is written into the location addressed by the stack pointer and then the stack pointer is decremented. When a word is popped from the stack, the stack pointer is incremented and then the word is read. In this way, the stack grows as words are entered and shrinks as words are removed. The stack pointer indicates the address of the next available location for writing. There are minor variations to this, mainly involving the way the stack pointer is changed.

When a simulated stack is used by a microprocessor, the stack pointer is generally included in the microprocessor. In this case, the stack pointer is automatically incremented or decremented for any stack operation that is to take place in the execution of a program instruction. The instructions affecting the stack generally include subroutine calls, subroutine returns, and explicit push and pop instructions.

PROBLEMS

6.1 Consider a model for a read/write random-access memory unit that uses a three-dimensional addressing scheme. In the model, three address decoders are to be used for selecting a memory word.

(a) Draw a diagram, such as in Fig. 6.4, showing the manner in which the select lines from the decoders are connected to the memory elements for one bit position in each word.

(b) Draw a logic network representing a memory element for this model. The element should be based on an unclocked SR flip-flop and should have separate data lines for input and output.

(c) Determine the number of word-select lines as a function of n (the total number of address lines).

6.2 Suppose that a two-dimensional addressing scheme (two address decoders) is to be used in a TTL read/write memory unit. Can the circuit for the memory elements used in the memory unit of Fig. 6.7 be easily modified to accommodate such a scheme? If so, draw a circuit for a modified element and explain its operation.

6.3 Show how the circuit for a memory element of the MOS read/write memory unit of Fig. 6.8 might be modified to accommodate a two-dimensional addressing scheme.

6.4 Draw a diode read-only memory unit that is programmed to implement the two functions c_{i+1} and s_i of a full adder.

6.5 One use of a memory stack is to provide operands in a proper order to an arithmetic unit so that a specified arithmetic expression can be evaluated. Suppose that an arithmetic unit, which is capable of performing the four basic operations (addition, subtraction, multiplication, and division), is connected to a memory stack, as shown in Fig. P6.5. The top stack location supplies the right-hand operand for any of the four operations to be performed by the arithmetic unit. Also, the left-hand operand is supplied by a separate register, which receives information from the top location of the stack when a stack pop operation is executed. Finally, the results of the last arithmetic operation, which are held in the arithmetic unit, are transferred to the top location of the stack when a stack push operation is executed.

Specify a sequence of operations (add, subtract, multiply, divide, push, and pop) and the order in which the operands (a, b, c, d, e) should initially appear in the stack so that the following arithmetic expression may be evaluated

$$\frac{a \times (b + c) - d}{e}$$

6.6 A certain read/write random-access memory unit has six address lines and eight bidirectional data lines. How many storage bits does it include altogether?

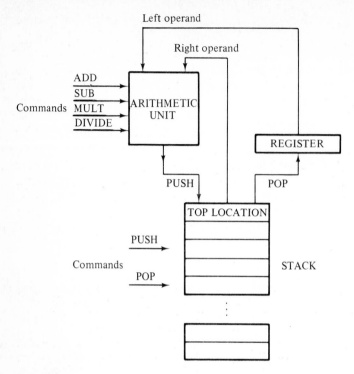

Figure P6.5.

It is desired to have a memory unit having the same number of bits, but with a word length chosen to minimize the total number of address and data lines. Determine the number of address lines and the number of data lines for the minimal unit.

Is there a second solution? If so, what is it?

6.7 Suppose that for a certain application a random-access memory system is needed that consists of 1024 8-bit words. Design such a system from memory units that are of size 256 words by 4 bits and characterized by the model of Fig. 6.1a. The overall memory system should also be characterized by the same model.

6.8 Suppose that a memory unit that fits the model of Fig. 6.1b (separate data lines) is needed but that only a memory unit of the form of Fig. 6.1a (bidirectional data lines) is available. With appropriate gates, show how the desired conversion can be made. Also, show how the opposite conversion can be made.

6.9 An engineer has acquired a number of memory units that were miswired during manufacture. The engineer knows that they are random-access read/write memory units of the form of Fig. 6.1a but that the address lines and the data lines had been mixed up and therefore do not agree with the published specifications. The engineer does know, however, which set of lines is for address and which for data, and also the function of both control lines. Are these units of any use to the engineer? Explain.

A MICROPROCESSOR ARCHITECTURE

Up to this point, emphasis has been on concepts that apply to the general study of digital systems. In the remaining chapters of this book, we will direct our efforts to the study of the operation and utilization of microprocessors and microcomputers.

Many microprocessors are at present commercially available. Each of them has its own distinct characterization. Rather than try to discuss the operation of all of them, an illustrative microprocessor will be defined having an *architecture*, i.e., structure and language, that is typical. In this way, emphasis can be placed on the fundamental aspects of microprocessor operations and applications without getting involved with the particular aspects of many different microprocessors. Although the illustrative microprocessor is not commercially available as such, it does have similarities to commercially existing microprocessors as, for example, the Intel 8000 series processors.

In Chap. 1, the basic organization and operation of a microcomputer were described. Rather than reiterate that discussion here, the reader should review Secs. 1.3 to 1.5 in Chap. 1 at this time, so that the overall operation and organization of a microcomputer is well understood. This will establish the framework for the illustrative microprocessor of this chapter.

7.1 THE MICROCOMPUTER

A microcomputer is a bus-oriented system of subassemblies that are implemented utilizing the technology of large-scale integration. Functions of these subassemblies provide for manipulation of information, ordering the sequence of instruction

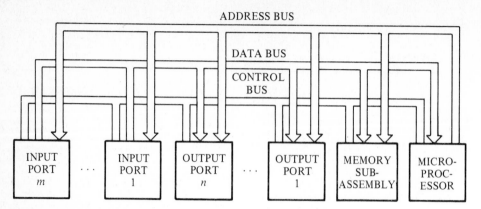

Figure 7.1 A microcomputer bus structure.

execution, interpretation of instructions, control and timing of bus operation, storage of instructions and data, and communication between the computer and the external environment. The first four of these functions are frequently handled by a single subassembly known as a microprocessor. The storage function is handled by a memory subassembly. This subassembly may consist of read-only memory and/or read/write memory. Finally, the external communication is performed by a set of subassemblies known as input and output ports. Each port provides an interface between the microprocessor and some external device, such as a terminal, a mass-storage unit, a process controller, or a measuring instrument. A possible structure for a microcomputer utilizing these subassemblies is shown in Fig. 7.1. Buses interconnecting the subassemblies provide a means for their interaction. In this structure, three buses are used—address, data, and control. Ensuing discussions will assume this structure, although other bus structures are possible.

7.2 STRUCTURE OF AN ILLUSTRATIVE MICROPROCESSOR

The general structure of an illustrative microprocessor is shown in Fig. 7.2. It consists of logical components that enable it to function as a programmable logic processor. Some of the components, i.e., the program counter, stack, and instruction register, provide for the management of a program. Other components, i.e., the ALU, carry flip-flop, scratchpad, and data-address register, provide for the manipulation of data. The remaining components, i.e., the decoder and the timing and control unit, specify and coordinate the operation of the other components. Internal pathways interconnect the components to provide for transferring data between designated components. Connection of the microprocessor to other units (memory and I/O devices) is done with the Address, Data, and Control buses.

This microprocessor operates with words consisting of bits that are grouped into units of eight. Eight-bit units, referred to as *bytes*, are manageable and convenient as arithmetic and logic operands and represent one of the more common

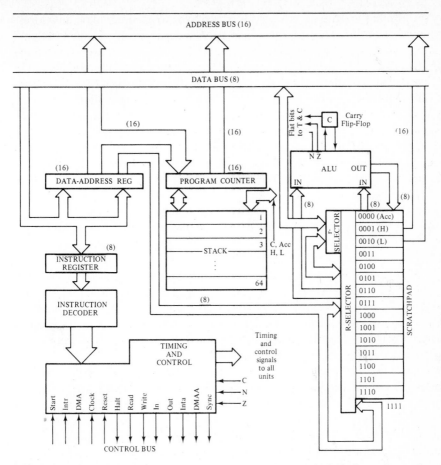

Figure 7.2 An illustrative microprocessor. The numbers in parentheses indicate the number of bits or lines.

data word lengths of commercially available microprocessors. Therefore, all data words will be assumed to be 8 bits long. Computations that require greater lengths are easily accommodated with multiple-precision programming.

On the other hand, an 8-bit address can only make direct reference to $2^8 = 256$ memory locations. Clearly, to accommodate real applications this is too restrictive. Therefore, in keeping with units of 8 bits, it is more convenient to have 16 bits for a memory address. This allows a total of $2^{16} = 65,536$† directly addressable memory locations.

Information is transferred to and from the microprocessor via the Address, Data, and Control buses. The Data bus consists of eight lines to accommodate a

---

† 65,536 is frequently designated as 64K. In computer terminology, the upper-case letter K denotes the quantity $2^{10} = 1024$.

data word, while the Address bus consists of 16 lines to accommodate an address for memory. In addition, as indicated in Fig. 7.1, the Address bus is unidirectional while the Data bus is bidirectional. The Control bus consists of five lines into the timing and control section of the microprocessor and eight outgoing lines. On these lines, control and timing information is conveyed between the microprocessor and the other component parts of a microcomputer system.

The microprocessor has a 16-bit *program counter* that holds the address of the next instruction byte to be fetched from memory. It is automatically incremented after each instruction byte is fetched. This program counter is connected to the top element of a 64-register push-down *stack*. One function of this stack is to save return addresses for subroutines. The stack can also save data from the top three scratchpad registers and carry flip-flop.

Whereas data words consist of a single byte, instruction words can consist of one, two, or three bytes. An *instruction register* is provided to accept the first byte of every instruction via the Data bus from memory. This first byte is presented to an *instruction decoder*, which determines the nature of the instruction. The instruction decoder determines, among other things, whether the instruction consists of more than 1 byte. In this case the additional bytes are transferred via the Data bus from memory to either the data-address register or one of the scratchpad registers.

The *data-address register* is used to hold the address of an operand for a memory reference instruction, the port designator for an input/output instruction, or the next address for a jump instruction.

A *scratchpad* memory consisting of fifteen 8-bit registers is provided to hold operands for all data operations. These registers are designated by a 4-bit code, 0000 through 1110. Register 0000 is referred to as the *accumulator* (Acc) and is used in every arithmetic or logic operation. In particular, the accumulator holds one of the operands prior to an operation and receives the result after the completion of the operation. Normally, access to and from the scratchpad memory is via the *R-selector* or *r-selector*. The R-selector is capable of referencing all the scratchpad registers, while the r-selector is only capable of referencing scratchpad registers 0000, 0001, and 0010.

A useful programming feature frequently found in computers is indirect addressing. This illustrative microprocessor implements a variation of indirect addressing.† The scratchpad register designation 1111 is used to indicate that a location in main memory is being referenced and is given by the 16-bit number formed from the content of two specific scratchpad registers. In particular, the high-order portion of the address is given by the content of scratchpad register 0001, which will be referred to as register H, while the low-order portion is given by the content of scratchpad register 0010, which will be referred to as register L. To illustrate this type of indirect addressing, assume that scratchpad register 0001, i.e., register H, contains 10111101 and scratchpad register 0010, i.e., register L,

---

† This indirect addressing variation is incorporated in the Intel 8080. Indirect addressing will be discussed in detail in Sec. 7.6.

contains 00101011. An instruction that refers to scratchpad register 1111 would cause an operand to be fetched from main memory location 1011110100101011.

All arithmetic and logic operations are performed in the *arithmetic-logic unit* (ALU). The ALU has two 8-bit input buses. One of the input buses comes from the accumulator (scratchpad register 0000) and the other comes from the R-selector that selects any one of the scratchpad registers 0000 through 1110 or a location in memory when the above indirect addressing scheme is used. An additional input line to the ALU comes from a single *carry flip-flop C*, which is used in certain arithmetic and logic operations. The results from the ALU are transferred over an 8-bit bus to the accumulator. The two additional lines emanating from the ALU and going to the timing and control unit indicate two special conditions: the accumulator contains all 0s (indicated by the status line Z) and the most-significant accumulator bit is 1 (indicated by the status line N). This second condition is useful when signed numbers in 2's-complement form are being processed. In this case the most-significant accumulator bit is the sign bit where a 1 indicates a negative quantity. The state of the carry flip-flop and the two status lines from the accumulator are *flag bits* that are used in conjunction with the conditional-jump instructions.

The final component of the microprocessor is the *timing and control unit*. The timing and control unit receives signals from the instruction decoder to determine the nature of an instruction to be executed. Also, as mentioned above, signals from the ALU and the carry flip-flop are sent to the unit to determine jump conditions. Timing and control signals are sent from the unit to all other units in the microprocessor in order to effect the execution of instructions. Thirteen external signals are connected to the timing and control unit to provide for a control interface to other modules in a microcomputer system. The purpose of these signals will be explained in the following section.

7.3 TIMING AND EXTERNAL CONTROL OF THE ILLUSTRATIVE MICROPROCESSOR

In general, a microprocessor is made up of flip-flops and combinational gates, which together operate in a synchronous fashion. The flip-flops, which comprise the registers and flags of the microprocessor, are connected to a common clock line that is driven externally by a periodic pulse source. Thus, any changes in the content of the registers or flags are confined to times that correspond to occurrences of pulses on the clock line.

The particular changes that occur in the contents of the registers and flags are determined by combinational circuits based upon the current contents of the registers and flags and upon the values of external signals. This scheme is depicted by Fig. 7.3. The combinational circuits perform functions that correspond to data transfers between registers, data manipulation, status maintenance, decision making, etc. Because of the complexity of some of these functions, the combinational circuits consist of many gate levels, resulting in a significant amount of

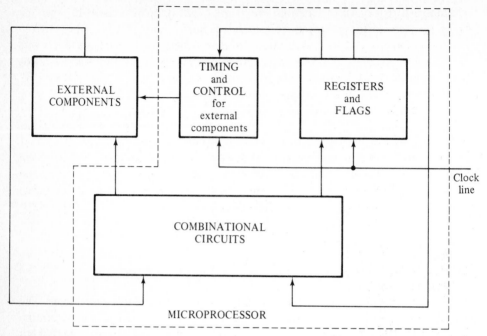

Figure 7.3 General scheme for the behavior of a microcomputer.

delay. The clock rate is adjusted so that there is sufficient time between the pulses to allow for both the time necessary for flip-flops to change state in response to a pulse and the time necessary for the worst-case delay in the combinational circuits.

A microcomputer consists of a microprocessor and components external to the microprocessor whose connections also are indicated in the scheme of Fig. 7.3. These external components generally include addressable memory and input/output devices. Information is transferred between the external components and the microprocessor over the buses in a synchronous fashion.

In the illustrative microprocessor of this chapter, an incoming control line labeled "Clock" is used to supply the clock pulses for timing purposes. Two clock-pulse periods are allocated to complete a data transfer involving an external component. This is to allow time for the operation of the buses and time for the external components themselves to respond. As a matter of fact, since all external transfers make use of common buses, they represent the major limitation in the speed of operation of the microprocessor. For this reason the basic timing of the microprocessor is organized around the transfer of information between the microprocessor and the external components. The sequence of clock pulses is broken into three clock-pulse periods, referred to as *machine cycles*. Exactly one external data transfer takes place for each machine cycle, when the microprocessor is running. The first and second clock pulses of a machine cycle are used to accomplish an external data transfer and possible internal processing, while the third clock pulse is used for any internal processing that must be done between successive external data transfers.

All the external data transfers make use of the Address and Data buses and may be placed into two categories, incoming and outgoing. External transfers of each category have a similar timing relationship with regard to signals on the buses. There are two types of outgoing external transfers. One involves the main memory, referred to as the *write* transfer, and another involves the output devices, referred to as the *output* transfer. There are three types of incoming external transfers. Two of them, referred to as the *read* transfer and the *input* transfer, involve, respectively, main memory and input devices. The third incoming transfer type concerns interrupts, which will be treated in Chap. 9.

Four control lines from the microprocessor—Write, Out, Read, and In—are used to specify which, if any, type of transfer occurs and its timing. Figure 7.4a

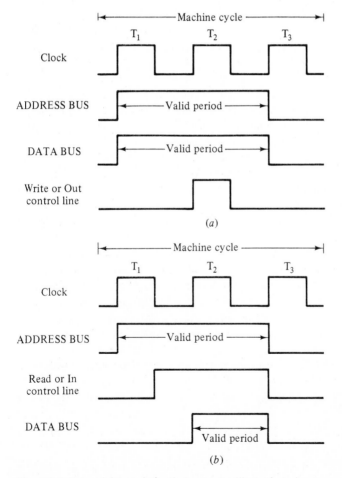

Figure 7.4 External data-transfer timing for the illustrative microprocessor. (*a*) Timing for outgoing data transfers. (*b*) Timing for incoming data transfers.

shows the timing relationship among the various signals during a machine cycle for which an outgoing data transfer occurs. The microprocessor specifies both the content of the Address bus, corresponding to a 16-bit memory address for a write transfer or an 8-bit device code for an output transfer, and the content of the Data bus. The contents of both buses are assumed to be valid, i.e., the information on the buses is correct and unchanging, during the time from the leading edge of pulse T_1 to the leading edge of pulse T_3.† For a write transfer, a pulse will occur on the Write control line coincident with T_2, which is used to strobe the content of the Data bus into the location of main memory that is addressed by the content of the Address bus. For an output transfer, a pulse will occur on the Out control line coincident with T_2, which is used to strobe the content of the Data bus into a register of the output device that has the 8-bit designator corresponding to the content of the low-order half of the Address bus.

Figure 7.4*b* shows the timing relationship among the various signals for an incoming data transfer. The content of the Address bus is specified by the microprocessor for the same time and manner as for an outgoing transfer. The content of the Data bus is, however, specified by the external component. The appropriate control line, Read or In, is set to logic-1 during the time between the trailing edge of T_1 to the leading edge of T_3, as a request to an external component to place data onto the Data bus. The Read line is used by the main memory, whereas the In line is used by the input devices. In each case the content of the Data bus is assumed to be valid during the time between the leading edges of T_2 and T_3 and is strobed into an appropriate register of the microprocessor at the time of the trailing edge of T_2.

Besides the control signals of the microprocessor mentioned so far, there are eight others—Start, Reset, Halt, Sync, Intr, Inta, DMA, and DMAA. The latter four concern program interrupts and direct memory access and will be discussed in detail in Chap. 9. Consider the first four of these control lines. Start is an input line to the microprocessor that is used to put it into a running mode. In particular, when a pulse appears on the Start line, program execution will begin with the next clock pulse at the location specified by the content of the program counter. Reset is an input line to the microprocessor that is used to put it into an initial state. In particular, when a pulse appears on the Reset line, program execution is terminated, the program counter is reset to zero, and the interrupt flag (to be discussed in Chap. 9) is reset. Halt is an output line from the microprocessor that indicates a logic-1 whenever the microprocessor is not executing instructions. Finally, Sync is an output line from the microprocessor that produces a pulse coincident with the third clock pulse of each machine cycle, which is used in some cases to synchronize external components to the machine-cycle timing of the microprocessor.

---

† In Fig. 7.4 the valid period of the Address and Data buses is indicated. The actual signal values on the lines of the buses will depend, of course, upon the specific address and data.

Table 7.1 Notation used in describing the instructions of Table 7.2

Notation	Description
( )	Content of
r	A 2-bit code that designates one of the scratchpad registers 0000, 0001, or 0010 (i.e., Acc, H, or L) by 00, 01, or 10, respectively
R	Any scratchpad register designator 0000 through 1111
d	Data-transfer direction indicator, 0 denotes "to" and 1 denotes "from"
→	Is transferred to
Acc	Accumulator, i.e., scratchpad register 0000
Acc_i	Bit position i of accumulator in the order of significance, $i = 0, 1, \ldots, 7$
C	Carry flip-flop
H	Scratchpad register 0001
L	Scratchpad register 0010
HL	Scratchpad register pair H and L
M	Location in main memory whose address is (H)(L); it has the scratchpad designation 1111
$\langle B_2 \rangle$	Second byte of an instruction
$\langle B_3 \rangle$	Third byte of an instruction
M[X]	Main memory location having the address X
PC	Program counter
$Stack_i$	Stack register i
$StackL_2$	Lower half of stack register 2
$StackH0_2$	Least-significant bit position of upper half of stack register 2
+	Arithmetic addition
∧	Logical AND
∨	Logical OR

7.4 AN INSTRUCTION REPERTOIRE

Microprocessors normally have a fixed set of distinct instructions that they are capable of performing. Clearly, such an instruction set differs from microprocessor to microprocessor. The details of the instruction set for our illustrative microprocessor are given by Tables 7.1 and 7.2. (Table 7.2 appears on pages 230–238.) For each instruction, the symbolic form, format, and symbolic and verbal descriptions are included. These are the only instructions that this microprocessor can perform; hence, any task that the microprocessor will be called upon to do must be described by a sequence of these instructions.

Table 7.2 Instruction repertoire for an illustrative microprocessor

Note: All transfers leave the source register unchanged unless otherwise specified.

MOVE INSTRUCTIONS

Instruction: MOVE
Symbolic form: MOV r to R   or   MOV r from R

Format:

0	r	d	R

Description: $(r) \xrightarrow{d=0} R$ or $(R) \xrightarrow{d=1} r$

If $d = 0$, then the content of scratchpad register r is transferred into scratchpad register R. If $d = 1$, then the content of scratchpad register R is transferred into scratchpad register r.

IMMEDIATE INSTRUCTIONS

Instruction: LOAD REGISTER IMMEDIATE
Symbolic form: LRI R

Format:

0	1	1	0	R	First byte
Data					Second byte

Description: $\langle B_2 \rangle \to R$

The second byte of the instruction is transferred into scratchpad register R.

MEMORY REFERENCE INSTRUCTIONS

Instruction: LOAD REGISTER
Symbolic form: LDR r

Format:

0	1	1	1	0	0	r	First byte
High-order address							Second byte
Low-order address							Third byte

Description: $(M[\langle B_2 \rangle \langle B_3 \rangle]) \to r$

The content of the main memory location whose address has the second byte as the high-order 8 bits and the third byte as the low-order 8 bits is transferred into scratchpad register r.

Instruction: STORE REGISTER
Symbolic form: STR r

Format:

0	1	1	1	0	1	r	First byte
High-order address							Second byte
Low-order address							Third byte

Description: $(r) \to M[\langle B_2 \rangle \langle B_3 \rangle]$

The content of scratchpad register r is transferred into the main memory location whose address has the second byte as the high-order 8 bits and the third byte as the low-order 8 bits.

Table 7.2 (*Continued*)

JUMP INSTRUCTIONS

Instruction: JUMP ON CARRY NOT-ZERO
Symbolic form: JCN

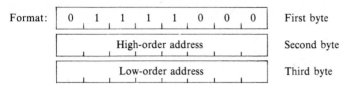

Format:

| 0 | 1 | 1 | 1 | 1 | 0 | 0 | 0 | First byte |

| High-order address | Second byte |

| Low-order address | Third byte |

Description: If (C) = 1, then $\langle B_2 \rangle \langle B_3 \rangle \rightarrow PC$

If the carry flip-flop contains a 1, then the content of the program counter is replaced by the second and third bytes of the instruction, where the second byte becomes the high-order 8 bits and the third byte becomes the low-order 8 bits of the program counter, thus effecting a jump to that location. Otherwise, the second and third bytes are ignored, and the next instruction in sequential order is executed.

Instruction: JUMP ON CARRY ZERO
Symbolic form: JCZ

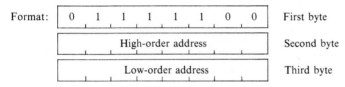

Format:

| 0 | 1 | 1 | 1 | 1 | 1 | 0 | 0 | First byte |

| High-order address | Second byte |

| Low-order address | Third byte |

Description: If (C) = 0, then $\langle B_2 \rangle \langle B_3 \rangle \rightarrow PC$

If the carry flip-flop contains a 0, then the content of the program counter is replaced by the second and third bytes of the instruction, where the second byte becomes the high-order 8 bits and the third byte becomes the low-order 8 bits of the program counter, thus effecting a jump to that location. Otherwise, the second and third bytes are ignored, and the next instruction in sequential order is executed.

Instruction: JUMP ON ACCUMULATOR ZERO
Symbolic form: JAZ

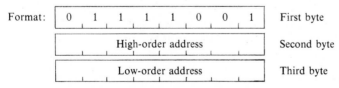

Format:

| 0 | 1 | 1 | 1 | 1 | 0 | 0 | 1 | First byte |

| High-order address | Second byte |

| Low-order address | Third byte |

Description: If (Acc) = 00000000, then $\langle B_2 \rangle \langle B_3 \rangle \rightarrow PC$

If the content of the accumulator is equal to zero, then the content of the program counter is replaced by the second and third bytes of the instruction, where the second byte becomes the high-order 8 bits and the third byte becomes the low-order 8 bits of the program counter, thus effecting a jump to that location. Otherwise, the second and third bytes are ignored, and the next instruction in sequential order is executed.

Table 7.2 (*Continued*)

Instruction: JUMP ON ACCUMULATOR NOT ZERO
Symbolic form: JAN

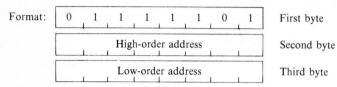

| Format: | 0 | 1 | 1 | 1 | 1 | 1 | 0 | 1 | First byte |

High-order address — Second byte

Low-order address — Third byte

Description: If (Acc) ≠ 00000000, then $\langle B_2 \rangle \langle B_3 \rangle \rightarrow$ PC

If the content of the accumulator is not equal to zero, then the content of the program counter is replaced by the second and third bytes of the instruction, where the second byte becomes the high-order 8 bits and the third byte becomes the low-order 8 bits of the program counter, thus effecting a jump to that location. Otherwise, the second and third bytes are ignored, and the next instruction in sequential order is executed.

Instruction: JUMP ON ACCUMULATOR POSITIVE
Symbolic form: JAP

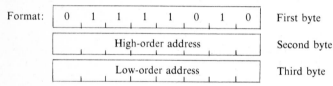

| Format: | 0 | 1 | 1 | 1 | 1 | 0 | 1 | 0 | First byte |

High-order address — Second byte

Low-order address — Third byte

Description: If $(Acc_7) = 0$, then $\langle B_2 \rangle \langle B_3 \rangle \rightarrow$ PC

If the leftmost bit of the accumulator is 0, then the content of the program counter is replaced by the second and third bytes of the instruction, where the second byte becomes the high-order 8 bits and the third byte becomes the low-order 8 bits of the program counter, thus effecting a jump to that location. Otherwise, the second and third bytes are ignored, and the next instruction in sequential order is executed.

Instruction: JUMP ON ACCUMULATOR MINUS
Symbolic form: JAM

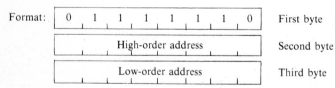

| Format: | 0 | 1 | 1 | 1 | 1 | 1 | 1 | 0 | First byte |

High-order address — Second byte

Low-order address — Third byte

Description: If $(Acc_7) = 1$, then $\langle B_2 \rangle \langle B_3 \rangle \rightarrow$ PC

If the leftmost bit of the accumulator is 1, then the content of the program counter is replaced by the second and third bytes of the instruction, where the second byte becomes the high-order 8 bits and the third byte becomes the low-order 8 bits of the program counter, thus effecting a jump to that location. Otherwise, the second and third bytes are ignored, and the next instruction in sequential order is executed.

Table 7.2 (*Continued*)

Instruction: JUMP UNCONDITIONALLY
Symbolic form: JMP

Format:

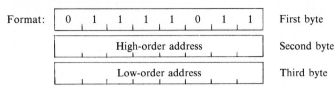

| 0 | 1 | 1 | 1 | 1 | 0 | 1 | 1 | First byte |

High-order address — Second byte

Low-order address — Third byte

Description: $\langle B_2 \rangle \langle B_3 \rangle \rightarrow PC$

The content of the program counter is replaced by the second and third bytes of the instruction, where the second byte becomes the high-order 8 bits and the third byte becomes the low-order 8 bits of the program counter, thus effecting a jump to that location.

Instruction: JUMP INDIRECT
Symbolic form: JHL

Format:

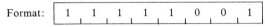

| 1 | 1 | 1 | 1 | 1 | 0 | 0 | 1 |

Description: $(H)(L) \rightarrow PC$

The content of the program counter is replaced by the content of the H and L scratchpad registers, where the H register content becomes the high-order 8 bits and the L register content becomes the low-order 8 bits of the program counter, thus effecting a jump to the location specified by the H and L registers.

SUBROUTINE INSTRUCTIONS

Instruction: JUMP TO SUBROUTINE
Symbolic form: JMS

Format:

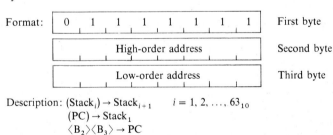

| 0 | 1 | 1 | 1 | 1 | 1 | 1 | 1 | First byte |

High-order address — Second byte

Low-order address — Third byte

Description: $(Stack_i) \rightarrow Stack_{i+1} \quad i = 1, 2, \ldots, 63_{10}$
$(PC) \rightarrow Stack_1$
$\langle B_2 \rangle \langle B_3 \rangle \rightarrow PC$

The stack is pushed down and the content of the program counter is entered into the top of the stack. The initial content of $Stack_{64}$ is lost. The content of the program counter is replaced by the second and third bytes of the instruction, where the second byte becomes the high-order 8 bits and the third byte becomes the low-order 8 bits of the program counter, thus effecting a jump to that location.

Instruction: RETURN FROM SUBROUTINE
Symbolic form: RET

Format:

| 1 | 1 | 1 | 1 | 1 | 0 | 0 | 0 |

Description: $(Stack_1) \rightarrow PC$
$(Stack_i) \rightarrow Stack_{i-1} \quad i = 2, 3, \ldots, 64_{10}$
$(Stack_{64}) \rightarrow Stack_{64}$

The content of the top register of the stack is transferred to the program counter and the stack is popped up. The content of $Stack_{64}$ is unchanged.

Table 7.2 (Continued)

ARITHMETIC AND LOGIC INSTRUCTIONS

Instruction: ADD REGISTER
Symbolic form: ADD R

Format:

1	0	0	0	R

Description: $(Acc) + (R) \to Acc$
    End Carry $\to$ C

The content of scratchpad register R is added to the content of the accumulator. The result of the addition becomes the new content of the accumulator and the end carry (i.e., the carry from the most-significant bit position) becomes the new content of the carry flip-flop C. All numbers are assumed to be unsigned integers.

Instruction: ADD REGISTER WITH CARRY
Symbolic form: ADC R

Format:

1	0	0	1	R

Description: $(Acc) + (R) + (C) \to Acc$
    End Carry $\to$ C

The content of scratchpad register R and the content of carry flip-flop C are added to the content of the accumulator. The result of the addition becomes the new content of the accumulator and the end carry (i.e., the carry from the most-significant bit position) becomes the new content of the carry flip-flop C. All numbers are assumed to be unsigned integers.

Instruction: SUBTRACT REGISTER
Symbolic form: SUB R

Format:

1	0	1	0	R

Description: $(Acc) - (R) \to Acc$
    End Borrow $\to$ C

The content of scratchpad register R is subtracted from the content of the accumulator. The result of the subtraction becomes the new content of the accumulator and the end borrow (i.e., the borrow by the most-significant bit position) becomes the new content of the carry flip-flop C. All numbers are assumed to be unsigned integers.

Instruction: SUBTRACT REGISTER WITH CARRY
Symbolic form: SBC R

Format:

1	0	1	1	R

Description: $(Acc) - (R) - (C) \to Acc$
    End Borrow $\to$ C

The content of scratchpad register R and the content of carry flip-flop C are subtracted from the content of the accumulator. The result of the subtraction becomes the new content of the accumulator and the end borrow (i.e., the borrow by the most-significant bit position) becomes the new content of the carry flip-flop C. All numbers are assumed to be unsigned integers.

Table 7.2 (*Continued*)

Instruction: LOGICAL AND
Symbolic form: AND R

Format:

1	1	0	0	R

Description: $(Acc) \wedge (R) \rightarrow Acc$

The content of scratchpad register R is logically ANDed bit by bit with the content of the accumulator. The result becomes the new content of the accumulator. The content of the carry flip-flop C is unaffected.

Instruction: LOGICAL OR
Symbolic form: OR R

Format:

1	1	0	1	R

Description: $(Acc) \vee (R) \rightarrow Acc$

The content of scratchpad register R is logically ORed bit by bit with the content of the accumulator. The result becomes the new content of the accumulator. The content of the carry flip-flop C is unaffected.

Instruction: LOGICAL EXCLUSIVE-OR
Symbolic form: XOR R

Format:

1	1	1	0	R

Description: $(Acc) \oplus (R) \rightarrow Acc$

The content of scratchpad register R is logically EXCLUSIVE-ORed bit by bit with the content of the accumulator. The result becomes the new content of the accumulator. The content of the carry flip-flop C is unaffected.

Instruction: COMPLEMENT ACCUMULATOR
Symbolic form: CMA

Format:

1	1	1	1	0	0	0	0

Description: $\overline{(Acc)} \rightarrow Acc$

Each 0 bit of the accumulator is changed to 1, and each 1 bit is changed to 0 (i.e., the 1's-complement is produced).

Instruction: COMPLEMENT CARRY
Symbolic form: CMC

Format:

1	1	1	1	0	0	1	1

Description: $\overline{(C)} \rightarrow C$

If the content of the carry flip-flop C is 0, then it is set to 1. If the content of the carry flip-flop C is 1, then it is reset to 0.

Table 7.2 (*Continued*)

Instruction: RESET CARRY
Symbolic form: RSC

Format:

1	1	1	1	0	1	0	0

Description: $0 \rightarrow C$

The carry flip-flop C is reset to 0.

Instruction: ROTATE ACCUMULATOR AND CARRY LEFT
Symbolic form: RTL

Format:

1	1	1	1	0	0	0	1

Description: $(C) \rightarrow Acc_0$
$\qquad (Acc_i) \rightarrow Acc_{i+1} \qquad i = 0, 1, \ldots, 6$
$\qquad (Acc_7) \rightarrow C$

The combined contents of the accumulator and the carry flip-flop C are shifted left by one bit position. The content of bit Acc_7 is entered into the carry flip-flop C, while the content of the carry flip-flop C is entered into bit position Acc_0.

Instruction: ROTATE ACCUMULATOR AND CARRY RIGHT
Symbolic form: RTR

Format:

1	1	1	1	0	0	1	0

Description: $(C) \rightarrow Acc_7$
$\qquad (Acc_i) \rightarrow Acc_{i-1} \qquad i = 1, 2, \ldots, 7$
$\qquad (Acc_0) \rightarrow C$

The combined contents of the accumulator and the carry flip-flop C are shifted right by one bit position. The content of bit Acc_0 is entered into the carry flip-flop C, while the content of the carry flip-flop C is entered into bit position Acc_7.

INPUT/OUTPUT INSTRUCTIONS

Instruction: INPUT
Symbolic form: INP

Format:

1	1	1	1	1	1	0	1	First byte

Device number	Second byte

Description: Input Device $[\langle B_2 \rangle] \rightarrow Acc$

A data byte is transferred into the accumulator from the input device designated by the second byte of the instruction.

Table 7.2 (*Continued*)

Instruction: OUTPUT
Symbolic form: OUT

Format:

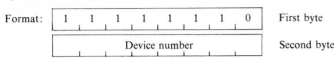

| First byte |
| Second byte |

Description: (Acc) → Output Device [⟨B₂⟩]

The content of the accumulator is transferred to the output device designated by the second byte of the instruction.

SPECIAL OPERATIONS INSTRUCTIONS

Instruction: INCREMENT REGISTER PAIR H AND L
Symbolic form: IHL

Format:

Description: $(H)(L) + 1 \rightarrow HL$

The 16-bit number contained in the register pair H and L is incremented by 1 modulo 2^{16}.

Instruction: DECREMENT REGISTER PAIR H AND L
Symbolic form: DHL

Format:

Description: $(H)(L) - 1 \rightarrow HL$

The 16-bit number contained in the register pair H and L is decremented by 1 modulo 2^{16}.

Instruction: PUSH DATA ONTO STACK
Symbolic form: PUSH

Format:

Description: $(Stack_i) \rightarrow Stack_{i+2}$ $i = 1, 2, \ldots, 62_{10}$
$0000000(C)(Acc) \rightarrow Stack_2$
$(H)(L) \rightarrow Stack_1$

The stack is pushed down twice. The combined contents of the carry flip-flop C and the accumulator are entered into the second top register of the stack, and the combined contents of H and L are entered into the top register of the stack.

Instruction: POP DATA FROM STACK
Symbolic form: POP

Format:

Description: $(Stack_1) \rightarrow HL$
$(Stack L_2) \rightarrow Acc$
$(Stack H0_2) \rightarrow C$
$(Stack_i) \rightarrow Stack_{i-2}$ $i = 3, 4, \ldots, 64_{10}$
$(Stack_j) \rightarrow Stack_j$ $j = 63, 64$

The content of the top register of the stack is transferred to the scratchpad register pair H and L. The content of the low-order half of the second top stack register is transferred to the accumulator and the least-significant bit of the high-order half of the second top stack register is transferred to the carry flip-flop C. The stack is popped up twice leaving the two bottom stack registers unchanged.

Table 7.2 (*Continued*)

Instruction: ENABLE INTERRUPT
Symbolic form: EIT

Format:

1	1	1	1	1	0	1	1

Description: $1 \rightarrow$ Interrupt Flag

A flip-flop called the Interrupt Flag is set to 1 at the end of the execution of the instruction following this instruction.

Instruction: DISABLE INTERRUPT
Symbolic form: DIT

Format:

1	1	1	1	1	1	0	0

Description: $0 \rightarrow$ Interrupt Flag

A flip-flop called the Interrupt Flag is reset to 0.

Instruction: NO OPERATION
Symbolic form: NOP

Format:

1	1	1	1	0	1	1	1

Description: No operation is performed during the execution of this instruction.

Instruction: HALT
Symbolic form: HLT

Format:

1	1	1	1	1	0	1	0

Description: No further instructions are executed until a pulse is encountered on the Start line.

The format version of each instruction in Table 7.2 indicates the exact structure of each instruction, as it must appear within the memory of the computer. That is, each instruction consists of a sequence of 0s and 1s. On the other hand, the symbolic form is presented so as to facilitate reference to each instruction. Thus, when writing programs, this form can be used, but it must be converted into its format version before it can be entered into the computer. The symbolic form will be used in most of our discussions for the sake of convenience.

Fetch-Decode Phase

As was indicated in Chap. 1, instructions are normally executed in sequential order. It will be assumed that all programs will commence with the instruction in location 0000_{16}. The time needed for each instruction to be fetched from memory, decoded, and executed is defined as an *instruction cycle*. In view of the fact that an instruction may have one, two, or three bytes and that the execution time for instructions can vary, the time for an instruction cycle is not constant. Thus, a smaller time unit is needed. As was indicated in the preceding section, this smaller basic time unit is the machine cycle, which consists of three clock pulses.

The first step in carrying out any instruction is fetching it from memory. Each byte of the instruction to be fetched from memory requires one machine cycle of the instruction cycle. Figure 7.5 illustrates information flow during the fetch-decode phase of an instruction cycle. The 16-bit address of the first instruction byte is sent to the memory over the Address bus from the program counter. A Read pulse is provided by the timing and control unit, causing the content of the addressed memory location to be placed onto the Data bus and then entered into the instruction register. This first byte, which contains the operation code, is interpreted by the decoder so as to determine if this is a multibyte instruction. Also during this time, the program counter is incremented. If it is determined that the instruction consists of one or two additional bytes, then one or two additional machine cycles are used to bring in the bytes from memory in a similar fashion. However, the destination of the additional byte or bytes is not the instruction

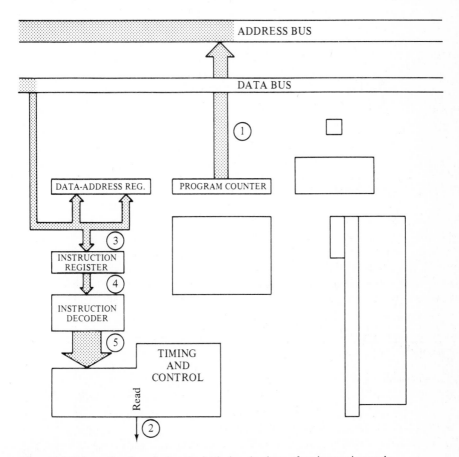

Figure 7.5 Information flow during the fetch-decode phase of an instruction cycle.

register but either the data-address register for nonimmediate instructions (which is indicated in Fig. 7.5) or some scratchpad register for immediate instructions. In any case, the fetch-decode phase is complete after the second clock pulse of the last of these machine cycles.

Execute Phase

After the instruction has been fetched, it must next be executed. For some instructions this is accomplished with the remaining clock pulse of the last machine cycle used for the fetch-decode phase, while for other instructions additional machine cycles must be utilized. It is the responsibility of the timing and control unit, knowing the operation requested, to determine the number of any additional machine cycles.

Let us now consider the execute phase for some of the instructions of our illustrative microprocessor. The reader should refer to Table 7.2 during the course of this discussion.

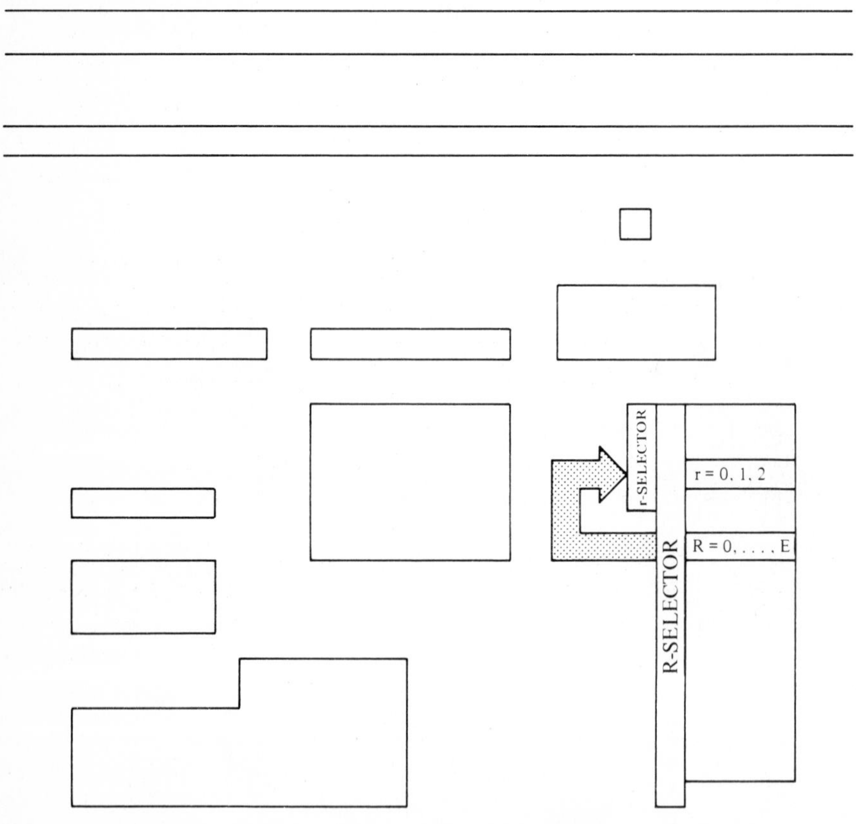

Figure 7.6 Information flow during the execute phase for a MOV r from R instruction, where $R \neq 1111_2$.

Move Instructions

First consider the execution of the move (MOV) instructions. The purpose of these instructions is to transfer information between two scratchpad registers or between a location in main memory and a scratchpad register. Figure 7.6 shows the information flow during the execution of the move instruction for the case of a data transfer between two scratchpad registers. In particular, if d equals 1 in the instruction format, then according to Table 7.2 the transfer is from any register 0_{16} through E_{16} designated by R to one of the registers 0_{16}, 1_{16}, 2_{16} designated by r. This transfer will occur during the third pulse of the same machine cycle that caused the 1-byte instruction to be fetched. Thus the instruction cycle in this case consists of a single machine cycle.

For the special case where $R = 1111_2$, the execution of the move instruction is different. In this case the indirect addressing scheme mentioned in Sec. 7.2 is used. Figure 7.7 illustrates this situation when again $d = 1$ in the instruction format. In

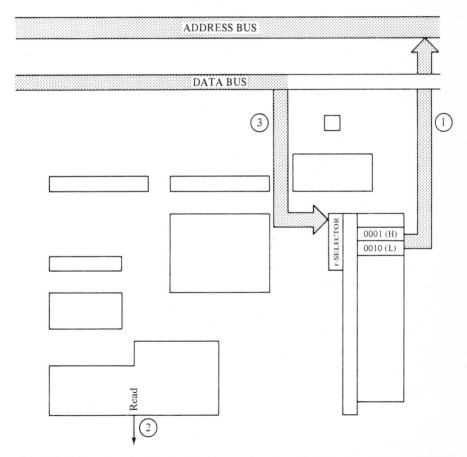

Figure 7.7 Information flow during the execute phase for a MOV r from R instruction, where $R = 1111_2$.

this case the contents of the scratchpad registers H and L, where H contains the 8 high-order bits of an address and L contains the 8 low-order bits, are placed onto the Address bus to designate a location in memory. Upon the issuance of a Read pulse the content of the addressed memory location is transferred over the Data bus to register r. In view of the fact that a move instruction that uses memory in this way requires an external data transfer, the instruction cycle necessitates a second machine cycle.

Immediate Instructions

Consider next the load register immediate instructions, LRI R. A characteristic of these instructions, as well as all immediate instructions in microprocessors, is that data is part of the instruction itself. Such instructions offer the programmer a convenient method of introducing constants into a program. As indicated earlier, it is necessary to have two machine cycles to fetch the instruction. The first machine cycle places the first byte into the instruction register and the second machine cycle places the second byte into the data-address register. Then, the third clock pulse of the second machine cycle is used to complete the execution of

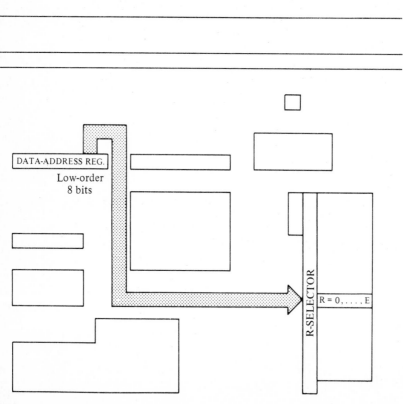

Figure 7.8 Information flow during the execute phase for an LRI R instruction, where R $\neq 1111_2$.

the instruction when R does not equal 1111_2. In this case, as illustrated in Fig. 7.8, the 8 low-order bits of the data-address register, which is the second byte of the instruction, is transferred to the scratchpad register R. As in the case of the move instructions, an additional machine cycle is necessary to perform the load-register-immediate instructions when R = 1111_2, since the data must be transferred from a location in memory.

Memory Reference Instructions

The next class of instructions to be considered is the memory reference instructions. These 3-byte instructions provide for the transfer of information between a location in main memory and one of the scratchpad registers 0_{16}, 1_{16}, 2_{16} designated by r. To illustrate a memory reference instruction, consider the store-register instruction STR r whose execution is shown in Fig. 7.9. The content of the data-address register, loaded during the fetch-decode phase with the second and third bytes of the instruction, is placed onto the Address bus, and the content of

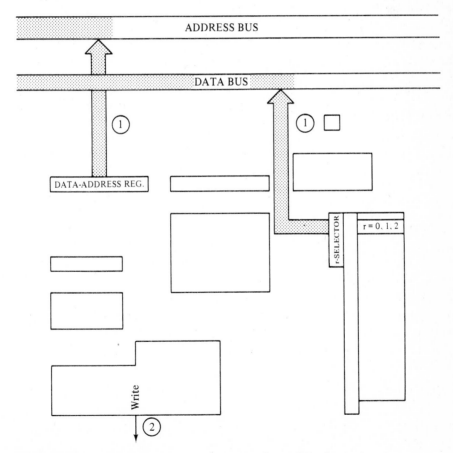

Figure 7.9 Information flow during the execute phase for an STR r instruction.

the scratchpad register r is placed onto the Data bus. Next a Write pulse from the timing and control unit is provided to strobe the data into the addressed memory location. The execution of this instruction requires one machine cycle owing to the single data transfer. Hence, the instruction cycle consists of a total of four machine cycles, i.e., three machine cycles for the fetch-decode phase and one for the execute phase.

Jump Instructions

The class of jump instructions are a very important part of a computer's instruction repertoire. These instructions provide the user with a means to alter the normal sequence of instruction execution, possibly as a result of decision-making tests. Microprocessors normally provide many instructions of this nature. A typical instruction is the jump-on-carry-not-zero (JCN) instruction. Since this is a 3-byte instruction according to Table 7.2, by the time of the third clock pulse of the third machine cycle the microprocessor is ready to start execution. During the third clock pulse the timing and control unit interrogates the carry flip-flop C. If the status condition of the flag bit is satisfied, i.e., $C = 1$, as illustrated in Fig. 7.10, then the content of the data-address register is transferred to the program counter. Thus, the second and third bytes of the instruction become the address of the next instruction to be fetched. On the other hand, if the status condition of the flag bit is not satisfied, i.e., $C = 0$, the program counter is not changed from its incremented value obtained during the fetch-decode phase. This results in the instruction not having any effect in the flow of the program. Jump instructions of this nature are called *conditional jump instructions* in view of the fact that the program counter is modified only if a certain condition is satisfied. Other typical instructions of this nature found in microprocessors are jump on accumulator zero, jump on the most-significant bit of the accumulator zero, etc.

Another type of jump instruction found in microprocessors is *jump unconditionally*. In this type of instruction the program counter is always changed to effect the jump. For our illustrative microprocessor this can be done in a direct manner by the instruction JMP (i.e., jump unconditionally) or in an indirect manner by the instruction JHL (i.e., jump indirect).

Closely akin to the jump instructions, some microprocessors provide *skip instructions*. In a skip instruction, when a specified condition is satisfied, e.g., the carry is equal to zero, the next instruction in sequence is skipped; otherwise, the next instruction is executed. One advantage of skip instructions over jump instructions is that an address does not have to be specified in the instruction itself. Thus, fewer bytes are required for the instruction.

Subroutine Instructions

Frequently in a computer program some procedure must be carried out several times. Rather than repeat the instructions corresponding to this procedure each time it is needed, it is convenient and efficient to express this procedure as a subprogram, which is referred to as a *subroutine*. As indicated in Fig. 7.11, the

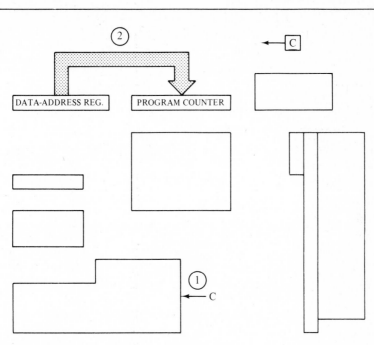

Figure 7.10 Information flow during the execute phase for a JCN instruction when C = 1. No transfer occurs when C = 0.

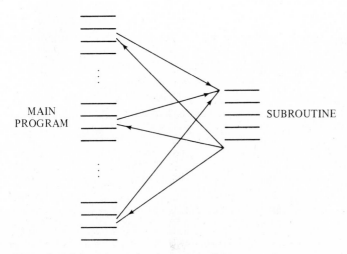

Figure 7.11 Subroutine and main program linkage.

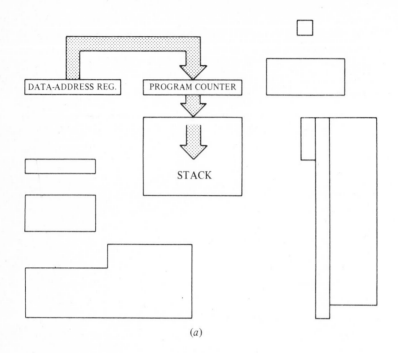

(a)

subroutine can be entered from several points in a main program. Clearly, provision must be made to reenter the main program at the same place, or some well-defined relative place, from which the exit had occurred. One common approach to provide for this capability is to include special instructions that allow the exit point of the main program to be stored and later recalled. In the case of our illustrative microprocessor this is achieved by the pair of instructions jump to subroutine (JMS) and return from subroutine (RET). The information flow for this pair of instructions is illustrated in Fig. 7.12. Consider first the JMS instruction. During the third pulse of the third machine cycle of the instruction cycle the content of the data-address register, which corresponds to the address of the first instruction of the subroutine, is entered into the program counter, thus accomplishing the jump. Simultaneously, the content of the program counter, which has already been incremented to the address of the instruction following the JMS instruction, is entered into the stack in a push-down fashion. Upon completion of a subroutine, the RET instruction provides for reentry into the main program. When this instruction is executed, the stack is popped, restoring the program counter to the address of the correct reentry point in the main program.

It should be clear that subroutines could call subroutines, referred to as

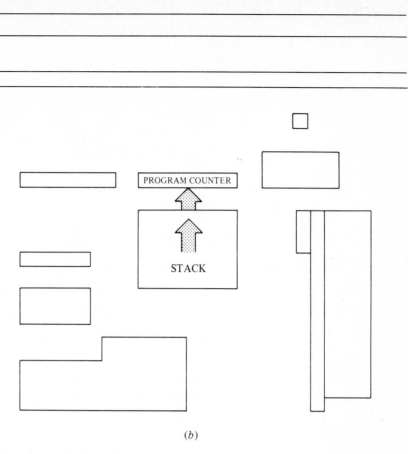

PROGRAM COUNTER

STACK

(*b*)

Figure 7.12 Subroutine instructions. (*a*) Information flow during the execute phase for the JMS instruction. (*b*) Information flow during the execute phase for the RET instruction.

subroutine nesting, in a simple manner with this pair of instructions. One limitation, however, is that the degree of nesting is limited to the number of registers that comprise the stack, since the content of the bottom register is lost when the stack is pushed down.

Since a subroutine is a program in itself, it frequently needs data on which to perform its computations. Furthermore, in general, this data, known as the *parameters* or *arguments* of the subroutine, will depend upon the point in the main program from which the subroutine was entered. One straightforward approach of passing the parameters from the main program to the subroutine is to have the main program place the parameters in the scratchpad memory prior to the JMS instruction. In this way, the subroutine can be written under the assumption that the necessary parameters are in the scratchpad memory and, hence, readily available to it. Similarly, the computed result from the subroutine can be passed to the main program by having the subroutine leave the result in the scratchpad memory. Subroutines will be considered in greater detail in the next chapter.

Arithmetic and Logic Instructions

All of the instructions discussed so far involve either decision making or information transfer. It is the class of arithmetic and logic instructions that provide for data manipulation. Such instructions as add, subtract, logic-AND, logic-OR, rotate, etc., typify this class. To illustrate this class of instructions, consider the add-register-with-carry instruction ADC R. Figure 7.13 shows the flow of information that occurs during the execution of this instruction when R is any scratch-pad register $0_{16}, \ldots, E_{16}$. According to Table 7.2, this is a single-byte instruction. Hence, after the second clock pulse of the single fetch machine cycle, the content of the accumulator and the content of scratchpad register R are each presented to the ALU as the operands. The ALU uses these two operands along with the content of the carry flip-flop C (as the carry into the least-significant bit position) to determine the 8-bit sum and a new carry. Thus, at the time of the third clock pulse the sum is transferred to the accumulator and the final carry is transferred to the carry flip-flop.

The ADC R instruction for $R = 1111_2$ is illustrated in Fig. 7.14. In this case a

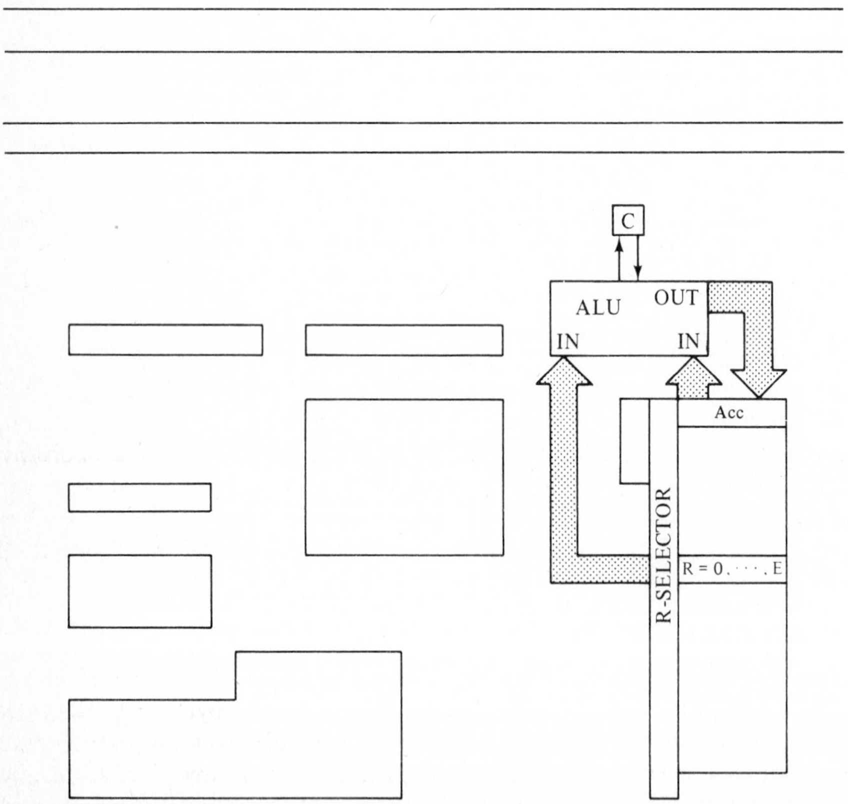

Figure 7.13 Information flow during the execute phase for the ADC R instruction, where $R \neq 1111_2$.

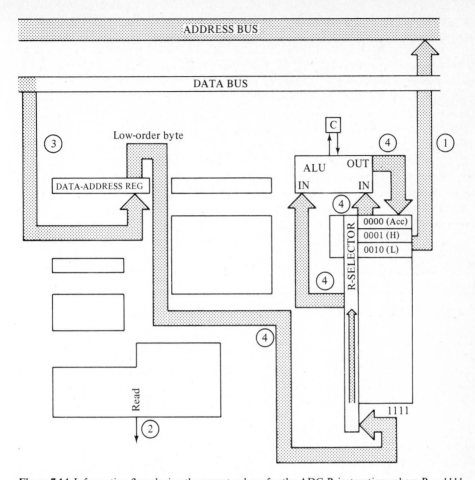

Figure 7.14 Information flow during the execute phase for the ADC R instruction, where R = 1111_2.

second machine cycle is needed to obtain an operand from the memory location addressed by the combined content of H and L. This operand is temporarily stored in the low-order half of the data-address register so that it may be presented through the R-selector to the ALU at the proper time.

Input/Output Instructions

Now consider the instruction class that provides for the transfer of information between the microprocessor and an input or output device. For the sake of discussion, the OUT instruction will be treated. Since this is a 2-byte instruction, the second byte is placed in the low-order half of the data-address register during the second machine cycle. To provide for the time delays incurred by the buses as well as the logic associated with the microprocessor and the output device, a third machine cycle is used for the execute phase of the instruction. This machine cycle

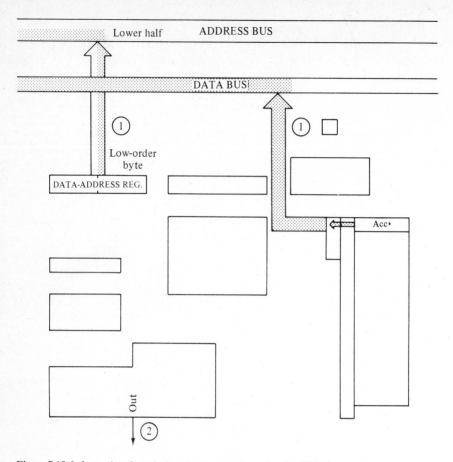

Figure 7.15 Information flow during the execute phase for the OUT instruction.

is illustrated in Fig. 7.15. At the first clock pulse of the third machine cycle, the content of the low-order half of the data-address register is placed onto the Address bus and the content of the accumulator is placed onto the Data bus through the r-selector. Each output device decodes the content of the lower-half of the Address bus. However, only within the output device that recognizes its code will a register be enabled to accept the data from the Data bus. At the second clock pulse period of the third machine cycle, the timing and control unit will place a pulse on the Out line of the Control bus, which is used to strobe the content of the Data bus into the enabled register.

Special-Operations Instructions

The final class of instructions included in the repertoire of our illustrative microprocessor is the special-operations instructions. These instructions are both necessary and convenient for writing efficient microprocessor programs.

Since the H and L scratchpad registers can be used to reference a memory location, the increment and decrement-register-pair-H-and-L instructions provide a convenient way of modifying these registers when used for indirect addressing. The enable- and disable-interrupt instructions will be described in detail in Chap. 9 when interrupts are discussed. The no-operation instruction provides time delay in a program. This can be important when a microprocessor must communicate with slower input and output devices. Clearly, the halt instruction allows the termination of a program.

The two remaining instructions in the special operations instructions class are the push-data-onto-stack and pop-data-from-stack instructions. When a subroutine or an interrupt service routine is executed, several scratchpad registers are usually needed by the routine to input, output, or manipulate data. However, it is often necessary for the routine not to disturb the current contents of the registers, since they might contain information important to the mainline program. For this purpose, the contents of the top three scratchpad registers Acc, H, and L, along with the content of the carry flip-flop C, can be saved with the push-data-onto-stack instruction and then later restored with the pop-data-from-stack instruction. This allows the accumulator, H register, L register, and C flip-flop to be used while still retaining their original contents. Furthermore, since the information is stored in a push-down stack, this procedure can be repeated for subsequent subroutine or interrupt service routine levels to allow for nesting.

The execution phase of the push-data-onto-stack instruction PUSH requires two clock pulses. During the third pulse of the instruction cycle the combined contents of the carry flip-flop C and the accumulator is entered into the stack in a push-down fashion. Then, during the next clock pulse, which is actually the first pulse of the next instruction cycle, the combined contents of the scratchpad registers H and L are entered into the stack in a push-down fashion. The overlap of the instruction cycle with the fetch-decode phase for the next instruction is permissible in this case, since no interference of information flow occurs.

The information flow during the execute phase of the pop-data-from-stack instruction POP is just the reverse of that for PUSH.

For the reader's convenience, the Appendix appearing at the end of the book summarizes the instruction repertoire of our illustrative microprocessor. Table A1 lists the instructions alphabetically and Table A2 lists them numerically.

7.5 ADDRESSING MODES

In the discussion of microprocessor instructions, it was seen that some of them refer to the memory for the purposes of obtaining or storing information involved in the operation of the instruction. Other instructions refer to the memory to indicate a location to which a program jump is to be made. In either case, the instruction must somehow specify the address of the memory location that is referenced. In general, the part of an instruction that provides an indication as to the memory location that is referenced is known as the *address field*. To illustrate a few different cases, the address field might contain the actual address of the referenced location, e.g., the load-register instruction LDR; the address field might refer to scratchpad registers that contain the address of the referenced location, e.g., the ADD instruction with R = 1111; or the address field of the instruction as it appears in memory might be the referenced location, e.g., the LRI instruction. It should be noted in this last case that the content of the address field itself is the information associated with the operation of the instruction. The manner in which the address field is interpreted with respect to the referenced memory location is known as the *addressing mode* of the instruction. As was noted, the instructions of a microprocessor generally consist of a variable number of words. For the case of our illustrative microprocessor it is 1, 2, or 3 bytes. The number of words needed for an instruction will be affected by the addressing mode as well as by the allowable size of the memory and the architectural structure of the micro-processor. Thus for the sake of program efficiency, manufacturers generally pro-vide for several addressing modes in a microprocessor.

At this time the most commonly occurring addressing modes will be con-sidered. In general, however, a particular microprocessor, including our illustra-tive one, does not utilize all of the modes to be discussed. For the sake of discussion, the content of the address field will be referred to as the *stated address*, while the address of the referenced memory location, which is the location of the information to be operated upon, will be referred to as the *effective address*.

Direct Addressing

The most straightforward method of accessing information in memory is *direct addressing*. In direct addressing the effective address is given in the instruction. That is, the stated address is the effective address. If all the locations in the computer memory are to be addressed directly, then the instruction must gen-erally consist of several words. With an 8-bit microprocessor, for example, if there are 65,536 memory locations to be directly addressed, then 2 bytes (i.e., 16 bits) are needed to specify just the address. Thus, allowing 1 byte to indicate the operation, a total of 3 bytes are required for the instruction.

An example of a direct address instruction for the illustrative microprocessor is the load-register instruction LDR. Two of the three bytes in this instruction indicate the actual address of the memory location that contains the operand that is to be placed into the specified scratchpad register.

Immediate Addressing

In the *immediate addressing* mode, the operand for the instruction is part of the instruction itself. In this case, the location of the operand immediately follows the memory location that contains the operation portion of the instruction. For example, in the load-register-immediate instruction LRI, the second byte of the instruction is a constant that is entered into a designated register.

Indexed Addressing

Several microprocessors allow the stated address in an instruction to be added to the content of a specified register to form the effective address. This is known as *indexed addressing*, and the specified register is called an *index register*.

Generally, special instructions are provided that increment or decrement an index register to facilitate accessing the entries of a table in a successive manner, especially in a program loop. Alternatively, the index register could be automatically incremented or decremented each time it is used to form an effective address. This mode of operation is known as *autoindexing*.

Indirect Addressing

A very useful and important addressing mode found in microprocessors is *indirect addressing*. With indirect addressing the stated address in the address field of the instruction serves as a pointer to the location in which the effective address can be found. Thus, the stated address is really the address of a location containing the address of the referenced memory location.

A special case of indirect addressing is when the stated address is used to point to a scratchpad register rather than a location in main memory. This restricted form is also called *register indirect addressing*. Register indirect addressing enhances program efficiency, since, generally, only a single word is needed for the instruction. This follows from the fact that the address field of the instruction need only contain a sufficient number of bits to designate a scratchpad register.

An example of the register-indirect-addressing mode is the ADD R instruction when R = 1111. In this case the 1111 in the 4 least-significant bits of the instruction serve as a pointer to the H and L scratchpad registers. The contents of these registers are then regarded as a 16-bit effective address corresponding to the referenced memory location.

Relative Addressing

Closely related to indexed addressing is *relative addressing*. In this addressing mode the stated address in the instruction is added to the content of the program counter to form the effective address. The stated address is regarded as a signed quantity, so that relative addressing in a jump instruction allows a jump forward or backward from the location indicated by the program counter by the amount indicated in the address field of the instruction. This addressing mode in a jump instruction is convenient and effective when the jump is to a nearby location, since the full address of the new location need not be specified.

Page Addressing Modes

Frequently the number of locations in a microcomputer memory is larger than can be directly addressed by an instruction. In this case the memory might be divided into *pages*, where the size of each page is determined by the maximum number of directly addressable locations. For example, if only 8 bits are allowed to designate a memory location, then each page consists of $2^8 = 256$ locations. Furthermore, each page of the memory is assigned a number in sequential order beginning with page 0. Thus, for the above example, page 0 consists of locations 0 to 255, page 1 consists of locations 256 to 511, etc. Under this concept the program counter can be regarded as consisting of two parts. The most-significant bits serve as the page number and the least-significant bits serve as the address within the page.

In the *present-page addressing mode* of an instruction, the effective address of the referenced memory location is the stated address relative to the beginning of the current page in which the instruction itself appears. That is, only the memory locations in the current page can be accessed, and the effective address is the sum of the starting address of the current page and the stated address appearing in the instruction. Thus, the most-significant bits of the effective address are simply the page portion of the program counter and the least-significant bits are the stated address in the instruction.

Another page addressing mode is the *page-0 addressing mode*, where the effective address is the page-0 location corresponding to the stated address appearing in the instruction. In this case the most-significant bits of the effective address are assumed to be just 0s, while the least-significant bits are the stated address. Since the present-page and page-0 modes relate to the program counter, they can be considered a form of relative addressing. Hence, these addressing modes are also called *page-relative addressing modes*.

With just present-page and page-0 addressing modes available, only memory locations in the current page and page 0 can be directly addressed. In order to address any other memory locations, indirect addressing might be used. For example, if a memory location in page 7 is to be addressed and the program counter indicates that the current instruction is in page 3, the address of the page 7 location must be stored in some location in page 0 or 3 so that the operand in page 7 may be accessed indirectly.

7.6 OTHER COMMON MICROPROCESSOR INSTRUCTIONS

Besides the types of instructions provided in the illustrative microprocessor, various other types are commonly found in actual microprocessors. Some of these other instruction types are variations of those in the illustrative microprocessor, others allow certain programming steps to be performed more conveniently, while still others enhance the computational power of a microprocessor. Rather than elaborate upon all such instructions, a few examples should help to illustrate the variety found among different microprocessors.

Performing Arithmetic and Logic Directly from Memory

Recall that the arithmetic and logic instructions for the illustrative microprocessor involve operands that are always located within the microprocessor or addressed indirectly via the H and L registers. An important variation to this scheme, found in many microprocessors, is to use an operand directly from a selected location in the main memory. For example, an add instruction according to this alternative scheme adds the content of a memory location to the content of an internal register serving as the accumulator and stores the results in an internal register. When the location of the operands in main memory must be specified for an arithmetic or logic operation, the instruction length is generally greater to accommodate an address.

Some microprocessors extend this scheme further by having the results of some arithmetic and logic operations go to a location in main memory. Examples of this are instructions that cause the content of a selected memory location to be complemented or incremented.

Decision-Making Instructions

To provide for decision making, the illustrative microprocessor has six conditional jump instructions, which are based on the three conditions: the accumulator is zero, the accumulator is positive, and the carry flip-flop is 0. Besides these three conditions, most microprocessors have various other conditions that serve as a basis for decision-making instructions. Some of these other conditions are

1. Overflow during 2's-complement arithmetic
2. Parity of a register, i.e., whether the number of bits equal to 1 in a register is even or odd
3. Whether the content of a register is strictly positive, i.e., positive but not zero
4. An external condition indicated by a special input line

For many microprocessors each of the conditions used by the decision-making instructions is represented by a flag bit corresponding to an individual flip-flop. These condition flags are generally determined at the time in which certain operations are performed. For example, a sign flag or a parity flag might be included that is affected only by the result of an arithmetic and/or logic operation. Other operations, such as load accumulator, do not affect these condition flags. Thus, the condition flags in such cases do not necessarily reflect the current contents of certain registers, but rather each flag reflects the results obtained from certain operations the last time that one of these operations was performed. This is in obvious contrast to the scheme used by the illustrative microprocessor for the two conditions involving the accumulator, indicated by the N and Z lines.

Generally, the condition flags in a microprocessor are arranged as the individual bit positions in a special register. The content of this register is frequently called the *program status word* and is used by all of the decision-making instructions in a microprocessor. This program status word can usually be transferred to other registers and to main memory. Particularly, in a program the program status word can be saved (say in a push-down stack) when a subroutine is called. In this way, even though the subroutine may change the program status word, the status condition of the main program can be retrieved after completing the subroutine.

In addition to (or instead of) conditional jump instructions, some microprocessors have other related instructions for decision making. The conditional skip instruction is an example that has already been discussed in Sec. 7.4. Other examples of decision-making instructions are conditional jump-to-subroutine instructions as well as conditional return-from-subroutine instructions.

Data-Manipulation Instructions

The types of operations performed by the arithmetic and logic instructions of the illustrative microprocessor are basic to most microprocessors. Some microprocessors, in addition to these basic operations, provide instructions for other data-manipulation operations, such as decimal arithmetic, binary multiplication, and binary division.

Decimal arithmetic appears in the instruction set of many microprocessors. The decimal numbers are generally represented in 8421 BCD with the 4-bit digits placed next to each other within a data word. Thus, a microprocessor with 8-bit data words, for example, treats each data word as a 2-digit unsigned decimal number. Decimal addition of two numbers is generally done, as described in Sec. 2.7, by first adding the numbers in binary and then correcting the results. The correction involves first determining which decimal-digit positions satisfy either of the two conditions: (1) the decimal digit in the binary sum exceeds 9, or (2) a carry was generated from the most-significant bit position of the decimal digit during the binary addition. For each such decimal-digit position, a correction of 6 is added in binary to the decimal digit while allowing any consequent carries to propagate to the higher-order digits.

This procedure is usually implemented by the instructions of a microprocessor in one of two ways. One way is to have a decimal add instruction that when executed performs both the binary addition and the correction. The other way is to provide an instruction that just performs the correction, which is often called a *decimal-adjust instruction*. In this case, decimal addition is performed by first executing the usual binary add instruction, which leaves the results in a register, and then executing the decimal-adjust instruction, which corrects the contents of that register. In order to operate, the decimal-adjust instruction needs information concerning the two conditions that determine when each decimal digit is to be corrected. In particular, there must be information available concerning the carry from each decimal digit that possibly occurred during the binary addition. For this purpose, auxiliary carry flip-flops are generally provided that record the carry bit from each fourth bit position during the execution of a binary add instruction. For an 8-bit data word only one auxiliary carry flip-flop is required, since the usual carry flip-flop is also available.

Multiplication and division are relatively powerful operations that are implemented in a few microprocessors. These two operations are generally performed on unsigned binary integers. A multiplication instruction typically multiplies the contents of two registers and stores the double-length product into two registers. A division instruction typically divides the combined contents of two registers (dividend) by the content of another register (divisor) and stores the integer quotient into one register and the remainder into another register. Before performing the division, however, the instruction usually tests for a possible quotient overflow. A quotient overflow occurs when the quotient must be expressed with a greater number of digits than the capacity of the register that will receive it. The test for a quotient overflow can be done by comparing the divisor with the high-order half of the dividend. No quotient overflow will occur if the divisor is not zero and is at least twice as large as the high-order half of the dividend.

Due to their complexity, the execution times for multiplication and division instructions are usually considerably longer than that of the other instructions. Each of the two operations consists of many steps that are performed sequentially in the microprocessor.

PROBLEMS

7.1 For each instruction in Table 7.2, determine the number of machine cycles needed for an instruction cycle. Be sure to differentiate any cases in which $R = 1111_2$.

7.2 Assume the accumulator (scratchpad register 0_{16}) contains the hexadecimal number $C6_{16}$, scratchpad register B_{16} contains the hexadecimal number 94_{16}, and the carry flip-flop C contains a 1. What are the contents of the accumulator and the carry flip-flop C after the execution of each of the following instructions:

    (a) ADD B   (b) ADC B   (c) SUB B   (d) SBC B   (e) AND B   (f) OR B
    (g) XOR B   (h) XOR 0   (i) RTL   (j) CMA   (k) STR 0

7.3 Sketch and explain the information flow during the execute phase for a MOV r to R instruction, where $R = 1111_2$.

EIGHT

MICROCOMPUTER PROGRAMMING

In order to perform information processing with a microcomputer, it is necessary to give it a step-by-step description on how the processing should be carried out. This description is called a *program*. Furthermore, an actual program to be executed by the microcomputer must only consist of the instructions that it has been designed to accept. These instructions are known as *machine language instructions.*

As was seen in Chap. 7, the machine language instructions that can be performed with a microprocessor's hardware are rather simple and limited in number. Nevertheless, the overall capability of a microprocessor, like all computers, is virtually without limit when these instructions are combined in the form of programs. In general, the totality of programs written for a microcomputer is known as its *software.*

Perhaps the reader is already familiar with procedure-oriented languages such as FORTRAN or PL/1. In general, it is more convenient to write programs in these languages rather than in machine language. However, since the actual program executed by the microcomputer must always be in machine language, it is necessary to translate a program written in a procedure-oriented language into a machine language program before it can be executed by the microcomputer.

In this chapter, we shall study microcomputer programming. Emphasis will be on machine language programming utilizing the illustrative microprocessor of the preceding chapter. Several programs will be written to illustrate basic programming techniques. This will also enable us to further understand the internal operations and limitations of a microprocessor. Finally, two types of programming aids, assemblers and compilers, will be discussed. *Assemblers* provide the necessary translation when the program is written in a symbolic form closely akin to machine language. *Compilers*, on the other hand, are translators for procedure-oriented languages.

8.1 MACHINE LANGUAGE PROGRAMMING

As was indicated above, a program must be in a form interpretable by the micro-processor. In particular, the instructions must be represented by sequences of 0s and 1s, since this is the only form acceptable by the microprocessor's hardware. Although all computers must have their instructions in this machine language form, the resulting long sequences of 0s and 1s make the programs cumbersome to write. For this reason, the more convenient hexadecimal notation is frequently used to write a machine language program. As indicated in Chap. 2, there is a simple conversion between hexadecimal notation and binary notation. In particular, each block of 4 binary digits corresponds to a single hexadecimal digit. Unless otherwise noted, all machine language programs in this book will be written in hexadecimal notation. For example, for the illustrative microprocessor of the preceding chapter the 3-byte machine language instruction that loads the accumulator with the content of the memory location addressed by 0110111111011011_2 is

$$01110000$$
$$01101111$$
$$11011011$$

In hexadecimal notation, this machine language instruction is written as

$$70$$
$$6F$$
$$DB$$

A difficulty with programs in binary or hexadecimal machine language form is that they are hard to read and write by humans. For this reason a symbolic form is often used for each instruction. This form utilizes mnemonics that are easily related to the instruction. For example, as was indicated in Table 7.2, the previous instruction can be written in symbolic form as

$$LDR \quad 0$$
$$6F$$
$$DB$$

It should be noted that the second and third bytes of the instruction are still given in hexadecimal form and the accumulator is given by its scratchpad designator 0. However, the operation is indicated by the three-letter mnemonic LDR. For convenience Tables A1 and A2 in the Appendix list the association between the hexadecimal form and the symbolic form of the instructions for our illustrative microprocessor.

At this time let us establish a convention that will be used throughout the rest of this book when dealing with the illustrative microprocessor. Unless otherwise indicated, all the programs will appear in symbolic form for ease of reading. Thus, the first byte of each instruction will be written using the "Symbolic form" indicated in Table 7.2 (or Tables A1 and A2). For those instructions involving a scratchpad register (or indirect addressing), a hexadecimal digit will always be used to designate the register (where F_{16} denotes indirect addressing). Finally, for those instructions requiring a second and third byte, these bytes will always be expressed in hexadecimal notation.

To illustrate the above convention and how a microcomputer proceeds through a program, let us consider a simple program that will add the hexadecimal constant 3C to a number that is in memory location $000A_{16}$. The program is shown in Table 8.1. The execution of this program proceeds as follows. First, a pulse is externally applied to the Reset terminal of the microprocessor, which initializes the program counter to zero. A pulse is then applied to the Start terminal that causes program execution to commence at location zero. The 3 bytes that make up the first instruction are fetched from memory with the program counter being incremented after each byte. This first instruction causes the content of memory location 000A to be transferred to the accumulator. Since the program counter was incremented 3 times, it now contains 0003. This is the address of the

Table 8.1 Illustrative program that adds a constant to a number in memory and places the result into memory

Memory location (hexadecimal)	Machine language instruction (hexadecimal)	Symbolic form of instruction	Remarks
0000	70	LDR 0	Transfer content of memory location 000A
0001	00	00	to accumulator
0002	0A	0A	
0003	61	LRI 1	Load register 1 with the quantity 3C
0004	3C	3C	
0005	81	ADD 1	Add contents of registers 0 and 1, place result in accumulator
0006	74	STR 0	Transfer content of accumulator to memory
0007	00	00	location 000B
0008	0B	0B	
0009	FA	HLT	Stop program
000A		X	
000B		Sum	

next instruction, which is a load-register-immediate instruction. The instruction contains the data within itself and is therefore useful for introducing a constant into the program. This instruction is fetched and its execution causes the hexadecimal quantity 3C, contained as the second byte in the instruction, to be transferred into scratchpad register 1. At this point the program counter contains 0005, which is the address of the third instruction. This instruction is fetched and its execution causes the content of scratchpad register 1 to be added to the accumulator and then the sum to be placed into the accumulator. The next instruction transfers the content of the accumulator to memory location 000B. Finally, the halt instruction is encountered causing the execution of the program to terminate.

8.2 A DECISION-MAKING PROGRAM

One of the more powerful features of a computer is its ability to make decisions given appropriate information. These decisions are normally based upon simple conditions that exist within the computer at the time the decision is to be made. Typically, the consequence of a decision is whether program execution is to continue in a sequential order or be transferred to another part of the program. By the use of a number of these simple branches more complex decisions can be made.

To illustrate this point, consider a program that will find the largest of the three 8-bit unsigned numbers x, y, and z. As a general approach, the larger of x and y can first be determined by testing for an end borrow when y is subtracted from x. If no end borrow occurs, then it can be concluded that x is greater than or equal to y. On the other hand, the occurrence of an end borrow indicates that y is greater than x. Then, in a similar manner, the larger of z and the previously determined larger of x and y can be established.

Figure 8.1 shows a diagrammatic interpretation of the above procedure. Such a graphical representation for the solution of a problem is known as a *flowchart*. Flowcharts are a convenient way of setting down on paper the approach that will be used to write a program.

A program for this decision-making problem is given in Table 8.2. The three unsigned numbers to be compared, x, y, and z, are assumed to be in the three memory locations 001B, 001C, and 001D. The program is to place the value of the largest into the accumulator. When program execution begins, the first instruction transfers the value of x into the accumulator and the second instruction transfers the value of y into scratchpad register 1. A comparison is then made by subtracting y from x. If y is strictly greater than x, then an end borrow occurs as indicated by a 1 in the carry flip-flop C. Before testing the content of C, however, the value of x is transferred to scratchpad register 2 as the tentative larger of x and y. This transfer does not affect the carry flip-flop. A conditional jump instruction is next used to test the value of C. The condition for a jump to occur is that C is equal to zero. If this condition is not met, then the tentative value x for the larger of x and y is replaced by y. This is done by the next instruction in sequence, which loads

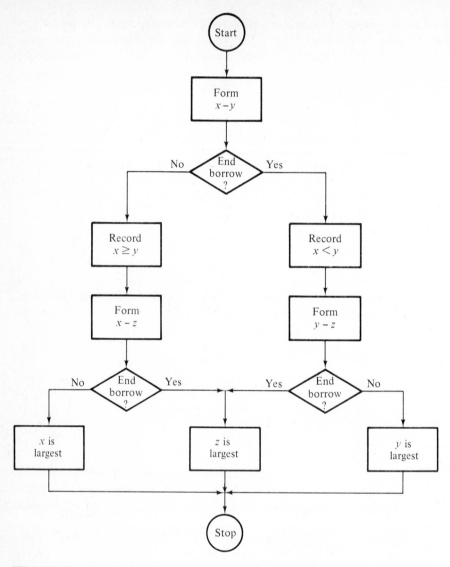

Figure 8.1 Flowchart for determining the largest of three unsigned numbers x, y, and z.

scratchpad register 2 from the location in memory containing y. If $C = 0$, then program execution is transferred to the instruction at location 0010. Thus the value of x in this case is retained as the larger of x and y. In either event, at this point in the program the larger of x and y is contained in scratchpad register 2, which is to be compared with z by a similar procedure. The value of z is transferred to scratchpad register 1 from memory by the LDR instruction at location 0010. The next instruction transfers the larger of x and y from scratchpad register 2 to the accumulator. A comparison is then made by subtracting z from the larger

Table 8.2 Program for determining the largest of three unsigned 8-bit numbers x, y, and z

Memory location	Machine language instruction	Symbolic form of instruction	Remarks
0000	70	LDR 0	Transfer x to accumulator from memory
0001	00	00	
0002	1B	1B	
0003	71	LDR 1	Transfer y to register 1 from memory
0004	00	00	
0005	1C	1C	
0006	A1	SUB 1	Subtract y from x. Flip-flop C is set if $y > x$
0007	72	LDR 2	Transfer x to register 2 from memory as the
0008	00	00	tentative larger
0009	1B	1B	
000A	7C	JCZ	Test C for an end borrow. If no end borrow, then
000B	00	00	x is the larger and the next instruction
000C	10	10	is skipped
000D	72	LDR 2	Transfer y to register 2, replacing x if y is
000E	00	00	the larger
000F	1C	1C	
0010	71	LDR 1	Transfer z to register 1 from memory
0011	00	00	
0012	1D	1D	
0013	12	MOV 0 from 2	Transfer the larger of x, y to accumulator from register 2
0014	A1	SUB 1	Subtract z from the larger of x, y. C is set if z is largest
0015	12	MOV 0 from 2	Transfer the larger of x, y to accumulator as the tentative largest
0016	7C	JCZ	Test C for an end borrow. If there is an end
0017	00	00	borrow, z is the largest; otherwise, the
0018	1A	1A	next instruction is skipped
0019	11	MOV 0 from 1	Transfer z to accumulator as largest
001A	FA	HLT	Stop execution with the largest number in the accumulator
001B		x	Unsigned number x
001C		y	Unsigned number y
001D		z	Unsigned number z

of x and y. An end borrow indicates that z is the larger. The larger of x and y is moved to the accumulator from scratchpad register 2 as the tentative largest of the three. The value of C is again tested by a jump-on-carry-zero instruction JCZ. If $C = 0$, indicating no end borrow occurred from the previous subtraction, then a jump is made to the halt instruction terminating the program. Otherwise, the move instruction that sequentially follows the conditional jump instruction is executed replacing the content of the accumulator with the value of z, and then the halt instruction is encountered. In either case, the resulting content of the accumulator is the largest value of the three numbers x, y, and z.

In general, the basic philosophy behind decision making is to set up a test such that the result after the test indicates what course of action the microprocessor should take. By means of the conditional jump instructions, the microprocessor is capable of carrying out the correct alternative without human intervention. Of course, it is the responsibility of the programmer to provide a course of action for the microprocessor under all possible outcomes of the test.

8.3 PROGRAM LOOPS

Program loops are a useful means for accomplishing a number of similar operations with a common sequence of instructions. In general, a program loop is a sequence of instructions that is repeatedly executed by having some instruction in the group return the computer to the first instruction in the same group until a terminating condition is satisfied. The ability to perform looping is one of the features of a digital computer. One of the advantages obtained by this concept is that it is possible to reuse instructions without duplicating them, resulting in shorter programs.

As an illustration, consider the task of finding the sum of N numbers. This involves the successive addition of each number to a running total. A program for the procedure can be written that includes a separate sequence of instructions for each number to be added. However, if N is large, it is more feasible to write a sequence of instructions in the form of a program loop. Instead of having N program segments to add up all the numbers, a program loop has a single segment that is executed iteratively N times. Of course, some means is needed for keeping track of the number of iterations, so that the process can be stopped when the appropriate number of iterations has been completed. For this purpose, a register can be used as a counter, which is initialized prior to the first iteration and tested and modified each time the loop segment is executed. Also, some means is needed for selecting the number to be added each time through the loop segment. Assuming that the numbers all appear in successive locations of the main memory, this selection can be done with a pointer that is altered for each number to be added.

Generally, a program involving a loop includes an initialization part prior to the loop and operation, testing, and modification parts within the loop. These parts can be observed in a program written for the addition example, which is shown in Table 8.3. In this example, the contents of ten consecutive memory

Table 8.3 Program for finding the sum of ten unsigned 8-bit numbers

Memory location	Machine language instruction	Symbolic form of instruction	Remarks
0000	61	LRI 1	Set H and L to address of first piece of data
0001	00	00	
0002	62	LRI 2	
0003	15	15	
0004	63	LRI 3	Initialize loop counter to ten
0005	0A	0A	
0006	64	LRI 4	Set partial sum to zero
0007	00	00	
0008	65	LRI 5	Load constant 1 for decrementing
0009	01	01	
000A	14	MOV 0 from 4	Add data
000B	8F	ADD F	
000C	04	MOV 0 to 4	
000D	F5	IHL	Increment H and L
000E	13	MOV 0 from 3	Decrement counter
000F	A5	SUB 5	
0010	03	MOV 0 to 3	
0011	7D	JAN	Test program loop
0012	00	00	
0013	0A	0A	
0014	FA	HLT	
0015		$data_1$	List of ten numbers to be added
0016		$data_2$	
⋮		⋮	
001E		$data_{10}$	

locations are to be added. The first five instructions constitute the initialization part. Scratchpad registers H and L together are used to form a 16-bit pointer that will contain the current address of the data to be added. The first two instructions initialize them to the first data address. Next, scratchpad register 3 is initialized to ten. This scratchpad register will be used as a counter to maintain a record of the number of pieces of data still to be summed. Scratchpad register 4 is used to hold the running sum during the course of computation. It is initialized to zero by the fourth instruction. Finally, scratchpad register 5 is loaded with the constant 1 so that it can be used to decrement the counter as the data is summed. The next three instructions constitute the operation part of the loop. First the running sum is transferred to the accumulator from scratchpad register 4. The ADD F instruction that follows refers to the special scratchpad register designator F, which actually corresponds to the location in main memory addressed by the scratchpad register pair H and L. The content of this memory location is added to the running sum contained in the accumulator. The result is then transferred by the next move instruction to scratchpad register 4. Testing and modification are performed by the remaining instructions of the program. First, the content of the H and L scratchpad register pair is modified by the IHL instruction to contain the address of the data for the next iteration. Then, the content of the loop counter is moved from scratchpad register 3 to the accumulator, decremented, and returned to scratchpad register 3. Since a copy of the counter remains in the accumulator, it can now be used to determine whether the program loop is to be repeated or if the computation is complete. In particular, the counter indicates the number of pieces of data still to be added. Hence, if the accumulator is zero, then the computation is complete. This condition is tested by the jump-on-accumulator-not-zero instruction. If the accumulator is zero, then no jump occurs and a halt is encountered; otherwise, another iteration is performed.

The reader should be conscious of the fact that in the above program it is conceivable that the sum obtained by the ADD F instruction can exceed the capacity of the accumulator. That is, the sum at that point can consist of 9 bits. This is the overflow condition that has been previously discussed. Clearly, if such a condition can occur with the data being used, the overflow should be detected (in this case, by the carry flip-flop being set to 1 at the end of the ADD F instruction) and provision made for handling sums consisting of more than 1 byte. Typically, a multiprecision addition procedure is used in problems of this type.

8.4 MULTIDECISION MAKING

The basic concept of decision making was discussed in Sec. 8.2. The procedure at that time was to set up a test condition, i.e., a result upon which a decision is to be predicated (such as the sign of the accumulator), and then to test this condition using an appropriate conditional jump instruction. In this way the microprocessor is able to make a decision between which of two possible courses of action to take. This procedure can be generalized to allow for multidecisions. That is, the microprocessor can decide among several courses of action rather than just two. Generally, this involves obtaining a test condition that is one of a set of several possible test conditions. Associated with each possible test condition is a specific course of action to be taken by the microprocessor. The microprocessor now must select the one course of action based on the existing test condition.

In one approach, the selection can be accomplished by having the microprocessor check the existing test condition against one of the possibilities. If the check is satisfied, a jump is made to a routine to carry out the corresponding course of action. If not, the existing test condition is checked against a second of the possibilities and a jump is made to a second routine if there is an agreement. Again, if not, the process is repeated until the appropriate jump is made. Figure 8.2 illustrates this method of handling multidecisions.

An alternate approach in the selection of the appropriate course of action for the microprocessor to take uses a *branch table*. The basic idea in this case is to have a test condition which serves as a pointer for the branch table. The branch table consists of a set of starting addresses. These starting addresses are those for the routines to be entered as a consequence of the multidecision.

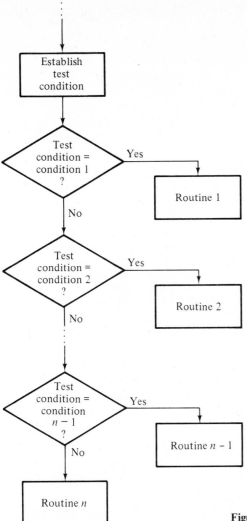

Figure 8.2 An approach to multidecision making.

To illustrate the branch table approach, assume a jump to one of eight possible routines is to be achieved as a consequence of a multidecision. Furthermore, assume the test condition has been set up according to the following scheme:

Jump to routine 1 if the accumulator contains 00000001.
Jump to routine 2 if the accumulator contains 00000010.
....
Jump to routine 8 if the accumulator contains 10000000.

The program in Table 8.4 provides for the appropriate jump once the test condition is in the accumulator. In this program, locations 2000 to 200F form the

Table 8.4 Multidecision making using a branch table

Memory location	Machine language instruction	Symbolic form of instruction	Remarks
1000	61	LRI 1	Load registers H and L with the starting address
1001	20	20	of the branch table
1002	62	LRI 2	
1003	00	00	
1004	F4	RSC	Reset C flip-flop
1005	F2	RTR	Place least-significant bit of accumulator
			into C flip-flop
1006	78	JCN	If C = 1, the content of H and L register pair
1007	10	10	points to branch table for the starting
1008	0E	0E	address of desired routine
1009	F5	IHL	If C = 0, increment the register pair H and L
100A	F5	IHL	twice, thus pointing to next location of
100B	7B	JMP	branch table, then jump to instruction in
100C	10	10	location 1005
100D	05	05	
100E	1F	MOV 0 from F	H and L point to the branch table location
100F	F5	IHL	containing the address of the routine to
1010	5F	MOV 2 from F	be executed. The address replaces the
1011	30	MOV 1 from 0	contents of registers H and L
1012	F9	JHL	Jump to desired routine
			Branch table:
2000	—	—	Routine 1 starting address
2001	—	—	
2002	—	—	Routine 2 starting address
2003	—	—	
200E	—	—	Routine 8 starting address
200F	—	—	

branch table and contain the eight starting addresses for the eight possible routines to be entered. The basic task for the program is to convert the pointer from the form in which it appears in the accumulator to the form of an address of the branch table. This will allow access to the appropriate location in the branch table so that its contents can be used as an address for a program jump. The first two instructions of Table 8.4 load the starting address of the branch table, i.e., 2000, into scratchpad registers H and L. A program loop is then entered for the purpose of determining the address of the location in the branch table that contains the starting address for the routine indicated by the accumulator. Initially in the program loop, the content of the accumulator is rotated so that the least-significant bit is entered into the carry flip-flop. If the carry flip-flop contains a 1 after the shift, the content of the H and L registers must indicate the address of the desired location in the branch table. On the other hand, if the carry flip-flop contains a 0, then the content of the register pair H and L is incremented and a jump is made to the beginning of the program loop. The process is then repeated in order to determine if the next entry of the branch table is the one associated with the original test condition.

Eventually, the conditional jump instruction in location 1006 will cause the microprocessor to leave the program loop and jump to the instruction in location 100E. When this occurs, the content of the scratchpad register pair H and L will be pointing to the location in the branch table that contains the starting address of the desired routine for the multidecision. Four instructions then load the starting address into the scratchpad register pair H and L. Of course, this destroys the branch table pointer already in H and L, so care must be taken to obtain the starting address information before the pointer is lost. For this purpose, the high-order part of the starting address is first moved to scratchpad register 0, rather than directly to scratchpad register H. The pointer in H and L is then incremented so as to point to the low-order part of the starting address, which is then moved to scratchpad register L since the pointer is no longer needed at this time. Next scratchpad register H is loaded with the high-order part of the starting address from scratchpad register 0. Finally, the jump-indirect instruction causes the content of the H and L scratchpad register pair to be entered into the program counter and program execution to continue with the correctly selected routine.

A difficulty that is common to both approaches just discussed is that either procedure involves sequencing through the test conditions for all courses of action in order to make the appropriate selection. This might require a great amount of time, especially if there is a large number of alternatives. To alleviate this difficulty, a procedure could be followed that searches through the test conditions in a *tree-like* fashion. Such a procedure successively eliminates half of the remaining test conditions until only one remains. Thus, for the example involving a branch table, the first step of the procedure could check to see whether the desired branch-table address is among the upper four or the lower four. Then, using the results of the first step, the second step could check to see whether the desired address is among the upper or lower two of the remaining four. Finally, the third step narrows it down to just the one address that is desired. As can be seen, just three steps are needed in this procedure, rather than the eight steps that are needed for the worst case in the previous procedure. In general, if the number of alternatives in a multidecision task is N, then the number of steps involved in a tree-like search procedure is equal to the smallest integer that is greater than or equal to $\log_2 N$. This represents a considerable savings in the number of steps over the previous procedure when N is large.

8.5 SUBROUTINES

Frequently, the same particular task must be performed at several different points in a program. A subroutine can be written for the particular task and used when necessary rather than rewriting the instructions for the particular task each time it is to be performed. Thus, a subroutine is an auxiliary program that is used by the main program. Since a subroutine is not really part of the main program, it is usually stored in a separate portion of the memory from the main program.

Entering and Exiting Subroutines

The concept of a subroutine requires that it can be entered from different points of the main program and that a subsequent return can be made to that point in the main program from which the subroutine was entered. Some means is therefore needed to store the address corresponding to the point in the main program to which execution is to return. Computers make use of various schemes for doing this. The use of a push-down stack, either in the microprocessor or in memory, is one such scheme. This scheme is used by the illustrative microprocessor. As was indicated in the last chapter, the jump-to-subroutine instruction of the illustrative microprocessor causes the content of the program counter (which at that time points to the next main-program instruction) to be pushed into the stack. This address is then available to be loaded back into the program counter when a return-from-subroutine instruction is encountered at the end of a subroutine. Another scheme involves saving the return address in a location within the portion of memory containing the subroutine. Still another scheme used by some computers involves saving the return address for a subroutine in a single register within the central processor.

It is generally desirable for subroutines to be able to jump to other subroutines. This is known as subroutine *nesting*. The three schemes just mentioned for saving subroutine return addresses differ in their ability to provide for subroutine nesting. The use of a push-down stack provides for the most general form of subroutine nesting. With a stack, not only can subroutines jump to other subroutines, but they can possibly jump to themselves. This is true, since each time a jump to a subroutine occurs the corresponding return address is placed into the stack, while all previously entered return addresses are pushed down and thus preserved. As return instructions are encountered, the stored return addresses are removed from the stack in the reverse order in which they were entered. This is the order in which they are needed in order to effect each return. Of course, the number of levels of subroutines (i.e., number of pending subroutines) is limited by the size of the stack, since each return address occupies a register in the stack. The illustrative microprocessor, for example, has a stack size of 64 registers, so that with it 64 levels of subroutines can be nested.

The scheme that involves placing the return address into a location within the subroutine will provide for a subroutine to jump to another subroutine, but not to itself. A subroutine may not jump to itself under this scheme because when the subroutine is in execution, the location for saving a return address is already occupied and may not therefore receive another return address. However, under this scheme, there is no limit to the number of levels in which subroutines can be nested, since the subroutine at each level provides a storage location for a return address. A disadvantage of this scheme is that subroutines cannot be placed into read-only memory, since the location for saving a return address needs to have both read and write capability. This can be a severe problem for a microprocessor, since many applications of microprocessors involve fixed programs.

The scheme making use of a single register within the central processor for saving a return address provides for no subroutine nesting at all, since obviously the return address for only one level can be saved in that register. However, this can be overcome with software by including instructions in each subroutine that save the content of the register in a memory location before any other subroutine is called. The memory location might be chosen to be in a different portion of memory from that of the subroutine, so that the subroutine could be put into a read-only memory. A return from such a subroutine could be effected by causing a jump to the location indicated by the saved address. With such software provision, nesting of subroutines under this scheme is comparable to the previous scheme in that a subroutine may call subroutines other than itself.

Each of the three mentioned subroutine schemes are used by various micro-processors, but the use of a push-down stack is the most dominate. With this approach, it is most common to have a *simulated stack* that uses locations in main memory, rather than a hardware push-down stack within the microprocessor. Such simulated stacks, as discussed in Chap. 6, make use of a special register, called the *stack pointer*, within the microprocessor. The stack pointer contains the address of a location in memory that is assumed to be the top of the stack. The stack pointer is generally initialized to a particular address at the beginning of a main program. Whenever information is entered into or removed from the stack, the stack pointer is adjusted automatically up or down so as to point to the new top of the stack. In this way, the stack is able to grow larger as more information is entered and to shrink as information is removed. Thus, there is virtually no limit to the number of return addresses for nested subroutines that can be saved in such a simulated stack.

Subroutine Arguments

An important aspect of the subroutine concept is the manner in which data, called the subroutine *arguments* or *parameters*, are passed, when necessary, between the main program and a subroutine. This problem can be handled in several ways. First, the arguments can be placed into the scratchpad registers by the main program before the jump-to-subroutine instruction is executed. The subroutine, written under the assumption that the arguments are in the scratchpad registers, then proceeds with its function and leaves the results in the scratchpad registers. Finally, after execution of the return instruction, the main program can pick up the results of the subroutine by referring to the scratchpad registers.

Table 8.5 Using the main program to pass arguments to a subroutine via the scratchpad registers

Memory location	Machine language instruction	Symbolic form of instruction	Remarks
0020	70	LDR 0	Place first argument into register D
0021	80	80	
0022	00	00	
0023	0D	MOV 0 to D	
0024	70	LDR 0	Place second argument into register E
0025	80	80	
0026	50	50	
0027	0E	MOV 0 to E	
0028	7F	JMS	Jump to subroutine at location 9000
0029	90	90	
002A	00	00	
002B	—	—	Reentry point from subroutine

This approach is illustrated in Table 8.5. Here it has been assumed that the arguments are in memory locations 8000 and 8050. The main program places the arguments into scratchpad registers D and E and then passes control to the subroutine in location 9000 by means of the jump-to-subroutine instruction.

If the arguments needed by the subroutine are in consecutive locations, an alternate approach to argument passing is to simply have the main program load the H and L scratchpad registers (or any other pair of scratchpad registers) with the address of the first argument and then jump to the subroutine. In this scheme the subroutine is responsible for obtaining the arguments. The advantage of this approach is that the arguments need not be entered into the scratchpad registers immediately, but rather fetched from memory by the subroutine when needed. Clearly, this is preferable when the number of arguments exceeds the number of available scratchpad registers. In addition, this approach also can be used for passing the results of a subroutine back to the main program. For example, part of the argument list can be reserved to hold the results of the subroutine.

In the above approach, a list of arguments is passed to the subroutine by having the main program load the H and L scratchpad registers with the address of the first argument. As a variation, the main program could pass to the subroutine a list of argument addresses rather than the arguments themselves. In this case, the main program loads the H and L scratchpad registers with the first location of the argument-address list. Thus, when the arguments are needed the subroutine must first obtain each address in the list and then proceed to obtain the corresponding argument. The advantage offered by this scheme is that the arguments themselves need not be in consecutive locations, since the argument-address list serves as a tabulation of the argument locations.

8.6 MULTIPRECISION ADDITION

The most commonly occurring word length in present commercial micro-processors consists of 8 bits. This precision roughly corresponds to 2.4 decimal digits. Clearly, this precision is not sufficient for many applications, and thus some means is needed for obtaining greater precision for number representation. This can be done in an obvious way by using two or more data words to comprise each number. Such multiprecision numbers can be stored within the memory in con-secutive word locations or within the microprocessor in consecutive scratchpad registers. The problem that remains then is to perform arithmetic on the multi-precision numbers using instructions that operate on single data words. The availability of the add-with-carry and subtract-with-carry instructions enable a rather simple program implementation of multiprecision addition and subtraction.

To implement unsigned double-precision addition, for example, the following procedure can be used. The low-order data words of the two numbers are added without an initial carry to generate the low-order sum and an end carry (carry from the most-significant bit position). The high-order data words are then added with an initial carry that is equal to the end carry from the low-order addition. The overall results are the double-precision sum of the two numbers and an end carry. This procedure is summarized by the flowchart of Fig. 8.3.

Table 8.6 shows a program written as a subroutine for this procedure. The two double-precision numbers to be added are referred to as X and Y and the sum as S. It is assumed that scratchpad registers 1 and 2 contain, respectively, the high- and low-order parts of X; and scratchpad registers 3 and 4 contain, respectively, the high- and low-order parts of Y. The high- and low-order parts of S are to be placed, respectively, into scratchpad registers 5 and 6.

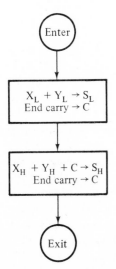

Figure 8.3 Flowchart for double-precision addition.

Table 8.6 Subroutine for double-precision addition

Scratchpad register allocation: R_1: X_H, R_3: Y_H, R_5: S_H
$\qquad\qquad\qquad\qquad\qquad$ R_2: X_L, R_4: Y_L, R_6: S_L

Memory location	Machine language instruction	Symbolic form of instruction	Remarks
0000	12	MOV 0 from 2	Transfer X_L to accumulator
0001	84	ADD 4	Add Y_L to X_L, C = end carry
0002	06	MOV 0 to 6	Transfer S_L to register 6
0003	11	MOV 0 from 1	Transfer X_H to accumulator
0004	93	ADC 3	Add Y_H to X_H with C as initial carry
0005	05	MOV 0 to 5	Transfer S_H to register 5
0006	F8	RET	Return from subroutine

The first instruction transfers the low-order part of X into the accumulator. The add instruction next adds the low-order part of Y to the low-order part of X with no initial carry. The carry flip-flop C is set equal to the end carry. The low-order part of S that results is next transferred to scratchpad register 6. The high-order part of X is then brought into the accumulator. An add-with-carry instruction is used to add the high-order part of Y to the high-order part of X using the content of C as the initial carry. The execution of this instruction places the high-order part of S into the accumulator and the overall end carry into C. This high-order part of S is transferred by the next instruction to scratchpad register 5. Finally, a return instruction causes the subroutine to be exited.

8.7 MULTIPLICATION

As can be noticed, there is no instruction in the illustrative microprocessor for multiplication. This lack of a multiplication instruction (as well as instructions for other arithmetic operations more complex than addition or subtraction, such as division) is typical of many microprocessors, although there are several exceptions. In those cases in which no multiplication instruction exists, a routine can be written using the available instructions to perform multiplication according to one of several known procedures. In particular, the common paper-and-pencil method of generating and summing partial products as discussed in Sec. 2.4 can be used.

Consider the multiplication of two unsigned 8-bit numbers. In general, the multiplication procedure can be carried out by forming a running sum of the partial products as they are encountered, starting with the partial product corresponding to the least-significant multiplier bit and ending with that for the most-significant multiplier bit. This is done by adding each partial product to the running sum. After each addition the running sum is shifted right to cause the proper alignment among the partial products. Each partial product is equal to either the multiplicand, if the corresponding multiplier bit is 1, or zero, if the multiplier bit is 0. After all eight partial products have been summed and the results shifted, the running sum will be equal to the desired 16-bit product.

The above procedure is detailed by the flowchart of Fig. 8.4. In the flowchart, the symbols X, Y, P_H, and P_L are used to represent, respectively, the 8-bit quantities for the multiplier, multiplicand, high-order product, and low-order product. The form of the flowchart is that of a loop. It begins with two blocks for initialization. The first block sets the high- and low-order parts of the product (used to contain the running sum) to zero. The second block sets a counter to 8 (corresponding to the number of multiplier bits), which keeps track of the number of times the loop is processed. The next block begins the loop segment. It causes the multiplier X to be shifted right with the least-significant bit entering the flag C to be tested. Actually, this least-significant bit corresponds to the current multiplier bit that is to be used to generate the partial product for the next addition to the running sum. The next block tests C. If $C = 1$, the multiplicand is added to the running sum with the end carry (carry from the most-significant bit) sent to the flag C. Otherwise, if $C = 0$, the addition is skipped, since the partial product is zero. In either case, the next block causes the high-order part of the running sum P_H and the end carry C to be circularly rotated right. By this rotation, the high-order part of the running sum P_H is shifted right; the content of the flag C, which prior to the rotation corresponds to the most-significant bit of the running sum, is transferred to the most-significant bit of P_H; and the least-significant bit of P_H is saved in the flag C. The following block then causes the low-order part of the running sum P_L to be shifted right, using the content of C for the new most-significant bit of P_L. This completes the operations for one iteration. The following block decrements the counter that keeps track of the loop iterations. The counter is then tested. If it is zero, the multiplication process is terminated; otherwise, another loop iteration is performed.

Using the above flowchart, a multiplication program can be written for the illustrative microprocessor in a straightforward manner. Actually, the flowchart was constructed with the illustrative microprocessor in mind, especially in the manner in which the flag C was used. However, most commercially available microprocessors do not differ significantly in the way their carry flag is treated, and they therefore may be generally programmed from the above flowchart with comparable ease.

Table 8.7 gives the multiplication program for the illustrative microprocessor written as a subroutine. In this program the scratchpad registers are used as follows: R_2 is the iteration counter, R_3 contains the multiplicand Y, R_4 contains the multiplier X, R_5 contains the high-order product P_H, and R_6 contains the low-order product P_L. The first three instructions of the program perform the initialization associated with the first two flowchart blocks. The next three instructions cause the multiplier X to be shifted right by moving X (in scratchpad register 4) into the accumulator, rotating right, and then moving the result back into scratchpad register 4. This leaves the multiplier bit that determines the next partial product in the carry flip-flop C. Next, the high-order product P_H is moved into

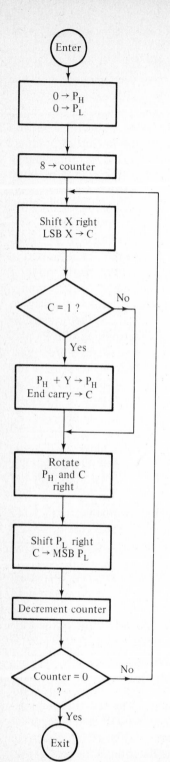

NOTATION:

X	8-bit multiplier
Y	8-bit multiplicand
P_H	8-bit high-order product
P_L	8-bit low-order product
C	Carry
LSB	Least-significant bit of
MSB	Most-significant bit of

Figure 8.4 Flowchart for unsigned multiplication.

Table 8.7 Subroutine for unsigned multiplication

Scratchpad register allocation: R_2: counter, R_3: multiplicand Y, R_4: multiplier X, R_5: high-order product P_H, R_6: low-order product P_L

Memory location	Machine language instruction	Symbolic form of instruction	Remarks
0000	65	LRI 5	Initialize product to zero
0001	00	00	
0002	66	LRI 6	
0003	00	00	
0004	62	LRI 2	Initialize iteration counter to 8
0005	08	08	
0006	14	MOV 0 from 4	Transfer multiplier into accumulator
0007	F2	RTR	Shift multiplier right, LSB goes into C
0008	04	MOV 0 to 4	Save new multiplier
0009	15	MOV 0 from 5	Transfer high-order product into accumulator
000A	7C	JCZ	Test multiplier bit. If 0, skip addition
000B	00	00	
000C	0E	0E	
000D	83	ADD 3	Add multiplicand to high-order product
000E	F2	RTR	Shift P_H right, save LSB in C
000F	05	MOV 0 to 5	Save new P_H
0010	16	MOV 0 from 6	Transfer low-order product into accumulator
0011	F2	RTR	Shift C and low-order product right
0012	06	MOV 0 to 6	Save new P_L
0013	F6	DHL	Decrement iteration counter
0014	12	MOV 0 from 2	Transfer counter into accumulator for testing
0015	7D	JAN	Test counter. If not zero begin new add-shift
0016	00	00	cycle
0017	06	06	
0018	F8	RET	Return from subroutine

the accumulator in preparation for the upcoming add and shift operations. The test for $C = 1$ indicated in the flowchart is accomplished with a jump-on-carry-zero instruction. This causes the next instruction to be skipped if $C = 0$. This next instruction adds the multiplicand Y to the accumulator (which contains P_H) and stores the end carry into C. P_H and C are then circularly rotated right by the RTR instruction. After the rotate operation, the new P_H is returned to scratchpad register 5. P_L and C are then shifted right together, as indicated by the next flowchart block, using three instructions that move P_L into the accumulator, rotate the accumulator, and return the new P_L to scratchpad register 6. The counter, corresponding to scratchpad register 2, is then decremented with a DHL instruction. The result is tested by moving it into the accumulator and executing a jump-on-accumulator-not-zero instruction. If the accumulator is zero, the subroutine is exited with a return instruction; otherwise, another iteration is performed.

8.8 PROGRAM LOADING

An important concern in the use of digital computers is the means by which programs are entered into the memory of the computer for execution. For many applications in which the microcomputer is dedicated to a set of fixed functions, the program appears in a read-only memory. However, for more flexible applications of microcomputers, various programs are entered into a read/write memory as needed. A way of accomplishing this is to provide a special program, called a *loader*, that performs the necessary input operations of bringing in any desired program from some input device and storing it in a read/write memory. The loader program itself might reside in a read-only memory, or it might be entered one instruction at a time into a read/write memory manually from front panel switches.

A loader used to bring general programs and perhaps data into the memory of a computer must be supplied with certain information for it to properly function. Typically, one of the following is needed:

1. The specification of the first and last memory addresses of the region to be occupied
2. The specification of the first memory address and a count of the number of words to be entered
3. The specification of the first memory address and a delimiter to mark the end of the information to be entered

In addition to providing the loading function, a loader program may also have additional features. For example, the loader program may have the capability to relocate programs in memory. This feature requires that the loader modify the memory references made by the instructions in a program that is being loaded so as to reflect the new location of that program in memory. Another feature of many loaders is the provision for error detection. That is, the loader checks for transmission errors between the input device and the memory.

Let us now consider a basic loader for the illustrative microprocessor. This will not only further illustrate the idea of a loader program, but will also help indicate how certain input operations are handled by a microcomputer. For the operation of this loader, it is assumed that the source of information to be loaded (either a program or data) comes from a specified input device. The input device obtains the information from a word-serial storage medium, such as magnetic or paper tape, and makes it available one word at a time to the microprocessor through an input port. Each word is assumed to be 8 bits long, the same as a data word of the microprocessor. The first two words to appear on the storage medium are assumed to be a 16-bit address (high-order byte first) to indicate to the loader the first memory location for the information to be loaded. The next two words are to specify a 16-bit address to indicate the last memory location. Finally, the remaining words are the information to be loaded between these two memory locations, inclusively.

In general, the loader brings in each word one at a time from the input device. The first four words are used as address information, as indicated above, and the remaining words are stored in memory. The input device, because of its mechanical nature, is typically much slower than the microprocessor in handling the words to be loaded. The microprocessor must therefore be programmed to wait until each word is made available by the device before it proceeds with inputting that word. For this purpose a second input port is used for status information. In this case, the input device sets a particular bit (the leftmost) at this status port to 1 each time a new word is available. The microprocessor must check this bit before it can input a word, waiting until it becomes a 1 if necessary. When the microprocessor does input a word, the bit is automatically reset to 0 by external circuitry so that the microprocessor does not input the same word twice.†

The operation of the loader program is outlined by the flowchart of Fig. 8.5. An input subroutine is used at a number of points in the mainline of the procedure. This subroutine first inputs the status of the input device, which it then tests to determine if a data word is ready to be inputted. If ready, the data word is brought in by the next block of the flowchart; otherwise, a jump is made back to repeat the status checking process. In this way, the microprocessor waits in a loop until a word is available. The mainline of the procedure uses this subroutine 4 times to bring in the first four words from the input device, followed each time with a transfer of the word into some register to be used as the appropriate half of the first- or last-word address. A loop is then entered that brings into memory the words to be loaded. Each word is inputted with the input subroutine and then transferred to the appropriate memory location, which is determined by the current value of the first-word address (FWA). FWA is incremented each time through the loop so that it will correspond to the proper location in memory for storing each word. A test is made at the end of the loop to determine if FWA exceeds the last-word address (LWA). If it does, the loading procedure is terminated; otherwise, another iteration of the loop is processed.

A program for the loader is given in Table 8.8. As it is written, it begins at location 0000. However, in actual use, the loader would probably be located elsewhere in the memory, say at the high end, to be out of the way of other programs. Two input ports are referenced by the program, port 00 for status and port 01 for data. The first set of instructions are for the mainline of the procedure, whereas the instructions beginning at location 001D are for the input subroutine. In this program, scratchpad registers 1, 2, 3, and 4 are used to contain FWA_H, FWA_L, LWA_H, and LWA_L, respectively. These are each loaded with address information from the input device. This is done in each case with a jump-to-subroutine instruction, which causes the input subroutine to be executed, followed by an appropriate move instruction. The loop indicated in the flowchart begins at location 0010 with a jump to the input subroutine. After the subroutine is executed, the accumulator contains the newly inputted word. This word is transferred to the appropriate location in memory with the use of the special feature of

---

† The details of this operation will be discussed in Sec. 9.2.

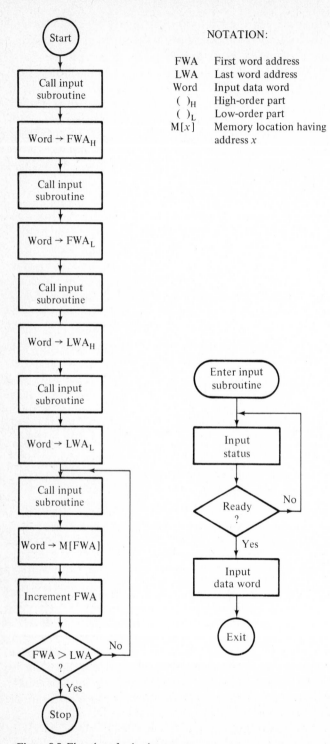

NOTATION:

FWA	First word address
LWA	Last word address
Word	Input data word
( )$_H$	High-order part
( )$_L$	Low-order part
M[x]	Memory location having address x

Figure 8.5 Flowchart for loader program.

Table 8.8 Loader program

Scratchpad register allocation: R_1: FWA$_H$, R_3: LWA$_H$,
 R_2: FWA$_L$, R_4: LWA$_L$

Memory location	Machine language instruction	Symbolic form of instruction	Remarks
0000	7F	JMS	Jump to input subroutine, bring in FWA$_H$
0001	00	00	
0002	1D	1D	
0003	01	MOV 0 to 1	
0004	7F	JMS	Bring in FWA$_L$
0005	00	00	
0006	1D	1D	
0007	02	MOV 0 to 2	
0008	7F	JMS	Bring in LWA$_H$
0009	00	00	
000A	1D	1D	
000B	03	MOV 0 to 3	
000C	7F	JMS	Bring in LWA$_L$
000D	00	00	
000E	1D	1D	
000F	04	MOV 0 to 4	
0010	7F	JMS	Begin loop, bring in data word
0011	00	00	
0012	1D	1D	
0013	0F	MOV 0 to F	Transfer word to M[FWA]
0014	F5	IHL	Increment FWA
0015	14	MOV 0 from 4	Subtract double precision FWA from LWA.
0016	A2	SUB 2	C is set if FWA > LWA
0017	13	MOV 0 from 3	
0018	B1	SBC 1	
0019	7C	JCZ	Test C for an end borrow. If no end borrow,
001A	00	00	bring in another word
001B	10	10	
001C	FA	HLT	Halt
001D	FD	INP	Begin input subroutine, input status
001E	00	00	
001F	7A	JAP	Test sign bit of status word, if 0 repeat
0020	00	00	status check
0021	1D	1D	
0022	FD	INP	Input data word into accumulator from
0023	01	01	input device
0024	F8	RET	Return from subroutine

the illustrative microprocessor that treats the scratchpad designator F as a memory reference. Specifically, a MOV 0 to F instruction transfers the content of the accumulator to the memory location whose address is specified by the combined content of scratchpad registers 1 and 2 (i.e., H and L). Since scratchpad registers 1 and 2 contain the current value of FWA, the word is placed into the desired location of memory. The next instruction, IHL, increments the value of

FWA. The test to determine whether FWA exceeds LWA is done with a double-precision subtraction and a conditional jump. The double-precision subtraction proceeds by first subtracting the low-order part of FWA from the low-order part of LWA and then subtracting the high-order part of FWA from the high-order part of LWA using the borrow from the low-order subtraction. The final end borrow is left in the C flip-flop. If the C flip-flop is 0, then FWA does not exceed LWA. The next instruction is the jump-on-carry-zero instruction to the beginning of the loop. If the C flip-flop is 0, then another loop iteration is processed; otherwise, the following halt instruction terminates the program.

The input subroutine begins by inputting a word from the status port 00 into the accumulator. The leftmost bit (i.e., the sign bit) is tested with a jump-on-accumulator-positive instruction. If the accumulator is positive, then the sign bit is 0, indicating that the input device is not ready. In that case, a jump is made back to the beginning of the subroutine to repeat the process. Otherwise, the following input instruction brings a data word from the input port 01 into the accumulator. A return instruction then terminates the subroutine.

It should be noted that the ready status bit was conveniently chosen to coincide with the sign bit of the status word, i.e., the word at the status input port. This allowed it to be tested with a single instruction. In a more general situation, the status bit of interest might appear at any position in the status word. In that case, it can be tested by first isolating it from the other status bits. This is easily done by ANDing the status word with another word, called a *mask*, having 1 in the desired bit position and 0 in all other bit positions. The result is then tested with either a jump-on-accumulator-zero or a jump-on-accumulator-not-zero instruction. Thus, the JAP instruction used to test the leftmost status bit in the loader program of Table 8.8 could be replaced by the following sequence

LRI 5

80 (mask)

AND 5

JAZ

00

1D

8.9 ASSEMBLY LANGUAGE PROGRAMMING

Up to this point our attention has been directed toward machine language programming. Because of its hardware design, programs written in machine language are the only type of programs that can be actually executed in a microcomputer. However, a problem does not have to be very complex before a long, tedious program must be written for its solution. For this reason manufacturers frequently provide special programs that aid in the preparation of a machine language program.

Assemblers

A definite convenience in writing a program is to allow the use of symbolic names to denote the operations, called *mnemonic operation codes*, as well as symbolic names to denote the addresses in instructions, rather than their numerical designators. For example, to load the content of memory location 5386_{16} into the accumulator in the microprocessor of the preceding chapter requires the 3-byte instruction (expressed in hexadecimal) 705386. Certainly a more convenient and readable way of writing this is LDR 0, X where LDR is the mnemonic operation code for the operation, 0 is the scratchpad designator for the accumulator, and X is the symbolic designator for memory location 5386.† This convenience can be achieved if a means is available for substituting numbers for the symbolic names (i.e., operation and address designators) after the program is written. This is precisely the main role of an *assembler*. A program written in this new convenient form is called an *assembly language program* and each instruction is known as an *assembly language statement*.

In general, a program written in an assembly language is essentially the same as a machine language program with symbolic names for the addresses of the operands, symbolic names for the addresses of the instructions, and mnemonic operation codes for the operations. The job of the assembler is to replace each mnemonic operation code by the corresponding machine language operation code, assign memory locations to each instruction and operand, and substitute numerical addresses for the symbolic addresses. Most frequently there is a one-to-one correspondence between each assembly language statement written by the programmer and each machine language instruction generated by the assembler. There are occasions, however, when several machine language instructions are generated from a single assembly language statement.

Figure 8.6 illustrates the manner in which an assembler is used. The assembly language program is called a *source program* and the machine language program that is generated is called an *object program*. The assembler, which serves as a translator, is entered into a computer along with the source program. The source program appears as "data" to the assembler. The net result is that an object program is generated. When the assembler is used in the same microcomputer as the final object program, it is called a *self assembler*. Frequently, however, the assembler is written so that a large, general-purpose computer is used to perform the translation process. This is known as a *cross assembler*.

When an assembly language program is translated, the assembler uses tables to assign numerical values to the mnemonic operation codes and symbolic addresses. Included in the assembler is a table that lists all the allowable mnemonic operation codes and their corresponding numerical operation codes. Thus, the substitution is readily performed. In order to assign a numerical address

---

† It should be noted that in all the programs written thus far, the entries in the column labeled "Machine language instruction" are the actual program (expressed in hexadecimal). The entries in the "Symbolic form of instruction" column have been included for ease of reading. What is being proposed at this time is that instructions similar to those in the "Symbolic form of instruction" column be used as the program.

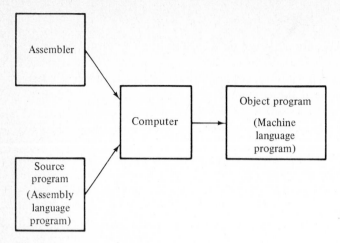

Figure 8.6 The assembly process.

to each symbolic address, the assembler first makes a table, called a *symbol table*, that lists all the symbolic addresses. Once this is done, the assembler assigns numerical memory locations to the symbolic addresses and then performs the necessary substitutions.

One of the advantages gained by using an assembly language is the ease in which statements can be inserted or deleted in the source program. For example, when writing a program, it is frequently realized that some additional instructions must be inserted at some earlier point in the program. If machine language is being used, the insertion of a group of instructions requires moving all the program words following the insertion. Furthermore, the address field of some of the instructions in the program may now refer to the displaced words (e.g., when program loops or jumps exist). This means that each of these address fields must be changed to account for the relocation of the displaced words. On the other hand, when an assembly language is used, this problem does not occur since addresses are not given by their actual numerical designators. Hence, statements can be inserted with no difficulty. In a similar manner, statements can be easily deleted from an assembly language program.

Another feature usually found in assemblers is that they have some error-detecting capability. Of course, in general, the assembler cannot check the logical reasoning behind the program; however, it can check for the adherence to the syntactical restrictions that have been placed on the assembly language and inform the programmer when these restrictions have not been followed.

The Assembly Language

To illustrate the close relationship between an assembly language program and a machine language program, again consider the program in Sec. 8.3 for finding the sum of ten unsigned 8-bit numbers. The machine language program for the illus-

Table 8.9 An assembly language program corresponding to Table 8.3

Label	Code	Operand	Comments
	LRI	1, H(NUM) ;	SET H AND L TO ADDRESS OF FIRST DATA
	LRI	2, L(NUM) ;	
	LRI	3, 10D ;	INITIALIZE LOOP COUNTER
	LRI	4, 0D ;	SET PARTIAL SUM TO ZERO
	LRI	5, 1D ;	LOAD CONSTANT 1 FOR DECREMENTING
LOOP:	MOV	0, 4 ;	ADD DATA
	ADD	F	
	MOV	4, 0	
	IHL	;	INCREMENT H AND L
	MOV	0, 3 ;	DECREMENT COUNTER
	SUB	5	
	MOV	3, 0	
	JAN	LOOP ;	TEST LOOP COUNTER
	HLT		
NUM:	RES	10D ;	RESERVE SPACE FOR TEN NUMBERS
	END		

trative microprocessor was given in Table 8.3. When this program is loaded into a microcomputer, only the numbers appearing in the column headed "Machine language instruction" are used.

An assembly language program for this same example is given in Table 8.9. Each line of the program corresponds to one assembly language statement. It should be noted that an assembly language statement consists of four parts: a label field, a code field, an operand field, and a comment field.

The purpose of the *label field* is to provide a reference to the address of an instruction if such is needed. That is, symbolic names are used in this field rather than numerical addresses. Usually there is a restriction on these names in that they must be fewer than a specified number of characters, the first character must be alphabetic, and certain reserved character combinations (e.g., the mnemonic operation codes) are not allowed. Thus, these are symbolic addresses that are selected to make the program easier to read and to provide a reference when the address of an instruction is needed. Since not every instruction needs to be referenced, the label field may be empty. In the program of Table 8.9, the label LOOP is used to indicate the start of the program loop and as a reference point for the jump-on-accumulator-not-zero instruction. Finally, the end of the label field in an assembly language statement is typically indicated by a delimiter, e.g., a colon.

The next field in the assembly language statement is the *code field*. This field contains the mnemonic name of the operation code of the instruction. Hence, it specifies the operation to be performed. Clearly, it is easier for a programmer to learn the set of mnemonic operation codes rather than the numerical designators for an operation.

The third field in an assembly language statement is the *operand field*. This field consists of any information needed by the code field to complete the specification of the instruction. For example, it may contain a symbolic reference address of memory, a scratchpad register designator, or data itself. Frequently, the assembler allows the specification of a computational procedure in the operand field. For example, arithmetic formulas may be allowed that result in the operand address or, in the case of a jump instruction, the number of locations, forward or backward, that must be skipped. If more than one piece of information is needed in the operand field, each is normally separated by a comma. When a symbolic reference address is given it must appear exactly as it appears in the label field. Typically, data information in the operand field can be specified in binary, octal, decimal, or hexadecimal form. By having a code letter appear at the end of the data (e.g., B, O, D, or H†) the assembler knows the base of the data being specified in the assembly language statement. In order to separate the code field from the operand field, at least one blank space is normally required.

To illustrate some of the above points, again consider the program in Table 8.9. The first two statements illustrate the idea of a computational procedure that may appear in the operand field. In this case H( ) is a computational procedure for masking the high-order 8 bits of what appears in parentheses. Thus, H(NUM) is interpreted to mean the high-order 8 bits of the numerical address assigned to NUM. In this program, NUM is used as the symbolic address for the first piece of data. When used in conjunction with the LRI instruction, these 8 bits form the immediate data of the instruction. Thus, LRI 1, H(NUM) is an assembly language statement causing the high-order 8 bits of the first data address to be entered into scratchpad register 1. Similarly, L( ) is the low-order 8-bit masking operation, and hence, L(NUM) is interpreted to mean the low-order 8 bits of the address assigned to NUM. These 8 bits are entered by the assembler as the second byte in the machine language instruction LRI 2, L(NUM).

Three more points should be noted in Table 8.9. First, when data is specified in the operand field, the base of the data is indicated. For example, in the third assembly language statement, the 10D indicates that the constant 10 is to be regarded as a decimal number. The assembler proceeds to convert this decimal number into binary during the assembly process. The second point that should be noted is that in the program all scratchpad registers are designated by their hexadecimal designator. Finally, the comma in the MOV statement is always interpreted as the word *from*. Thus, the statement MOV 0,4 means to load scratchpad register 0 (the accumulator) from scratchpad register 4. It should be recalled that the illustrative microprocessor requires at least one of the registers in a MOV instruction to be 0, 1, or 2. If the programmer violates this restriction, the assembler detects the error and the programmer is notified. This is typical of the type of error-detecting capability found in assemblers.

---

† When the data is hexadecimal, the restriction is placed that the first digit must be one of the symbols 0, 1, ..., 9.

The final field in an assembly language statement is the *comment field*. The purpose of this field is to provide the programmer with the convenience of appending any remarks to the statement to make the program easier to read. This field is ignored by the assembler when the source program is translated into an object program. Typically, the only restriction placed on this field is that it must be preceded by a delimiter (e.g., a semicolon).

Assembler Directives

Typical of all assembly languages, assembler directives are introduced for special purposes. An assembler directive, when used in an assembly language program, provides information that is needed to control the translation from the source language to the object language, but is never performed as an actual instruction during the execution of the object program. Assembler directives, however, are assigned mnemonics that appear in the code field of assembly language statements.

One type of assembler directive is used to define a word of data. Its function is to allow the assembler to insert a constant into a memory location. In particular, when the assembler translates such a statement, the numerical constant appearing in the operand field is stored at the symbolic address indicated by the label field of the assembler directive statement. Similarly, there are assembler directives to define an ASCII character. As an illustration, assume the mnemonic code DB corresponds to the assembler directive to define a byte. Then, when the assembler translates the statement

CONST: DB 53H

the hexadecimal number 53 is placed into the memory location whose address is denoted by CONST.

Another type of assembler directive is used to reserve and name a series of memory locations. This is useful when a group of memory locations must be set aside for data and when temporary storage locations must be named. The number of locations reserved is given by the quantity appearing in the operand field of the assembly language statement. The symbolic address given to the first of these reserved locations is the symbolic address of the defining assembler directive. This type of directive appears in the assembly language program of Table 8.9. Here, RES is the mnemonic code for the assembler directive which reserves a set of memory locations. The statement

NUM: RES 10D

causes the assembler to reserve ten memory locations (since D indicates a decimal quantity), where NUM is the symbolic address of the first of these locations.

In addition to the aforementioned assembler directives, others are used to define an absolute address in the object program and to define the end of the source program. The second case is illustrated by the END directive appearing at the end of the program in Table 8.9. This directive simply serves to inform the assembler that the physical end of the source program has been reached. To illustrate the address-assigning directive, let ORG be its mnemonic. Then, the assembly language statement

ORG 1000H

informs the assembler that the first machine language word for the statement immediately following the assembler directive statement should be assigned the hexadecimal memory location 1000. Thus, if this statement were to appear as the first statement of the program in Table 8.9, the address of the LRI 1,H(NUM) instruction would be 1000; while if it appeared between the HLT and RES statements, NUM would be assigned the memory location 1000.

Macroinstructions

Some assemblers permit the programmer to expand upon the assembly language of the microprocessor by means of *macroinstructions*. Macroinstructions are particularly convenient when the programmer finds that a certain set of operations has to be used repeatedly. The programmer can define this sequence of operations as a macroinstruction. Then, it becomes part of the assembly language repertoire and can be used as often as the programmer wishes. Each time the macroinstruction appears in the assembly language program, the assembler replaces it by the sequence of machine language instructions that forms its definition.

The reader should not confuse a macroinstruction with a subroutine. A subroutine is a subprogram that is entered by a jump-to-subroutine instruction and exited by a return instruction. The subroutine itself appears only once within the microcomputer, but, in general, is referenced several times. A macroinstruction, on the other hand, is a sequence of instructions that are inserted into the object program by the assembler every time reference is made to the macroinstruction. Thus, the same set of instructions is duplicated in the object program with only changes made to the addresses of the operands, if necessary. Thus, in general, a program using macroinstructions requires more memory space than a program using subroutines. However, there is no linkage needed, and hence, the program tends to be faster in execution.

8.10 COMPILERS

There is another class of translators, called *compilers*, that are available. FORTRAN, PL/1, and PASCAL are all examples of programming languages that are translated by compilers. Programming languages that are translated into machine language by a compiler are frequently referred to as *higher-level languages*. These languages are characterized by the fact that they are designed to allow the description of algorithmic processes in a relatively machine-independent form. Thus, the programmer can avoid having to be familiar with the idiosyncrasies of the particular microcomputer that will be used. Also, the program can be run on many different computers, as long as they each have an appropriate compiler.

When a higher-level language is translated into machine language, generally each statement in the source language translates into several machine language instructions. This is in contrast to assemblers which basically involve a one-to-one translation. Thus, higher-level languages enable the writing of a source program in a very compact manner.

In comparison to machine or assembly language, higher-level languages are powerful and convenient to use. However, to achieve convenience and generality, compilers are long programs and require a large amount of memory for their storage during program translation. Furthermore, their use is generally not as flexible as machine language. For example, they do not provide for the direct manipulation of data in registers. This inflexibility is a handicap in many applications that are pertinent to microprocessors, especially those involving real-time control.

PROBLEMS

8.1 Write a program that will rearrange three unsigned numbers in memory so that they appear in ascending order.

8.2 Rewrite the multidecision program in Sec. 8.4 using the tree-like search procedure described in that section.

8.3 Write a program for triple-precision addition.

8.4 Write a program for double-precision subtraction.

8.5 Write a program for adding two 2-digit decimal numbers. The numbers are to be represented in 8421 binary-coded decimal, with both digits contained in 1 byte. After the addition is performed, the 2-digit sum is to be in the accumulator and the end carry in the carry flip-flop.

8.6 Write a program to divide one 8-bit integer by another 8-bit integer. Make appropriate assumptions regarding overflow and truncation.

8.7 Write a program to multiply a 2-byte number by a 1-byte number. What is the maximum possible length of the result?

8.8 Write a program that inputs eight numbers from a relatively slow device and computes their average. Assume that the device has two input ports, one for data and the other for status. The leftmost status bit will be 1 when a new number is available in the data input port.

8.9 Write a loader program for the illustrative microprocessor assuming the following format for the information to be loaded.

First-word address, high order
First-word address, low order
Word count, high order
Word count, low order
Words to be loaded

The first-word address specifies the beginning of the memory region to be loaded and the word count specifies the number of words to be loaded.

8.10 Frequently, microcomputer applications involve items of information that are smaller than a data word. In such cases, a programmer might place two or more of the items into a single data word so that they can be stored in memory more compactly. This is referred to as *packing* a word. Generally, before the items of information can be used, the data words must be separated into individual items. This is known as *unpacking*. Suppose decimal digits, encoded in 8421 BCD, are to be stored 2 digits per byte. Write a subroutine to perform the packing and another to perform the unpacking. In either case, scratchpad registers 1 and 2 are allocated to contain the individual digits in their 4 least-significant bit positions and the accumulator is allocated to contain the packed word.

8.11 Write a program to output all the odd numbers appearing in memory locations 80_{16} to FF_{16}. Assume that the output device accepts information as fast as the microprocessor can output it.

8.12 Write a subroutine to determine if an overflow occurs when two unsigned arguments, appearing in scratchpad registers 1 and 2, are added. If there is an overflow, the subroutine is to halt; otherwise, it is to return to the main program.

8.13 Write a program to reverse the order of the bits of the number appearing in the accumulator and leave the results in the accumulator. For example, the number 00010011 would become 11001000.

8.14 Suppose that it is desirable to determine which leftmost bit is equal to 1 in the accumulator of the illustrative microprocessor. For this purpose, let the accumulator bits be assigned the numbers 0, 1, ..., 7 from right to left, as usual. Write a subroutine to determine the number corresponding to the leftmost 1 in the accumulator. The result is to be placed into the accumulator. Such a subroutine is useful in determining the highest-priority event from a number of possible events, as will be seen in discussing program interrupts in Chap. 9.

8.15 It was mentioned in Chap. 2 that alphanumeric information when transferred between a computer and a peripheral device is generally represented by some sort of code, such as ASCII. Suppose that hexadecimal numbers are to be entered into a microcomputer from an ASCII-coded keyboard and also that hexadecimal numbers are to be outputted to an ASCII-coded printer. In either case, each hexadecimal digit is encoded in ASCII and transferred separately. However, when the numbers are used for computation within the microcomputer, they should be represented in binary. For this purpose, subroutines could be provided to convert between the binary representation of numbers and their ASCII-coded hexadecimal representation. Write a subroutine to convert two ASCII-encoded hexadecimal digits into an 8-bit binary number. Also, write another subroutine to convert an 8-bit binary number into two ASCII-encoded hexadecimal digits. In either case, scratchpad registers 1 and 2 are allocated to contain the ASCII digits and the accumulator is allocated to contain the binary number. Assume the 8-bit ASCII code with the parity bit always equal to 0. In performing either conversion, note that the decimal digits are encoded sequentially and so are the hexadecimal characters A through F, but that a gap of seven characters separates 9 from A.

8.16 Write a program to input two 2-digit hexadecimal numbers from an ASCII keyboard, add them, and then output the 8-bit sum as a 2-digit hexadecimal number to an ASCII printer. Use the subroutines of Prob. 8.15 to convert between ASCII and binary. Assume that the data ports for both the keyboard and printer have device code 00. Furthermore, an input port having the code 01 provides status for both devices. Specifically, the leftmost status bit is 1 when a character is available from the keyboard; whereas, the rightmost status bit is 0 when the printer can accept another character to be printed. The program should check these two status bits before proceeding with a corresponding I/O data transfer.

NINE

INTERFACING CONCEPTS

A microcomputer system is made up of different types of components, which generally include a microprocessor, memory units, I/O registers, and peripheral devices. The interconnection of these components, which is a primary concern in the design of a microcomputer system, must take into account the nature and timing of the signals that appear at the interfaces between components. For the purpose of achieving compatibility of signals, it is generally necessary to select appropriate components and design supplementary circuits. This is referred to as *interfacing*. In regard to microcomputer systems, interfacing can be separated into two areas of concern. One area involves the connection of the components, such as memory units and input/output registers, to the buses of a microprocessor. Such interfacing is primarily concerned with the timing and control of the buses and the selection of a component so as to effect a data transfer at a given time between the selected component and the microprocessor.

The other area of concern involves interfacing components external to the microcomputer, such as peripheral devices, data channels, and controllers, to a part of the microcomputer. Such interfacing does not directly involve the buses of the microprocessor; so it is comparatively less structured. It is concerned with converting signals associated with the external components, which might be of any nature (including analog), to signals compatible with the buses and vice versa.

9.1 INPUT/OUTPUT PORTS

By convention, the direction of input and output information flow involving a microprocessor is normally regarded relative to the microprocessor itself. Thus, an *input port* refers to any source of data, such as a register, that is connected in a selectable manner to a microprocessor data bus. It supplies a data word to the microprocessor when selected. An *output port* refers to a receptacle of data, such as a register, that is connected in a selectable manner to a microprocessor data bus. It receives a data word from the microprocessor when selected. Most microprocessors use all or part of their address bus to designate which input or output port is selected. Also, input ports and output ports are often distinguished from each other and memory locations by certain control lines.

I/O Ports for the Illustrative Microprocessor

Figure 9.1 shows a network consisting of a typical input port and a typical output port for the illustrative microprocessor. A unique 8-bit device code is assigned to these two ports so that the microprocessor can distinguish them from all other input or output ports. In this case, both ports are assigned the same device code (01100101), which is allowed since the two ports are further distinguished by the separate control lines In and Out. During the execution of an input or output instruction, the device code for the port to be accessed is obtained from the instruction and placed onto the lower half of the Address bus. To detect the presence of the particular device code assigned to the ports of Fig. 9.1, an 8-bit AND gate with the appropriate lines inverted is connected to the lower half of the Address bus. The output line of this AND gate, labeled "Select," is used in the selection of either of the two ports.

The input port includes an 8-bit register that is assumed to contain information supplied by some external device. Eight 3-state drivers couple the output lines of this register to the Data bus. These 3-state drivers are all enabled by the AND of the Select signal and the In control signal from the microprocessor. Thus, the content of the register is placed onto the Data bus when (1) Select is logic-1, indicating that the device code assigned to this input port has been specified, and (2) In is logic-1, indicating that an input instruction is being executed and that it is the proper time in the instruction cycle to input information. Once information is placed onto the Data bus, it is the responsibility of the microprocessor to transfer it to the proper destination within the microprocessor, which is the accumulator.

One machine cycle, the third of an input instruction, is used to perform an input data transfer. The timing relationship among the various signals during this machine cycle is shown in Fig. 9.2. Three clock pulses comprise the machine cycle. At the beginning of the first clock pulse T_1 the microprocessor places the appropriate device code onto the lower half of the Address bus. The In control line becomes logic-1 with the trailing edge of T_1 and remains at logic-1 until the leading edge of the third clock pulse T_3. It is assumed that the Data bus, in response to the In signal, will contain valid data from the input port during the time between the leading edges of T_2 and T_3. Finally, this data on the bus is strobed into the microprocessor accumulator at the end of T_2.

It should be noticed that two timing constraints are placed upon the circuitry for the input port with this scheme. One time constraint is that the Data bus must

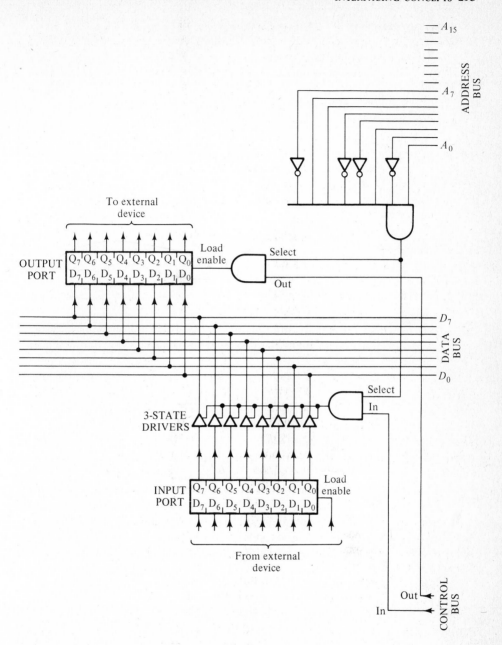

Figure 9.1 Typical network for an input port and an output port for the illustrative microprocessor.

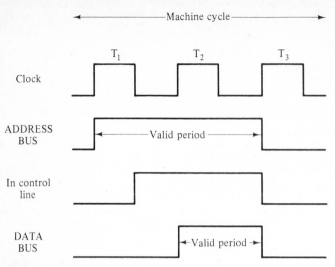

Figure 9.2 Timing diagram for an input data transfer to the illustrative microprocessor.

become valid within a certain amount of time (i.e., one-half of a clock period) after the In control signal becomes logic-1. This constraint implies that the delay encountered in the 3-state drivers plus the delay encountered in the two-input AND gate connected to the drivers must be no greater than one-half of a clock period.

The second time constraint is that the Data bus must become valid within one clock period after the device code appears on the Address bus. This constraint implies that the sum of the delay encountered in the 8-input AND gate and the connected inverters used to generate the Select signal plus the previously indicated delay must be no greater than one clock period.

Schemes for inputting data used by various microprocessors may differ somewhat from this scheme, but similar time constraints exist for them. These constraints on the external components are usually quite liberal. This is due to the fact that the components comprising an input or output port are usually of a higher speed than that of the microprocessor. For example, medium-scale integrated TTL, which is relatively fast, might be used to implement an input port for a microprocessor that is fabricated with large-scale integrated MOS logic, which is relatively slow.

The output port shown in Fig. 9.1 has an 8-bit register, which is assumed to supply information to an external device. The register consists of D-type clocked latches that are controlled by a common load-enable line. The D input terminals are connected directly to the Data bus. A two-input AND gate that drives the load-enable line combines the Select signal with the Out control signal. Thus, the content of the Data bus, which comes from the accumulator of the microprocessor, is transferred into the output-port register when (1) Select is logic-1, indicating that the device code assigned to this output port has been specified, and

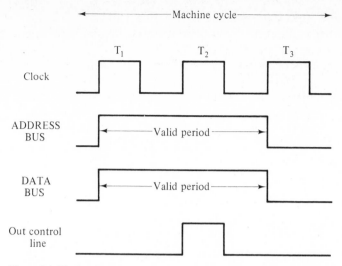

Figure 9.3 Timing diagram for an output data transfer from the illustrative microprocessor.

(2) Out is logic-1, indicating that an output instruction is being executed and that it is the proper time in the instruction cycle to output information.

The third machine cycle for the execution of an output instruction is used to perform the output data transfer. The timing relationship among the various signals during this machine cycle is shown in Fig. 9.3. At the beginning of clock pulse T_1 the lower-half of the Address bus and the Data bus become valid as determined by the microprocessor. That is, both address and data information are placed onto the appropriate buses. The data is then strobed into the output register by a pulse on the Out control line that occurs coincident with the T_2 clock pulse.

Time constraints are placed on the circuitry for an output port that are similar to those for an input port. Again they are normally of little concern due to the relatively fast components that are usually used to implement input and output ports.

I/O Variations

The differences between the I/O scheme just discussed for the illustrative microprocessor and some I/O schemes for commercial microprocessors primarily concern the nature of the control signals that determine the type and timing of data transfers. The In and Out control signals of the illustrative microprocessor serve as strobes that provide for both the necessary timing and control of the I/O transfers. Many schemes for commercial microprocessors, however, require that signals similar to In and Out be derived by logically combining other control signals.

In some cases, a control line from the microprocessor is provided that has the purpose of specifying the direction of the data bus. This control line, referred to as say Data-out, indicates the output direction when at one logic value, say logic-1, and the input direction when at the other logic value. A clock line to the micro-processor or a second control line is then used as a strobe to determine the times of data transfers. Interfacing I/O ports to such microprocessors can be done in a manner similar to that indicated for the illustrative microprocessor by forming signals corresponding to In and Out, as follows:

$$\text{In} = \overline{(\text{Data-out})}\ \text{Strobe}$$

$$\text{Out} = (\text{Data-out})\ \text{Strobe}$$

where Strobe refers to the control line that determines the transfer time.

Some data-transfer schemes of microprocessors involve sending a control word over the data bus during the beginning of a machine cycle that specifies precisely what type of data transfer is to occur, such as data-in, data-out, memory-read, or memory-write. This control word is then stored in an external register so that it may be used in combination with the clock or other control signals to derive such signals as In, Out, Read, and Write of the illustrative microprocessor. In this way, the corresponding control lines from the microprocessor need not be provided.

9.2 HANDSHAKING

As was indicated in the previous section, input and output ports provide the means for coupling external devices to a microprocessor. An external device can be anything that supplies or accepts digital information, such as a mass storage unit, a data terminal, a data-acquisition instrument, a machine-tool controller, or even another microprocessor. Most external devices operate in a manner that is inherently independent of the timing of the microprocessor. For example, a data terminal having a keyboard and a printer produces a unit of data each time a key is depressed manually and accepts data at a rate dictated by the mechanical limitations of the printer. Some means is needed to coordinate the timing of an external device to the timing of the microprocessor. Otherwise, a data transfer from a given input port might be performed before it contains the desired data or that a data transfer to a given output port might be performed before previous data in that port is used. This coordination of timing is generally known as *handshaking*.

Generally, the operation of an external device involves a specific action based on the mechanism of the device. The end result of this *device action* is either the utilization of one data word at an output port or the provision of one data word to an input port. For example, the device action of a keyboard consists of the depression of a key and the subsequent supply of information to an input port of a microprocessor. Also, the device action of a printer is the activation of the appro-priate hammer solenoid for the character that corresponds to the data present at an output port of a microprocessor. It is generally assumed that the data port is engaged by the device during the device action and, therefore, should not be accessed at that time by the microprocessor. Only at times after the completion of the device action is the data port for the device available or ready for either an input or output data transfer, as the case may be, by the microprocessor. There are three overall aspects to the handling of data between a device and a microprocessor:

1. The initiation of the device action
2. The checking for device port availability by the microprocessor
3. The actual transfer of data between the device port and the microprocessor

There are several ways of coordinating data handling based upon the possible combinations of employing the first and second aspects.

Program-Initiated Data Handling

One way of coordinating data handling for some devices is to have the program initiate the action of the device for each data transfer. This is done by a signal sent from the microprocessor to the device at times determined by the program. The device responds to this signal by supplying new data in the case of an input port or using the data in a prescribed manner in the case of an output port. After a sufficient amount of time has elapsed to allow for the device action, the program can access the data port. Very often such access to the port serves as the signal to initiate device action (which, in the case of an input port, is actually for the next access to be made).

A device consisting of a paper-tape reader and punch serves to illustrate program-initiated data handling. Assume that the paper-tape reader is connected to an input port and the punch to an output port. The paper tape consists of a sequence of 8-bit data words. Initially, the input port is filled from the reader with the first data word of an input tape. At various points in a running program, access is made to the input port. In addition to obtaining the data, this access also serves as a signal to operate the reader. The reader responds by reading the next data word from the input tape to replace the previous content of the input port. Likewise, at other points in the running program, access is made to the output port. In addition to loading the output-port register, this access also serves as a signal to operate the punch. It responds by punching the new content of the output port into an output tape.

Figure 9.4 illustrates, in general, how the signals that cause device action can be produced with the illustrative microprocessor. Networks are shown both for input devices and for output devices. Each network involves an unclocked *SR* flip-flop, which serves as a flag to the external device. Each flag is set by the signal, in either case, that was used in the network of Fig. 9.1 to produce a transfer between the microprocessor and the appropriate port register. Specifically, the output-port flag is set by the AND of the Select signal from the device selection

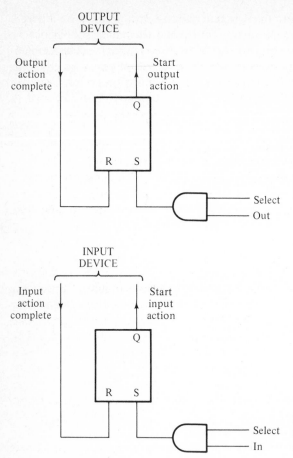

Figure 9.4 Flags for signaling an external device to perform an input or output action.

network and the Out control signal from the microprocessor. Likewise, the input-port flag is set by the AND of Select and the In control signal. The output of each flag is sent to the device to cause its action to occur, such as activating the drive motor and punch solenoids of a paper-tape punch. In any case, the result of the device action is the utilization of data from an output port or the provision of data to an input port. After such action takes place, the device places logic-1 onto the reset terminal of the appropriate flag flip-flop. The flag is thus reset at the completion of the action so that the action is not repeated until after the corresponding port is accessed again by the microprocessor.

Device-Initiated Data Handling

A second way of coordinating data handling is to have the device initiate its own action for each data transfer. In this case, after the completion of the device action, information must be provided to the program that the data port connected to the device is available for another data transfer. This is done by having the device set a port-ready flag that is repetitively checked by the program during times the program expects to perform a data transfer with the port. Usually an auxiliary input port is used for this purpose that corresponds to the status of one or more devices. The separate bits making up this status port correspond to different conditions that may occur in regard to a group of devices, specifically including a ready condition for each data port.

In a segment of a program in which access to a certain data port is to be made, the ready status of the data port is checked by first inputting the content of the associated status port. The bit that indicates the ready condition for the particular data port is then isolated and tested by the program. If it is determined that the data port is not ready, then this status-checking operation is repeated until the data port is ready.

A magnetic-tape unit is an example that typifies devices that involve device-initiated data handling. Data words are usually grouped on the magnetic tape in blocks, called *records*, with empty spaces in between the records. In operation, the tape is accelerated, within a space between records, to a specified velocity. Thus, during reading or writing, data words in a record are successively encountered and transferred at a fixed rate. The encountering of each data word is the device action.

Generalized Handshaking

A more general scheme for coordinating data handling is to combine the aspects of the first two schemes. In this case, the program initiates the device action and checks the ready status of the data port.

Figure 9.5 illustrates how an interface for this general scheme, including both a data input port and a data output port, might be implemented for the illustrative microprocessor. A single input/output device is assumed to be connected to the two data ports. Besides the two data ports there is a status port and a control port.

The status port is an input port that provides the microprocessor with information concerning the set of prevailing device conditions. Two particular conditions are "data input port not ready," corresponding to status bit 7, and "data output port not ready," corresponding to status bit 0. These two status bits each come from the output of an unclocked *SR* flip-flop. Each flip-flop is set at the time that a data transfer occurs between the microprocessor and the corresponding data port, which indicates that the port is not available for another data transfer. This also informs the device to perform the appropriate device action, which obtains new data in the case of the input port or utilizes the data in the case of the output port. Upon completion of a device action, the device resets the corresponding status bit, which is an indication to the microprocessor that the corresponding data port is ready. The remaining six status bits may be used to represent other device conditions such as "end of tape," "end of block," "input error," etc.

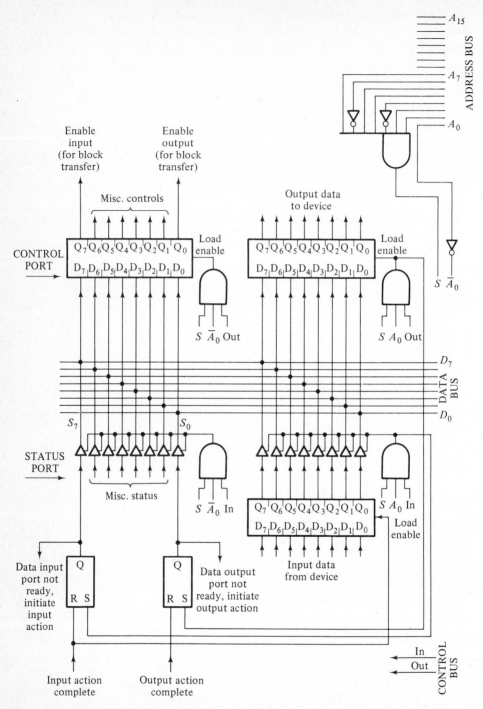

Figure 9.5 General I/O interface to the illustrative microprocessor including input, output, status, and control ports.

The control port is an output port, which is used to convey commands to the device from the microprocessor. Two particular commands are "enable input," corresponding to control bit 7, and "enable output," corresponding to control bit 0. The purpose of these two commands is to allow an entire block of data words to be inputted or outputted. For example, to read paper or magnetic tape, the enable-input bit is set to 1 at the beginning of a record and then reset to 0 when all data words in a record have been encountered. The device ANDs each of these enable commands with the corresponding port-not-ready status bit as a signal to start or continue the device action for each data transfer. Thus, in the example, tape motion and reading continues from one data word to the next only if both the enable-input and data-input-port-not-ready bits are 1. The remaining six control bits may be used to perform other device functions such as "rewind input tape," "skip a page," "reset error flags," etc.

A selection network is used to partially select the four ports. This network consists of a 7-input AND gate, with some inputs inverted, which is connected to the lower half of the Address bus excluding bit A_0. The output line S of this network will be logic-1 if either of the two device codes 10110110 or 10110111 is present on the Address bus. The first of these codes corresponds to the status and control ports, whereas the second corresponds to the data ports. Each port is controlled by a 3-input AND gate. The line S is connected to an input line of each of these AND gates. The complement of the least significant address line $\overline{A}_0$ is connected to an input line of the two AND gates for the status and control ports, while A_0 is connected to an input line of the two AND gates for the data ports. In this way, each port is conditioned upon an assigned device code. The third input line of each AND gate is connected to either the In control signal, if it is for an input port, or the Out control signal, if it is for an output port. Thus, each port is uniquely determined and will respond appropriately when designated by the microprocessor. Also, the output lines of the AND gates controlling the two data ports are connected to the set terminals of the corresponding status flip-flops so that they behave as previously discussed.

Table 9.1 shows program segments for input and output that could be used with the network of Fig. 9.5. The input segment is shown starting at memory location 1000_{16}. The first instruction inputs the device status word from the input port $B6_{16}$. The bit in position 7, corresponding to the condition "data input port not ready," is isolated by ANDing the status word with the mask 80_{16}. If bit 7 of the status word is 0, indicating that data is available for input, then the entire accumulator will be zero. If this condition is not met then the next instruction, jump on accumulator not zero, will cause this status checking operation to be repeated. Otherwise, the next instruction will input the data from input port B7, which concludes the input segment.

The output program segment is shown starting at memory location 2000_{16}. It is similar to the input segment except that bit 0 of the device status word is used to indicate "data output port not ready." This status bit is isolated using the mask 01_{16}. Also, of course, the last instruction is an output instruction.

Table 9.1 Program segments for input and output

Memory location	Machine language instruction	Symbolic form of instruction	Remarks
1000	FD	INP	Input device status word
1001	B6	B6	
1002	61	LRI 1	Load H with mask
1003	80	80	
1004	81	AND 1	Isolate bit 7
1005	7D	JAN	Test bit 7; if equal to 1, then recheck status
1006	10	10	
1007	00	00	
1008	FD	INP	Input data
1009	B7	B7	
2000	FD	INP	Input device status word
2001	B6	B6	
2002	61	LRI 1	Load H with mask
2003	01	01	
2004	81	AND 1	Isolate bit 0
2005	7D	JAN	Test bit 0; if equal to 1, then recheck status
2006	20	20	
2007	00	00	
2008	FE	OUT	Output data
2009	B7	B7	

9.3 PROGRAM INTERRUPTS

A powerful facility of most microprocessors is the ability to have a running program interrupted in response to an external event so that a special routine dealing with the event may be executed. This is generally referred to as a *program interrupt*. For example, an interrupting event could be the completion of a data-handling action by an external device for which the microprocessor was waiting. Thus, such interrupt capability provides an alternative to having the microprocessor continually check a status port to determine when a particular I/O port is ready for a data transfer. A considerable advantage is gained by the use of program interrupts because during the waiting time for an I/O port, the microprocessor is free to independently perform other functions, including attending to other I/O ports.

A program interrupt, for most computers, generally resembles a jump to a subroutine. However, it is invoked by an external signal appearing on a specific control line rather than by a program instruction. Such an interrupt signal is referred to as an *interrupt request*. As for a subroutine, an interrupt routine, written to perform a desired task, is placed in memory beginning at the location to which program control is to be transferred. When the microprocessor recognizes an interrupt request while executing a program, it suspends execution of that program and begins execution of the interrupt routine. At the end of an interrupt routine, a return instruction is normally included to cause the microprocessor to resume execution of the suspended program at the point of interruption. Usually, a microprocessor has the capability of disabling interrupts during times in which they are inappropriate. When interrupts are disabled, then any interrupt request will be ignored.

It is common for a microcomputer system to contain more than one device that can request a program interrupt. A need therefore exists in such systems to be able to determine which, if any, device is requesting an interrupt so that the appropriate action can be taken. There are two basic ways in which this determination is made. One way is to have a master interrupt service routine that, when an interrupt request does occur, checks the status of each device to see if it is making the request. This is often referred to as a *polled-interrupt* scheme. The second way is to have a network that provides the microprocessor with information that " points " to a device requesting an interrupt. This is usually referred to as a *vectored-interrupt* scheme.

Polled Interrupts

For the polled-interrupt scheme only a single control line to the microprocessor is necessary for the purpose of requesting an interrupt. This interrupt-request control line is driven by the OR of individual interrupt-request lines from the various devices, so that any device can send an interrupt signal to the microprocessor. Associated with each device is generally a status input port in which one bit position is used to indicate an interrupt request by that device. When an interrupt signal from any device appears on the interrupt-request control line to the microprocessor, a jump will be made to a fixed location upon completing the current instruction provided that interrupts are enabled by the microprocessor. That location is the beginning of a master interrupt service routine, which will successively input the content of each status port in order to test its interrupt-request bit. When a device requesting an interrupt is found, the master routine will then branch to a specific routine that deals with that device.

When two or more devices are simultaneously requesting an interrupt, a conflict arises that must be resolved. The resolution of such conflicts is built into the polled-interrupt scheme. The first interrupting device in the polling order is the one serviced. Of course, after one device is serviced any other pending interrupt requests will cause another program interrupt to occur, which will cause the next device to be serviced, and so on. The order of polling therefore determines a priority for servicing interrupting devices.

The major disadvantage with the polled-interrupt scheme is the amount of time required for the master service routine to poll the separate devices. This polling time is frequently of little concern, since the applications of microprocessors, unlike large-scale computers, often involve a relatively small number of devices. However, there are microprocessor applications in which timing is critical, so that the polling time is of concern. For such applications a vectored-interrupt scheme is a valuable alternative, since then the interrupting device is directly determined.

Vectored Interrupts

For a vectored-interrupt scheme, circuitry external to the microprocessor is provided for the determination of an interrupting device. Of course, this circuitry must be able to resolve conflicts arising when two or more devices simultaneously request an interrupt so that a single device at a time is selected for service.

There are various ways in which an interrupting device can be identified. One way involves a microprocessor with more than one interrupt-request line, each one of which is connected to a separate device. In this case, a signal on any one of the lines causes a program jump to a different location in memory, unless inhibited internally by a higher priority interrupt signal. At each of these locations a specialized service routine begins that treats the particular device. This method is quite common for large-scale computers and is used to a small extent with some microprocessors. However, as can be appreciated, if the number of interrupt-causing devices is not very small, then the necessary number of interrupt-request lines to the microprocessor will be excessive.

Vectored Interrupts Based on Distinguishing Addresses

One scheme for interrupt vectoring, which can be directly or indirectly used with any microprocessor, is to have the beginning address of the service routine corresponding to an interrupting device sent to the microprocessor over the data bus. The address is determined by an external network that selects one of the devices requesting an interrupt according to some priority scheme. Of course, if only one device is requesting an interrupt at the time, it is the one selected.

The illustrative microprocessor was specified with this scheme in mind and will therefore be used to explain it. To handle interrupts, the illustrative microprocessor has two specific control lines, Intr (Interrupt Request) and Inta (Interrupt Acknowledge). The control Intr is an input line to the microprocessor that conveys an external request for an interrupt when it is placed at logic-1. All interrupt requests, however, are conditioned on the internal Interrupt Flag. Only if this flag is set will a request for an interrupt be honored. The control Inta is an output line from the microprocessor that is used to strobe an externally supplied jump address onto the Data bus in response to a program interrupt.

Figure 9.6a shows the interrupt circuitry for one device. The device is assumed to include one input port for inputting data (not shown in figure), a second input port for status, and an output port for control. One bit of the status port, the leftmost, is of particular importance in this case. This status bit is used, as it was in Fig. 9.5, to signal the device to begin an input operation. Also, it is available to the microprocessor to indicate when the device is busy with the input operation, and

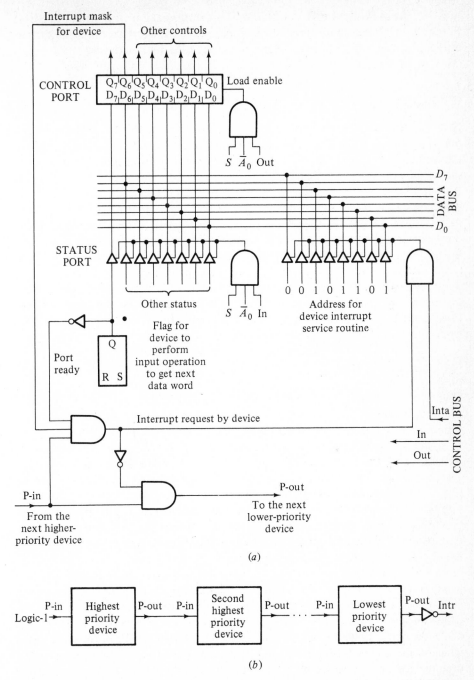

Figure 9.6 Vectored-interrupt scheme based on device-supplied addresses, which uses a daisy-chain to determine priority. (*a*) Network to provide interrupt address from one device. (*b*) Daisy-chain interconnections.

thus the input data port is not ready. The complement of this status bit, Port Ready, is the basis for an interrupt request by the device. Two other conditions must hold, however, before an interrupt is requested by this device.

One of these conditions is that a certain bit, labeled "Interrupt Mask," of the control register is equal to 1. This allows a program to inhibit interrupts by this particular device at times when an interrupt by the device is not appropriate.

The remaining condition for an interrupt request to be made by the device is that the device be given priority by other devices. For this purpose a priority network, in the form of a so-called *daisy-chain*, as shown in Fig. 9.6*b*, interconnects all devices in an order according to an assigned priority. Each device has an incoming priority line, labeled "P-in," and an outgoing priority line, labeled "P-out." The P-in line to each particular device is defined to be logic-1 when no device having a higher assigned priority is requesting an interrupt. It is connected to the P-out line of the device that has the next higher priority. The particular device in turn computes the value of its P-out line, which is connected to the P-in line of the device that has the next lower priority. Logically, the P-out line of the device is the AND of the P-in line and the negation of an interrupt request by that device. That is, the next device is given priority if its predecessor device is given priority but is not requesting an interrupt. The three signals, Interrupt Mask, Port Ready, and P-in, which correspond to the just mentioned conditions, are ANDed to produce the interrupt-request signal by the device.

When the interrupt-request signal from any of the devices becomes logic-1, the Intr control line to the microprocessor also becomes logic-1. This is accomplished by connecting the Intr control line to the complement of the last P-out line. This last P-out line is logic-0 if any device is requesting an interrupt. When the microprocessor recognizes an interrupt request, it will respond at the proper time with a pulse on the Inta (Interrupt Acknowledge) control line. The Inta line is ANDed with the interrupt-request signal from the device. The output of the AND gate for each device is used to enable a bank of 3-state drivers that couple a specified 8-bit address (which is particular to the device) to the Data bus. In this way, the specified address is brought into the microprocessor to indicate the beginning location of the interrupt service routine. The timing for the transfer of the address into the microprocessor involves one machine cycle and is similar to that for a data transfer from an input port. In this case, however, the Inta control line determines the timing rather than the In control line.

The sequence of events inside the microprocessor for an interrupt is as follows. If the internal Interrupt Flag is logic-0, then any interrupt request is ignored. If this flag is logic-1, then whenever a logic-1 appears on the Interrupt Request line Intr, a program interrupt will be recognized. In this case, however, the execution of the current instruction is first completed. The content of the program counter, which is the address of the next instruction that would otherwise be executed, is then pushed down into the stack. The Interrupt Flag is reset to block any more interrupts until it is set by an instruction. Finally, one machine cycle is used to bring in the 8-bit address from the interrupting device. This 8-bit address forms the lower half of the new content of the program counter, and the upper half is made zero. Consequently, a jump is effected to this address, which is somewhere within the first 256_{10} locations of memory.

The first instruction of an interrupt service routine is often a jump to a location outside of the first 256_{10} locations in order to conserve space there for other interrupt service routines. The routine is especially written to treat the device that caused the interrupt. During the routine the Interrupt Flag of the microprocessor, which was automatically reset (interrupts disabled), might be set (interrupts enabled) by an instruction in order to allow other devices, especially higher-priority devices, to interrupt the routine. Otherwise, the second last instruction of the routine is usually the enable-interrupt instruction, so that the same device or other devices could cause an interrupt in the future. A delay of one instruction is built into the enable-interrupt instruction so that one final instruction of the routine can be executed before any other interrupts are recognized. The last instruction of the routine is always a return instruction, which causes the stack to be popped up into the program counter. This restores the program counter to the address of the location where the program was interrupted.

Priority Encoders for Vectored Interrupts

A second vectored-interrupt scheme, which can be used with any microprocessor, provides the microprocessor with a unique code number representing the interrupting device. In such a scheme, an interrupt causes a jump to a fixed location where a master interrupt service routine begins. This routine then inputs the content of a special port that has been provided to contain the code number for the interrupting device. Based on this code number, a subsequent jump is made to another routine that is particular to the interrupting device. As in other schemes, conflicts which result from more than one device at a time requesting an interrupt are resolved by a priority assignment.

This scheme can be implemented in a manner similar to the previous scheme, in which priority is determined by a daisy-chain network, and in which the code number is supplied by the device requesting an interrupt. However, these two functions can be combined by an alternative manner of implementation, which is often used. In this alternative implementation, a combinational circuit, called a *priority encoder*, produces the code number of the highest priority device requesting an interrupt. The encoder has a number of input lines, each of which corresponds to an interrupt request signal from some device. These input lines are labeled with the code numbers of the devices to which they are connected. In this case, the code numbers are assigned consecutively starting from 0. A sufficient number of output lines from the encoder are provided to represent in binary the number of the highest active (i.e., equal to logic-1) input line.

In particular, consider the design of a priority encoder having eight input lines, labeled $I_0, I_1, \ldots, I_7$. Assume that the priority assignment is the same as the code number assignment with the highest priority corresponding to the highest code number. Since there are eight code numbers there must be three output lines to correspond to the 3-bit binary representation of the selected code number.

Label these output bits b_2, b_1, b_0 according to their significance. Using intuitive reasoning to find logic expressions for these 3 output bits, first note that b_2 is to be 1 whenever any input line for a code number greater than or equal to 4 is active. Thus,

$$b_2 = I_7 + I_6 + I_5 + I_4$$

Next, note that b_1 is to be 1 whenever I_6 or I_7 are active, since the binary representation of either 6 or 7 has a 1 in the b_1 position. Also, b_1 is to be 1 whenever I_2 or I_3 are active provided that neither I_4 or I_5 are active, since a 1 appears in the corresponding b_1 position of the binary representation of 2 and 3 but not of 4 and 5. The combination of these two conditions yields the following expression for b_1

$$b_1 = I_7 + I_6 + \bar{I}_5 \bar{I}_4 (I_3 + I_2)$$

Finally, note that b_0 is to be 1 if any input line for an odd code number is active, provided no input line for a higher even code number is active. The combination of these conditions for the four odd numbers yields the following expression for b_0

$$b_0 = I_7 + \bar{I}_6 I_5 + \bar{I}_6 \bar{I}_4 I_3 + \bar{I}_6 \bar{I}_4 \bar{I}_2 I_1$$

As a check on these equations, consider the case when the active input lines are I_1, I_2, I_4, and I_5. Substituting 1 for each of these into the three equations the resulting output bits become $b_2 = 1$, $b_1 = 0$, and $b_0 = 1$. These values of b_2, b_1, b_0 form the binary representation of 5, which is the number of the highest active input line in this case.

Figure 9.7 illustrates how this vectored-interrupt scheme using a priority encoder can be used with the illustrative microprocessor. Interrupt-request lines from up to eight devices are connected to the priority encoder, which computes the highest code number of the active lines. The resulting code number, represented by 3 bits, is presented to an input port, so that the microprocessor has access to it.

The interrupt-request lines from the devices are also connected to an OR gate whose output is connected to the Intr line to the microprocessor. Thus, when one or more device interrupt-request line becomes active an interrupt request will be made to the microprocessor. A pulse at the proper time will appear on the Inta control line in response to the recognition of an interrupt request by the microprocessor. This Inta pulse is used to place the fixed address of the master interrupt service routine onto the Data bus, so that it may then be transferred into the microprocessor. Execution of the master interrupt service routine then begins. This routine first inputs the code number of the highest priority device requesting an interrupt. The routine might then use this code number in one of two ways. It could use the code number as a basis to jump to a special routine that treats the corresponding device. Alternatively, it could proceed with a routine that is common to all devices and uses the code number to specify the device code for any accessed ports. This second possibility is especially suitable if the individual devices are similar in the way they are to be handled.

As was mentioned above, this particular vectored-interrupt scheme can be used with any microprocessor. This is true, since only an input port is necessary to

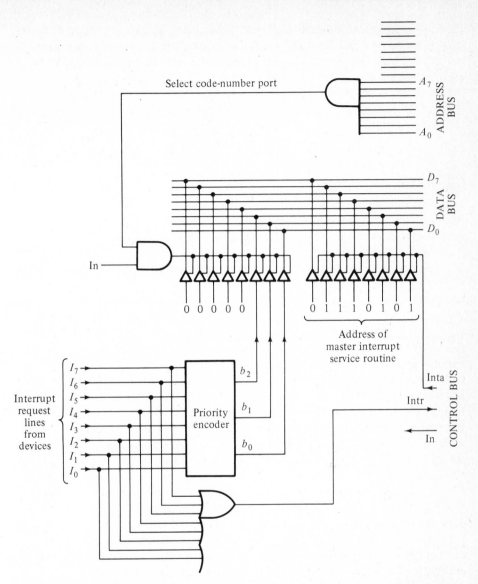

Figure 9.7 Vectored-interrupt scheme for the illustrative microprocessor using a priority encoder to select the code of one interrupting device.

convey to the microprocessor the information that points to the interrupting device.

Vectored Interrupts Using Device-Originated Instructions

Some microprocessors use a vectored-interrupt scheme that involves an instruction sent to the microprocessor from the interrupting device. When an interrupt request is recognized by such microprocessors, the response is to fetch the next instruction to be executed from the interface network for the interrupting device rather than from memory. The program counter is not automatically saved when an interrupt occurs as it is in other schemes.

Sometimes the single instruction fetched from the interrupting device is sufficient to accomplish the purpose of the interrupt. For example, an event counter might be implemented in software that simply keeps track of the number of times a certain type of interrupt occurs. This could be accomplished by a single instruction that increments a particular register or memory location. In such cases, after the single interrupt instruction is executed, the microprocessor resumes the sequence of instructions it had been executing.

Most of the time, however, a single instruction is not sufficient to service an interrupt. In such cases the instruction fetched from the interrupting device could be a jump to subroutine. The subroutine is then a particular one to treat the interrupting device.

There are various other schemes for carrying out program interrupts, some of which are special to certain microprocessors. Generally, they are variations of schemes that were just discussed.

Programming Considerations for Interrupts

From a programming point of view it is interesting to compare program interrupts with subroutine jumps. They both correspond to the suspension of a given program while a subsidiary routine is executed. Consequently, they both require a linkage between the given program and the subsidiary routine, so that execution can be returned to the given program upon completion of the subsidiary routine. This linkage involves saving the content of the program counter in a place from where it may be retrieved, such as in a pushdown stack or a location in the subsidiary routine.

The fact that program interrupts are invoked by external events while subroutine jumps are caused by program instructions brings about an important difference between the two. The programmer has full control over what points in a program that a subroutine jump can occur. In particular, the programmer has knowledge of what registers and flags are being used by the program at the time a subroutine jump occurs and may save the contents of any of these that are also used by the subroutine. A program interrupt, however, might occur anywhere in a program, thereby hindering the programmer's knowledge of register and flag usage. In this case, all registers and flags used by the interrupt routine must be saved. Some microprocessors, in acknowledgment of this difference, automatically save the contents of all registers and flags into a stack or a special work area whenever an interrupt occurs, but not when a subroutine jump is made. This necessitates two types of return instructions for such microprocessors, one for interrupts that restores the contents of all registers and flags including the program counter, and another for subroutines that only restores the program counter. This automatic saving of registers and flags for interrupts has advantages and disadvantages. It does eliminate the need for extra instructions in an interrupt service routine for the purpose of saving registers. This, however, does not always save time and may actually waste time in cases where no registers and flags need to be saved.

The illustrative microprocessor, for example, does not make such a distinction in the treatment of subroutine jumps and program interrupts. In either case, only the content of the program counter is automatically saved in the stack. Data from the first three scratchpad registers and the content of the carry flag C can be saved and then restored with the use of the instruction pair PUSH and POP. Generally, these three scratchpad registers should be adequate to perform the tasks required of an interrupt routine. In such a case, before any of these three registers or the carry flip-flop is used by the interrupt routine their content is pushed onto the stack. Then, after the interrupt routine has completed its tasks involving these three registers and the carry flip-flop, their original content is restored by popping the stack.

As an example of an interrupt routine for the illustrative microprocessor consider the following simple task. An input/output device supplies 8-bit unsigned integers to the microprocessor. The microprocessor compares each such number with a constant, say $5B_{16}$, and outputs the number only if it is less than the constant. It is assumed that the microprocessor is also performing other computations so that this task will be handled on an interrupt basis. Furthermore, it is assumed that this is the only type of program interrupt that can occur. An interrupt routine for this task is shown in Table 9.2. Whenever a number is available at an input port from the device, a program interrupt occurs causing the interrupt routine to begin. The first instruction is PUSH, which saves the contents of the

Table 9.2 Example of an interrupt service routine

Memory location	Machine language instruction	Symbolic form of instruction	Remarks
0080	77	PUSH	Save Acc, H, L, C in stack
0081	FD	INP	Input number
0082	12	12	
0083	61	LRI 1	Load H with constant 5B
0084	5B	5B	
0085	A1	SUB 1	Subtract 5B from number
0086	7C	JCZ	Test difference, if not negative skip output step
0087	00	00	
0088	8C	8C	
0089	81	ADD 1	Add 5B to restore number
008A	FE	OUT	Output number
008B	12	12	
008C	73	POP	Restore Acc, H, L, C
008D	FB	EIT	Enable future interrupts
008E	F8	RET	Return to interrupted program

first three scratchpad registers and the carry flip-flop C. The next instruction inputs the available number from the device (which is assumed to have device code 12_{16}) and places it into the accumulator. Constant 5B is subtracted from the inputted number by first loading 5B into register 1 and then subtracting register 1 from the accumulator. The carry flip-flop C is set if the difference is negative, which indicates that the inputted number is less than the constant 5B. This condition is tested by the jump-on-carry-zero instruction, which causes the next two instructions to be bypassed if C = 0. These next two instructions first add back the constant 5B to the accumulator to restore the inputted number and then output the number to the device (where the same device code 12 is assumed). The POP instruction is then used to restore the values of the first three registers and the carry flip-flop. Before returning to the interrupted program, the Interrupt Flag is set (it had been automatically reset at the beginning of the program interrupt), thus allowing future interrupt requests to be recognized. Finally, the last instruction returns control to the interrupted program.

9.4 MAIN-MEMORY INTERFACING

Main memory is a basic part of a microcomputer that is used to contain program instructions and data. In a few microcomputers, instructions are stored in a separate portion of memory from that of data. In such cases, the basic word size, means of addressing, method of access, and speed may be different for the two portions of memory. Most microcomputers, however, allow arbitrary intermixing of instructions and data within the same portion of memory. The discussion in this section will apply separately to each portion of memory in the former case and to the entire memory in the latter case.

Generally, the main memory of a computer has random access and is made up of a number of words each consisting of a certain number of bits. An address is assigned to each word so that it may be uniquely accessed by the computer. Main memory for a microcomputer is most often implemented with a collection of *memory units* in the form of integrated circuits. The integrated circuits are interconnected in a way that each word is of the appropriate size and has a distinguishing address. Different types of read-only and read/write memory units can be intermixed to serve certain purposes. In particular, some memory locations might be allocated to contain a fixed program or constant data and are therefore implemented with read-only memory units, whereas other locations, allocated to contain variable data, are implemented with read/write memory units. Some or all of the memory units might have a smaller word size than that needed by the microprocessor. In that case, several such units, whose combined word length is equal to that of the microprocessor, are connected so that they are accessed in parallel.

The timing of data transfers between the main memory and a microprocessor is an important concern. Because of the relatively large scale of integration of memory units, they generally operate considerably slower in the transfer of data than do the components for I/O ports. Thus, certain time specifications for a memory unit must be taken into account to ensure that they are met with the timing of the microprocessor.

Prototype Memory Unit

The interfacing of memory units to a microprocessor can be summarized briefly by the two considerations, addressing and timing. In order to proceed with this interfacing, let us assume a prototype for a memory unit that represents most static types of random-access memory. Figure 9.8 indicates the assumed signal lines for the prototype. There are m incoming lines used to address the words in the unit and n bidirectional lines for data corresponding to the bits comprising each word. Thus, the unit consists of 2^m words of n bits each. Finally, there are two incoming control lines, R/W and Enable, which work together to cause a read or write operation to occur. The unit is in a read mode whenever the R/W signal is logic-1; otherwise, it is in a write mode. Neither operation occurs, however, unless the Enable signal is logic-1. When the Enable line is logic-0, the data lines will be in the third state (floating). In the case of read-only memory units, the R/W line is deleted and the unit is always in the read mode. Actual memory integrated circuits might vary from this prototype in ways that include (1) additional enable lines (sometimes called *chip-select* lines) may be provided, which are internally ANDed together; (2) the bidirectional data lines may be replaced by separate input and output data lines; (3) the Enable line might be replaced by two separate control lines to enable the read operation and the write operation; and (4) the data lines may be open-collector or open-emitter rather than 3-state. These variations, however, should not seriously affect the following treatment of interfacing memory units to a microprocessor.

Memory Space of a Microprocessor

In configuring a memory system from memory units for a certain microcomputer it may be useful to think of it as filling a "memory space." The memory space for a particular microprocessor may be viewed as a rectangular area that is divided into

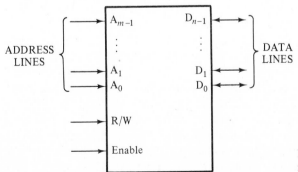

Figure 9.8 Prototype for a static memory unit.

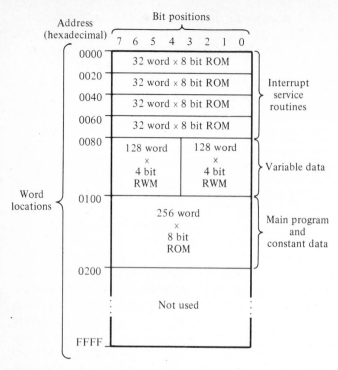

Figure 9.9 An example of a memory space allocation for the illustrative microprocessor.

rows corresponding to possible address combinations. Each row consists of the number of bits making up a data word for the microprocessor. The illustrative microprocessor, for example, has a memory space that is 2^{16} rows by 8 bits. Memory units of various type and size are placed into the memory space as needed for a specific application. Figure 9.9 indicates how the memory space of the illustrative microprocessor might be allocated.

Once the placement of memory units in the memory space of a microprocessor has been decided, it remains to specify the necessary interconnections. The data lines of every memory unit are each connected to the corresponding line of the microprocessor data bus. The address lines of the microprocessor are used to first select a memory unit or a parallel group of units and then a word location within the selected unit or units. Since the words in a unit usually correspond to consecutive words in the memory space, the address lines of a unit are connected to the lower-order address lines of the microprocessor. The remaining address lines of the microprocessor then are used to select that unit. The selection of a prototype unit is done with the use of the Enable control line.

The Enable control line of each memory unit is also used in conjunction with the R/W control line to both effect and time read and write operations. Certain microprocessor control lines are connected in an appropriate manner with the Enable and R/W lines. For a read operation, the R/W line of each memory unit is placed at logic-1, and at the proper time the Enable line of the selected unit or units is placed at logic-1. This causes the content of the addressed word in the selected unit or units to be placed onto the data bus and subsequently transferred into the microprocessor. For a write operation, the R/W line of each memory unit is placed at logic-0, and at the proper time the Enable line of the selected unit or units is placed at logic-1. This causes the content of the data bus as specified by the microprocessor to be transferred into the addressed word location of the selected unit or units.

Example of a Memory System

The manner in which the prototype memory units might be connected to the illustrative microprocessor is shown in Fig. 9.10. The figure assumes the same memory allocation indicated by Fig. 9.9. There are a total of seven memory units of varying size. For each unit, the address lines are connected to the lower lines of the Address bus, and the data lines are connected to the appropriate lines of the Data bus. The Enable line of each memory unit is driven by some combination of Address bus lines ANDed either with the microprocessor control signal Read, in the case of ROM units, or the OR of the microprocessor control signals Read and Write, in the case of RWM units. Thus, a memory unit is enabled only if selected by the Address bus and when a read or write data transfer is to occur.

The particular conditions that enable each memory unit can be seen more clearly, perhaps, by determining the logic expressions corresponding to each Enable line. Let E_i represent the Enable line of unit i, and A_i represent the Address bus line i. Notice that all Enable lines have the AND of the complements of the highest seven Address bus lines in common. Further conditions for E_1 through E_4 are Read, $\bar{A}_7$, $\bar{A}_8$, and some combination of A_5 and A_6. These first four enable signals are specifically expressed as

$$E_1 = \text{Read}\,\bar{A}_{15}\bar{A}_{14}\bar{A}_{13}\bar{A}_{12}\bar{A}_{11}\bar{A}_{10}\bar{A}_9\bar{A}_8\bar{A}_7\bar{A}_6\bar{A}_5$$

$$E_2 = \text{Read}\,\bar{A}_{15}\bar{A}_{14}\bar{A}_{13}\bar{A}_{12}\bar{A}_{11}\bar{A}_{10}\bar{A}_9\bar{A}_8\bar{A}_7\bar{A}_6 A_5$$

$$E_3 = \text{Read}\,\bar{A}_{15}\bar{A}_{14}\bar{A}_{13}\bar{A}_{12}\bar{A}_{11}\bar{A}_{10}\bar{A}_9\bar{A}_8\bar{A}_7 A_6\bar{A}_5$$

$$E_4 = \text{Read}\,\bar{A}_{15}\bar{A}_{14}\bar{A}_{13}\bar{A}_{12}\bar{A}_{11}\bar{A}_{10}\bar{A}_9\bar{A}_8\bar{A}_7 A_6 A_5$$

E_5 and E_6 have Read + Write, A_7, and $\bar{A}_8$ as conditions. They are equal to each other and may be expressed as

$$E_5, E_6 = (\text{Read} + \text{Write})\bar{A}_{15}\bar{A}_{14}\bar{A}_{13}\bar{A}_{12}\bar{A}_{11}\bar{A}_{10}\bar{A}_9\bar{A}_8 A_7$$

Finally, E_7 has Read and A_8 as conditions and is expressed as

$$E_7 = \text{Read}\,\bar{A}_{15}\bar{A}_{14}\bar{A}_{13}\bar{A}_{12}\bar{A}_{11}\bar{A}_{10}\bar{A}_9 A_8$$

It can be noticed that except for E_5 and E_6, which pertain to parallel memory units, the E_i's are mutually exclusive. Also, a simplification might be made to Fig.

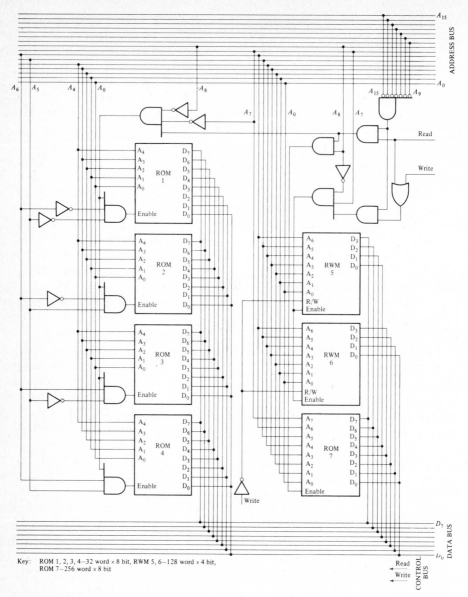

Key: ROM 1, 2, 3, 4–32 word × 8 bit, RWM 5, 6–128 word × 4 bit,
ROM 7–256 word × 8 bit

Figure 9.10 The manner in which prototype memory units might be connected to the illustrative microprocessor for the example of Fig. 9.9.

9.10 if it is known that there will be no future memory expansion. In that case, the common factor $\bar{A}_{15} \cdots \bar{A}_9$ could be deleted from each E_i. As a result, each word in the memory units will respond to many different addresses in addition to its intended address. This causes no difficulty and might even be exploited in programming.

Timing of Memory Data Transfers

The timing of data transfers to and from the memory is often critical, since memory units are relatively slow in operation, especially when compared to the small-scale integrated components used for I/O ports. Certain delays arising in the sequence of events for the read and write operations of memory units must be taken into account to assure proper operation. The read operation generally involves first sending an address to a memory unit, then placing logic-1 onto its Enable line, and finally using the data when it appears on the data lines. Of prime concern is the delay between the time the address is sent and the time data becomes available. This delay, referred to as the *read-access time*, must be taken into account in the operation of the microprocessor, so that the contents of the data bus are not transferred into the microprocessor before valid data is placed onto the data bus by the memory unit. Also important is the amount of delay between setting the Enable line of a memory unit to logic-1 and the time that the data lines become valid. This delay time, which is usually less than the read-access time, must also be taken into account in the operation of the microprocessor. These read time requirements are illustrated in Fig. 9.11.

A write operation is slightly more complicated as compared to a read operation and consequently involves more time considerations. The sequence of events for a write operation generally involves sending an address and data word to a memory unit and holding these while the Enable and R/W lines are momentarily placed at logic-1 and logic-0, respectively. Several periods of time in this sequence are of prime concern and are illustrated by Fig. 9.12. After an address has been specified, a certain amount of time is necessary before the decoding circuit internal to a memory unit can respond. If, while the Enable line is logic-1, the R/W line is brought to logic-0 before the decoding circuit has time to respond to the address, then data may be written into the wrong memory location. This required period of time is often referred to as the *address setup time*. Data presented to a memory unit is written into a word location during the time in which the R/W line is logic-0 and the Enable line is logic-1. This length of time, referred to as the *write-pulse width*, must be sufficient for the memory elements to accept the data being written. The values that are stored in the addressed word location are those that appear on the data lines at the end of this " write pulse " time, provided those values appeared for a sufficient length of time before the end of the write pulse, referred to as the *data*

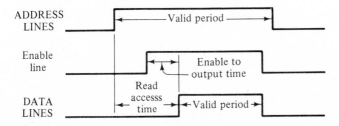

Figure 9.11 Time requirements for the prototype memory units under a read operation.

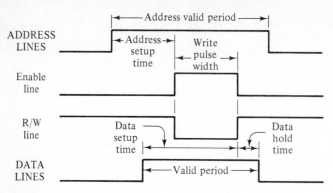

Figure 9.12 Time requirements for the prototype memory units under a write operation.

setup time, and a sufficient length of time after the end of the write pulse, referred to as the *data hold time*.

In meeting the above time requirements of the memory units, the additional delays due to the auxiliary gates involved in the interface must be taken into account. Often these additional delays are negligible since the interfacing gates may be relatively high speed owing to their small-scale integration.

Let us now consider how the time requirements of the memory units could be met by the illustrative microprocessor. Consider first the timing diagram shown in Fig. 9.13 for the read operation. A machine cycle consisting of three clock pulses is used to perform this operation. The Data bus is assumed by the microprocessor to contain valid data from memory during the time between the leading edges of clock pulses T_2 and T_3. To provide for the read-access time of the memory units, the address of the location to be read is sent over the Address bus one clock cycle earlier, that is, at the time of the leading edge of the first clock pulse T_1. This

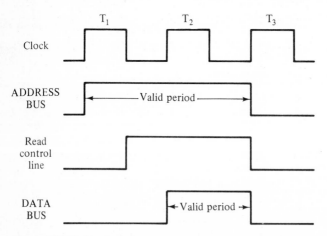

Figure 9.13 Timing diagram for the read operation of the illustrative microprocessor.

address specifies the memory unit (or parallel group of units) and the word location in that unit (or units) to be accessed. A little later, at the trailing edge of T_1, the Read control line of the microprocessor is activated, which causes the selected unit or units to be enabled. The clock-off time between T_1 and T_2 is used to provide for the Enable-to-output delay in the memory units plus delay associated with the gates driving the Enable lines.

The R/W lines of all the memory units are at logic-1 throughout a read operation, since they are driven by the complement of the microprocessor Write line (which is at logic-0). Consequently, the content of the addressed word location in the selected memory units will be placed onto the Data bus, sometime after the units have been enabled. At the end of clock pulse T_2 this data is strobed into a destination register within the microprocessor.

The timing diagram for the write operation of the illustrative microprocessor is shown in Fig. 9.14. For a write operation, data is strobed into a selected memory location during the second clock pulse T_2. To provide for the address and data setup times, both the address and data are placed onto their respective buses beginning with the leading edge of the first clock pulse T_1. The time between the leading edges of T_1 and T_2 is allowed for address setup, while the time between the leading edge of T_1 and the trailing edge of T_2 is allowed for data setup. A pulse occurs on the microprocessor Write control line in coincidence with T_2. This pulse affects the network driving the Enable lines of the memory units so as to enable those units selected by the specified address. The pulse on the Write line also causes the R/W lines of the RWM units to go to logic-0, placing them into the write mode. The time allowed for the write-pulse-width requirement of the memory units is thus approximately the time of duration of a clock pulse, altered by the delay associated with the gates of the enable circuitry. The address and data are held until the leading edge of T_3, allowing the clock-off time between T_2 and T_3 for the data-hold-time requirement of the memory units.

Each of the mentioned time requirements for the memory units must be satisfied. If one or more of the requirements are not met, then the clock repetition rate might be decreased to accommodate the limiting requirement.

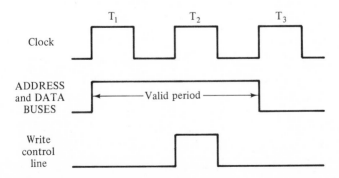

Figure 9.14 Timing diagram for the write operation of the illustrative microprocessor.

It should be mentioned at this point that actual microprocessors vary considerably from one another in their basic time relationships between signals. Some microprocessors have been designed to work with certain types of memory units having a particular time-requirement " profile " that is considerably different from that of other memory unit types. If a different type of memory unit were to be used than that assumed in the design of a microprocessor, then the clock rate might have to be drastically reduced just to meet one time requirement. For example, some microprocessors are designed for memory units that have a data-hold requirement of almost zero. If a memory unit having an appreciable data-hold requirement were to be used with such microprocessors, the clock might have to be reduced to an unreasonable rate. Such situations are sometimes remedied by providing a delayed clock pulse source for either the microprocessor or the memory system.

Dynamic Memory Systems

Dynamic memory units differ in their use from static memory units mainly in their need to be periodically refreshed. Generally, this refreshing is accomplished by performing a read and/or write operation. Let us consider a particular form for a dynamic memory unit that is refreshed by reading it. One control line in addition to those for the static prototype will be assumed for this dynamic-memory prototype, as is indicated in Fig. 9.15. The two control lines Enable and Select operate together to perform a function similar to that of the static-prototype Enable line. The Enable line controls functions that are internal to a memory unit, whereas the Select line controls the data lines by placing them into the third state when Select is at logic-0. These two lines are activated together when a read or write operation is to be performed. However, only the Enable line is used to perform a refresh operation.

Each refresh operation restores the contents of several word locations in a memory unit. Internally, a memory unit has its words placed in an array of columns and rows. The address of a word then consists of two parts, a column address and a row address. The bits in each word can be thought of as lying in a third dimension. All words in a specified row are refreshed during one operation.

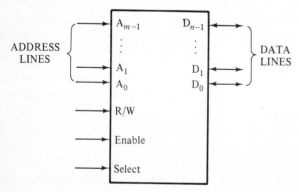

Figure 9.15 Prototype for a dynamic memory unit.

A refresh operation consists of specifying a row address and then activating the Enable line while the R/W line is kept at logic-1. The Select line and column address lines are not used during a refresh operation and may be either logic value. Each row of a dynamic memory unit must be refreshed within a certain period of time from the previous refresh. This period of time is generally in the order of a few milliseconds. During this time, as many refresh operations must be performed as there are rows in a memory unit.

Since a refresh operation generally interferes with the use of a memory unit by the microprocessor, some means is necessary to suspend the operation of the microprocessor during the time in which a memory row is to be refreshed. This is done in many ways by the various microprocessors. For some microprocessors a certain control signal is provided that when activated momentarily delays the operation of the microprocessor to allow for a memory refresh. Alternatively, a direct memory access facility of a microprocessor, as discussed in the next section, might be used. Still another way for allowing for memory refresh is to momentarily alter the clock to the microprocessor.

In any case, once the operation of the microprocessor is suspended, the refresh procedure is generally carried out by external circuitry. This external circuitry also determines the time and row address for each memory refresh operation.

Example of a Refresh Scheme

A possible scheme that might be used with the illustrative microprocessor to refresh dynamic memory units is shown in Fig. 9.16. The operation of the microprocessor is suspended during the time a refresh is to occur by the inhibition of the clock line. This will always occur just before a machine cycle begins, at which time it is assumed that the Address bus is placed into the third state by the microprocessor.

In the network of Fig. 9.16, the beginning of a machine cycle is determined with the use of the Sync control line from the microprocessor. A pulse occurs on the Sync control line in coincidence with the third clock pulse of each machine cycle. To determine the time that a refresh operation is to occur, a k-bit up counter is used that is driven by the Sync line. Connected to the output lines of this counter is a k-input AND gate, whose output will be logic-1 when the counter contains all 1s. This condition indicates that it is time for a refresh operation to occur. The next clock pulse is inhibited from reaching the microprocessor and is used for the refresh.

In performing the refresh operation, the content of a 4-bit counter is sent to the row-address lines of the memory unit. Three-state drivers are used for this purpose. Then, the Enable line is activated by a pulse from the clock source that is coupled through several gates. This refresh pulse is used also to increment the row-address counter for the next refresh operation. In addition, the pulse increments the k-bit counter that determines the refresh time. As a consequence, the k-bit counter becomes all 0s and terminates the refresh operation. The next clock pulse is allowed to pass to the microprocessor as the first pulse of a new machine

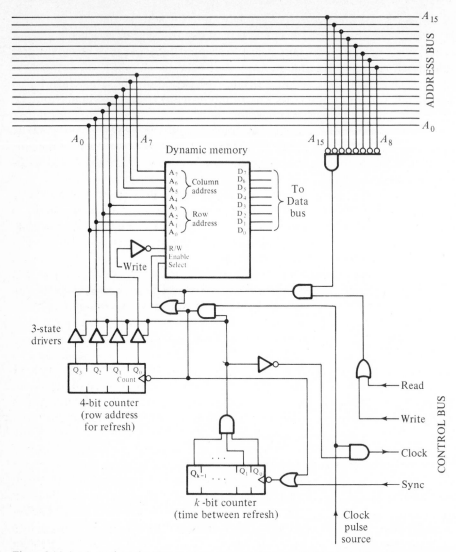

Figure 9.16 A scheme for refreshing dynamic memory for use with the illustrative microprocessor.

cycle. The k-bit counter will then be counting Sync pulses to determine the time for the next refresh operation.

It should be noted that methods used for refreshing dynamic memory units vary considerably from one microprocessor to another and even from one application to another for the same microprocessor. Consequently, the method shown here is used to illustrate what might be involved only in the most general sense. An actual design of a memory refreshing circuit requires a careful consideration of the microprocessor to be used as well as the particular memory units and the application for which they are to be used.

9.5 DIRECT MEMORY ACCESS

So far in this chapter, the discussion has been concerned with data transfers between a microprocessor and external devices or between a microprocessor and main memory. As might be expected, data transfers between external devices and main memory are also of concern. For example, such data transfers could be made to initially load a program into memory from an input device. Also, during the execution of a program, data might be transferred from a device into memory to be manipulated later by the microprocessor, or for that matter, results produced by the microprocessor might be stored in memory to be transferred later to an external device.

When a facility exists in a microcomputer system to transfer data directly between memory and external devices without the immediate intervention of a program, it is referred to as *direct memory access* (DMA). Certainly, by providing sufficient supportive circuitry, a microcomputer system based upon any microprocessor can be made to have direct memory access. In order, though, to keep the number of data pathways to a minimum most microprocessors have a special provision that allows their normal bus system to be used for direct memory access. This is done by releasing the microprocessor's control of the bus system at the time a DMA data transfer is to occur. An external device may then make use of the bus system to perform a data transfer between itself and memory.

Program execution, since it inherently depends upon data transfers to and from memory, usually must be suspended during the time the bus system is released by the microprocessor. Although there are variations among microprocessors, the action of releasing the buses typically occurs whenever a special DMA request control line is activated. The illustrative microprocessor, for example, has the two control lines DMA and DMAA, which are used respectively to request and to acknowledge direct memory access. Whenever logic-1 is placed externally on the DMA control line, the microprocessor will, after completing the current machine cycle, suspend program execution and then release the Address and Data buses by placing each of their lines into the third state (floating). To acknowledge that the Data and Address bus lines are in the third state, the DMAA control line is set to logic-1 by the microprocessor. During this time, the microprocessor retains control of the other outgoing lines of the Control bus. This is necessary so that unintentional events do not arise from undefined control signals, such as writing randomly into memory.

In particular, the control lines Read and Write from the microprocessor are kept at logic-0 during the time DMAA is 1. Normally, these two control lines are connected to the memory system. However, with direct memory access, a modification is necessary in order to allow an external device to determine a memory read or write operation. This modification involves ORing the Read and Write lines from the microprocessor with similar lines from the external device, the result of which is connected to the corresponding lines of the memory system. A particular device may perform a direct-memory-access transfer by first setting DMA to logic-1. It then waits for logic-1 to appear on DMAA. At that time, the device uses the Address bus, Data bus, and its read and write control lines to perform data transfers between itself and memory in a manner similar to that of the microprocessor. When no more such transfers are to be made the device places logic-0 onto the DMA control line, which returns control of the buses back to the microprocessor.

Data transfers using direct memory access can be considered a form of I/O with regard to a microcomputer, which differs from programmed I/O in that it is done under the supervision of external circuitry instead of a program. A savings in program time is gained in the use of direct memory access, since the program is not directly involved in such data transfers. This savings becomes quite important in the case of high-speed data devices, such as disk or tape storage units, which might exceed the capability of a program to keep up with the data flow.

Data Block Transfer Using DMA

Direct-memory-access schemes for high-speed data devices usually involve the transfer of data words in blocks. The microprocessor under program control often initiates the transfer of a block of data and might specify the number of words comprising the block. The transfer of the individual data words is, however, controlled by circuitry that is separate from the microprocessor. For example, a program might involve the inputting of a number of data words from magnetic tape into memory. In this case, the program might include instructions that output to the direct-memory-access control circuitry the number of data words to be transferred and the beginning address of where they are to be located in memory. The program would then set a flag to commence the transfer of data. From that point the program could go on to some other function, while the external control circuitry attended to the data transfer.

Figure 9.17 depicts a network to be used with the illustrative microprocessor for controlling direct-memory-access block transfers from a general input device. In the network, an 8-bit latch is provided to receive input data from the device and place it onto the Data bus at the proper time. Two 8-bit binary up counters are provided to contain each half of the memory address indicating where the input data is to be written. These two counters are connected in cascade to count in unison. The number of data words to be transferred for a block is controlled by an 8-bit binary down counter. The two address counters and the word counter are connected to the microprocessor as output ports.

A program initiates a block transfer by outputting each half of a 16-bit address to the address counters and then outputting an 8-bit number to the word counter. An AND gate with inverted input lines is connected to the word counter as a zero detector. Whenever the word counter contains a nonzero quantity the output of the zero detector will be logic-0, which is a signal to the device to allow the inputting of data. The device responds by sending an input data word each time it obtains one from its source, e.g., magnetic tape. The input data word is strobed by a pulse from the device into the 8-bit latch provided to receive it. This same strobe pulse also sets a flip-flop whose output line is connected to the DMA control line to the microprocessor.

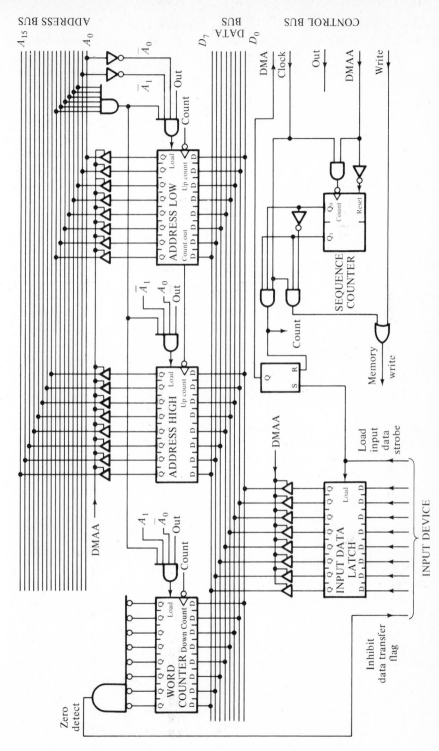

Figure 9.17 Direct-memory-access controller for an input device connected to the illustrative microprocessor.

When DMA becomes logic-1, the microprocessor will suspend program execution at the end of the current machine cycle and then release the Address and Data buses. The outgoing control line DMAA becomes logic-1 at this point, causing the start of a 4-pulse sequence that transfers the content of the input-data latch into memory. The sequence is controlled by a 2-bit counter that is driven by the microprocessor clock conditioned on DMAA.

When DMAA first becomes logic-1 the contents of the two address counters are placed onto the Address bus and the content of the input-data latch is placed onto the Data bus. Each clock pulse increments the 2-bit sequence counter. Nothing else happens for the first two clock pulses, but the third clock pulse causes a write pulse to be sent to memory. This is done by ORing the clock conditioned on the output combination 10 of the sequence counter with the Write control line. The write pulse causes the input data to be stored into the memory location specified by the Address bus.

The clock pulse following the memory write brings the sequence counter to 00 and causes a pulse to be generated on the line labeled "Count." This count pulse causes the 16-bit address counter to be incremented and the word counter to be decremented. It also resets the flip-flop connected to the DMA line. Thus, at this time the counters are ready for the next input data transfer and the microprocessor is allowed to resume program execution. When the word counter eventually reaches zero, the zero-detector output will become logic-1, indicating the end of the block transfer. No further data will be transferred from the device until another block transfer is initiated by the microprocessor.

This type of direct memory access is often referred to as *cycle stealing*, or other similar phrase, since it suspends the execution of a program for about one machine cycle at a time. An alternative type of direct memory access involves stopping program execution while an entire block of data is transferred.

9.6 FURTHER MICROPROCESSOR BUS CONCEPTS

The general arrangement of microprocessor buses assumed in the previous sections basically represents that for most microprocessors and their applications. There are, however, several other bus concepts that should be discussed, which are important to certain microprocessors or are valuable in the application of any microprocessor. These concepts include memory-mapped I/O, multiplexed buses, and memory-bank switching.

Memory-Mapped I/O

To handle input/output transfers many microprocessors, like the illustrative model, have instructions and control lines that are separate from those for handling memory transfers. This allows the assignment of I/O device codes to be independent from the assignment of memory addresses. It is often desirable, however, to treat I/O ports in the same manner as memory locations. That is, the

I/O ports for a particular system are given assigned addresses and are accessed as if they were memory locations. This is often referred to as *memory-mapped I/O*. Memory-mapped I/O can be used with any microprocessor, but there are certain microprocessors in which I/O handling must be memory-mapped since separate I/O instructions and control lines are not provided.

An advantage of memory-mapped I/O is that with it all memory-reference instructions in the instruction set of a microprocessor may also reference I/O ports. For some microprocessors the set of memory-reference instructions is very rich, providing various addressing modes and other flexibility. Often, instructions that perform arithmetic or logic with memory operands are included in the set for a microprocessor. With such microprocessors memory-mapped I/O is especially advantageous.

The illustrative microprocessor, as an example, does not have a very rich set of memory-reference instructions, but memory-mapped I/O can still be used to advantage. The two specific I/O instructions only allow a transfer to be made between the accumulator and an I/O port. However, with memory-mapped I/O a transfer can be made between any of the first three scratchpad registers and an I/O port by using the load register, store register, or move instructions. Interfacing I/O ports to the illustrative microprocessor under memory-mapped I/O involves the use of the Read and Write control lines in place of the In and Out lines, respectively.

Multiplexed Buses

The bus system for the illustrative microprocessor, like that for many actual microprocessors, consists of three explicit buses for conveying address, data, and control information. By having a separate bus for each of these three functions, the interfacing of I/O ports and memory units to the microprocessor is accomplished in a simple and straightforward manner. However, some microprocessors combine two of these interfacing functions with the use of one bus. As mentioned in Sec. 9.1, for example, several microprocessors make use of the data bus at certain times to send control information for a data transfer. This is done primarily to keep the pin count of the integrated circuit from exceeding a specified amount (say, 40 pins).

Some microprocessors gain a particular advantage by combining the function of the address bus with that of the data bus. This is done by having a *multiplexed bus*, which will be called the *address-data bus*, that conveys address information at certain times and data at other times. There are several variations to this scheme that primarily concern which address bits are sent over the common address-data bus. If the number of address bits is equal to the number of data bits, which is the case for several microprocessors, then all address bits could be simultaneously sent over the address-data bus. However, if the number of address bits exceeds the number of data bits, as is the case for the illustrative microprocessor and many others, then either additional address lines might be provided or portions of the address could be sent separately over the address-data bus.

In any case, some external means is necessary for recording the address information when it appears on the address-data bus so that it can be used to select the appropriate memory location or I/O port. One way of doing this is with a control line from the microprocessor that is used to strobe the address information into a register at the proper time.

Special memory units having internal address registers are often made available for use with a particular microprocessor having a multiplexed address-data bus. Generally, each such memory unit records from the address-data bus the relevant address information (i.e., the lower-order address bits) needed to designate a memory location within that unit. The high-order bits of an address are then used to select the appropriate memory unit from among all memory units in the system. This step might be done in several ways. The high-order address bits might be obtained either directly from additional address lines of the microprocessor or from a central register in the memory system that recorded these bits from the address-data bus earlier. Alternatively, the selection of the appropriate memory unit might be done with the use of a selection flag within each memory unit. In this case, the selection flag in each memory unit is conditioned to be set when an assigned combination of high-order address bits appear at the proper time on the address-data bus. Once the address of the appropriate memory location is determined, data is then transferred to or from that location over the address-data bus in the usual manner.

As can be seen, a reduction in the number of pins is gained by using a multiplexed address-data bus for a microprocessor. Furthermore, when the special memory units having an address register are used with such a microprocessor, a significant reduction is also gained in the number of wires needed to connect the memory units to the microprocessor. However, the overall operation of such a microprocessor system will tend to be slower due to the need to time share the bus for addresses and data.

Memory-Bank Switching

Typically, the addressable memory space of a microprocessor, as determined by the number of its address bits, is sufficiently large to accommodate the requirements of most microprocessor applications. However, in the event that a particular application has a memory requirement that exceeds the address capability of the microprocessor, the memory space can be extended with the concept of memory-bank switching. To do this, the required memory is divided into memory banks. The selection of a desired memory bank is then determined from the content of a register, called bank designate, that is connected as an output port to the microprocessor.

Let us assume that memory-bank switching is to be done with only that part of the memory containing data and not the part containing the program instructions, since otherwise, switching banks could interfere with the instruction execution sequence. For this purpose, assume that all program instructions are located in the lower half of the normal memory space of the microprocessor. Bank switching, then, will only be done with addresses corresponding to the upper half of the normal memory space. Thus, when the most-significant address bit of the microprocessor is 0 a memory location in the program portion of memory will be designated by just the remaining address bits of the microprocessor. On the other hand, when the most-significant address bit is 1 a memory location in the selected bank will be designated.

With this arrangement a program can determine the memory bank for transferring data by outputting the corresponding number to the bank-designate register. This memory bank will then remain in effect until the program switches to another bank by outputting its corresponding number.

This scheme of switching memory banks can be extended to as large a memory as desired. If the number of bits in an output port is not sufficient to designate all of the required memory banks, then two or more output ports can be used for this purpose.

9.7 ANALOG CONVERSION

Many applications of microcomputers involve physical parameters that take on a continuous range of values. In a mechanical control application, for example, parameters such as speed, position, and force might be monitored or controlled. These parameters are generally represented by some electrical parameter, which will be assumed to be a voltage. Such voltages that directly represent physical parameters are referred to as *analog* quantities. In the case of monitored parameters, the corresponding voltages are generated by appropriate transducers (e.g., tachometers for speed, pressure transducers for force or pressure, and potentiometers for position). Parameters that are controlled are determined from their corresponding voltages by actuators of some sort (e.g., motors for force, speed or position, and heaters for temperature). Now, of course, microcomputers are inherently digital and therefore work with quantities that are digitally represented. In order for microcomputers to handle analog quantities, some means of converting from digital to analog representation and from analog to digital representation is necessary.

Digital-to-Analog Conversion

First, consider the conversion from the digital representation of a quantity into its analog representation. Positive quantities will be assumed at first for simplicity. The digital representation of a quantity N in binary notation consists of just a string of k bits,

$$a_{k-1}a_{k-2} \cdots a_1 a_0$$

The meaning of these bits is specified by the corresponding polynomial expansion of the quantity N, i.e.,

$$N = a_{k-1}2^{k-1} + a_{k-2}2^{k-2} + \cdots + a_1 2 + a_0$$

This expansion equates N to the result of weighting each bit by an appropriate power of 2 and then adding all such terms together. This operation corresponds to a linear combination of the bits. Such a linear combination is easily performed with a network of resistors. If the voltage equivalent of each bit is available, then the network will effectively yield the analog equivalent of the binary number. One such resistive network, shown in Fig. 9.18a, is in the form of a "ladder" having resistors of just two different values. The number of bits in this case is assumed to be 8. Connected to the resistive network are eight ideal voltage generators each corresponding to one of the bits a_i. Each generator produces either 0 or 1 V depending on the value, 0 or 1, respectively, of the corresponding bit. That is, the voltage of each generator is numerically the same as the value of the corresponding bit a_i. The output voltage V_{out} will be seen to be proportional to the power-of-2-weighted sum of the generator voltages. The resistor ladder therefore performs the desired digital-to-analog conversion of N.

Derivation of Resistor-Ladder Operation

To show that the resistor ladder in Fig. 9.18a performs the indicated weighted summation, the principle of superposition for linear circuits will be used. Each generator acts as a source of an input signal to the linear circuit composed of just the resistors. According to the principle of superposition the output voltage V_{out} can be computed by summing the effect that each individual input signal has upon the output voltage. The effect of a particular input signal is computed by considering the output voltage while that particular signal is present on its input line and all other input lines are at zero voltage.

Consider the effect that the input voltage for a_i has upon the output. The generator for a_i is connected to a resistor of R Ω. Refer to the node at the other side of this resistor as P_i. The resistance to ground looking to the left of the node P_i (not counting the R-Ω resistor connected to the a_i generator) happens to be R Ω, as indicated in Fig. 9.18b. This is seen by combining resistances starting from the left. The R-Ω resistor on the left going directly to ground may be combined in parallel with the R-Ω resistor leading to the a_7 generator (which is effectively grounded since that input line is set at 0 V). The parallel combination yields a value of $R/2$ Ω, which may then be combined in series with the $R/2$-Ω resistor toward the right. This series combination yields a value of R Ω to ground. This process is repeated until node P_i is reached, yielding a combined value of R Ω as stated. In a similar manner, it is seen that the resistance looking to the right between node P_i and ground is R Ω. Thus, the resistor ladder can be represented by the equivalent circuit in Fig. 9.18b.

The voltage at node P_i with respect to ground due to the a_i voltage generator may now be determined using the voltage divider rule for resistances in series. First the resistance looking to the left and to the right of node P_i may be combined in parallel to yield a value of $R/2$ Ω, as indicated by Fig. 9.18c. This resistance and the resistor connecting the a_i generator to node P_i form a voltage divider. This voltage divider produces at the node P_i a fractional amount of the input voltage a_i

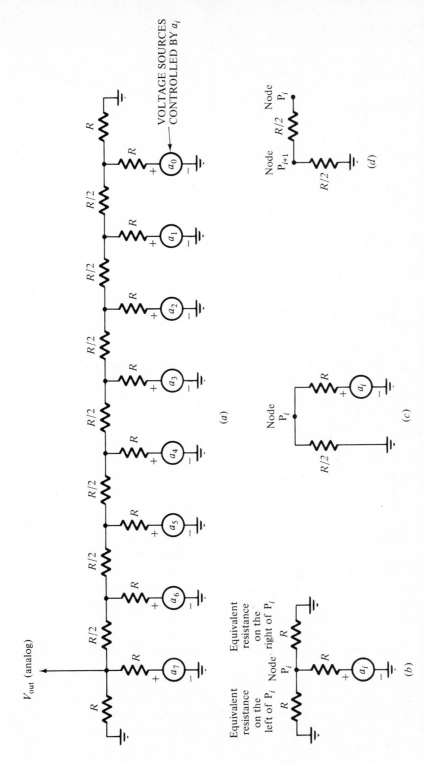

Figure 9.18 Resistor ladder for digital-to-analog conversion. (*a*) Resistor ladder. (*b*) Equivalent resistances on each side of node P_i. (*c*) Equivalent voltage divider determining effect of a_i upon the voltage at node P_i. (*d*) Equivalent voltage divider determining effect of the voltage at node P_i upon the voltage at node P_{i+1}.

331

given by the relation

$$\text{Voltage at } \mathbf{P}_i = \frac{R/2}{R + R/2}\, a_i = \tfrac{1}{3} a_i$$

The effect that this voltage of $\tfrac{1}{3} a_i$ V at node $\mathbf{P}_i$ has upon the output can be determined by working node by node to the left.

The voltage at the next left node $\mathbf{P}_{i+1}$ due to the voltage at node $\mathbf{P}_i$ is seen to be one-half of the value. This is determined again by the voltage divider rule. Note that the resistance between the node $\mathbf{P}_{i+1}$ and ground, excluding the resistor connecting node $\mathbf{P}_i$ to node $\mathbf{P}_{i+1}$, is $R/2$ Ω, as indicated in Fig. 9.18d. This value comes from the parallel combination of the R-Ω resistor from node $\mathbf{P}_{i+1}$ to the a_{i+1} generator and the resistance for node $\mathbf{P}_{i+1}$ looking to the left, which is also R Ω. This $R/2$-Ω resistance between node $\mathbf{P}_{i+1}$ and ground and the $R/2$-Ω resistor connecting node $\mathbf{P}_i$ to node $\mathbf{P}_{i+1}$ form the voltage divider shown in Fig. 9.18d. This voltage divider produces a voltage at node $\mathbf{P}_{i+1}$ equal to one-half that at node $\mathbf{P}_i$. Thus, the voltage at node $\mathbf{P}_{i+1}$ due to a_i is given by the relation

$$\text{Voltage at } \mathbf{P}_{i+1} = \frac{R/2}{R/2 + R/2} \times \text{voltage at } \mathbf{P}_i$$

$$= \frac{1}{2}\frac{a_i}{3}$$

This voltage is further halved for each node that is encountered going to the left. The output voltage due to a_i is the voltage at node $\mathbf{P}_7$, which is now seen to be given by the relation

$$\text{Voltage at } \mathbf{P}_7 = \left(\frac{1}{2}\right)^{7-i}\frac{a_i}{3}$$

The total output voltage is next obtained by summing the effects due to all generator voltages, i.e.,

$$V_{\text{out}} = \sum_{i=0}^{7} \left(\frac{1}{2}\right)^{7-i}\frac{a_i}{3}$$

$$= \left(\frac{1}{2}\right)^{7}\frac{1}{3}\sum_{i=0}^{7}\left(\frac{1}{2}\right)^{-i} a_i$$

$$= \left(\frac{1}{2}\right)^{7}\frac{1}{3}\sum_{i=0}^{7} 2^i a_i$$

The summation in the expression above is just the polynomial expansion for the quantity N. Thus V_{out} is proportional to N. The constant of proportionality is $(\tfrac{1}{2})^7\tfrac{1}{3}$ or generally $(\tfrac{1}{2})^{k-1}\tfrac{1}{3}$.

The conversion of numbers represented by the 2's-complement number system, each of which may be positive or negative, can be accomplished by a slight modification of the scheme for unsigned numbers. The 2's-complement representation for a number may be thought of as a weighted code, similar to unsigned binary representation, with the most-significant bit (the sign bit) having a negative weight. That is, a number N represented in 2's-complement form by the k bits

$$a_{k-1} a_{k-2} \cdots a_1 a_0$$

is given by the polynomial expression

$$N = a_{k-1}(-2^{k-1}) + a_{k-2} 2^{k-2} + \cdots + a_1 2^1 + a_0$$

This expression can be implemented in analog by a resistor ladder similar to that of Fig. 9.18, where the polarity of the voltage generator for a_{k-1} is reversed.

Implementation of Voltage Generators

Consider now the implementation of the voltage generators that produce the input signals to the resistor ladder. They are each to be controlled by an a_i bit, so as to produce a voltage equal or proportional to the a_i bit. It is important that the generators be close to ideal so that their output voltage is not affected by the load from the resistor ladder. Also, the voltages must be specified in a precise manner, since they directly affect the accuracy of the output voltage. These requirements can be met by the use of analog switches that connect each input line of the resistor ladder to a precise reference voltage or to ground depending upon the value of the corresponding a_i bit. These analog switches might be just bipolar transistors connected in a "totem pole" arrangement, as shown in Fig. 9.19. In this case, it is assumed that the voltage level corresponding to logic-1 is somewhat greater than $V_{\text{reference}}$. When a_i is at logic-1 the upper transistor will be in saturation, which brings the output to the reference voltage. When a_i is logic-0 the lower transistor is in saturation, which brings the output to ground. The transistors should be chosen to have a negligible voltage drop from collector to emitter when saturated. That is, $V_{ce}(\text{sat})$ should be approximately zero.

For a small number of bits (8 or less), reasonably good results can be obtained with the use of totem-pole output TTL gates and pull-up resistors for the voltage generators, as shown in Fig. 9.20. Normally, the pull-up circuit in a TTL gate, unlike the pull-down circuit, will have a significant voltage drop. The added

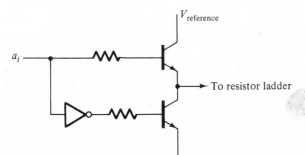

Figure 9.19 Circuit for voltage generator controlled by a_i using two transistors.

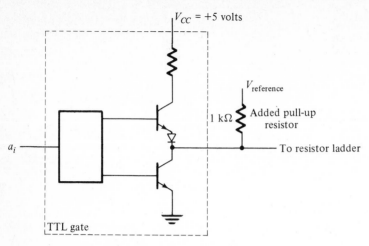

Figure 9.20 Use of a TTL gate with an added pull-up resistor to a reference voltage as a voltage generator for a resistor ladder.

resistor connected between the output line of the TTL gate and a reference voltage (nominally $+5$ V) will bring the output reasonably close to the reference voltage, provided that the load from the resistor ladder is kept small. The value of 1 kΩ is chosen for this pull-up resistor, since that is about the minimum value to assure that the pull-down transistor is not overloaded. The input resistors to the ladder should then be set at a much higher value to prevent loading of the 1-kΩ pull-up resistor. A value of 20 kΩ for the input resistors is reasonable.

Use of Operational Amplifiers

In place of a resistor ladder, an *operational amplifier* can be used to perform the weighted summation indicated by the polynomial expansion of a binary number. An operational amplifier is a voltage amplifier having a high negative gain $(-A)$, which may be programmed to perform various operations. This programming is done with the interconnection of resistors and other passive components. Figure 9.21 depicts one way an operational amplifier can be programmed to convert a binary number into an analog voltage. The signals labeled V_i are input voltages corresponding to the bit values a_i of the number to be converted. The circuit produces an output voltage V_{out} that is proportional to the quantity represented by the binary number. To verify this, let us analyze the circuit by summing currents into the node labeled "summing junction." The voltage of the summing junction is referred to as V. Each input voltage source V_i is connected to the summing junction through a resistor, which for generalization will be referred to as R_i. Using Ohm's law, the current through each of these resistors into the summing junction can be expressed as $(V_i - V)/R_i$. Also, the output line is connected via the resistor R to the summing junction, contributing a current given by

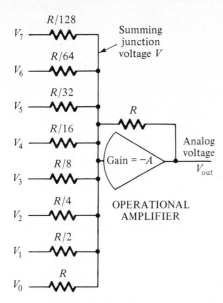

Figure 9.21 Binary digital-to-analog converter using an operational amplifier.

$(V_{out} - V)/R$. The sum of these currents may be equated to 0 as follows:

$$\frac{V_0 - V}{R_0} + \frac{V_1 - V}{R_1} + \cdots + \frac{V_7 - V}{R_7} + \frac{V_{out} - V}{R} = 0$$

Now, since V is the input voltage of the operational amplifier the output voltage V_{out} is equal to $-AV$, where A is the gain. This relationship can be rewritten equivalently as $V = -V_{out}/A$. Making this substitution for V and transposing terms involving V_{out}, the previous equation becomes

$$\frac{V_0}{R_0} + \frac{V_1}{R_1} + \cdots + \frac{V_7}{R_7} = \frac{-V_{out}}{A} \left(\frac{1}{R_0} + \frac{1}{R_1} + \cdots + \frac{1}{R_7} + \frac{A}{R} + \frac{1}{R} \right)$$

This equation may be simplified by making an approximation based on the high gain of an operational amplifier. The gain A is normally 50,000 or greater, causing the term A/R on the right side of the equation to be much greater than the other terms to which it is added. The parenthetical quantity on the right side is thus approximated by just the term A/R. The right side of the equation then becomes

$$\frac{-V_{out}}{A} \left(\frac{A}{R} \right) = \frac{-V_{out}}{R}$$

The output voltage V_{out} is therefore given by the expression

$$V_{out} = -R \left(\frac{V_0}{R_0} + \frac{V_1}{R_1} + \cdots + \frac{V_7}{R_7} \right)$$

Now using the values given in Fig. 9.20 for each R_i the expression for V_{out} becomes

$$V_{out} = -R\left(\frac{V_0}{R} + \frac{V_1}{R/2} + \cdots + \frac{V_7}{R/128}\right)$$

$$= -(V_0 + 2V_1 + \cdots + 128V_7)$$

$$= -\sum_{i=0}^{7} V_i 2^i$$

This indicates that the output voltage is equal to the negative of the quantity represented by the input binary number.

A similar circuit can be used to convert numbers represented in 8421 BCD (binary-coded decimal) to analog by adjusting the values of the input resistors to match the weights associated with the bits of a BCD number. A 2-digit 8421 BCD number represented by the sequence of bits

$$N = b_3 b_2 b_1 b_0 a_3 a_2 a_1 a_0$$

has the following polynomial expansion

$$N = (b_3 2^3 + b_2 2^2 + b_1 2^1 + b_0)10^1 + (a_3 2^3 + a_2 2^2 + a_1 2^1 + a_0)$$

The weights for the bits of N are therefore (in the order that the bits appear above) 80, 40, 20, 10, 8, 4, 2, 1. The corresponding input resistor values for a circuit similar to that of Fig. 9.21 are therefore

$$\frac{R}{80} \quad \frac{R}{40} \quad \frac{R}{20} \quad \frac{R}{10} \quad \frac{R}{8} \quad \frac{R}{4} \quad \frac{R}{2} \quad R$$

Analog-to-Digital Conversion

Several methods for converting an analog quantity into a digital representation will be discussed, all of which use a digital-to-analog (D/A) converter in a "trial and error" manner. Each such method starts with a trial digital number, which is converted with a D/A converter to produce an analog voltage. This analog voltage is then compared to the given analog voltage. Based on the comparison the trial number is either adjusted or left along. The process is repeated with the new trial number and so on, until an appropriate digital number is found corresponding to the given analog voltage. It is assumed that the input analog quantities are properly scaled so that they fall within the range of the digital-to-analog converter. The methods differ from each other primarily in the way that the trial number is adjusted.

The simplest method of adjusting the trial number is to start with the lowest number in the range (which is zero for positive numbers) and continually increment it until the converted voltage first exceeds or equals the given voltage. Figure 9.22 shows how this may be done with an up counter. The bits of the counter are connected to a D/A converter. The analog output voltage of this converter and the

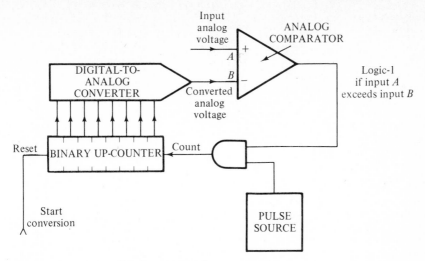

Figure 9.22 Analog-to-digital converter using an up counter.

given input analog voltage are connected to an analog comparator, which produces a logic-1 on its output line if the given voltage exceeds the D/A voltage. This comparator output line and a pulse source are connected to an AND gate, the output of which is connected to the count line of the counter.

The analog-to-digital (A/D) conversion process is started by resetting the counter to zero. The counter is then incremented with each pulse from the pulse source until the comparator output becomes logic-0. This occurs when the content of the binary counter is sufficient to cause the output of the D/A converter to exceed or equal the given analog voltage. At that time the content of the counter is used as the converted digital number.

A significant improvement to this first method for A/D conversion involves replacing the up counter with an up-down counter. The trial number may then be adjusted by incrementing or decrementing the counter. This allows the counter to track the given analog voltage if it varies in a continuous manner. Figure 9.23 depicts a circuit for this modified method. An analog comparator with two output lines, H and L, is used to compare the given analog voltage with the D/A converter output voltage. The comparator output line H will indicate with a logic-1 when the converted analog voltage exceeds the given analog voltage by at least a certain amount Δ. The other comparator output line L, on the other hand, will indicate with a logic-1 when the converted analog voltage falls short of the given analog voltage by at least the amount Δ. There is thus a "dead zone" of width 2Δ in which neither comparator output line is logic-1. Each of the two comparator output lines, H and L, are used to gate pulses that are applied, respectively, to the down-count and up-count lines of the counter.

The conversion process may start with an arbitrary number in the counter. If the content of the counter is too high compared to the given analog voltage, then the comparator output line H will be at logic-1, causing the counter to decrement

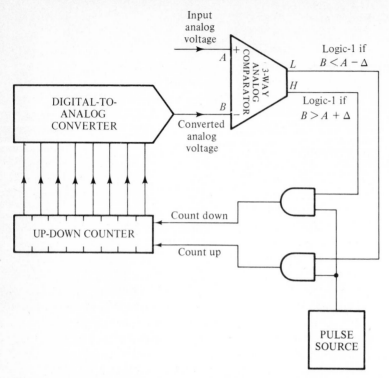

Figure 9.23 Analog-to-digital converter using an up-down counter.

with the next pulse. If the content of the counter is too low compared to the given analog voltage, then the line L will be at logic-1, causing the counter to increment with the next pulse. When the content of the counter becomes within $\pm \Delta$ of the given analog voltage, both H and L will be at logic-0, causing the counter to become stationary. If the analog voltage were to subsequently vary, the counter would be incremented or decremented accordingly.

It should be noted that the margin Δ of the comparator should be suitably chosen so that just one number of the counter will fall within the dead zone. The dead-zone width 2Δ should be greater than the amount in which the converted analog voltage varies between successive numbers, which is equal to the analog weight associated with the least-significant bit (W_{LSB}). However, the dead-zone width should not be greater than twice the analog weight of the least-significant bit. That is,

$$W_{LSB} < 2\Delta < 2W_{LSB}$$

The time required for A/D conversion using an up-down counter depends on how far the initial content of the counter is from the value to be determined. The number of pulses can vary from 0 to the range of the counter. In situations where the analog voltage to be converted varies slowly, just a few pulses are needed to complete conversions after the first conversion.

Successive Approximation

In many situations, however, the analog voltage to be converted can vary greatly from one conversion to the next. This is especially true if the A/D converter is shared (multiplexed) among several analog sources in a sequential manner, which is often the case. Furthermore, many applications making use of an A/D converter require that conversions be performed at regular intervals, so that the worst-case time must be assumed regardless of the actual time for conversion. For these latter situations, an alternative method for A/D conversion is available that will complete a conversion in a fixed amount of time that is relatively small. The method, referred to as *successive approximation*, involves adjusting each bit in a successive manner in order to achieve an increasingly-close approximation to the analog voltage to be converted. For converters that work with positive numbers, the method begins with a trial digital number having all bits equal to 0. The most-significant bit is set to 1, and the resulting number is converted to analog and compared with the given input analog voltage. If the comparison indicates that the trial number is too large then the most-significant bit is reset to 0. Otherwise, it is kept at 1. Next, the second most-significant bit is set to 1, and the resulting number is again converted to analog and compared with the input voltage. If this comparison indicates that the trial number is too large, then the second most-significant bit is reset to 0. This process continues with each of the remaining bits, using the values that have been determined for the more-significant bits. When the least-significant bit is tested and adjusted, the A/D conversion is complete.

A circuit that performs A/D conversion by successive approximation is shown in Fig. 9.24. A register consisting of eight negative-edge-triggered *SR* flip-flops is provided to contain the trial number. As before, the content of this register is presented to a D/A converter. The output voltage from the D/A converter and the input analog voltage to be converted are presented to an analog comparator, the output of which is used to determine whether the bit under trial is to be reset. A 4-bit binary up counter and a 1-out-of-8 decoder are provided to scan the bits of the trial number from left to right. The lower 3 bits of the counter are connected to the input lines of the decoder, to determine which of the eight output lines is to be active (logic-1). A pulse source is connected to the counter and also to the clock lines of the flip-flops comprising the trial-number register. The behavior of the counter and register will therefore be synchronized and state changes of either will occur only at the negative edges of the pulses. The most-significant bit of the counter, which will be 1 for a count of 8, is used to disable the pulse source after eight pulses and thus stop the conversion process. The decoder output lines are each used to select the reset terminal of the corresponding flip-flop in the trial-number register and the set terminal of the next flip-flop. Each reset terminal is also conditioned on the output of the comparator. In this way, when a pulse occurs, the flip-flop corresponding to the active decoder output line will be reset if the trial number is too large, and the next flip-flop will always be set.

The circuit operates as follows. A pulse on the line labeled "start conversion," which is assumed to be synchronized to the pulse source, will initialize the trial-

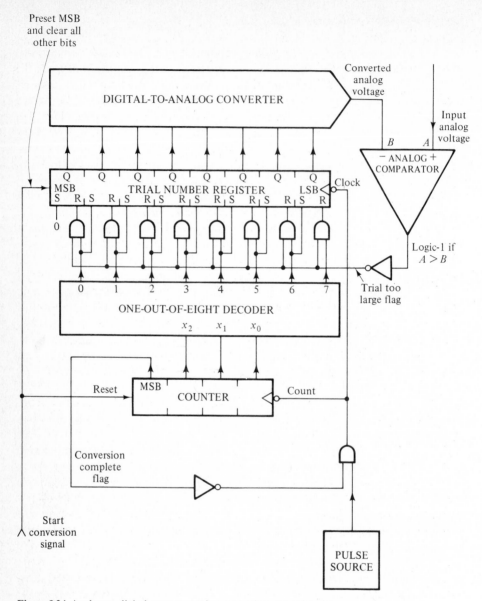

Figure 9.24 Analog-to-digital converter using successive approximation.

number register with 1 for the most-significant bit and 0 for the rest of the bits. This start pulse also resets the 4-bit counter to zero, which enables pulses from the pulse source. The initial trial number is converted to analog and compared with the input voltage. When the negative edge of a pulse from the pulse source occurs, the most-significant bit of the trial number is reset if the trial number is too large. In any event, the second most-significant bit is set. The counter is also incremented to one. This process is repeated for succeeding bits. When the counter reaches eight, all bits of the trial-number register will have been tested and adjusted. The process stops at this point, with the converted number in the trial-number register.

Generally, successive approximation requires only k pulses to perform the conversion of an analog voltage to a k-bit number. This is compared to $2^k - 1$ pulses in the worst case for a conversion using the circuit with an up-down counter.

A/D Conversion with a Microprocessor

When analog data is to be converted into digital form for use with a microprocessor, it is possible and often advantageous to have the microprocessor partake in the conversion process. By allowing the microprocessor to perform part of the conversion task, the external circuitry can be simplified. Furthermore, there will be fewer required interconnections between the microprocessor and the external circuitry.

The use of a microprocessor in the conversion process becomes especially advantageous when more than one analog signal is to be converted. In this case, a single D/A converter connected to an output port suffices to convert the trial numbers for all analog signals. A separate comparator for each analog signal is provided to compare that analog signal with the output of the D/A converter. The comparison results for each analog signal are sent to the microprocessor over one line of an input port.

To be more specific, consider a scheme for converting the signals of eight analog channels into digital making use of the illustrative microprocessor. Figure 9.25 shows a circuit to implement this scheme. Included in the circuit are an 8-bit output port and an 8-bit input port, each having the same device code. The output port has an 8-bit register connected to the Data bus to receive trial numbers from the microprocessor. The output lines of this register are connected to a D/A converter, the output line of which is connected to an input line of each of eight analog comparators. The other input line of each comparator is connected to one of the eight analog input channels. Output lines from the comparators are connected to a bank of 3-state drivers that form the input port.

These components provide for sufficient information to and from the microprocessor for a program to be able to perform an analog-to-digital conversion for all eight channels. Generally, the program will begin the conversion for a particular channel by outputting a trial number. This trial number is converted to analog by the D/A converter and then compared with the voltage on each input channel. The results of all eight comparisons are brought in through the input port. The program will then isolate and test the comparison bit corresponding to the particular channel in order to determine a new trial number for this channel. After determining the correct number for the voltage of one channel, the microprocessor will go on to repeat the process for another channel. In this way, all channels are converted in a time-multiplexed manner. It should be noted that no

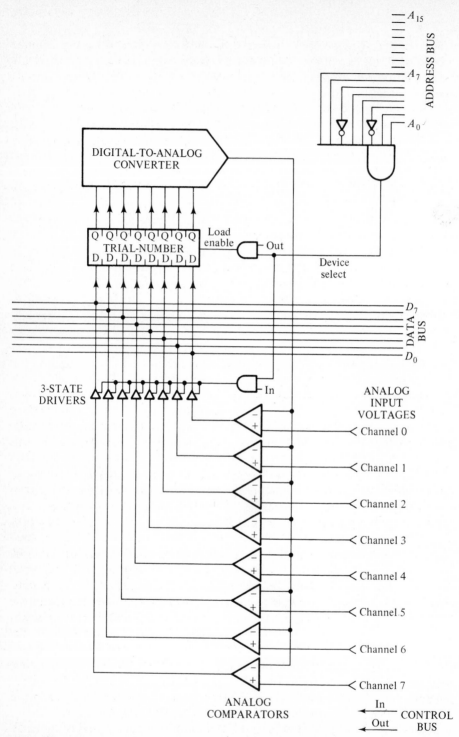

Figure 9.25 Interface for the illustrative microprocessor to perform A/D conversion for eight analog channels.

status information concerning the start and completion of the conversion process need be transferred between the microprocessor and the external circuit. This is due to the fact that the conversion is done by the microprocessor, which therefore has control of the starting of the process, as well as knowledge of its completion. If, alternatively, the conversion were done entirely by external components, then such status information would have to be transferred through special I/O ports.

The method used by the program to perform the conversions might be any one of many, including successive approximation, a counting method, or some special method.

There is an interesting programming method that is comparatively fast if the number of bits is rather small (say 4) and the number of channels is large (say 16 or more). The method involves trying every possible number starting from zero and going through the range. As each number is tried, the results from all comparators are noted. If the comparator for any channel has just changed, then the current trial number is used as the value for that channel. After all numbers have been tried, all channels will have been converted. For 4 bits and 16 channels, this method involves just 16 trials to convert all channels, which is an average of one trial per channel.

9.8 SERIAL I/O

In handling I/O data, serial techniques are often used to transfer information between a microcomputer and some I/O device (such as a terminal) or to store information for a microcomputer within a memory unit (such as magnetic cassette tape). Generally, such serial techniques involve a single line that is shared in time to convey a number of bits comprising a data word. The two situations, data transfer and data storage, can be thought of in a similar manner. Each involves an information source and destination. Data is taken from the source and is then either transferred a bit at a time over a line to the destination or stored a bit at a time onto some medium to be later retrieved at the destination. The data path connecting the source to the destination in each case is referred to as a *channel*.

The data is often in a parallel form at the source and/or the destination of a serial channel. In such cases, some means of converting between parallel and serial form is needed. A shift register fills this need quite naturally. To convert parallel data into serial form, first the bits comprising a data word are simultaneously loaded into a shift register. The shift register is then repeatedly shifted in a specified direction, causing each bit of the word to appear sequentially on the output line of the end flip-flop. To convert serial data into parallel form, the line in which the serial data appears is connected to the serial input line at the appropriate end of a shift register. The shift register is then shifted as many times as there are bits in a data word. The bits forming a data word are then available at the output lines of the appropriate flip-flops in the shift register.

There are basically two modes in which information is conveyed over a serial channel, *synchronous* and *asynchronous*. For the synchronous mode, a clock line is provided that is common to the source and destination. Pulses appearing on the clock line serve to separate the individual bits that are conveyed through the channel. Both the source and the destination use the same clock pulses as a time reference for the occurrence of each data bit. As a consequence, the operation of a serial channel in the synchronous mode does not require precision in absolute time. For the asynchronous mode, no clock line common to the source and destination is provided. Instead, the source and the destination each determine the time for each bit by precisely measuring the time from the beginning of a word. For this purpose, the source must mark the beginning of a word in a way recognizable to the destination.

Synchronous Mode

To illustrate the synchronous mode for a serial data channel, consider the network of Fig. 9.26. The network is configured for words of 8 bits, one of which is a parity check bit.

At the data source, an 8-bit shift register is provided to convert the parallel input data into serial form. The shift register has input lines controlled by a strobe line, labeled "Load," for the parallel loading of data into the eight flip-flops. Seven bits of input information are presented to the parallel-load input lines of the seven rightmost flip-flops in the shift register. A parity-generator network based on these 7 information bits produces an eighth bit (parity bit) that is presented to the parallel-load input line of the remaining flip-flop. A pulse source is provided to serve as the clock for both the data source and destination. A 3-bit counter is included at the source to keep track of the number of clock pulses modulo 8. Each time the counter reaches seven a pulse occurs on the Load strobe line of the shift register with the next clock pulse. This causes the source shift register to be loaded with the next data word assumed to be present on its parallel-input lines. When the counter is at a number other than seven, clock pulses are applied to the shift line of the shift register. This causes the 8 bits to appear sequentially on the data line of the channel. The rightmost bit is on the data line immediately after loading, which corresponds to a count of zero. The leftmost bit will appear on the data line after seven clock pulses occur, which corresponds to a count of 7.

An 8-bit shift register is provided at the destination to accept serial data from the channel and convert it into parallel form. Data from the channel is presented to the serial input line on the left end of the shift register. Clock pulses, sent on a second line of the channel from the source, are applied to the shift line of the destination shift register. This causes the shift register to shift in data toward the right. As at the source, a 3-bit counter is provided at the destination to keep track of the clock pulses modulo 8. It is assumed that the 3-bit counters at the source and destination have been reset together at some time and therefore agree in content. Each time the 3-bit counter at the destination reaches zero, a flag labeled "Word Received" is placed at logic-1 signifying that a word has been received and is available at the output lines of the shift register. A network to check parity of a

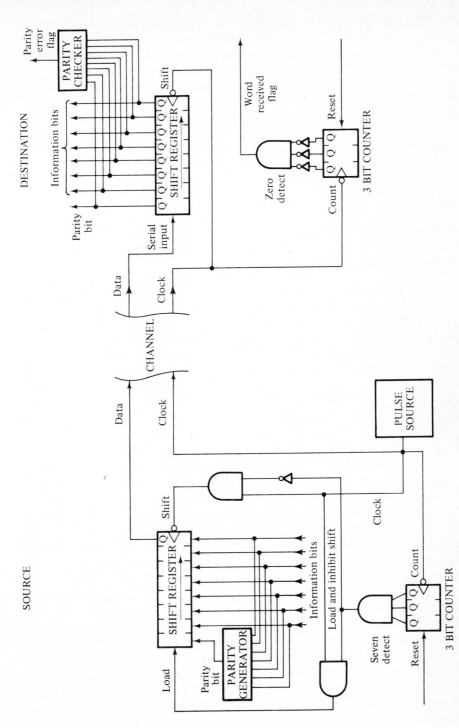

Figure 9.26 Synchronous serial data channel.

received word is provided that indicates an error if the received word has incorrect parity.

The channel connecting the source and destination could correspond to many types of communication links or storage media. For example, it could consist of two lines connecting a computer I/O port to a peripheral device, a complex communication link utilizing a modulator and a demodulator for a telephone or radio channel, or a pair of tracks of a magnetic-cassette-tape unit. It is important that any time delay occurring in a synchronous channel affects the data and clock lines in the same way, so that their relative time relationship is maintained.

The particular scheme illustrated in Fig. 9.26 is synchronous with respect to the bits comprising a word and also with respect to the words themselves. This is true, since words begin always at a periodic time, specifically the eighth clock pulse. Alternatively, a scheme might be bit synchronous, but word asynchronous. In such a case, a word begins with an externally specified clock pulse.

Asynchronous Mode

With the asynchronous mode of operation, a channel is asynchronous with respect to both bits and words. This means that there is no common clock line connecting the source and destination to delineate bit times and that a word may begin at any time. Some means is necessary to mark the beginning of a word so that the time of appearance of each bit in the word can be determined at the destination. A standard way of doing this is to frame each word with a start bit and a stop bit. During intervals of time in which no word is being transferred the channel is specified to be a certain logic value, say 1. The stop bit, occurring at the end of a word, is assigned this same value 1. The start bit occurring at the beginning of a word is then assigned the opposite value 0. In this way, the front edge of the start bit always corresponds to a transition in values, 1 to 0, and is therefore discernible at the destination. This front edge of the start bit is used at the destination to signify the beginning of a new word and also as a reference to determine the times for all bits in that word.

A network to implement this scheme for an asynchronous serial channel is shown in Fig. 9.27. The network is configured to handle words having 8 information bits. No provision for generating or checking parity is shown in the network to keep it simple. As in the synchronous case, a shift register at the source and at the destination provide respectively for parallel-to-serial and serial-to-parallel conversion. The shift register at the source is 10 bits long to accommodate the start bit, 8 data bits, and the stop bit. The data bits are supplied in parallel to the shift register from a buffer register. The buffer register in turn receives parallel input data that is externally supplied. This external data is loaded into the buffer register by a pulse externally applied to the line labeled "Load buffer strobe." This may be done during the time that another word is being shifted out of the shift register. In that case, the content of the buffer will be loaded into the shift register as soon as the shift register becomes empty. On the other hand, if the buffer is loaded with data while the shift register is idle, this data will be relayed to the shift register with the

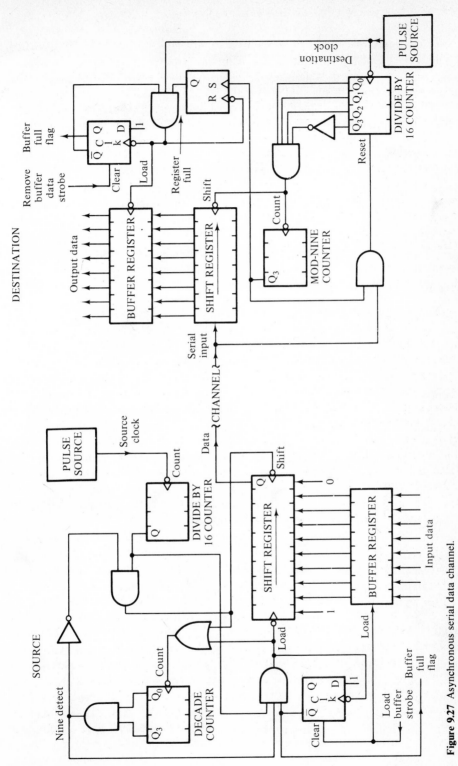

Figure 9.27 Asynchronous serial data channel.

347

next clock pulse. A D flip-flop is used as a flag to signify when the buffer does not contain data ready to be transferred. This flip-flop is cleared when the buffer is loaded and is set (by pulsing its clock line with $D = 1$) when the buffer content is transferred to the shift register.

The pulses used throughout the source network are derived from a pulse source connected to a divide-by-16 counter. It will be seen that this allows the frequencies of the source and destination clocks to be similar.

A decade counter is provided at the source to control the number of shift pulses. Each pulse to the shift register is also applied to the decade counter. A count of 9 (corresponding to the end of a transmitted word) is detected by an AND gate. This nine-detect signal is used to block further pulses from reaching the shift register and the decade counter. The source network at this time is in the idle condition.

While in the idle condition another word can be loaded into the shift register from the buffer. This is done with a pulse that is enabled by the AND of the nine-detect signal and the buffer-full condition. The decade counter is also incremented by this load-shift-register pulse, causing it to go to zero. Consequently, the shift register begins shifting out the new word.

At the destination, an 8-bit shift register is used to accommodate just the 8 data bits. To shift in each bit, a shift pulse is generated at the approximate center of each bit time. These shift pulses are presented to both the shift register and a mod-9 counter. The mod-9 counter starts with a count of 8 before a new word from the channel is encountered. As shift pulses occur for a word, the counter will first go to zero and then count back up to 8, which signifies the end of a new word. This allows 9 bits to be shifted into the register; however, the start bit is lost at the right end.

The shift pulses are generated with the use of a divide-by-16 counter connected to the destination clock. The destination clock is adjusted as close as possible to the pulse rate of the source clock. Connected to the divide-by-16 counter is a seven detector, which produces a shift pulse each time the counter passes through seven. When the mod-9 counter reaches 8, further shift pulses are inhibited by the resetting of the divide-by-16 counter. This is done with the AND of the channel line (which should be logic-1 corresponding to a stop bit) and the most-significant bit of the mod-9 counter. The divide-by-16 counter is kept reset during idle periods of the channel. With the divide-by-16 counter in reset, no shift pulses will be generated.

When the leading edge of a start bit appears on the channel, its 0 value will cause the reset terminal of the divide-by-16 counter to become logic-0. This allows the divide-by-16 counter to begin counting clock pulses. With the seventh clock pulse a shift pulse is generated, which is at the approximate center of the start bit. Every 16 clock pulses later another shift pulse is generated, which will be at the approximate center of a data bit.

It should be noted that if after the start bit begins, but before the first shift pulse, the channel were to return to 1, then the divide-by-16 counter would again be reset. This would signify a false start that is attributed to noise. The network in this case simply continues to wait for a true start bit.

Included at the destination is a buffer register. This buffer register is loaded from the shift register whenever the buffer is empty and the shift register is full. Two flip-flops are used to indicate the full conditions of the two registers. The flip-flop used to indicate the full condition of the shift register is assumed to be of a special type having edge-triggered S and R input terminals. The S terminal is activated by the most-significant bit of the mod-9 counter, which indicates that a new word has been received. The R terminal is activated whenever the content of the shift register is moved to the buffer. A D flip-flop is used to indicate the full condition of the buffer. This flip-flop is cleared by an external strobe whenever the buffer register is read, and is set (by pulsing its clock line with $D = 1$) whenever the buffer is loaded from the shift register.

The buffers at the source and destination are a convenience that allow the channel to operate at full speed while providing time (10 bit times) for external devices to supply and to accept data. This extra time is important when a computer is involved, since a certain amount of program execution time is required before the computer can respond to the status information such as source buffer empty or destination buffer full.

It should be pointed out that the source and destination clocks are not physically the same. They should, however, be adjusted so that their pulse rates are as close as possible. If the two pulse rates differ by some amount, then the destination network will drift away from the center of each bit time as a word progresses. Starting with the front edge of the start bit, the destination circuit must not drift more than one-half of a bit time by the time the 10th bit is received. Otherwise, it will have drifted outside of the time for the tenth bit. This corresponds to a tolerance of 5 percent between the two pulse rates.

There are integrated-circuit modules available that incorporate both a source network and a destination network for synchronous and for asynchronous serial channels. Two such modules thus provide all components for a two-way channel. The source network (referred to as a *transmitter*) of one module is connected to the destination network (referred to as a *receiver*) of the other module and vice versa. In the case where the channel corresponds to a storage medium (such as a magnetic-tape cassette unit), a single module provides both the source and destination networks.

Such modules have various forms and include additional components to make them more flexible. For the asynchronous mode, one available module, referred to as a *universal asynchronous receiver/transmitter (UART)*, can be programmed to handle 5, 6, 7, or 8 data bits per word with a possible extra bit for odd or even parity and with 1 or 2 stop bits. The programming is done by wiring certain control lines high or low. The module has additional status lines to indicate various error conditions that might arise, such as wrong parity, framing error (no stop bit when expected), buffer overrun (data supplied too fast to transmitter buffer or removed too slow from receiver buffer). A similar module is available for the synchronous mode, which is referred to as a *universal synchronous receiver/transmitter* (*USRT*).

Other similar modules are available that are intended to be used with particular microprocessors. They usually have 3-state output lines so that they can conveniently form an I/O port. Programming the options for some of these modules is done by writing a control word from a microprocessor into a special internal register rather than by wiring control lines. This saves a few pins for the module.

The channel connecting the source to the destination often makes use of interface circuits that convert the electrical signals to a certain form. In the case of a two-way asynchronous channel between a terminal and a computer, two standard interface schemes are commonly used. One, which is specified for teletypes or teletype-like terminals, encodes logic-1 as a current of magnitude 20 mA and logic-0 as a zero current. The other scheme, which is part of the EIA RS232C standard, encodes logic-1 as a voltage that is nominally -5 V and logic-0 as a voltage that is nominally $+5$ V.

In the case of asynchronous channels involving long-distance communication, such as telephone lines, or information storage, such as magnetic-tape units, modulators and demodulators of various forms are used. In particular, modules, referred to as *modems*, incorporating a modulator and a demodulator for frequency-shift keying are available for use with telephone channels. Such modems use two frequency bands, one for each direction, so that a two-way channel can be obtained from a single telephone line. One frequency band commonly encodes a logic-1 with a frequency of 1270 Hz and a logic-0 with a frequency of 1070 Hz. The other band commonly uses the frequencies of 2225 Hz for logic-1 and 2025 Hz for logic-0. A modem is needed at each end of a two-way channel. Such modems are also useful to store information asynchronously on audio magnetic tape, since the frequency bands used by the modem fall nicely in the audio range.

9.9 BIT-SLICE MICROPROCESSORS

As has been indicated, a microcomputer is a system of modules that generally includes a microprocessor along with memory and I/O units. The microprocessor might be broken down further into subunits in order to achieve greater flexibility. One such approach involves separating the data-handling portion of a microprocessor from that which generally handles instructions and their sequencing. The data-handling portion, consisting of the arithmetic-logic unit and various data registers, is then formed by cascading several identical data units. Each such data unit, referred to as a *microprocessor slice*, consists of an arithmetic-logic unit and various registers for a certain number of bits.

Many different versions of bit-slice microprocessors are available, each having a particular arrangement of data registers and set of arithmetic-logic functions. No one model can therefore encompass the details involved in each of them. In

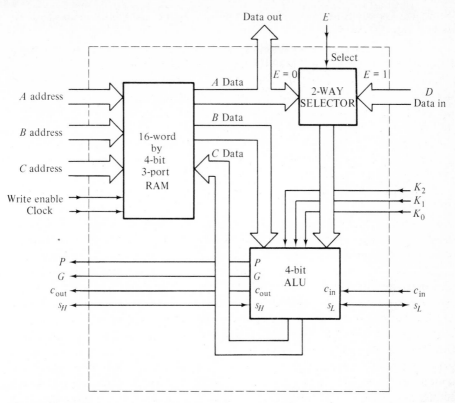

Figure 9.28 Model for a microprocessor slice.

order to illustrate the general concept, a simplified model will be considered that is representative of the various versions of bit-slice microprocessors. This model, shown in Fig. 9.28, is composed of a 4-bit arithmetic-logic unit (ALU) and a 16-word × 4-bit scratchpad memory unit. The ALU can perform eight different functions upon two 4-bit operands, A and B, to produce a 4-bit result. Three control lines, K_0, K_1, and K_2, are provided to specify which function is to be performed as shown in Table 9.3. Six lines are provided to the ALU to allow for the cascading of several microprocessor slices. Four of the lines, c_{in}, c_{out}, P, and G, are used to convey carry information for the two arithmetic operations, addition and subtraction; whereas the other two lines, s_H and s_L, are used to convey information for the two shift operations. In particular, c_{in} is an incoming line that provides the value of a carry or borrow to the low-order bit and c_{out} is an outgoing line that transmits the value of the carry or borrow produced from the high-order bit. The two lines P and G are outgoing lines that convey additional carry information to allow cascading microprocessor slices with a look-ahead-carry generator. It is assumed that the look-ahead-carry scheme, as discussed in Sec. 5.6, is internally used in the implementation of the two arithmetic operations. The two lines s_H and s_L are bidirectional. The line s_H provides the value of the bit shifted

Table 9.3 Functions performed by the ALU in the model bit-slice microprocessor

K_2	K_1	K_0	Function	Effect
0	0	0	Add B to A	Result $= A + B + c_{in}$, $c_{out} =$ final carry
0	0	1	Subtract B from A	Result $= A - B - c_{in}$, $c_{out} =$ final borrow
0	1	0	AND A with B	$r_i = a_i \wedge b_i$
0	1	1	OR A with B	$r_i = a_i \vee b_i$
1	0	0	EXCLUSIVE OR A with B	$r_i = a_i \oplus b_i$
1	0	1	Shift A left	$r_i = a_{i-1}$ $i \neq 0$, $r_0 = s_L$, $s_H = a_3$
1	1	0	Shift A right	$r_i = a_{i+1}$ $i \neq 3$, $r_3 = s_H$, $s_L = a_0$
1	1	1	Pass A	Result $= A$

Note: $A = a_3 a_2 a_1 a_0$, $B = b_3 b_2 b_1 b_0$, and Result $= r_3 r_2 r_1 r_0$.

into the high-order position during a right shift and receives the bit shifted from the high-order position during a left shift. The line s_L provides the value of the bit shifted into the low-order position during a left shift and receives the bit shifted from the low-order position during a right shift.

The 16-word × 4-bit scratchpad memory unit is assumed to have three ports. Each port consists of a set of four data lines with an associated set of four address lines, and each port can access any of the 16 words of the scratchpad independently from the other ports. Two of the ports, A and B, are for reading the scratchpad memory, while the third, C, is for writing. Each of the two read ports continuously reflects the content of the word in the scratchpad that is addressed by the corresponding address lines. The scratchpad contents are altered only by means of port C. Two control lines, Write-enable and Clock, are provided to coordinate the transfer of data through port C into the scratchpad. If Write-enable is at logic-1, the content of the data lines of port C is written, with the trailing edge of the Clock line, into the word location of the scratchpad that is designated by the address lines of port C.

The two read ports A and B of the scratchpad are connected to provide data for the respective A and B operands of the ALU, while the write port C is connected to receive the results from the ALU. The A-operand data to the ALU can also be supplied externally. For this purpose, a two-way 4-bit selector is provided to determine whether the A-operand data is to come from the A port of the scratchpad or from the four incoming data lines labeled as D. This selector is controlled by the external line E, which when at logic-1 causes the external data to be selected. Finally, four outgoing lines are connected directly to port A of the scratchpad, to allow data from the scratchpad to be brought to the outside of the microprocessor.

In summary, the microprocessor slice performs basic operations upon data obtained from the scratchpad to produce results that are returned to the scratchpad. In addition, external data for an operation can be brought directly in from a set of four lines and data from the scratchpad can be sent out over another set of four lines. The operation to be performed, the source of operand data, and the destination of the results are controlled externally with various control lines to the microprocessor slice. The signals on these control lines are specified by outside circuitry so as to achieve a desired operation of the microprocessor slice. In this way, a microprocessor slice can be adapted for use in a customized micro-computer having a particular behavior. This represents a greater flexibility for bit-slice microprocessors as compared to self-contained microprocessors.

The fact that microprocessor slices can be readily cascaded to achieve a desired data precision represents still more flexibility. Several microprocessor slices in the form of the model may be cascaded by interconnecting their shift and carry lines. In all cases, this involves connecting the shift line s_H of one slice to the shift line s_L of the slice in the next higher position. The carry lines, however, may be interconnected in two different ways. The simplest way is to connect the carry-out line c_{out} of one slice to the carry-in line c_{in} of the next higher slice. This results in a rippling of the carry from one slice to the next.

To take full advantage, however, of the look-ahead-carry scheme used in the microprocessor slices, the carry interconnection might make use of a look-ahead-carry generator network, as discussed in Sec. 5.6. In this case, the look-ahead-carry generator will have the P and G lines from each slice as inputs and will produce as outputs the value for the c_{in} lines to each slice. The c_{out} lines from each slice are not used in this case. Figure 9.29 shows the connections that are made to cascade four microprocessor slices using a look-ahead-carry generator.

To form a complete microprocessor from microprocessor slices, additional components are needed to handle the sequencing and decoding of instructions. Included among these additional components would be a program counter, an instruction register, a timing and control unit, an instruction decoder, perhaps a push-down stack, and other registers to accommodate memory and I/O interfac-ing. Generally, these components provide for fetching an instruction from main memory according to the program counter and transferring it to the instruction register. The instruction decoder along with the timing and control unit, using the

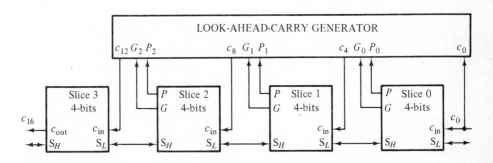

NOTE: The three address buses A, B, and C
and the six control lines K_2, K_1, K_0, Clock,
Write enable, and E are tied in common.

Figure 9.29 The cascading of four microprocessor slices using a look-ahead-carry generator.

content of the instruction register as input, produce values for the control signals and other input lines to the microprocessor slices in a way to carry out the instruction. The program counter is incremented after each instruction and is appropriately altered in the case of jump instructions.

Implementation of the Illustrative Microprocessor Using Microprocessor Slices

As an example, consider how the illustrative microprocessor might be implemented from the model microprocessor slices. Two slices are cascaded to achieve an 8-bit data width. These two slices contain the ALU and the 16-word scratchpad of the illustrative microprocessor. The remaining necessary components consist of a 16-bit program counter, a 64-word × 16-bit stack, an 8-bit instruction register, a 16-bit data-address register, an instruction decoder, a carry flip-flop, certain control and timing circuitry, and various bus-driving gates. The interconnection of these components is depicted in Fig. 9.30.

In the figure the block labeled " general logic " directs the flow of data between the various components. Its timing is determined by signals sent to it from the block labeled " timing-and-control logic."

The block labeled " instruction decoder " accepts the content of the instruction register and provides control signals to the general-logic block and to the microprocessor slices. The specific information that the decoder supplies to the microprocessor slices consists of the A, B, C addresses of the scratchpad for operands and results, as well as the 6 control signals K_2, K_1, K_0, Write-enable, Clock, and E. The information sent to the general-logic block by the instruction decoder concerns either address modification of the program counter (in the case of jump instructions) or data transfer to or from the microprocessor slices. The time in which specific information is sent by the decoder is influenced by signals from the timing-and-control-logic block.

The timing-and-control-logic block as just indicated determines the timing of all operations performed by other blocks. It also receives signals on the incoming lines of the Control bus and sends signals on the outgoing lines. A major component of this block is a 4-bit sequence counter. This sequence counter is connected to the incoming clock line so that it is incremented with each clock pulse. At the end of each instruction, the sequence counter is reset to zero. The state of the counter is used to determine the clock pulse time of each step in the execution of an instruction. For this purpose the 4 bits of the counter are presented to a 1-out-of-16 decoder, as shown in Fig. 9.31. The output lines of this decoder, labeled S_i, are enabled by the clock line. Thus, for each clock pulse during the execution of an instruction, a pulse will occur on one output line of the decoder, corresponding to the number of clock pulses since the beginning of the instruction cycle. These S_i signals are sent to the blocks labeled " general logic " and " instruction decoder." These two blocks combine the S_i signals with other logic signals to generate pulses on lines that strobe data into the various registers and flags. The timing-and-control block uses the S_i lines also to generate pulses on the outgoing lines of the Control bus.

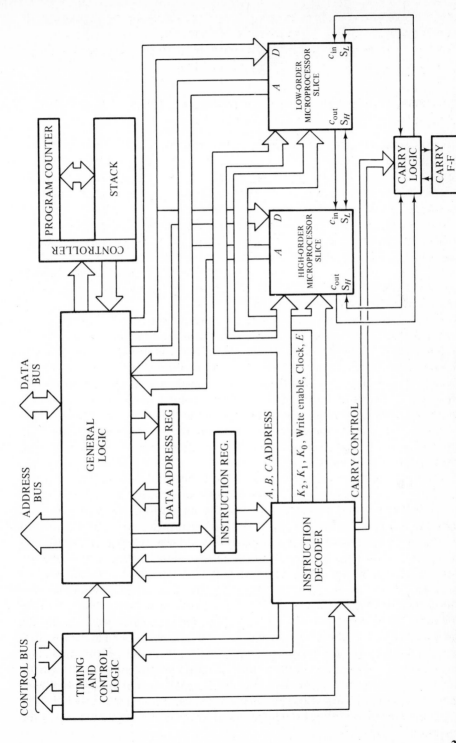

Figure 9.30 Implementation of the illustrative microprocessor using microprocessor slices.

355

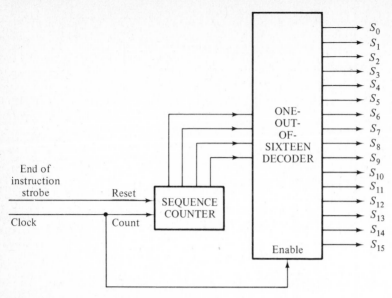

Figure 9.31 Sequence counter and decoder.

The general operation of the overall network will now be illustrated by considering the execution of two instructions. The first two clock pulses are common to all instructions, since it is during this time that the operation code of an instruction is fetched from main memory. A pulse on S_0 is used to send an address over the Address bus, commencing with the leading edge. The Read control line is then set to logic-1. This causes the first byte of an instruction to be placed onto the Data bus by main memory. This first byte is then strobed into the instruction register with the trailing edge of the S_1 pulse. The instruction decoder then determines the type of instruction and indicates to the general-logic block to bring in additional bytes in the case of a multibyte instruction.

Suppose, for example, that the instruction is add-with-carry. Since this is a single byte instruction no additional bytes will be brought in. This instruction is carried out by the microprocessor slices during the next clock pulse. It involves the addition of the content of some scratchpad register R to the accumulator, which is scratchpad register 0. The results of the addition are stored into the accumulator. To set this up, the instruction decoder places 0000 onto the A and C Address lines to the microprocessor slices, and the specific designator R onto the B Address lines. The control lines $K_2 K_1 K_0$ are set at 000, corresponding to ADD, and E is set at logic-0, corresponding to select A data. The carry logic is directed to place the value of the carry flip-flop onto the c_{in} line. Finally, the Write-enable control line is set at logic-1 to allow the results to be written into the scratchpad. At this time, the pulse on the S_2 line is passed to the clock line of the microprocessor slices. This causes the computed sum to be written into the accumulator (i.e., scratchpad register 0). At the same time, a pulse is sent to the carry logic that is used to strobe the final carry into the carry flip-flop. The sequence counter is also reset at this time since the execution of the instruction has been completed.

For a second example, consider the unconditional jump instruction, which will not involve the microprocessor slices at all. After the first byte of this instruction is brought into the instruction register, the instruction decoder informs the general-logic block to bring in the two additional bytes. Consequently, the second instruction byte is fetched from main memory and stored into the high-order portion of the data-address register, using pulses on S_3 and S_4 (corresponding to the first two clock pulses of the second machine cycle). The third instruction byte is then fetched and stored into the low-order portion of the data-address register, using pulses on S_6 and S_7 (corresponding to the first two clock pulses of the third machine cycle). The execution of the instruction is completed by transferring the new content of the data-address register to the program counter using the pulse on S_8. This S_8 pulse is also used to reset the sequence counter, since the instruction execution will be completed at this point.

Considerations in the Use of Bit-Slice Microprocessors

It can be generally said that bit-slice microprocessors offer more flexibility as compared to self-contained microprocessors. In particular, the bit slices can be easily cascaded to achieve any degree of data precision. Moreover, the slices can be grouped so as to operate on different components of a vector quantity, allowing the implementation of a microprocessor that deals with vectors instead of individual numbers. Also, the instruction repertoire of a microprocessor using slices can be freely specified by the way the other logic blocks are designed.

Microprocessors constructed from bit slices tend to also have an advantage in speed over self-contained microprocessors, due to the lower scale of integration involved. A disadvantage of bit-slice microprocessors is the need to provide the additional circuitry that is necessary for a complete microprocessor. This causes them to be less convenient to use for most applications. To alleviate this inconvenience, manufacturers generally make modules available that handle the sequencing of instructions. Using such modules in conjunction with microprocessor slices usually requires just the addition of an instruction register, an instruction decoder, and any other registers that are particular to an application. By excluding the instruction register and decoder from the sequencing module the flexibility advantage is retained.

A common approach taken in the design of instruction sequencing modules is to perform the various operations involved in the execution of an instruction as a sequence of microinstructions. These microinstructions reside in a special memory unit and are fetched and executed in a manner similar to that of regular instructions. Fetching the microinstructions in the proper sequence is handled by the instruction sequencing module. A portion of each microinstruction is decoded by additional circuitry to determine the signals to the microprocessor slices. These microinstructions also manage an external program counter and instruction register for handling the regular instructions. The regular instructions (those making up the instruction repertoire) reside in main memory and are fetched into the instruction register according to the program counter. This is done by a routine made up of several microinstructions. The content of the instruction register is then used as an address of a microinstruction subroutine that is especially written to carry out the execution of the regular instruction. Thus, in this case, there exists a computer within a computer, in which the inner computer is programmed with microinstructions to carry out the instructions of the outer computer.

It should be pointed out that *microprogramming* does not refer to the programming of a microcomputer, but rather to the implementation of the instructions in the repertoire of any computer by routines of microinstructions.

9.10 MICROPROCESSOR CLOCKS

Many microprocessors, unlike the illustrative model, require a clock having two or more phases. The phases correspond to separate pulse lines having the same period and a fixed time relationship among each other. Generally, the phases are used within the microprocessor to control different types of data transfers. For instance, two-phase master-slave flip-flops may be used for registers in a microprocessor. In this case, one clock phase is used to strobe information into the master sections of all flip-flops and the other clock phase is used to strobe the content of each master section into the corresponding slave section.

A network that may be used to derive two nonoverlapping phases from a single pulse source is shown in Fig. 9.32. The pulse source is connected to the

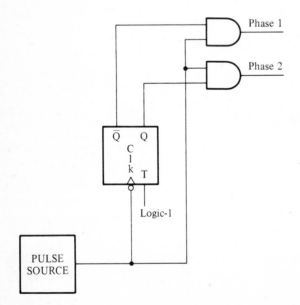

Figure 9.32 Phase-splitting circuit.

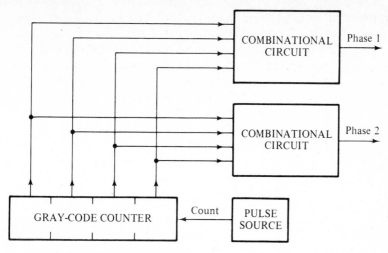

Figure 9.33 Generalized phase-splitting circuit.

clock line of a T-type flip-flop, with the T terminal tied to logic-1. The flip-flop therefore changes state after each pulse. The output line of the flip-flop and its complement are each ANDed with the pulse source to produce the two derived phases. When the state Q of the flip-flop is logic-0, a pulse from the source will produce a pulse on the phase-1 line. When Q is logic-1, a pulse from the source will produce a pulse on the phase-2 line. In this way, pulses from the source are alternately applied to the two phases. The "dead time" between phases is equal to the off time of the pulse source, which can be adjusted to meet whatever requirement is specified for a microprocessor. The pulse rate of the two phases is one-half of that of the pulse source. The pulse-duration time for each phase will be equal to that of the pulse source.

A more general time relationship between two phases can be achieved with the network of Fig. 9.33. The network makes use of a Gray-code counter driven by a pulse source. Each phase is derived having an arbitrary pulse duration and position relative to the other phase by combining selected successive counts in the Gray code. Hazard-free† combinational circuits are used for this purpose. The Gray code rather than straight binary is used to prevent the occurrence of "glitches" due to multiple bit changes. With a 4-bit counter, as shown in the figure, the pulse rate of the source needs to be 16 times the desired pulse rate of the two phases. This network can be extended to more than two phases by simply including additional combinational circuits to derive the extra phases.

---

† For a treatment of the design of hazard-free combinational circuits see a text on switching circuit theory, such as D. D. Givone, "Introduction to Switching Circuit Theory," McGraw-Hill Book Company, New York, 1970.

PROBLEMS

9.1 Draw a network for an input port for the illustrative microprocessor using open-collector TTL gates rather than 3-state drivers. No inversion of the input data should occur. Include a network for detecting the device code 23_{16}, which is to be assigned to the port. Also, include a register to serve as the source of the input data.

9.2 A function that is encountered in various types of computation is that of reversing the order of bits in a number. It is a rather simple function in concept, but one that is rather cumbersome to implement with the instructions that are available with a typical microprocessor. It can be easily accomplished, though, using an input/output operation.

Design a device for the illustrative microprocessor having an input and an output port that may be used for this purpose. Specifically, the device should be such that when an 8-bit number is sent to the output port the number becomes available with the order of the bits reversed at the input port. Both ports should have the device code $B2_{16}$. Provide a register with either port only if needed.

9.3 A certain device to be connected to the illustrative microprocessor is to have eight sources of input data of 8 bits each. Design an interface that provides for selecting and coupling the data sources to the Data bus, using a 1-out-of-8 decoder and eight sets of 3-state drivers.

9.4 Redesign the interface network for Prob. 9.3 using an eight-way 8-bit data selector and one set of eight 3-state drivers.

9.5 The interface for the device of Prob. 9.3 is to be changed so that the selection of the eight data sources is done automatically in a cyclic order. Rather than have a separate device code for each of the eight data sources, just one device code (say 49_{16}) is used for all eight data sources. Each time this device code is specified in an input instruction, the next data source from the previous one is selected in a cyclic fashion. For this purpose a 3-bit binary counter can be used to point to the selected source, which is connected to count input accesses to the device. Design a network for this device using a 3-bit counter, a 1-out-of-8 decoder, 3-state drivers, and whatever logic gates are needed.

9.6 Design a network for an interval timer to be used by the illustrative microprocessor. Specifically, the network is to include a binary down counter that provides an indication when a specified time interval has elapsed. This is done by loading the counter with a number from an output port. The counter will then down count with pulses from a precise source and set a status flag when it reaches zero. The status flag is to be available to the microprocessor as a certain bit of an input port. A program might make use of such a timer to determine when a certain event (e.g., an input operation) is to take place relative to a certain point in time (e.g., the time of the previous input operation). The design should include an 8-bit down counter, the output port connections to the counter, the status flag network, and the device-code detection network. Note that the status flag should be reset when the counter is loaded and set when the counter reaches zero.

9.7 Design an interval timer similar to that of Prob. 9.6 except that when the interval has elapsed an interrupt is requested rather than a status flag set. This will alleviate the need for the program to continually check the status flag. The network should present the address 48_{16} to the Data bus when an interrupt from the timer is acknowledged to be used as the starting address of an interrupt service routine.

9.8 Consider an application of the illustrative microprocessor involving the control of engine and vehicle dynamics of an automobile. Suppose that part of the microprocessor's task is to monitor four particular parameters and to take corrective action if any of the four parameters become critical. The four critical conditions specifically are

1. Engine temperature exceeds limit.
2. Certain exhaust emissions exceed limit.
3. Hydraulic brake pressure is low.
4. Vehicle speed is beyond legal limit.

Each of these conditions is to cause a program interrupt and a particular service routine to be executed that will take the appropriate corrective action.

Assign a priority to each of these conditions and design a network that will cause an interrupt request if any of the conditions become true. In the network, provide for an address (your choice) of a service routine that is particular to each condition to be sent over the Data bus in response to an interrupt acknowledgment from the microprocessor. Use a daisy-chain arrangement for determining priority. Assume that each condition is indicated by a logic-1 on a particular line. No external flags for disabling these interrupts should be provided. Finally, no input or output ports of any kind need to be provided.

9.9 In Sec. 9.3 the equations for a priority encoder that has eight input lines were derived. The encoder indicates the 3-bit binary number corresponding to the highest active (logic-1) input line. Extend this to a similar circuit having 16 input lines and 4 output lines. In other words, derive the equation for each of the four output lines so that the 4-bit binary number is generated that corresponds to the active input having the highest assigned number from 0 to 15.

9.10 Quite often a priority encoder such as described in Prob. 9.9 is implemented with a read-only memory unit rather than with logic gates. For this purpose, determine the truth table for such an encoder having four input lines and two output lines.

9.11 Design the memory system for an application of the illustrative microprocessor consisting of 1024 words of read-only memory beginning at location 0 followed by 512 words of read/write memory. The memory units to be used are of the form of the prototype in Fig. 9.8. They are of two types:

1. Read-only of size 512 words $\times$ 4 bits
2. Read/write of size 128 words $\times$ 8 bits

9.12 For each of the read/write memory units specified below determine the maximum clock rate for the illustrative microprocessor so that the indicated timing requirements are met. Refer to Figs. 9.13 and 9.14 for the timing of the microprocessor. Neglect the time delay associated with any gates involved in the interface. Assume that the only important parameters for the memory units are the read-access time T_{RA}, the address setup time for write T_{AS}, the data setup time for write T_{DS}, and the data hold time for write T_{DH}. These four parameters are illustrated by the timing diagrams of Figs. 9.11 and 9.12. Consider memory units having the following values for these parameters (in microseconds):

1. $T_{RA} = 1.2$; $T_{AS} = 1.0$; $T_{DS} = 1.0$; $T_{DH} = 0.05$
2. $T_{RA} = 0.9$; $T_{AS} = 1.5$; $T_{DS} = 2.0$; $T_{DH} = 0.8$
3. $T_{RA} = 0.5$; $T_{AS} = 1.2$; $T_{DS} = 2.0$; $T_{DH} = 0.1$
4. $T_{RA} = 0.8$; $T_{AS} = 1.4$; $T_{DS} = 1.6$; $T_{DH} = 0.2$

9.13 Design a simple "front panel" for a general-purpose microcomputer that uses the illustrative microprocessor. The front panel is to have switches and lights that allow a user to deposit a word into any memory location and to examine the content of any memory location. This is to be done using the direct memory access facility of the microprocessor. The front panel should have 16 switches for address, 8 switches for data, 8 lights for data, 1 switch to activate the DMA line, and 1 switch for deposit. The design should use the DMAA line from the microprocessor to enable the address and data switches.

To operate the front panel, the DMA switch is first activated. A memory location may then be examined by setting the address switches to the desired address and leaving the deposit switch deactivated. A word is written into a memory location by setting the address switches to the desired address, the data switches to the desired word, and then momentarily activating the deposit switch. Other functions such as start, examine and alter registers, etc., are not to be implemented.

9.14 A special digital-to-analog converter is needed to produce a voltage proportional to the time of day expressed digitally as hours, minutes, and seconds. Each of the three time units is represented by 2 binary-coded digits. Design a circuit for this special D/A converter using an operational amplifier and resistors of the appropriate value. Note that the representation of time is in a hybrid base. Some digits are base ten and others are base six.

9.15 Design a 2-digit 8421 binary-coded decimal analog-to-digital converter using an up-down counter.

9.16 Write a program for the illustrative microprocessor to perform analog-to-digital conversion using the circuit of Fig. 9.25. The program should use the successive approximation method. All eight channels shown in the figure are to be converted with the results stored in designated memory locations.

9.17 Design the receiver and transmitter for a serial channel that is bit synchronous but word asynchronous. Such a channel has a clock that is common to the receiver and transmitter to specify the bit times, but words might commence with any clock pulse. Words are to have a format that begins with a start bit (logic-0), followed by 8 data bits, followed by a stop bit (logic-1). Assuming that a formatted word is contained in a shift register at the transmitter, transmission begins when a certain line at the transmitter is activated. The receiver waits for a start bit from the data channel and then begins to shift the following data bits into a shift register. Counters at the receiver and the transmitter keep track of the number of bits and cause the shifting process in each case to stop when the appropriate number of bits have been encountered.

9.18 Microprocessor slices, as discussed in Sec. 9.9, can be cascaded to achieve any degree of precision for numbers upon which they operate. They can be combined in other ways, however, to perform various types of parallel processing. One approach is to use a number of microprocessor slices operating in unison to perform computations with vectors. In this case one or more microprocessor slices is assigned to each component of a vector so that a vector computation will take no longer than the time for one component.

Suppose that such a system is desired to operate with three-dimensional vectors having a component precision of 8 bits. Show how 4-bit microprocessor slices described by the model of Fig. 9.28 can be interconnected to form the computational part of the desired system.

9.19 Consider the phase-splitting circuit of Fig. 9.32. Plot a timing diagram showing the relationship among phase 1, phase 2, and the pulse source when the pulse source has each of the three duty cycles 25, 50, and 75 percent. Duty cycle refers to the percentage of time in which the signal from a pulse source is at logic-1.

SAMPLE APPLICATIONS

In order to gain a perspective of the way components interact within a microcomputer system, three specific applications will be considered. The applications have been kept relatively simple for the sake of illustration, but are believed nevertheless to typify practical microcomputer systems. They have been chosen to bring out various forms of input and output. Each application is based on the illustrative microprocessor and its treatment includes the configuration of components, the design of interfaces, and the necessary program.†

10.1 CALCULATING WEIGHT SCALE

The first sample application involves a scale that might be found at a candy counter, butcher shop, or other location where goods are sold by weight. Its function is to provide a digital display of the weight and the price for an amount of goods. Input information appears in two forms: (1) an analog quantity corresponding to the weight and (2) a digital quantity corresponding to the cost per pound. A pressure transducer is used to generate a voltage that corresponds to the weight of the goods being measured. This voltage is converted within the microprocessor into an 8421 binary-coded decimal representation of the weight. The weight is multiplied by a binary-coded decimal quantity corresponding to the cost per pound, which is brought into the microprocessor from thumbwheel switches. These two operations, analog-to-digital conversion and multiplication, constitute most of the overall task.

---

† The programs in this chapter are not necessarily the most efficient possible. They have been written to retain simplicity in reading them.

Assumptions need to be made concerning the range of values that each quantity may take on. It will be assumed that the weight ranges between 0.00 to 9.99 lb and that the cost per pound ranges between \$0.00 and \$9.99/lb. Each of these quantities will be represented by three BCD digits. The total price of a given quantity may therefore range between \$00.0000 and \$99.8001. However, since transactions do not usually involve fractions of a cent, the total price of a given quantity will be truncated to four BCD digits. In the microprocessor a separate 8-bit data word will be allocated to contain each BCD digit. This might be considered wasteful since each BCD digit consists of just 4 bits. However, it simplifies programming considerably, since each digit can then be treated separately. The digit in each case will occupy the lower 4 bits of a data word.

The operation of the scale proceeds generally as follows. The pressure transducer senses the weight placed on the scale and produces a voltage that is proportional to this weight. This voltage is amplified and conditioned by a signal amplifier. The weight analog signal is then converted into digital form as part of the input process. This is done by having the microprocessor partake in a successive approximation procedure for converting the weight. The procedure consists of successively trying values for each bit of each digit. Three 4-bit output registers are provided to receive trial values for the 3 weight digits. The combined contents of the output registers are converted to analog form and compared to the voltage corresponding to the actual weight. The single-bit result of the comparison, whether high or low, is the only information concerning weight that is inputted to the microprocessor. This result is used to adjust the trial weight. After all bits have been tried and adjusted, the microcomputer will have the BCD representation of the weight. Each of the 3 digits of the weight are then outputted to three additional registers for display.

The 3-digit weight is multiplied by a 3-digit multiplier, which corresponds to the cost per pound. This multiplier is brought into the microprocessor from three thumbwheel switches, a digit at a time, as the multiplication is being carried out. Only the 4 most-significant digits of the product are retained. These digits are outputted to four registers for display as the price of the goods. This whole operation is continually repeated.

Flowchart

The procedure of operation is specified in detail by the flowchart in Fig. 10.1. The procedure begins with the block labeled "Reset, Start," which indicates that the corresponding control signals of the microprocessor are activated. This is done whenever power is first supplied to the system, causing program execution to begin with location zero. Three loops are then encountered that determine the three weight digits by successive approximation. The 3 weight digits are each referred to by W with a subscript H, M, or L depending on whether the digit is high, middle, or low order. Thus, the weight W is expressed by $(W_H W_M W_L)$. Each loop starts with an initial value for all 3 trial weight digits. Each bit of a trial weight digit, beginning with the most-significant bit, is tested by setting it to 1 and

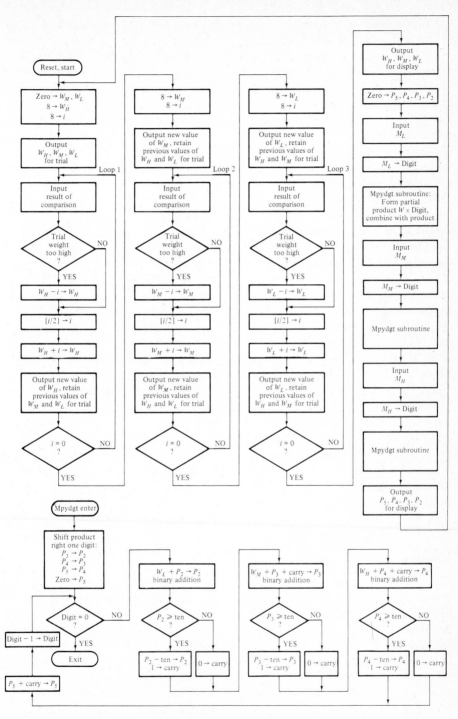

Figure 10.1 Flowchart for the calculating weight scale.

comparing the resulting analog trial weight with the actual weight. If the trial weight is determined to be too high, then the bit under test is reset to 0. It should be pointed out that in some cases with this method the trial value for a digit exceeds 9 and it is therefore a nonvalid decimal digit. This is allowed to happen for simplicity. If it is assumed that the D/A converter is capable of working with digits greater than 9, then the comparison result in such cases will always indicate that the trial value is too high. Consequently, the bit under test will be reset which will result in a valid decimal digit.

The test bit position is controlled by an index i. The index i starts with the value of 8, corresponding to the weight of the most-significant bit of a digit, and is divided by two each time through the loop. Only the integer part is retained, as indicated by the brackets [ ], so that after all 4 bits have been determined the index i will be 0. This condition causes the particular loop to terminate. When all 3 weight digits have been determined they are displayed.

The remaining portion of the flowchart corresponds to the multiplication of the weight by the cost per pound. Each digit of the BCD representation for the total price is referred to by P with a subscript that corresponds to the significance of the digit. Thus, the total price P is expressed by $(\$P_5 P_4 . P_3 P_2 P_1 P_0)$. The lower two digits of the total price are never displayed and are each discarded during the multiplication as soon as its influence on higher digits has been taken into account. Each of the three multiplier digits, i.e., the cost per pound, is referred to by M with a subscript H, M, or L. Thus, the cost per pound is expressed by $(M_H M_M M_L)$. The multiplication involves multiplying the 3-digit weight by each multiplier digit to determine a partial product. The partial product in each case is added, a digit at a time as it is generated, to the sum of previous partial products. The sum of partial products is retained in the digits P_5, P_4, P_3, and P_2, which are the same digits that refer to the total price.

A subroutine flowchart, referred to as Mpydgt (for multiply digit), is shown in Fig. 10.1, which performs multiplication by a single digit. The particular digit of the multiplier is referred to as simply *Digit*. The subroutine begins by shifting the 4 digits corresponding to the sum of previous partial sums to the right. During this right shift the previous least-significant digit is lost and the most-significant digit becomes 0. The purpose of this right shift is to bring the sum of previous partial products into proper alignment with the current partial product. The current partial product corresponds to the result of multiplying the weight by the value of Digit. This is actually done by adding the value of the weight to the sum of partial products the number of times indicated by Digit. The addition process is done in 8421 BCD and is done a digit position at a time. There are four digit positions that are involved.

The addition of the first 3 digits is accomplished by three similar segments of the flowchart. Each segment starts by adding in binary one weight digit to the corresponding product digit, taking into account any carry from the previous digit position. The result in each case is then adjusted, if necessary, to make it conform to a BCD digit. The adjustment involves determining whether the result exceeds 9 and if so, subtracting ten and setting the carry to 1. Addition in the fourth-digit position involves no weight digit and is simply accomplished by adding just the carry from the third bit position.

After this 4-digit addition is performed the value of Digit is decremented by 1. If the resulting value of Digit is 0, then the subroutine is exited; otherwise, the addition is repeated.

The mainline flowchart uses this subroutine to perform the overall multiplication as follows. First the 4 product digits are initialized to 0. Then, each of three similar segments of the mainline flowchart brings in a multiplier digit and uses it as the value of Digit in the Mpydgt subroutine. When all three segments have been processed, the product is contained in the digits P_5, P_4, P_3, P_2. The values of these digits are then displayed as the price of the goods. The entire procedure is then repeated.

Input/Output Interface

The necessary components for input and output and their interconnections are shown in Fig. 10.2. As can be seen, there are 4 input ports and 10 output ports. A 1-out-of-10 decoder is used as a port selector. The low-4 Address-bus bits are connected to the four basic input lines of the decoder. The decoder also has an enable input line that must be at logic-1 for any output line to be logic-1. This enable input line is driven by a network that ANDs the complement of the remaining 4 Address-bus bits that specify a device code. Consequently, the output lines of the decoder correspond to the first ten hexadecimal device codes, 00 to 09. These lines are labeled with s subscripted with the corresponding device code.

One input port provides the means to bring in the single-bit result obtained from comparing the trial weight with the actual weight. This port is assigned device code 00_{16} and consists of a 3-state driver that is used to couple the output line of a comparator to bit 0 of the Data bus. The enable line of the 3-state driver is determined by the AND of the s_0 port selector line and the microprocessor In control line. The other three input ports provide the means to input the 3 multiplier digits M_H, M_M, and M_L from thumbwheel switches. They are respectively assigned the hexadecimal device codes 01, 02, and 03. Each of these ports uses four 3-state drivers, which are controlled by the AND of the appropriate port selector line and the In control line.

Each thumbwheel switch has ten positions which are encoded into 4 bits corresponding to the 8421 BCD code. The encoding may be done within the switches if a sufficient number of poles is provided. Figure 10.3 shows one way of encoding the 10 positions using switches with three poles each.

Each of the 10 output ports uses a 4-bit latch to receive the information sent from the microprocessor over the four low-order lines of the Data bus. The load enable line of each latch is driven by the AND of the appropriate port selector line and the Out control line. Three output ports, which have hexadecimal device codes 00, 01, and 02, receive the digits of the trial weight. These digits are presented to a BCD digital-to-analog converter, which produces a voltage proportional to the trial weight.

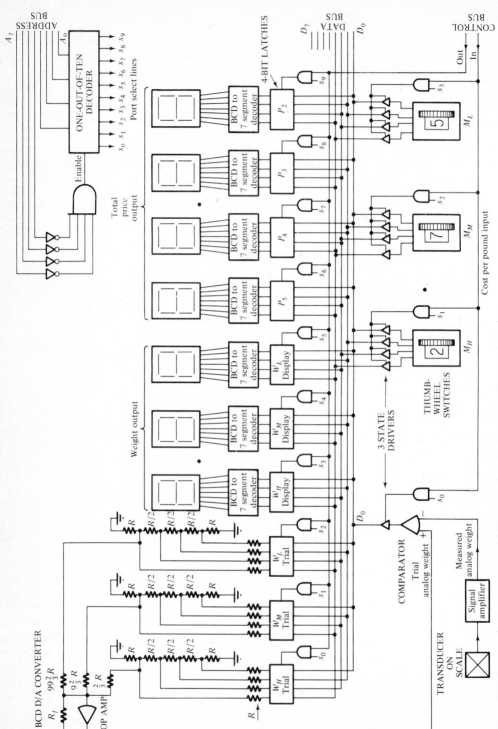

Figure 10.2 Input and output component interconnections for the calculating weight scale.

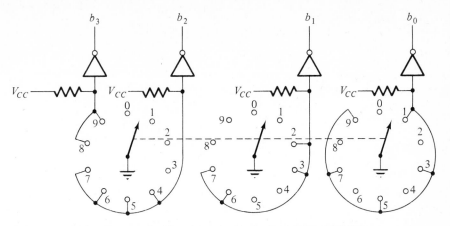

Figure 10.3 Wiring diagram of a 10-position thumbwheel switch for 8421 BCD.

The BCD digital-to-analog converter consists of three 4-bit resistor ladders, one for each digit, and a three-input operational-amplifier summer. The resistor ladders produce a voltage proportional to the value of each digit, and the summer multiplies each of these voltages by the appropriate power of ten and sums the results. The input resistors to the summer determine the values of the multiplying factors. These resistor values have been adjusted to compensate for the effective output resistance from each resistor ladder, which is $R/3$. The effective input resistances to the summer for the high-, middle-, and low-order digits are seen to be R, $10R$, $100R$, respectively, which have the proper relationship.

Three other output ports, having device codes 03, 04, and 05, receive the weight digits to be displayed. Each of these digits is presented to a special decoder that generates the proper values for the segments of a seven-segment numerical display. The remaining four output ports, having device codes 06, 07, 08, and 09, receive and display the total price digits.

Note that the lines connecting the entire input/output network to the microprocessor consist of just the lower eight Address bus lines, the lower four Data bus lines, and the In and Out control lines.

Program

A program to perform the procedure outlined by the flowchart of Fig. 10.1 is shown in Table 10.1. It follows the flowchart quite closely and is explained by the remarks column of the table.

Notice that the instructions of the program occupy $BA_{16} = 186_{10}$ memory locations. Thus a 256_{10}-byte read-only memory unit will serve to adequately contain the entire program. Also note that the 15 register scratchpad in the microprocessor is sufficient to contain all variable data that is used by the program. Consequently, no read/write memory is needed in the main memory system. The 256-byte ROM is therefore the only additional component needed, aside from the microprocessor and the input/output network.

Table 10.1 Program for the calculating weight scale

Scratchpad register allocation:

R_1: bit position index i R_6: P_5 ⎫
R_2: multiplier digit R_7: P_4 ⎪ Total R_A: constant ten
R_3: W_H ⎫ R_8: P_3 ⎬ price R_B: constant 01_{16}
R_4: W_M ⎬ Weight R_9: P_2 ⎭ R_C: constant $0F_{16}$
R_5: W_L ⎭

Memory location	Machine language instruction	Symbolic form of instruction	Remarks
0000	6A	LRI A	Load constants into allocated registers
0001	0A	0A	
0002	6B	LRI B	
0003	01	01	
0004	6C	LRI C	
0005	0F	0F	
0006	E0	XOR 0	Clear accumulator by doing EXCLUSIVE OR with itself
0007	FE	OUT	Output zero as trial weight digits W_M and W_L
0008	01	01	
0009	FE	OUT	
000A	02	02	
000B	61	LRI 1	Set index i equal to 8
000C	08	08	
000D	23	MOV 1 to 3	Load the value of i as trial weight digit W_H.
000E	13	MOV 0 from 3	both internal and external to the
000F	FE	OUT	microprocessor
0010	00	00	
0011	FD	INP	Begin loop 1: Input and mask result of
0012	00	00	analog comparison
0013	CB	AND B	
0014	79	JAZ	Test comparison result. If trial not too high,
0015	00	00	skip resetting bit
0016	1A	1A	
0017	13	MOV 0 from 3	Reset bit of W_H corresponding to index i,
0018	A1	SUB 1	since trial was too high
0019	03	MOV 0 to 3	
001A	11	MOV 0 from 1	Change i to correspond to next lower bit
001B	F4	RSC	position. Set carry flip-flop if i becomes 0
001C	F2	RTR	
001D	01	MOV 0 to 1	
001E	D3	OR 3	Set bit of W_H corresponding to i
001F	03	MOV 0 to 3	
0020	FE	OUT	Output new W_H for trial
0021	00	00	
0022	7C	JCZ	Test if i is 0. If not, repeat loop 1 to adjust
0023	00	00	next bit of W_H; otherwise, go on to W_M
0024	11	11	
0025	61	LRI 1	Set i to 8
0026	08	08	

Table 10.1 (*Continued*)

Memory location	Machine language instruction	Symbolic form of instruction	Remarks
0027	24	MOV 1 to 4	Load 8 as W_M, both internally and externally
0028	14	MOV 0 from 4	
0029	FE	OUT	
002A	01	01	
002B	FD	INP	Begin loop 2: Input and mask result of
002C	00	00	analog comparison
002D	CB	AND B	
002E	79	JAZ	Test comparison result. If trial not too
002F	00	00	high, skip resetting bit
0030	34	34	
0031	14	MOV 0 from 4	Reset bit of W_M corresponding to index i,
0032	A1	SUB 1	since trial was too high
0033	04	MOV 0 to 4	
0034	11	MOV 0 from 1	Change i to correspond to next lower bit
0035	F4	RSC	position. Set carry flip-flop if i becomes 0
0036	F2	RTR	
0037	01	MOV 0 to 1	
0038	D4	OR 4	Set bit of W_M corresponding to i
0039	04	MOV 0 to 4	
003A	FE	OUT	Output new W_M for trial
003B	01	01	
003C	7C	JCZ	Test if i is 0. If not, repeat loop 2 to adjust
003D	00	00	next bit of W_M; otherwise, go on to W_L
003E	2B	2B	
003F	61	LRI 1	Set i to 8
0040	08	08	
0041	25	MOV 1 to 5	Load 8 as W_L, both internally and externally
0042	15	MOV 0 from 5	
0043	FE	OUT	
0044	02	02	
0045	FD	INP	Begin loop 3: Input and mask result of
0046	00	00	analog comparison
0047	CB	AND B	
0048	79	JAZ	Test comparison result. If trial not too
0049	00	00	high, skip resetting bit
004A	4E	4E	
004B	15	MOV 0 from 5	Reset bit of W_L corresponding to index i,
004C	A1	SUB 1	since trial was too high
004D	05	MOV 0 to 5	
004E	11	MOV 0 from 1	Change i to correspond to next lower bit
004F	F4	RSC	position. Set carry flip-flop if i becomes 0
0050	F2	RTR	
0051	01	MOV 0 to 1	
0052	D5	OR 5	Set bit of W_L corresponding to i
0053	05	MOV 0 to 5	
0054	FE	OUT	Output new W_L for trial
0055	02	02	

(*continued overleaf*)

Table 10.1 (*Continued*)

Memory location	Machine language instruction	Symbolic form of instruction	Remarks
0056	7C	JCZ	Test if i is 0. If not, repeat loop 3 to adjust next
0057	00	00	bit of W_L; otherwise, go on to output weight
0058	45	45	
0059	13	MOV 0 from 3	Output W_H for display
005A	FE	OUT	
005B	03	03	
005C	14	MOV 0 from 4	Output W_M for display
005D	FE	OUT	
005E	04	04	
005F	15	MOV 0 from 5	Output W_L for display
0060	FE	OUT	
0061	05	05	
0062	E0	XOR 0	Begin multiplication: Initialize the
0063	06	MOV 0 to 6	product digits to 0
0064	07	MOV 0 to 7	
0065	08	MOV 0 to 8	
0066	09	MOV 0 to 9	
0067	FD	INP	Input and mask M_L to use as multiplier digit
0068	03	03	for subroutine
0069	CC	AND C	
006A	02	MOV 0 to 2	
006B	7F	JMS	Jump to Mpydgt subroutine, which generates
006C	00	00	the first partial product
006D	8B	8B	
006E	FD	INP	Input and mask M_M to use as multiplier
006F	02	02	digit for subroutine
0070	CC	AND C	
0071	02	MOV 0 to 2	
0072	7F	JMS	Jump to Mpydgt subroutine, which adds the
0073	00	00	second partial product to the first
0074	8B	8B	
0075	FD	INP	Input and mask M_H to use as multiplier
0076	01	01	digit for subroutine
0077	CC	AND C	
0078	02	MOV 0 to 2	
0079	7F	JMS	Jump to Mpydgt subroutine, which adds the
007A	00	00	third partial product to the sum of the
007B	8B	8B	other two, completing multiplication
007C	16	MOV 0 from 6	Output P_5 for display
007D	FE	OUT	
007E	06	06	
007F	17	MOV 0 from 7	Output P_4 for display
0080	FE	OUT	
0081	07	07	
0082	18	MOV 0 from 8	Output P_3 for display
0083	FE	OUT	
0084	08	08	

Table 10.1 (*Continued*)

Memory location	Machine language instruction	Symbolic form of instruction	Remarks
0085	19	MOV 0 from 9	Output P_2 for display
0086	FE	OUT	
0087	09	09	
0088	7B	JMP	Jump to beginning of program to repeat
0089	00	00	
008A	06	06	
008B	18	MOV 0 from 8	Beginning of Mpydgt subroutine: Shift
008C	09	MOV 0 to 9	product digits P_5, P_4, P_3, P_2 right one
008D	17	MOV 0 from 7	digit position. The previous value of
008E	08	MOV 0 to 8	P_2 is lost and P_5 becomes 0
008F	16	MOV 0 from 6	
0090	07	MOV 0 to 7	
0091	66	LRI 6	
0092	00	00	
0093	12	MOV 0 from 2	Test multiplier digit for 0. If not 0, go on
0094	79	JAZ	to add weight to the product; otherwise,
0095	00	00	exit subroutine
0096	B9	B9	
0097	19	MOV 0 from 9	Add W_L to P_2 in binary
0098	85	ADD 5	
0099	09	MOV 0 to 9	
009A	AA	SUB A	Test if result exceeds 9. If so, reduce by
009B	78	JCN	ten and set the carry flip-flop
009C	00	00	
009D	9F	9F	
009E	09	MOV 0 to 9	
009F	F3	CMC	
00A0	18	MOV 0 from 8	Add W_M to P_3 with carry
00A1	94	ADC 4	
00A2	08	MOV 0 to 8	
00A3	AA	SUB A	Test if result exceeds 9. If so, reduce by
00A4	78	JCN	ten and set the carry flip-flop
00A5	00	00	
00A6	A8	A8	
00A7	08	MOV 0 to 8	
00A8	F3	CMC	
00A9	17	MOV 0 from 7	Add W_H to P_4 with carry
00AA	93	ADC 3	
00AB	07	MOV 0 to 7	
00AC	AA	SUB A	Test if result exceeds 9. If so, reduce by
00AD	78	JCN	ten and set the carry flip-flop
00AE	00	00	
00AF	B1	B1	
00B0	07	MOV 0 to 7	
00B1	F3	CMC	
00B2	E0	XOR 0	Add carry to P_5. Result can never exceed 9
00B3	96	ADC 6	

(*continued overleaf*)

Table 10.1 (*Continued*)

Memory location	Machine language instruction	Symbolic form of instruction	Remarks
00B4	06	MOV 0 to 6	
00B5	F6	DHL	Decrement the multiplier digit
00B6	7B	JMP	Jump back to test multiplier digit for 0
00B7	00	00	and repeat addition process if not 0
00B8	93	93	
00B9	F8	RET	Exit subroutine

It is interesting to determine just how fast the microcomputer can update the total price of the weighed item. When the program is examined it is ascertained that the number of encountered machine cycles for the worst case is roughly 1700_{10}. Each machine cycle consists of three clock pulses. If the clock period is assumed to be 1 μs, then the total processing time for each price update is equal to (in decimal) 3×1700 μs $= 5100$ μs $= 5.1$ ms. This delay should not be discernible by humans.

10.2 TRAFFIC LIGHT CONTROLLER

Traffic lights are something that we all encounter frequently. At times they can be a source of considerable frustration. They are generally timed with usual traffic patterns in mind, which may change with the time of day. This is normally quite satisfactory. However, traffic patterns that deviate from the usual can lead to poor traffic flow when using the preplanned timing of a traffic light. In particular, during rush hour the timing of a traffic light for each direction is set to accommodate the expected flow of traffic. However, if the actual flow in one direction is greater than expected, even though the increase might be slight, an accumulative effect could occur that results in a back up of traffic.

Microcomputers might be applied to the control of traffic lights to help alleviate some of the difficulties. If a microcomputer is to be effective in such an application, some means of monitoring traffic conditions is necessary. For this purpose, sensors can be employed that detect the presence of vehicles at certain points and times.

Figure 10.4 illustrates an intersection with a traffic light that is to be controlled by a microcomputer. The intersection is formed by two 4-lane roads. Left turns are allowed from the left lane of each direction and for this purpose left-turn arrows are provided. Overhead sensors are located in each lane just before the intersection. The sensors are magnetic and indicate the presence of a vehicle underneath them (assuming the vehicle has a sufficient amount of iron). Corresponding lights facing in opposing directions operate in unison as a pair.

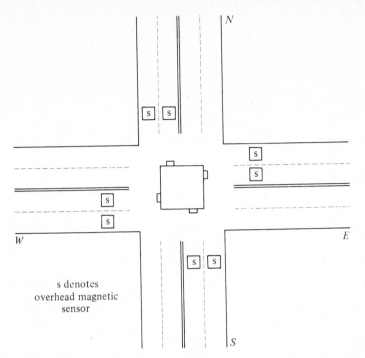

Figure 10.4 Configuration of the intersection with the traffic light to be controlled.

For each direction there are four lights consisting of green, amber, red, and left-turn arrow.

The timing pattern that will be used for the operation of the lights is shown in Fig. 10.5. A circular ring is shown for each of the eight pairs of lights. The on condition of a pair of lights is indicated by black appearing in the corresponding ring. The timing pattern consists of a cycle of six phases. Each phase corresponds to a combination of lights that are on for an amount of time. The six phases are specifically: green, amber, red with left arrow for the horizontal (east-west) road, while the vertical (north-south) road is held at red; followed by green, amber, red with left arrow for the vertical road, while the horizontal road is held at red. The phases other than amber are variable in duration and are to depend in some way upon traffic conditions.

A performance objective must be chosen to serve as a basis for specifying the phase-duration times. The objective that will be used is the avoidance of situations in which traffic cumulatively backs up along some direction because of insufficient green time. In order to meet this objective, the controller will use the following strategy. At the end of each phase of the light cycle having a variable duration time, the controller is to use the appropriate sensors to determine whether cars are about to enter the intersection. At each such time, if a vehicle is sensed from a direction in which motion was allowed by the particular phase, then it is assumed that vehicles are still waiting and that insufficient time had been allocated. On the

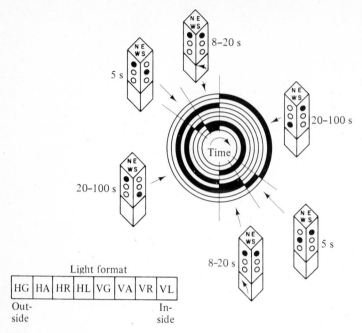

Figure 10.5 Light operation cycle for the traffic-light controller.

other hand, if no vehicle is sensed, then it is assumed that too much time had been allocated. The duration time of the phase is adjusted for the future accordingly, up or down.

This strategy might be considered questionable since it involves a decision based on the presence or absence of a single vehicle. There are different reasons why a vehicle might be present at the end of a phase. The vehicle could be at the end or the middle of a string of vehicles or it could be alone or perhaps stalled. It would not be desirable to increase the duration time if the vehicle was the only one waiting to traverse the intersection. However, the strategy does generally serve its purpose, which is to avoid traffic backing up in a cumulative manner.

Flowchart

Figure 10.6 is a flowchart that specifies the details of the controller operation using the strategy just mentioned. The operation during each of the six phases includes the two steps (1) turning on the appropriate lights for the phase and (2) waiting the specified length of time. The phases having variable duration times have additional steps that input and select the appropriate sensor values and then increase or decrease the phase-duration time. In the flowchart, the duration times are referred to by T with two subscripts signifying the phase. The first subscript is either H or V, for the horizontal or vertical road; and the second subscript is either G or L, for green light or left arrow. Values for the four duration times are

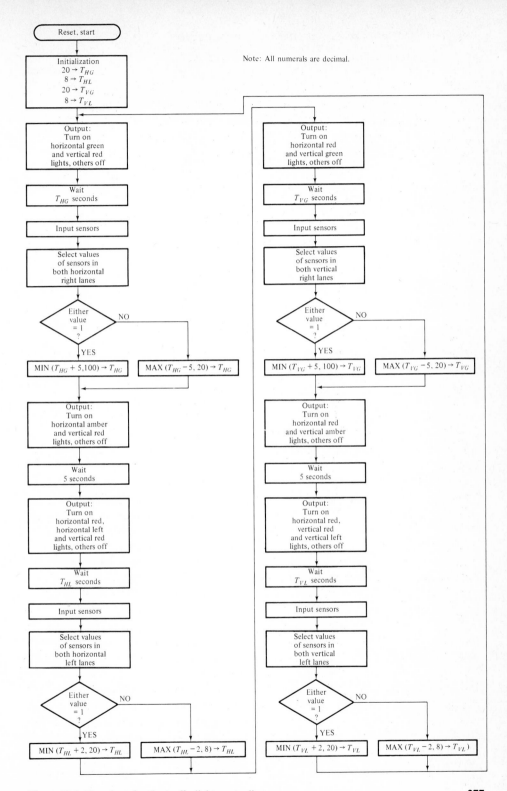

Figure 10.6 Flowchart for the traffic-light controller.

377

initialized at the beginning of the procedure to their minimum allowed values. These minimum values are 20 s and 8 s for the green light and left arrow phases, respectively. Also, the amount of adjustment, up or down, in the duration times will be 5 s and 2 s for the green light and left arrow phases, respectively. The duration times also have maximum values, which are 100 s for the green light and 20 s for the left arrow. The flowchart indicates that an adjustment will never take a duration time beyond the minimum or maximum allowed values. This is done by setting the new duration time to the smaller of either the increased time or the maximum allowed value in the case of an upward adjustment and to the larger of either the decreased time or the minimum allowed value in the case of a downward adjustment.

Input/Output Interface

Note that there are eight sensors and eight pairs of lights. These can be accommodated with just one 8-bit input port for the sensors and just one 8-bit output port for the lights. The input/output section of the traffic light controller is therefore rather simple. Figure 10.7 shows the components and their connections that comprise the input/output section. The sensor signals are amplified and then coupled to the Data bus with eight 3-state drivers, which form one input port. An 8-bit latch is connected to the Data bus to receive the on-off signals for each light pair. The outputs of the latch control the lights using light-driver circuits. A selection network comprising the AND of the complemented bits of the lower half of the Address bus is used to select both the input and the output port. Each port, therefore, has device code 00_{16}. The two ports are selected further by the appropriate Control bus signal, In or Out.

The remaining portion of the input/output section involves the interrupt facility of the microprocessor. The interrupt facility is used to implement a timer that provides the program with an indication of the remaining time for each phase. For this purpose, a 1-s pulse source is used to set a D flip-flop (by pulsing its clock line while $D = 1$) that is connected to the interrupt request line Intr. Each pulse causes a program interrupt to occur, which is similar to a jump to subroutine. A service routine is provided that decrements a counter each time it is invoked by an interrupt. This counter is initialized with the phase-duration time at the beginning of each phase. In this way, the counter keeps track of the remaining time for a phase in seconds independently from the program execution time.

The illustrative microprocessor responds to an interrupt request with a pulse on the interrupt-acknowledge line Inta of the Control bus. At this time, an 8-bit address is provided externally that is used to specify the location to which the jump for the interrupt is made. In Fig. 10.7, eight 3-state drivers are used to couple a constant to the Data bus. The 3-state drivers are controlled by Inta, so that the constant is placed on the Data bus as the address for the interrupt jump when Inta is activated. The Inta pulse is also used to clear the flip-flop connected to the interrupt request line. Note that the pulse on Inta is timed in a manner similar to In, as was explained in Sec. 9.3.

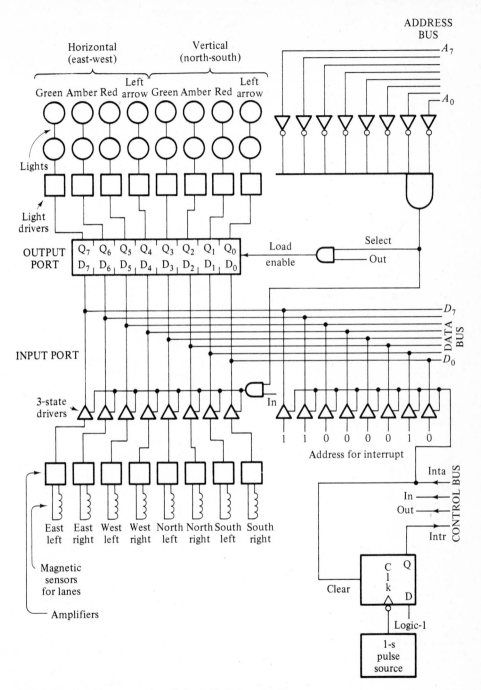

Figure 10.7 Input/output section of the traffic-light controller.

Program

The scheme shown in the flowchart is carried out by the program shown in Table 10.2. The main program begins at location 0000_{16} and the interrupt-service routine begins at location $00C2_{16}$. Notice that the interrupt-service routine makes use of scratchpad register 2, which is the lower half of the pair HL. It requires only three instructions altogether.

The entire program requires only $C5_{16} = 197_{10}$ bytes, which fits within a 256×8 bit ROM unit. Also, since no variable data is stored in the main memory, no read/write memory units are needed.

Table 10.2 Program for the traffic light controller

Sensor input format:

L	R	L	R	L	R	L	R
E		W		N		S	

Light output format:

G	A	R	L	G	A	R	L
Horiz.				Vert.			

Scratchpad register allocation:

R_2: interval timer (seconds)
R_3: horizontal green time T_{HG}
R_4: horizontal left-arrow time T_{HL}
R_5: vertical green time T_{VG}

R_6: vertical left-arrow time T_{VL}
R_7: constant 5
R_8: constant 2

Memory location	Machine language instruction	Symbolic form of instruction	Remarks
0000	FB	EIT	Enable interrupts
0001	67	LRI 7	Load constants 5 and 2 into allocated registers
0002	05	05	
0003	68	LRI 8	
0004	02	02	
0005	63	LRI 3	Initialize duration times to minimums
0006	14	14	
0007	64	LRI 4	
0008	08	08	
0009	65	LRI 5	
000A	14	14	
000B	66	LRI 6	
000C	08	08	
000D	60	LRI 0	Turn on horizontal green and vertical red lights
000E	82	82	
000F	FE	OUT	
0010	00	00	
0011	53	MOV 2 from 3	Initialize timer with T_{HG}
0012	12	MOV 0 from 2	Transfer timer content to accumulator
0013	7D	JAN	If remaining time is not 0, go back and continue
0014	00	00	to wait
0015	12	12	

Table 10.2 (*Continued*)

Memory location	Machine language instruction	Symbolic form of instruction	Remarks
0016	FD	INP	Input sensors
0017	00	00	
0018	61	LRI 1	Select horizontal right lane sensors by masking
0019	50	50	
001A	C1	AND 1	
001B	7D	JAN	Test for either selected sensor equal to 1. If so,
001C	00	00	jump to increase T_{HG}; otherwise, decrease T_{HG}
001D	2B	2B	
001E	13	MOV 0 from 3	Decrease T_{HG} by 5 s
001F	A7	SUB 7	
0020	03	MOV 0 to 3	
0021	61	LRI 1	Test new T_{HG}. If less than 20_{10}, replace with 20_{10}
0022	14	14	
0023	A1	SUB 1	
0024	7A	JAP	
0025	00	00	
0026	35	35	
0027	23	MOV 1 to 3	
0028	7B	JMP	Skip over increasing T_{HG}
0029	00	00	
002A	35	35	
002B	13	MOV 0 from 3	Increase T_{HG} by 5 s
002C	87	ADD 7	
002D	03	MOV 0 to 3	
002E	61	LRI 1	Test new T_{HG}. If greater than 100_{10}, replace
002F	64	64	with 100_{10}
0030	A1	SUB 1	
0031	7E	JAM	
0032	00	00	
0033	35	35	
0034	23	MOV 1 to 3	
0035	60	LRI 0	Turn on horizontal amber and vertical red lights
0036	42	42	
0037	FE	OUT	
0038	00	00	
0039	57	MOV 2 from 7	Wait 5 s
003A	12	MOV 0 from 2	
003B	7D	JAN	
003C	00	00	
003D	3A	3A	
003E	60	LRI 0	Turn on horizontal red, horizontal left-arrow,
003F	32	32	and vertical red lights
0040	FE	OUT	
0041	00	00	
0042	54	MOV 2 from 4	Wait T_{HL} s
0043	12	MOV 0 from 2	
0044	7D	JAN	
0045	00	00	
0046	43	43	

(*continued overleaf*)

Table 10.2 (*Continued*)

Memory location	Machine language instruction	Symbolic form of instruction	Remarks
0047	FD	INP	Input sensors
0048	00	00	
0049	61	LRI 1	Select horizontal left lane sensors by masking
004A	A0	A0	
004B	C1	AND 1	
004C	7D	JAN	Test for either selected sensor equal to 1. If so,
004D	00	00	jump to increase T_{HL}; otherwise, decrease T_{HL}
004E	5C	5C	
004F	14	MOV 0 from 4	Decrease T_{HL} by 2 s
0050	A8	SUB 8	
0051	04	MOV 0 to 4	
0052	61	LRI 1	Test new T_{HL}. If less than 8, replace with 8
0053	08	08	
0054	A1	SUB 1	
0055	7A	JAP	
0056	00	00	
0057	66	66	
0058	24	MOV 1 to 4	
0059	7B	JMP	Skip over increasing T_{HL}
005A	00	00	
005B	66	66	
005C	14	MOV 0 from 4	Increase T_{HL} by 2 s
005D	88	ADD 8	
005E	04	MOV 0 to 4	
005F	61	LRI 1	Test new T_{HL}. If greater than 20_{10},
0060	14	14	replace with 20_{10}
0061	A1	SUB 1	
0062	7E	JAM	
0063	00	00	
0064	66	66	
0065	24	MOV 1 to 4	
0066	60	LRI 0	Turn on horizontal red and vertical green lights
0067	28	28	
0068	FE	OUT	
0069	00	00	
006A	55	MOV 2 from 5	Wait T_{VG} s
006B	12	MOV 0 from 2	
006C	7D	JAN	
006D	00	00	
006E	6B	6B	
006F	FD	INP	Input sensors
0070	00	00	
0071	61	LRI 1	Select vertical right lane sensors by masking
0072	05	05	
0073	C1	AND 1	

Table 10.2 (*Continued*)

Memory location	Machine language instruction	Symbolic form of instruction	Remarks
0074	7D	JAN	Test for either selected sensor equal to 1. If so,
0075	00	00	jump to increase T_{VG}; otherwise, decrease T_{VG}
0076	84	84	
0077	15	MOV 0 from 5	Decrease T_{VG} by 5 s
0078	A7	SUB 7	
0079	05	MOV 0 to 5	
007A	61	LRI 1	Test new T_{VG}. If less than 20_{10}, replace with 20_{10}
007B	14	14	
007C	A1	SUB 1	
007D	7A	JAP	
007E	00	00	
007F	8E	8E	
0080	25	MOV 1 to 5	
0081	7B	JMP	Skip over increasing T_{VG}
0082	00	00	
0083	8E	8E	
0084	15	MOV 0 from 5	Increase T_{VG} by 5 s
0085	87	ADD 7	
0086	05	MOV 0 to 5	
0087	61	LRI 1	Test new T_{VG}. If greater than 100_{10}, replace
0088	64	64	with 100_{10}
0089	A1	SUB 1	
008A	7E	JAM	
008B	00	00	
008C	8E	8E	
008D	25	MOV 1 to 5	
008E	60	LRI 0	Turn on horizontal red and vertical amber lights
008F	24	24	
0090	FE	OUT	
0091	00	00	
0092	57	MOV 2 from 7	Wait 5 s
0093	12	MOV 0 from 2	
0094	7D	JAN	
0095	00	00	
0096	93	93	
0097	60	LRI 0	Turn on horizontal red, vertical red, and
0098	23	23	vertical left-arrow lights
0099	FE	OUT	
009A	00	00	
009B	56	MOV 2 from 6	Wait T_{VL} s
009C	12	MOV 0 from 2	
009D	7D	JAN	
009E	00	00	
009F	9C	9C	
00A0	FD	INP	Input sensors
00A1	00	00	

(*continued overleaf*)

Table 10.2 (*Continued*)

Memory location	Machine language instruction	Symbolic form of instruction	Remarks
00A2	61	LRI 1	Select vertical left lane sensors by masking
00A3	0A	0A	
00A4	C1	AND 1	
00A5	7D	JAN	Test for either selected sensor equal to 1. If so,
00A6	00	00	jump to increase T_{VL}; otherwise, decrease T_{VL}
00A7	B5	B5	
00A8	16	MOV 0 from 6	Decrease T_{VL} by 2 s
00A9	A8	SUB 8	
00AA	06	MOV 0 to 6	
00AB	61	LRI 1	Test new T_{VL}. If less than 8, replace with 8
00AC	08	08	
00AD	A1	SUB 1	
00AE	7A	JAP	
00AF	00	00	
00B0	0D	0D	
00B1	26	MOV 1 to 6	
00B2	7B	JMP	Go back to beginning of entire cycle
00B3	00	00	
00B4	0D	0D	
00B5	16	MOV 0 from 6	Increase T_{VL} by 2 s
00B6	88	ADD 8	
00B7	06	MOV 0 to 6	
00B8	61	LRI 1	Test new T_{VL}. If greater than 20_{10},
00B9	14	14	replace with 20_{10}
00BA	A1	SUB 1	
00BB	7E	JAM	
00BC	00	00	
00BD	0D	0D	
00BE	26	MOV 1 to 6	
00BF	7B	JMP	Go back to beginning of entire cycle
00C0	00	00	
00C1	0D	0D	
00C2	F6	DHL	Interrupt routine: Decrease remaining
00C3	FB	EIT	time by 1 s
00C4	F8	RET	

10.3 SIMPLE GENERAL-PURPOSE COMPUTING SYSTEM

One important application of computers in general is as a facility for executing many different programs that are written for unrelated processing tasks. The diversity of such facilities justifies the cost of large general-purpose computers. However, microprocessors, even though they are relatively inexpensive, are sufficiently powerful to be used in a general-purpose computing facility.

Let us consider a rather simple system that consists of the illustrative microprocessor, a keyboard as an input device, a cathode-ray-tube (CRT) display as an output device, and up to 64K bytes of memory. A simple operating system will be included that resides in read-only memory. The operating system is to interpret and carry out commands issued from the keyboard. Such commands could include alter or display the content of a register or a memory location, run a program stored in memory, list a program or data string on the CRT display, and so forth. Perhaps an implementation of a higher-level language, such as a BASIC interpreter or a FORTRAN compiler, would be included in read-only memory, which could be invoked by a command of the operating system.

The design of the system will concern the manner in which the microprocessor interacts with the keyboard and the CRT display in order to input and output information. For the sake of illustration, the types of interface for the keyboard and the CRT display have been chosen to be quite different from each other. The keyboard will utilize a standard bit-serial interface that will be under program control; whereas, the CRT display will utilize a bit-parallel interface that will have direct access to memory.

Keyboard

The keyboard is assumed to be ASCII-encoded, having a key for each character in the ASCII code. The character codes consist of 8 bits that are sent over a single line to the microprocessor in an asynchronous serial fashion. The serial format for transmission is shown in Fig. 10.8. As discussed in Sec. 9.8, a universal asynchronous receiver/transmitter (UART) could be used at the input port of the microprocessor to accept the 8-bit character. However, for illustrative purposes let us assume that the microprocessor itself is to perform this function.

As shown in part of Fig. 10.9, a line receiver is provided at the microprocessor that accepts the signal from the keyboard and translates it to the proper voltage levels for the microprocessor. The line receiver is coupled to the microprocessor with a 3-state driver as a single-bit input port, having the device code 00_{16}. The microprocessor then has the responsibility of converting the serial format for each character into an 8-bit data word. This conversion is done by a subroutine that is called by the operating system each time a character is expected from the keyboard.

The flowchart of Fig. 10.10 shows the process for accepting the serial transmission of a character and converting it into parallel form. It is first necessary to wait for the leading edge of a start bit as indicated by the first 1 to 0 transition of

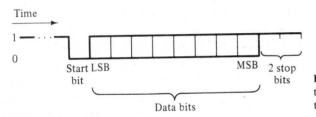

Figure 10.8 Format for the serial transmission of a character from the keyboard.

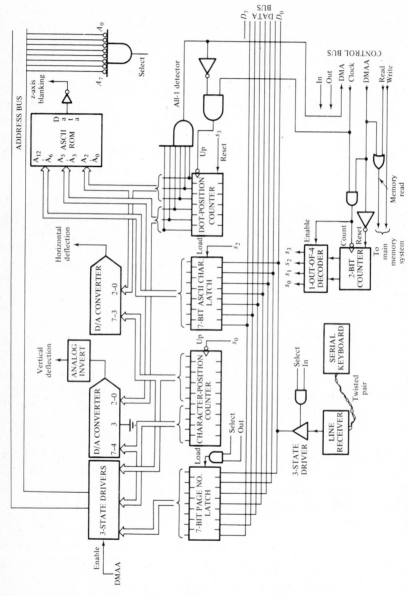

Figure 10.9 Input/output section for a general-purpose computing system.

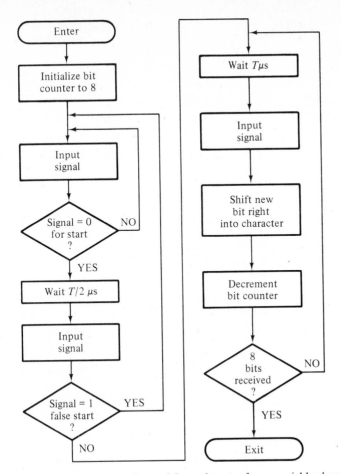

Figure 10.10 Flowchart for receiving a character from a serial keyboard.

the signal from the keyboard. The start bit corresponds to a 0 level lasting for an amount of time equal to T μs. After $T/2$ μs from the beginning of the start pulse, the signal is examined to verify that it is still at 0 corresponding to an actual start bit. This is important, since it is possible that the initial 1 to 0 transition was caused by a random noise spike; whereas, it is relatively improbable that a second random noise spike would occur at a specific time, such as at $T/2$ μs later. If the signal is 1 at this midpoint then a false start is assumed and the process starts over. Otherwise, the signal is sampled 8 times, each T μs after the midpoint of the start bit. Each of these sample times is assumed to correspond to the midpoint of a character bit. The logic value of the signal at every sample time is shifted right into a data word. After eight shifts, the data word will contain the eight bits of the transmitted character in their proper order.

A subroutine for the process described by the flowchart is given in Table 10.3 beginning in memory location 1000_{16}. The subroutine follows the flowchart fairly

Table 10.3 Subroutine for receiving a character from a serial keyboard

Scratchpad register allocation:

R_2: bit counter R_4: constant 1
R_3: time-delay counter R_5: received character

Memory location	Machine language instruction	Symbolic form of instruction	Remarks
1000	64	LRI 4	Load constant 1 into register 4
1001	01	01	
1002	62	LRI 2	Initialize bit counter to 8
1003	08	08	
1004	FD	INP	Input and isolate keyboard signal to test for
1005	00	00	start bit
1006	C4	AND 4	
1007	7D	JAN	Test signal. If 0, start bit is detected;
1008	10	10	otherwise, go back and continue search
1009	04	04	
100A	63	LRI 3	Wait 4524 μs, about $\frac{1}{2}$ bit time
100B	FB	FB	
100C	13	MOV 0 from 3	
100D	A4	SUB 4	
100E	03	MOV 0 to 3	
100F	7D	JAN	
1010	10	10	
1011	0C	0C	
1012	FD	INP	Input and isolate keyboard signal to test for
1013	00	00	false start
1014	C4	AND 4	
1015	7D	JAN	Test signal. If not 0, assume false start and go
1016	10	10	back to beginning
1017	04	04	
1018	63	LRI 3	Wait 9042 μs, about 1 bit time
1019	FB	FB	
101A	F7	NOP	
101B	F7	NOP	
101C	F7	NOP	
101D	F7	NOP	
101E	F7	NOP	
101F	F7	NOP	
1020	13	MOV 0 from 3	
1021	A4	SUB 4	
1022	03	MOV 0 to 3	
1023	7D	JAN	
1024	10	10	
1025	1A	1A	
1026	FD	INP	Input and isolate keyboard signal to obtain
1027	00	00	next bit
1028	C4	AND 4	
1029	F2	RTR	Shift bit into the carry flip-flop
102A	15	MOV 0 from 5	Transfer previous bits to accumulator
102B	F2	RTR	Shift new bit into character

Table 10.3 (*Continued*)

Memory location	Machine language instruction	Symbolic form of instruction	Remarks
102C	05	MOV 0 to 5	Transfer character back to register 5
102D	F6	DHL	Decrement bit counter
102E	12	MOV 0 from 2	Test bit counter. If zero, complete character has
102F	7D	JAN	been received; otherwise, go back for
1030	10	10	another bit
1031	18	18	
1032	15	MOV 0 from 5	Transfer complete character to accumulator
1033	F8	RET	Exit subroutine

close and should be easily understood from the included remarks. Note that the waiting times shown in the flowchart are implemented by loops in the program. Each loop involves decrementing a counter until it reaches zero. The counter in each case is initialized by a number chosen for an appropriate amount of delay, based on an assumed microprocessor clock period of 1 μs.

The bit time T used by the subroutine is determined according to a character rate of 10 characters per second. Since a total of 11 bits is transmitted serially for each character, the bit rate is seen to be 110 bits per second. The time T is then computed as the reciprocal of this bit rate. Thus,

$$T = \frac{1}{110} \text{ s} \approx 9091 \ \mu s$$

The subroutine, as noted before, is called by the operating system or other program whenever a character is to be received from the keyboard. The character is placed into the accumulator by the subroutine and is used in a manner that is determined by the calling program. Note that if a key of the keyboard is depressed at a time when a character is not anticipated by a call to the subroutine, then the bits will not be received. Thus, keys are to be depressed only when specific information is expected, such as commands requested by the operating system, instructions to be loaded by a loading program, or data expected by a running program.

CRT Display

The CRT display device will be based upon the use of an oscilloscope, which is to have a z-axis blanking input terminal as well as horizontal- and vertical-deflection input terminals. The device will display alphanumeric characters in the form of a pattern of dots. On the screen of the oscilloscope, there will be 16 rows of 32 character positions each. A character position will consist of an 8 × 8 array of dot positions.

In operation, the dot positions over the entire screen are continually scanned by appropriately driving the horizontal- and vertical-deflection terminals. The

z-axis blanking terminal is controlled during the scan so that the dots of each character to be displayed are illuminated.

This display device is interfaced to the microcomputer using a direct-memory-access scheme. Information to be displayed will come from a specified region, called a *page*, of main memory without the direct intervention of the micro-processor. The page will consist of $16 \times 32 = 512$ memory locations corresponding to the number of character positions on the screen. Each memory location consists of 8 bits, which conveniently agrees with the number of bits of one character in the ASCII code. The content of each memory location to be displayed is transferred from memory to a buffer register using the Data and Address buses, while the microprocessor is momentarily stopped.

In order to minimize the number of transfers from memory, a certain scanning sequence is used for this display device. The dot positions of each character are completely scanned before any dot positions of another character. In particular, each character is scanned left to right, top to bottom. The different character positions are scanned in a similar manner. The result, as seen in Fig. 10.11, is a scan pattern or raster that looks quite different from that of television.

A circuit to implement this CRT display device and its interface to the micro-computer is also shown in Fig. 10.9. There are two 8-bit D/A converters in the circuit that supply the voltages for vertical and horizontal deflection. The output voltage from the vertical D/A converter is inverted (multiplied by -1), so that low numbers to the D/A converter correspond to the top of the screen. The input lines of the D/A converters are connected to two counters in a manner that causes the vertical and horizontal deflection to follow the desired scan pattern. One counter, consisting of 6 bits, specifies the dot position within a character. The lower 3 bits of this dot-position counter correspond to the horizontal dot position and are

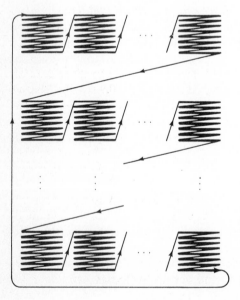

Figure 10.11 Raster for the CRT display device.

connected to the lower 3 bits of the horizontal D/A converter. Likewise, the upper 3 bits of the dot-position counter correspond to the vertical dot position and are connected to the lower 3 bits of the vertical D/A converter. If the other bits of the two D/A converters are kept constant while the dot-position counter is incremented from all 0s to all 1s, then the desired dot scan pattern for one character is obtained.

The other bits of the two D/A converters are connected to the second counter, which specifies the character position. This character-position counter consists of 9 bits. The lower 5 bits of this counter correspond to the horizontal character position and are connected to the remaining bits of the horizontal D/A converter. The upper 4 bits of this counter correspond to the vertical character position and are connected to the four highest-order bits of the vertical D/A converter. The remaining bit of the vertical D/A converter, bit 3, is grounded corresponding to constant 0. This grounding of bit 3 causes every other character row to be skipped, thereby providing a space between displayed lines. As the character-position counter is incremented from all 0s to all 1s, 16 rows are generated vertically from top to bottom each containing 32 horizontal character positions that are scanned left to right.

Each character to be displayed is generated with a read-only memory unit. This read-only memory is organized as 2^{13} words by 1 bit. Its contents consist of the 8×8 dot patterns for each of the 2^7 characters in the ASCII code. The actual characters displayed on the CRT generally will occupy an 8-dot vertical by 5-dot horizontal array, leaving the three right dot-columns vacant. This allows for horizontal spacing between displayed characters. The dot patterns are arranged in the ROM so that the lower six address lines of the ROM correspond to the dot position in a character and the upper seven address lines correspond to the bits of the ASCII code (with no parity bit) of the characters. The lower six address lines of the ROM are connected to the dot-position counter so that the dots of a character agree with the dot position on the screen. The upper seven address lines of the ROM are connected to a 7-bit latch that contains the ASCII code of the character to be displayed.

The character latch obtains a character from main memory over the Data bus using a direct-memory-access scheme. Two registers in Fig. 10.9 specify the main memory location from where the displayed character is to be taken. One of these registers is a 7-bit latch that specifies the high seven main-memory address bits. It in effect determines one out of the 128 pages of main memory from which all characters to be displayed are taken. Each page consists of $2^9 = 512$ memory locations. The particular location in a page is determined by the character-position counter, whose 9 bits form the low-order portion of the main-memory address. In this way, all characters of the specified page are displayed in order. The 7-bit page latch is connected to the microprocessor as an output port with device code 00_{16}. Thus, the page of memory to be displayed can be specified by a program by outputting a page number to this port.

The series of events that occur for displaying a page of characters is as follows. Assume that there is the ASCII code of a character in the character latch and that the dot-position counter is at zero. These two registers specify the address for the character-generator ROM. If the character specified by the character latch has a dot in position zero (upper left corner) then a 1 is produced by the ROM, which is inverted and then presented to the z-axis blanking terminal of the oscilloscope. A 0 at this z-axis terminal causes no blanking, resulting in an illuminated dot. Otherwise, blanking occurs, resulting in no illuminated dot.

The dot-position counter is driven by a gated form of the microprocessor clock. An AND gate is connected to the output lines of the dot-position counter to serve as an all-1 detector. The output of this all-1 detector is inverted and then ANDed with the microprocessor clock to generate the gated clock that drives the counter. Thus the counter will vary from all 0s up to all 1s causing the corresponding dots of the character to be displayed. When the counter reaches all 1s the gated clock is blocked, causing the counter to stop counting.

At this point the next character in the page is obtained for display. A sequence of four clock pulses is used to fetch the next character from main memory. A 2-bit counter is provided to keep track of clock pulses during the sequence. This 2-bit counter is connected to the input lines of a 1-out-of-4 decoder. The output lines from the decoder are controlled by its enable line that is connected to the AND of the clock and the direct-memory-access acknowledge (DMAA) control line from the microprocessor. Each of the four decoder output lines s_i therefore produces one pulse in synchronism with the clock when DMAA is logic-1. The four-pulse sequence begins after DMA, which is connected to the all-1 detector line of the dot-position counter, becomes logic-1. When DMA is set to logic-1, the microprocessor, after finishing the current machine cycle, stops program execution, puts the Data and Address buses into the floating state, and then sets DMAA to logic-1. When DMAA becomes logic-1 the 2-bit sequence counter begins counting clock pulses. With the first clock pulse the counter goes to 01 and a pulse occurs at s_0. This pulse at s_0 is used to increment the character-position counter, so that it corresponds to the next character to be displayed and its position on the screen.

The address of this next character, consisting of the combined contents of the page latch and the character-position counter, is placed onto the Address bus. This is done with a bank of sixteen 3-state drivers enabled by DMAA. Also, the read line to the main memory system is forced to logic-1 during the time that DMAA is logic-1. Consequently, after some delay the Data bus will contain the next character to be displayed. Two clock periods are provided to allow for the memory read-access time. The next clock pulse increments the 2-bit sequence counter to 10, but nothing else occurs. The clock pulse after that increments the counter to 11 and a pulse occurs at s_2, which is used to strobe the content of the Data bus into the character latch.

Finally, when the next clock pulse occurs, the 2-bit sequence counter goes to 00 and a pulse occurs at s_3, which is used to reset the dot-position counter. This terminates the four-pulse direct-memory-access sequence, since when the dot-position counter is reset the DMA control line goes to logic-0. In turn, the microprocessor causes DMAA to go to logic-0, which resets the 2-bit sequence counter.

At this point the character latch contains the ASCII code of the new character. Also, the dot-position counter is at zero and enabled to count. Thus the dots of the new character will be scanned and displayed at the proper character position on the screen.

This process is continued so that all characters in the page are repeatedly displayed. The repetition rate should be great enough so that no flicker is discernible by the human eye. To determine the repetition rate assume that the clock period is 1 μs. The number of clock periods per character displayed is equal to the number of dot positions of a character, which is 64, plus 4 more for fetching the character. There are 512 characters in a page, so the repetition time is equal to $512 \times 68 = 34,816 \mu$s. The repetition rate is therefore approximately 28.7 repetitions/s, which is fairly close to the frame repetition rate of 30 for U.S. television.

Note that this display device continuously displays a page of main memory regardless of what is in the page. It is the responsibility of the operating system or the user's program to maintain the contents of the displayed page. Up to 128 pages may be stored in memory for display, and each one is selected by a program by outputting the page number to port 00_{16}.

10.4 CONCLUDING REMARKS

It should be apparent that microprocessors, because of their programmability and interface flexibility, are highly versatile devices. Their range of applications is further enhanced by their low cost and small size. However, the number of additional components needed and the complexity of their interconnections are an important concern in the implementation of a microprocessor system for a given application. For the purpose of simplifying design, manufacturers commonly make available various subsystems, packaged as integrated circuits, to accompany their microprocessors (or other microprocessors). Generally, each of these packaged subsystems performs a basic interfacing function and has a certain amount of flexibility to allow for its adaptation to particular situations. To provide for serial I/O, for example, manufacturers provide various forms of universal asynchronous receiver/transmitters (UARTs) having certain selectable options, as was mentioned in Sec. 9.8.

In general, if a packaged subsystem has a number of selectable options, it is said to be *programmable*. The programming might be done by the means of control lines that are tied to logic-0 or logic-1; otherwise, the programming might be done by loading a control word into a register from the microprocessor, which eliminates the need for the control lines. Included among the available packaged subsystems are the following:

1. Programmable I/O ports, which generally include circuitry for several data ports as well as status and control ports for handshaking. The options might

include the specification of the port configuration and the manner in which handshaking is to be performed. Also, circuitry is often included to provide for interrupt requests based on the information contained in the status port.

2. Programmable interval timers, which generally consist of one or more up-down counters connected as both an input and an output port to a microprocessor having selectable modes of operation. In one mode, a counter provides an indication to the microprocessor when a specified amount of time has elapsed. In this case, the counter is loaded with an initial count from the microprocessor. It then downcounts pulses from an external source until zero is reached. At that time, either a status flag is set or a program interrupt is requested. Other modes might allow a counter to be used as a real-time clock, an event counter, or a variable-rate pulse source.

3. Vectored-interrupt controllers, which include circuitry to resolve interrupt request conflicts and to provide the appropriate information to the microprocessor.

4. Direct-memory-access controllers, which provide the necessary circuitry to coordinate the transfer of a block of data words between memory and a device.

5. Dynamic-memory refresh controllers, which include the necessary circuitry to periodically refresh dynamic memory units connected to a microprocessor.

6. Clock generators, which provide the clock phases having the required time relationship for a microprocessor, and also other special timing signals.

7. Data acquisition units, which might include one or more D/A converters and/or one or more A/D converters that are connected to appropriate I/O ports.

8. Extended arithmetic units, such as multipliers, dividers, and trigonometric function generators, which are operated through I/O ports included in the unit.

Generally, these subsystem units are organized such that the number of necessary interconnections between them and the microprocessor is kept to a minimum. Furthermore, their signal levels and timing are made to agree with those of the accompanying microprocessor. Consequently, a large part in the design of many microprocessor systems is reduced to just connecting such subsystem units and the microprocessor together. Of course, there will usually be other aspects in the design of a system that are particular to the specific application and will therefore require specially designed circuitry and components.

To further enhance the ease of implementing microcomputer systems, manufacturers also make available so-called *single-chip microcomputers*. Besides a microprocessor, these single-chip microcomputers generally include a small amount of read/write and read-only memory, several input and output ports, and some of the other basic subsystem functions. This leads to a significant reduction in the number of required interconnections for microcomputer systems that involve a small amount of memory and I/O connections. Usually most of the normal bus lines are eliminated with such chips to provide room for the external lines to the I/O ports. In some cases, certain lines may be programmed to serve either as bus lines (for address and/or data) or as I/O port connections.

Besides the manner of implementation, the development of a microcomputer system involves the testing and verification of its proper operation. This includes the debugging of both the software and the hardware. Because of the interaction between the software and hardware and the complexity of component interconnections, the debugging aspects of system development can be very challenging. For this reason, various development tools and aids are made available both from the manufacturers and from instrument companies. These tools and aids generally allow some isolation between the software and hardware debugging processes. Included are

1. Development systems for particular microprocessors, which include a console and prepackaged hardware modules, such as microprocessor boards, read/write and programmable read-only memory systems, I/O ports, and other interfacing functions. These allow for the prototyping of systems during their initial design phases.
2. Evaluation kits, which consist of a small microcomputer system on one or more printed-circuit boards.
3. Microprocessor analyzers, which record and display the contents of the buses and other lines in a microcomputer during each machine cycle while the microprocessor is executing a program.
4. Hardware emulators, which allow specified portions of a microcomputer system to be simulated so that the various signals and timing between portions can be studied.
5. Software aides, such as microprocessor simulation programs to be run on general-purpose computers, as well as cross assemblers and compilers.

DESIGN PROJECTS

10.1 Design a "front panel" for a general-purpose microcomputer based on the illustrative microprocessor. The front panel is to have switches and lights that are used to perform each of the following functions:

1. Examine the content of any memory location.
2. Deposit a word into any memory location.
3. Examine the content of any scratchpad register.
4. Deposit a word into any scratchpad register.
5. Examine the carry flag.
6. Examine the program counter.
7. Deposit an address into the program counter.
8. Start and stop the microprocessor.
9. Reset the microprocessor.

The following should be included: 16 switches for address, 8 switches for data, 8 lights for displaying data and the lower half of the program counter, 8 more lights for the upper half of the program counter, and switches for activating each of the 9 functions above. The four low-order address switches are also to be used to specify a particular register for the two functions that involve the scratchpad. The front panel switches are to be effective only when the microprocessor is stopped, except for the start-stop and reset switches.

When the microprocessor is halted, the Address and Data buses will be floating. These buses can therefore be used to access memory with the switches to accomplish the first two functions. The other functions cannot be accomplished so directly since they involve registers internal to the microprocessor. These other functions could be accomplished, though, by having the microprocessor execute one or more fixed instructions that are selected in each case to bring about the desired transfer. For example, the content of a scratchpad register (say 5) can be examined by executing the instruction MOV 5 to F. The desired information can then be intercepted when it appears on the Data bus and latched into a register for display. Of course, the information should be prevented from reaching main memory.

It is important that all registers of the microprocessor not involved in the function being performed should not be disturbed. For this reason, the program counter needs to be treated in a special way, since the execution of an instruction causes it to be incremented. A 16-bit register could be provided to temporarily hold the desired content of the program counter. Whenever the microprocessor is stopped, the current content of the program counter could be transferred to the temporary register. This can be done by executing an NOP instruction and noting the Address bus when the NOP is fetched. This temporary register may then be examined or altered by the two program counter functions of the front panel. When the microprocessor is eventually restarted, the content of the temporary register could be transferred back to the program counter, which can be done by executing a jump instruction.

Note that the instructions executed in carrying out the front panel functions are to come from the logic of the front panel, rather than from main memory. They are forced onto the Data bus at the appropriate time independent from the Address bus.

10.2 Using the illustrative microprocessor or one that is commercially available, design a simple microcomputer as follows. The microcomputer is to have some read/write memory (say 1K words or more) and several general-purpose input and output ports. For controlling and monitoring the operation of the microcomputer, a small keyboard and several seven-segment LED displays are to be provided that work with a special program residing in a read-only portion of main memory. The keyboard is to consist of 16 keys for the hexadecimal digits 0 through F, plus several keys for activating various functions including

1. Examine and/or alter a memory location.
2. Examine and/or alter a scratchpad register (or whatever registers exist for the particular microprocessor).
3. Examine and/or alter the program counter.
4. Reset.
5. Start.
6. Stop.

Additional keys might be provided to perform such things as to load information from a peripheral storage device (such as cassette tape) into a section of memory or to dump information from memory to the storage device. The hexadecimal digit keys are used to specify numerical information such as memory addresses and data words to be entered. At least 6 seven-segment displays are to be provided, four for generally displaying addresses in hexadecimal and two for displaying data in hexadecimal.

The special program residing in read-only memory is to serve as a small *operating system*, which interprets the keyboard, carries out any requested function, and generates appropriate information for display. For example, the examine and/or alter memory function might be carried out as follows. While the operating system is running, the key for this function is depressed. The operating system then waits for a 4-digit address to be entered from the digit keys. As each address digit is entered, it is shown in the corresponding seven-segment display. After all 4 address digits have been entered, the operating system causes the data contained in the specified memory location to be shown in the 2 seven-segment displays for data. This data could then be altered, if desired, by simply entering 2 digits for the replacement data.

The operating system is to be running whenever a user's program is not. The start key causes a user's program to commence with the current value of the program counter. Either the stop or reset key is used to terminate a user's program.

10.3 Music production is an interesting application of microprocessors. Based on any microprocessor, design a music synthesizer that will play tunes stored in main memory. The following approach is suggested, although many variations and alternatives are possible. Eight (more or less) variable-frequency tone generators controlled by the microprocessor are used to generate individual notes making up a chord. Each tone generator consists of a 5-bit counter driven by a voltage-controlled oscillator (VCO), whose output frequency is proportional to the input voltage. The binary counter serves as a frequency divider that allows the frequency range of a tone to be selected from one of five octaves. The frequency of a tone within an octave is determined by the input voltage applied to the VCO. Each tone generator could be controlled by two 8-bit output ports (this depends on the word length of the microprocessor). One port would be connected to a D/A converter to produce the input voltage for the VCO, whereas the other port would be used to digitally select the output from the desired stage of the binary counter. Filters might be provided to shape the wave from each tone generator. In this case, a separate filter for each counter stage should be used so that they may be designed to work with a narrow range of frequencies (one octave). The outputs from selected tone generators are combined and amplified. A variable gain amplifier controlled by another output port might be used to allow for loudness variations.

In operation, a program would obtain a representation for each chord from memory one at a time and generate it. The representation of a chord includes the pitch of each constituent note, the loudness of the chord, and the time duration.

10.4 Design a game-playing machine based on some microprocessor to play Tic-Tac-Toe against a human opponent. The game board is to consist of a 3-by-3 array of cells. Each cell is to have two different colored lights, one for each opponent, and a pushbutton switch for the human. The microprocessor is to control the game board through appropriate input and output ports. Additional switches and lights should be provided to start the microprocessor, to select the opponent to go first, to display the winner, and perhaps to display the number of human wins for a series of games.

10.5 Design a game-playing machine based on some microprocessor to play three-dimensional Tic-Tac-Toe against a human opponent. The machine is to be similar to the Tic-Tac-Toe machine of Prob. 10.4, except that the game board is to be a 3-by-3-by-3 array of cells. Alternatively, the machine might be designed for a 4-by-4-by-4 array.

The strategy for the program for three-dimensional Tic-Tac-Toe is considerably more challenging than that for the two-dimensional case. This is especially true for the 4-by-4-by-4 game. Consequently, a strategy might be sought that plays a good game based on "rules of thumb" rather than a strategy that plays a perfect game.

10.6 Design a checker-playing machine using any microprocessor. Computer programs for playing checkers, as well as chess, have been the subject of considerable research in artificial intelligence. There are checker-playing programs that play an excellent game, whereas the best chess-playing programs can usually be beaten by good players. At any rate, devising a strategy for the program for the checker-playing machine should be the most challenging aspect in its design. It is therefore suggested for the sake of feasibility that the strategy be kept relatively simple. Emphasis should be placed on the interfacing aspects of the design.

The machine is to have a game board, arranged as an ordinary checkerboard, with three lights (different colors) and a pushbutton switch in each of the 32 playing squares. Two of the lights will represent the two opponents' checkers, and the third light will indicate whether or not a checker occupying the square is a kinger. The pushbuttons are used by the human to enter moves. A move is to be entered by first depressing the button in the square containing the checker to be moved and then depressing the button in the destination square. In the case of multiple jumps, the button in each intermediate square should also be depressed in order. Besides playing its game, the microprocessor is to control the game board, including monitoring the switches and displaying the position of all checkers. In addition, the microprocessor is to declare the winner at the end of a game and check for illegal moves by the human.

10.7 The digital control of machine tools, such as punch presses, milling machines, and boring machines, is an important part of industrial automation. It is commonly referred to as numerical control, if the controller is made up of digital components and gates, or computer control, if a computer is involved.

Consider the problem of controlling a punch press for sheet metal. The press consists of a table that moves along two horizontal axes to position the sheet metal and an overhead punch that moves vertically to pierce the metal with the aid of a mating die on the other side. The table is moved by means of screw gears along each axis, which are rotated by stepper motors. Assume that each stepper motor is driven by a circuit, referred to as a translator, that causes one unit of rotation in the clockwise direction for each pulse on one input line and one unit of rotation in the counterclockwise direction for each pulse on a second input line. The punch head is operated by a motor, which is controlled by a circuit that causes one punch cycle for each pulse applied to its input line.

Design a controller using any microprocessor to operate such a punch press. The controller is to position the sheet metal according to coordinates stored in the memory and then cause the punch to produce a hole. This is repeated for as many holes that are to be punched. The sheet metal is positioned by issuing the appropriate number of pulses to the stepper motor translators to account for the difference in each direction between the new position and the current position. The operation begins with the sheet metal in a specified fixed position relative to the punch head, which is referred to as the origin. All coordinates are specified relative to this origin, which is in the lower left hand corner of the metal. Limit switches are used to determine the origin by having the sheet metal move toward the switches until they are actuated. The microprocessor has the responsibility for this initialization.

For simplicity, the coordinates for the holes to be punched might be assumed to be already in memory and that no provision be made to bring in this information from an external device. On the other hand, a more complete design might be undertaken that includes a terminal for inputting hole coordinates both manually or from paper tape. In addition, a design might include the generation of the hole coordinates by a program according to specified geometric patterns, such as a circle of specified radius and a specified number of evenly spaced holes.

10.8 Design a microprocessor-controlled trainable robot arm. The arm is to consist of a base, two rigid cylindrical links, and a two-finger hand, as shown in Fig. P10.8a. There are two joints, a shoulder that connects the base to one link and an elbow that connects the two links together. Each joint allows for two types of rotational motion, twist and pivot, of one element (the one closest to the hand) relative to the other element. Twist refers to the rotation of an element along its axis; whereas, pivot refers to the swinging of an element in a certain plane. For the shoulder joint the pivotal plane is just the horizontal plane. For the elbow joint the pivotal plane rotates with the link attached to the base. The hand is rigidly connected to one link, so that no wrist motion is allowed. The two fingers of the hand move toward or away from each other, while remaining parallel. As can be seen there are altogether five types of motion. To produce each of these, a dc servomotor should be provided. In order to monitor each motion a spatial encoder is attached to the shaft of each servomotor.

The spatial encoders to be used should be similar to that depicted in Fig. P10.8b. It includes a transparent disk having two circular tracks of evenly-spaced opaque marks. The marks and spaces are of equal width. The disk is illuminated on one side by lights. A photo detector is placed on the other side for each track. An amplifier attached to each photo detector produces a logic-1 on an output channel when a mark is under the detector, and a logic-0 otherwise. As can be noticed from the figure, the marks of one track are shifted with respect to the marks of the other track by an amount equal to one-half the width of a mark. This results in a corresponding shift of the logic signals of the output channels (which is referred to as quadrature phase). The direction of rotation can be determined by observing the time relationship of the two channels. A simple sequential circuit can be designed to do this. The amount of rotation can be determined by counting the number of level transitions for both channels. For this purpose, an up-down binary counter could be used in which the count direction is specified by the determined direction of shaft rotation. The counter will then track the position of the shaft relative to an initial position. The initial position could be determined by limit switches.

The arm is to be interfaced to a microprocessor by supplying driver circuits connected to output ports for the servomotors and connecting the up-down counters to input ports. Each motor-driving circuit will require 2 bits of an output port, 1 bit for each direction of rotation. The number of input port bits required by each counter, of course, depends on the number of bits making up the counter, which depends on the desired resolution. For 8 bits, the resolution is 1 unit out of 256. For the rotational movements, this resolution corresponds to approximately 1.5° per step (assuming the range of rotation is 360°). This represents a fairly good resolution for many purposes. In this case, one 8-bit

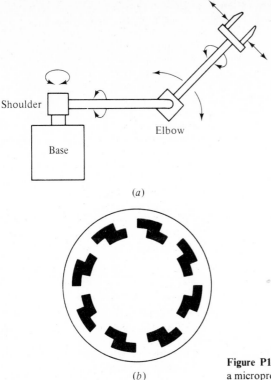

Shoulder

Base

Elbow

(a)

(b)

Figure P10.8 (a) Robot arm to be controlled by a microprocessor. (b) Two-channel spatial encoder.

input port per counter will suffice. In any case, the amount of resolution is determined by the number of marks in a track of the spatial encoder and the gearing involved between the shaft and the particular joint of the arm.

The interfacing just mentioned allows the microprocessor to both cause the arm to move and to determine its position. Thus, the microprocessor could be programmed to move the arm through predetermined positions. To allow for training, a pushbutton is provided that when pushed causes the microprocessor to input the contents of all five counters. This could be done as a program interrupt or with a status bit that is checked by the program. The training can then be done by a person taking the arm by the hand (literally and figuratively) and moving it from position to position with the motors off. This is to include the possible grasping of objects by the fingers. At each intermediate position the person presses the pushbutton, causing the positional coordinates to be accepted by the micro-processor. The microprocessor should be programmed to store these coordinates in the form of a list in main memory. The microprocessor could then use this list of coordinates at a later time to cause the arm to repeatedly make the same motions.

10.9 Design a microprocessor-based controller for a model railroad. Consider a layout for dc-type trains consisting of at least two trains and a track configuration having several loops and spurs connected together with track switches. A possible objective for the controller is to allow for the routing of each train according to instructions entered through a keyboard. The routing instructions might have several forms, such as

1. To proceed along the shortest path from the present location to a specified destination and then stop
2. To follow a closed path until otherwise instructed
3. To back up onto a spur

It should be the responsibility of the microprocessor to carry out these instructions without incurring an accident, such as two trains colliding or a train entering a closed track switch. To do this, the microprocessor is to perform certain tasks, including: determining the location of each train at various points in time, controlling the speed and direction of each train, and controlling the track switches. In order to determine the location of the trains and to control their motion, the track is to be divided into a number of sections. The voltage applied to each section is to be separately controlled. The presence of an engine on any section could be determined by sensing the current drawn by the section. This may be done with a resistor placed on the negative side of each section as shown by Fig. P10.9. If current flows into the track, a voltage will appear across the resistor, which is converted to a logic signal by a special amplifier circuit. This assumes that the track polarity is never reversed. If the polarity is to be reversed, however, then an arrangement of diodes connected to each side of the track in an AND gate fashion could be used instead.

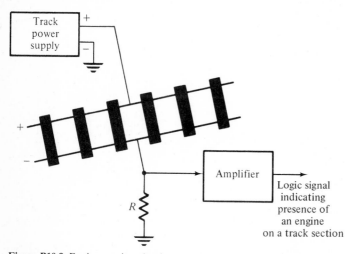

Figure P10.9 Engine sensing circuit.

Interfacing the track to the microprocessor will involve an output port for the voltage applied to each section, an input port bit for detecting a train for each section, and an output port bit to control each switch. A D/A converter with a current-driving circuit at its output could be used to produce the voltage applied to a section. A simple keyboard could also be interfaced to an input port of the microprocessor.

The trains are to be started from a known initial position. It is then the responsibility of the microprocessor to keep track of each train, while causing them to move according to instructions entered from the keyboard. The microprocessor should be programmed to determine when each section of track is to be energized and when each switch is to change. Also, the program could determine such things as minimal paths for train routes, etc.

Various embellishments might be added to this arrangement such as crossing gates, blocking signals, car decouplers, log loaders, etc. Each of these additions could also be controlled by the microprocessor.

10.10 Design a home weather station that uses a microprocessor to make measurements of weather variables and to predict short-term weather. Included in the measurements might be the following five variables: temperature, air pressure, relative humidity, wind speed, and wind direction. Temperature could be measured with the use of a thermistor, which is a semiconductor device for which resistance decreases with an increase in temperature. Air pressure could be measured with a pressure transducer or perhaps with a strain gauge attached to the surface of a sealed container. Relative humidity could be measured with a type of hygrometer. In the hygrometer would be two thermistors, one of which is kept dry, while the other is kept wet with a wick having one end submerged in water. Air from a fan is then directed at the wet thermistor, which would produce a cooling effect due to evaporation. The relative humidity could then be determined from the temperatures of the two thermistors with the use of a standard table. Wind speed could be measured with an anemometer to which a small dc generator is attached. An anemometer involves a rotor having cups that catch the wind causing it to spin. Finally, wind direction could be measured with a weather vane to which is attached a special potentiometer. The potentiometer should have a resistance element that nearly covers 360° and should not have stops to limit its rotation.

The microprocessor is to convert voltages from the measuring devices to digital form and input this information. The information may then be formatted and outputted for display. Also, the information may be used by the microprocessor to form simple weather predictions for the near future, which are then outputted to a special display. For the purpose of making predictions, various rules of thumb[†] could be followed, such as

1. Fair weather will tend to continue if the air pressure remains steady or rises and wind blows gently from the west or northwest.
2. An approaching rainstorm is probable if the air pressure is falling and wind is blowing from the south or southwest.
3. Rain or snow will tend to continue if the air pressure is falling and wind is blowing from the southeast.
4. Temperatures will tend to fall if the air pressure steadily rises and wind blows gently from the north or northwest.

Such rules will depend on the area and time of year, which may be taken into account. Also, the rules might be altered in an adaptive fashion by the microprocessor, making use of past performance.

10.11 Design a sportscar rally computer. A sportscar rally is a competitive event in which teams, consisting of a driver and a navigator, follow a prescribed course of roads at prescribed speeds. The navigator interprets a set of course instructions, which are sometimes rather obscure, and informs the driver accordingly. Along the course are placed checkpoints to record the elapsed running time for each car from the previous checkpoint or point of beginning. This elapsed running time is compared with the theoretical time that would elapse if a car traveled at the precise specified speeds for the leg. Penalty points are issued for each unit of time (usually seconds) in which a car is early or late. This is the only check that is made on speed, so only average speed is important. The navigator normally keeps track of the theoretical time throughout a leg by calculating it from odometer readings and the speeds specified in the course instructions. This theoretical time is continually compared to the actual running time from a watch. The driver is informed of the results of the comparisons and makes adjustments in speed to compensate for being early or late. Sometimes so-called unmanned checkpoints are included in a rally, for which the theoretical time is to be recorded but not compared with the running time.

One aspect that should be taken into account in the calculations is any difference between the odometer readings for a particular car and those for the car that was used to lay out the course. The difference is usually appreciable, since odometer readings are affected by tire diameter and tire wear. For this purpose, a correction factor is generally used in the calculations, which is determined over a special calibration leg at the beginning of the course.

The rally computer to be designed is to perform the calculations normally done by the navigator. Specifically, the computer should calculate and display the following:

1. Theoretical time
2. Actual time
3. Difference between theoretical and actual time
4. Corrected odometer reading

---

† Taken from the article Weather, in "The World Book Encyclopedia," Field Enterprises, Chicago, 1976.

The information necessary for these calculations includes measured distance, elapsed time, specified speed, and the calculated correction factor. The measured distance is to be determined from a pulse generator attached to the odometer cable. The pulse generator is to produce a pulse for each unit of distance traveled. These pulses are counted (perhaps with program interrupts) to produce a value for measured distance. Elapsed time is to be determined from a precise pulse source, the pulses of which are counted (perhaps with program interrupts again). Finally, the specified speed and the correction factor are to be entered from a decimal keyboard, and also displayed.

10.12 The computational power of a microprocessor can be improved by providing an external arithmetic unit to perform operations beyond those that are included within the instructions of the microprocessor. Taking multiplication as an example, a unit could be provided that receives the multiplier and multiplicand from the microprocessor through output ports, performs multiplication, and then supplies the results to the microprocessor through one or more input port.

Design such a multiplier unit for a particular microprocessor. Assume that the two operands are each as wide as a data word for the microprocessor. The product will be twice this width (16 bits for an 8-bit microprocessor). Therefore, an output port is to be provided for each operand and two input ports for the product. A status port might also be provided if the multiplication operation requires a considerable amount of time compared to an instruction time. One bit of the status port is to be used to start the multiplication and a second status bit is to be used to inform the microprocessor that the multiplication has been completed.

The design might make use of multiplication modules that are commercially available. Besides multiplication, other operations might be considered such as division, floating-point addition and subtraction, and trigonometric functions.

10.13 Since microprocessors are generally inexpensive, it is tempting to consider ways of interconnecting a number of them so that they would work together to achieve a greater computational speed and power. There are, of course, many possible arrangements for interconnecting the microprocessors. In particular, consider an arrangement that has a master microprocessor that controls several slave microprocessors. The master microprocessor is to be programmed to follow an algorithm and to use the slave microprocessors to carry out some of the individual steps (such as extended arithmetic operations, function evaluation, or input/output operations) that are involved in the algorithm.

Design such a system of multimicroprocessors having one master microprocessor controlling two or more slaves. Each microprocessor is to have its own memory system to contain both instructions and data. Transfer of data between the master microprocessor and each slave microprocessor is to be done by means of input and output ports having intermediate storage registers.

Each slave microprocessor is to have a library of routines in its memory system. The master microprocessor causes a slave to execute one of its routines by requesting a program interrupt of the slave. The slave responds by executing the routine specified by the interrupt, after which it requests a program interrupt of the master to indicate completion of the routine. While not executing a requested routine, each slave simply idles. This might be done by having the slave execute an instruction that causes a jump to itself or, in some cases, executing a halt instruction.

10.14 Design a microprocessor-based Morse-code generator. The generator is to produce the dot and dash patterns for characters on an output line, which is used to key an audio oscillator or a transmitter. The patterns for the characters can be determined from a table that is located in memory. Each entry in the table is to represent the sequence of dots and dashes making up a character.

For an 8-bit memory word length, a convenient way of representing the character patterns is as follows. The dots and dashes, represented by 0 and 1 respectively, of a character are placed left-justified into a memory word. An additional 1 is placed into the position at the right of the last dot or dash and 0 is placed into any remaining bit positions of the word. In this way, the additional 1 will always be the rightmost 1 encountered in a word and will therefore serve to delimit the end of a character.

To generate a selected character the microprocessor could transfer the representation of the character to the accumulator (or similar register). The dots and dashes could then be left shifted one at a time into the carry flag (or similar flag), where they could be used to determine the time duration in which the output line is to be at 1. Eventually, when the delimiter 1 is shifted into the carry flag the accumulator will become zero, indicating that the generation of the character has been completed.

The time for the different events should all be based on a selected dot time according to the following standard specifications:

1. Dash time is 3 dot times.
2. Space time between dots and dashes is 1 dot time.
3. Space time between characters is 3 dot times.
4. Space time between words is 5 dot times.

This generator could be used in several ways depending on the manner in which the characters are selected. Characters could be entered one at a time from an ASCII-encoded keyboard. The microprocessor would then decode each character to determine the table location for its Morse-code representation. Characters could be specified according to messages (such as a call sign or a CQ protocol) stored in memory. Finally, for code practice, characters could be selected at random based on a random-number generator.

10.15 Design a microprocessor-based Morse-code interpreter. The interpreter is to accept the dot-dash patterns of Morse-code characters appearing on an input line and convert them to the corresponding ASCII code so that they can be outputted to an ASCII-encoded printer. To do this the interpreter will need to measure the 1 and 0 duration times of the input line so that it may detect the occurrence of a dot, dash, character space, or word space.

Since Morse code is usually sent by hand, the code speed will not generally be known and in fact must be assumed to vary during a message. Thus, the timing of the interpreter must adapt to the actual code speed. This might be done by first estimating the time of a dot and then using multiples of this dot time for the other times in accordance with the time relationships given in the previous problem. A threshold could be established between the estimated dot and dash times (say two dot times) in order to discern between a received dot or dash. Likewise, a threshold could be established between the estimated character and word space times (say 4 dot times) and between the mark and character space times (say 2 dot times). The most difficult part of this scheme is estimating the dot time. There are various ways of doing this, but the following method is suggested. An initial estimate of the dot time is made by averaging the times of the first few spaces between dots and dashes. The estimated dot time is then continually adjusted by setting it equal to the average of the times for the last few received dots. To guard against locking into a gross misestimate, the dot time could be reinitialized any time an invalid pattern of dots and dashes is detected.

The measurement of duration times could be done by sampling the input line at regular intervals. A programmed counter could then be used to keep track of the number of samples for each event. The sampling time should be considerably shorter than the dot time that corresponds to the fastest allowed code speed.

Once a character is received it could be stored in memory in the format given in the previous problem to be converted later to ASCII. Otherwise, it could be converted immediately to ASCII using a table in memory. The table could be arranged so that its entries are ASCII codes for possible characters with the corresponding addresses related in a simple fashion to the representation of received Morse-code characters.

10.16 Design a microprocessor-based graphic display unit. The unit is to generate a dot pattern on an oscilloscope according to image information stored in memory. The possible dot positions on the screen are to form an array of size 256×256. A pattern of dots is to be produced by having the beam repeatedly scan just those positions to be illuminated. For this purpose, the x and y axes can be driven by 8-bit digital-to-analog converters, each connected to an output port. The microprocessor is to supply the coordinates to these ports for each point to be illuminated.

To simplify manipulation of a stored image and to reduce storage requirements the following often used scheme for representing stored images is suggested. In this scheme, an image is made up of a variable number (up to some maximum) of subimages. Each subimage is represented in memory by a list of coordinate pairs, each pair indicating the position of a dot relative to a center point of the subimage. The list for each subimage can be of arbitrary length and is terminated by a delimiter word (consisting of all 1s). An overall image is then represented by another list, consisting of ordered triples. Each triple corresponds to a subimage to be included in the image. The first two elements of a triple specifies the center position of a subimage on the screen. The third element corresponds to an address indicating the beginning location of the subimage's representation in memory. This list is also terminated by the delimiter consisting of all 1s. These lists provide all of the information needed by the microprocessor to compute the coordinates of all dots to be illuminated.

This scheme of composing an image from subimages allows the description of a subimage to be used several times in the overall image. This is advantageous when a scene containing similar objects (such as people, cars, trees, etc.) is to be displayed. Furthermore, these subimages can be easily moved around the image by simply changing the coordinate information specifying their centers.

10.17 Design a microprocessor-controlled animated scoreboard. The animated part of the scoreboard is to consist of a 32-by-32 array of lights. Each light is to be driven by an SCR (or other electronic device) connected to an ac power source. Each SCR could be controlled by a flip-flop in an output port. For an 8-bit microprocessor, this will involve 128 8-bit output ports for the entire array.

To produce apparent motion the board should be updated periodically at a rate of say 4 times per second. Each new image could be generated by making changes to the representation of the previous image. This is facilitated if a scheme of composing an image from subimages such as indicated in the previous problem is used. Then, only certain subimages need to be changed and others relocated to simulate motion. Using such a scheme, it is suggested that a region of memory be allocated to assemble a new image into the form in which it will appear at the output ports. The assembly of an image consists of first resetting all locations in the memory region to zero and then setting certain bits in the region to 1 as specified by the list representation of the image. Once an image is assembled in memory it may then be transferred a word at a time to the output ports that control the lights.

10.18 Design a computing digital voltmeter for ac waveforms. The voltmeter is to be able to indicate each of the following values: maximum, minimum, peak-to-peak, root mean square (RMS), average of absolute values, and algebraic average. To do this, it is to take samples of the voltage waveform over a cycle and from these compute the selected value. A cycle could be assumed to be the segment of the waveform between two consecutive positive peaks. Each sample is to be converted to digital form. This could be done by the microprocessor with the use of a D/A converter and a comparator. Assume that the voltage to be converted has been scaled to a range between -1 and $+1$ V. This could be done with a resistor voltage dividing network connected to a range switch.

Assume that the allowable frequency range is from 40 to 120 Hz. To ensure that a sufficient number of samples is obtained, a sampling rate of around 10,000 samples per second is suggested. As the samples are obtained and converted, they could be stored in memory. Then after the sampling cycle, the particular value selected is computed, converted to decimal, and outputted to a numerical display. The selection of which value to compute could be done with switches connected to an input port.

The number of bits used to represent each sample will limit the precision of the voltmeter. For an 8-bit microprocessor, an 8-bit representation of the samples is convenient. This corresponds approximately to $2\frac{1}{2}$ decimal digits and an error of about 0.4 percent. This is generally acceptable, but a greater precision might be considered.

10.19 Redesign the calculating weight scale of Sec. 10.1 using a commercially available microprocessor and/or incorporating one or more additional features. One additional feature could be a provision for specifying the cost rate in dollars per kilogram as well as in dollars per pound.

10.20 Redesign the traffic light controller of Sec. 10.2 using a commercially available microprocessor and/or a different strategy. Perhaps additional sensors could be used that are located on the incoming lanes at some distance away from the intersection so as to detect a line of waiting vehicles.

APPENDIX

Table A1 Alphabetic listing of instructions for the illustrative microprocessor

Symbolic form $(R = 0, 1, \ldots, F)$	Hexadecimal code $(R = 0, 1, \ldots, F)$	Number of bytes
ADC R	9R	1
ADD R	8R	1
AND R	CR	1
CMA	F0	1
CMC	F3	1
DHL	F6	1
DIT	FC	1
EIT	FB	1
HLT	FA	1
IHL	F5	1
INP	FD	2
JAM	7E	3
JAN	7D	3
JAP	7A	3
JAZ	79	3
JCN	78	3
JCZ	7C	3
JHL	F9	1
JMP	7B	3
JMS	7F	3
LDR 0	70	3
LDR 1	71	3
LDR 2	72	3
LRI R	6R	2
MOV 0 from R	1R	1
MOV 0 to R	0R	1
MOV 1 from R	3R	1
MOV 1 to R	2R	1
MOV 2 from R	5R	1
MOV 2 to R	4R	1
NOP	F7	1
OR R	DR	1
OUT	FE	2
POP	73	1
PUSH	77	1
RET	F8	1
RSC	F4	1
RTL	F1	1
RTR	F2	1
SBC R	BR	1
STR 0	74	3
STR 1	75	3
STR 2	76	3
SUB R	AR	1
XOR R	ER	1

Table A2 Numeric listing of instructions for the illustrative microprocessor

Hexadecimal code $(R = 0, 1, \ldots, F)$	Symbolic form $(R = 0, 1, \ldots, F)$	Number of bytes
0R	MOV 0 to R	1
1R	MOV 0 from R	1
2R	MOV 1 to R	1
3R	MOV 1 from R	1
4R	MOV 2 to R	1
5R	MOV 2 from R	1
6R	LRI R	2
70	LDR 0	3
71	LDR 1	3
72	LDR 2	3
73	POP	1
74	STR 0	3
75	STR 1	3
76	STR 2	3
77	PUSH	1
78	JCN	3
79	JAZ	3
7A	JAP	3
7B	JMP	3
7C	JCZ	3
7D	JAN	3
7E	JAM	3
7F	JMS	3
8R	ADD R	1
9R	ADC R	1
AR	SUB R	1
BR	SBC R	1
CR	AND R	1
DR	OR R	1
ER	XOR R	1
F0	CMA	1
F1	RTL	1
F2	RTR	1
F3	CMC	1
F4	RSC	1
F5	IHL	1
F6	DHL	1
F7	NOP	1
F8	RET	1
F9	JHL	1
FA	HLT	1
FB	EIT	1
FC	DIT	1
FD	INP	2
FE	OUT	2
FF	(Not used)	

SELECTED BIBLIOGRAPHY

The following is a list of books dealing with microprocessors and micro-computers. Manufacturer's literature and journal articles have not been included.

Agerwala, Tilak, Gerald Masson, and Roger Westgate: "Designing with Microprocessors," Institute of Electrical and Electronics Engineers, Inc., New York, 1976.

Altman, Laurence (ed.): " Microprocessors," Electronics Book Series, McGraw-Hill Publications, New York, 1975.

Aspinall, D., and E. L. Dagless (eds.): "Introduction to Microprocessors," Academic Press, Inc., New York, 1977.

Barna, Arpad, and Dan I. Porat: "Introduction to Microcomputers and Microprocessors," John Wiley & Sons, Inc., New York, 1976.

Bibbero, Robert J.: "Microprocessors in Instruments and Control," John Wiley & Sons, Inc., New York, 1977.

EDN Staff: "EDN Microprocessor Design Series," Cahners Publishing Company, Boston, Mass., 1974.

————: "EDN Microprocessor Design Series Volume II," Cahners Publishing Company, Boston, Mass., 1975.

Garland, Harry: "Introduction to Microprocessor System Design," McGraw-Hill Book Company, New York, 1979.

Hilburn, John L., and Paul M. Julich: " Microcomputers/Microprocessors: Hardware, Software, and Applications," Prentice-Hall, Inc., Englewood Cliffs, N.J., 1976.

Klingman, Edwin E.: "Microprocessor Systems Design," Prentice-Hall, Inc., Englewood Cliffs, N.J., 1977.

Korn, Granino A.: "Microprocessors and Small Digital Computer Systems for Engineers and Scientists," McGraw-Hill Book Company, New York, 1977.

Leahy, William F.: "Microprocessor Architecture and Programming," John Wiley & Sons, Inc., New York, 1977.

Lee, Samuel C. (ed.): "Microcomputer Design and Application," Academic Press, Inc., New York, 1977.

Lesea, Austin, and Rodnay Zaks: "Microprocessor Interfacing Techniques," 2d ed., SYBEX Inc., Berkeley, Calif., 1978.

Leventhal, Lance A.: "Introduction to Microprocessors: Software, Hardware, Programming," Prentice-Hall, Inc., Englewood Cliffs, N.J., 1978.

Lin, Wen C. (ed.): "Microprocessors: Fundamentals and Applications," IEEE Press, New York, 1977.

McGlynn, Daniel R.: "Microprocessors: Technology, Architecture, and Applications," John Wiley & Sons, Inc., New York, 1976.

Motorola Semiconductor Products, Inc.: "Microprocessor Applications Manual," McGraw-Hill Book Company, New York, 1975.

Osborne, Adam: "An Introduction to Microcomputers Volume I: Basic Concepts," Adam Osborne and Associates, Inc., Berkeley, Calif., 1976.

————: "An Introduction to Microcomputers Volume II: Some Real Products," Adam Osborne and Associates, Inc., Berkeley, Calif., 1976.

————: "8080 Programming for Logic Design," Adam Osborne and Associates, Inc., Berkeley, Calif., 1976.

Peatman, John B.: "Microcomputer-Based Design," McGraw-Hill Book Company, New York, 1977.

Rao, Guthikonda V.: "Microprocessors and Microcomputer Systems," Van Nostrand Reinhold Company, New York, 1978.

Sippl, Charles J.: "Microcomputer Dictionary and Guide," Matrix Publishers, Inc., Champaigne, Ill., 1975.

————: "Microcomputer Handbook," Petrocilli/Charter, New York, 1977.

Souček, Branko: "Microprocessors and Microcomputers," John Wiley & Sons, Inc., New York, 1976.

Veronis, Andrew: "Microprocessors: Design and Applications," Reston Publishing Company, Inc., Reston, Va., 1978.

Weller, W. J., A. V. Shatzel, and H. Y. Nice: "Practical Microcomputer Programming: The Intel 8080," Northern Technology Books, Evanston, Ill., 1976.

Zaks, Rodnay: "Microprocessors: From Chips to Systems," SYBEX Inc., Berkeley, Calif., 1977.

INDEX

INDEX